The Etiology and

Treatment of

Bulimia Nervosa

THE ETIOLOGY AND TREATMENT OF BULIMIA NERVOSA

A Biopsychosocial Perspective

CRAIG JOHNSON, Ph.D.

MARY E. CONNORS, Ph.D.

Basic Books, Inc., Publishers *New York*

Library of Congress Cataloging-in-Publication Data

Johnson, Craig, 1950–
   The etiology and treatment of bulimia nervosa.

   Bibliography: p. 306
   Includes index.
   1. Bulimia. I. Connors, Mary E., 1953–
II. Title. [DNLM: 1. Bulimia—etiology. 2. Bulimia—
therapy. WM 175 J66e]
RC552.B84J64 1987   616.85′2   86–47734
ISBN 0–465–02092–5

For Patti, Laura, Jeff, and my parents

and

For Roger, my parents, and Bob

CONTENTS

PART I

DESCRIPTION OF THE SYNDROME

PART II

ASSESSMENT AND TREATMENT

FOREWORD

It is an honor and a sincere pleasure to have been asked to provide introductory remarks to a volume from investigators who, with their colleagues, have shaped and greatly enriched the literature related to bulimia. It is hard to believe that only a decade ago the disorder that has come to be known as bulimia or bulimia nervosa simply did not appear in the psychiatric nomenclature. Prior to the 1940s, the symptoms of bulimia were reported almost exclusively within the context of anorexia nervosa. Reports appearing in the late 1970s and early 1980s identifying the symptom of binge eating in nonemaciated individuals spawned a veritable explosion of research aimed at the identification, understanding, and treatment of this disorder. Reading this volume has made us aware of just how far our understanding of this disorder has come in a relatively brief span of time. We thought that it might be useful to highlight, from our own (admittedly biased) perspective, some of the most interesting things we have learned about this disorder as well as some fundamental questions that remain to be answered.

Less than a decade ago, virtually nothing was known about the clinical features and the epidemiology of bulimia nervosa. There has been remarkable consistency in the clinical description of the signs and symptoms characteristic of the syndrome. In contrast to early reports that emphasized the uniformity across patients, bulimia nervosa is now largely viewed as a more heterogeneous syndrome that can be associated with a variety of personality profiles. Patients' sense that their eating is out of control, and the variety of weight-losing behaviors they engage in, has been described consistently. Whether they have the necessary and sufficient features to warrant a diagnosis of bulimia nervosa is another matter, and will be discussed later.

During the past few years much has been learned about the epidemiology of the disorder. Early reports were plagued by methodological flaws and overly inclusive definitions, but in the past few years more reliable estimates have indicated that between 1 and 5 percent of adolescent and young adult women from the upper and middle socioeconomic strata have serious cases of bulimia nervosa. Although the prevalence for men is not as high, cases do exist and these may have been under-reported because of men's reluctance to admit to what has been viewed as a "woman's disorder." Further work is needed to distinguish high-risk subgroups from those whose risk for the disorder is relatively low. This work will add to our understanding of the factors responsible for the expression of bulimia nervosa and will lay the groundwork for primary and secondary intervention programs.

Another area of tremendous advancement in the last several years has been diagnosis. Some confusion resulted from the wide acceptance of two sets of diagnostic criteria that defined overlapping but not identical populations (DSM-III, 1980; Russell, 1979). There have been many criticisms of the original DSM-III criteria, but it must be remembered that these were advanced at a time when very little was known about the epidemiology and nature of the disorder. The original DSM-III criteria were interpreted as clearly distinguishing bulimia from anorexia nervosa, and this view has shaped much of the early literature on etiology and treatment. The proposed revisions to the DSM-III criteria address most of the criticisms directed to the earlier version. Recently there has been greater recognition that bulimia nervosa and anorexia nervosa share many common features and that variability within each group is probably greater than the variance between the groups. This relates to the whole question of the importance of body weight as a diagnostic parameter. We have presented data that are consistent with the observations in this volume, which indicate that many bulimia nervosa patients presenting at tertiary centers have lost as much body weight as patients with anorexia nervosa. The difference between the two groups is that many so-called "normal weight bulimic" patients have started at a much higher weight. The identification of meaningful subgroups using either psychological or biological markers is currently the focus of intense research efforts at centers in North America and Europe. It is not yet certain whether having a history of anorexia nervosa is associated with a poor response to treatment for bulimia. The theoretical and practical implications of body weight and personality features are of great interest and have been thoughtfully addressed by Craig Johnson and Mary Connors.

Probably the area in which our understanding is the least advanced relates to the etiology of bulimia nervosa. Some models of causality have been clearly outlined; others have been implied by the interventions advocated. Binge eating has been attributed to stress, anxiety, habitual behavior, lack of assertiveness, poor labeling of emotional states, deficits in identifying hunger or satiety, sexual conflicts, addiction, faulty mothering, current relationship conflicts, personality deficits, depression, primary or secondary disturbances of the hypothalamic-pituitary-endocrine axes, and cravings associated with dieting or the maintenance of a suboptimal weight. It appears that any one-factor theory of this complex disorder is far too limited. The "risk factor" model of causality has gained greater acceptance in the understanding of anorexia nervosa and it would seem that it also applies to bulimia nervosa, as well as a myriad of other psychological disorders.

Johnson and Connors are to be commended for dispelling the "uniformity myth" in their conceptualization of bulimia nervosa as a multidetermined disorder. In attempting to specify different paths leading to the disorder, they go beyond the simple statement of multidimensionality. We hope that the next decade of eating disorders research will lead to greater refinement of etiological parameters and more specific knowledge of how they interact to produce bulimia nervosa. We can expect to learn more about the relationship between affective disorders and eating disorders. It is likely that primary neuroendocrine abnormalities will be further distinguished from changes that are secondary to the disorder or its sequelae. Psychological disturbances related to body image, self-esteem, interoceptive awareness, identity formation, and others identified in eating disorder patients will be specified in greater detail. It is hoped that this will clarify distinguishing mechanisms of different subgroups based on personality attributes.

We still do not understand why some individuals are able to control their weight without developing the pattern of binge eating. The possibility of hereditary predisposition toward eating disorders constitutes a fascinating area of study that we are only beginning to explore. Is there a greater aggregation of eating disorders in the families of eating disorder patients? Are there other genetic markers that confer a vulnerability to eating disorders? The roles of cultural and familial influences are undoubtedly complex, but they have generated a great deal of interest. Further research will add to our understanding of their contributions to eating disorders. Johnson and Connors cover each of these areas by reviewing and synthesizing the research evidence to date and adding valuable theoretical speculations on which future empirical work may be based. Their developmental speculations indicate tremendous clinical sensitivity as well as a firm grounding in neo-analytic schools of thought. Unlike many analytically oriented theorists, they are able to integrate psychodynamic theory with an understanding of the cultural factors central to the disorder.

It is sometimes difficult to separate primary causal factors from those that perpetuate bulimia nervosa. One of the most fascinating areas of study has been the elucidation of the starvation-based perpetuating mechanisms for anorexia nervosa. Some of the changes observed in emaciated patients also seem to apply to bulimia nervosa, particularly to those patients who have lost a large proportion of their body weight. We are just beginning to understand the interplay between central mechanisms and eating patterns. Promising work is being done on the effects of the serotonergic, noradrenergic, endogenous opioid, and hypothalamic-pituitary systems upon feeding patterns. During the next decade we hope to learn more about the role of metabolic factors in weight regulation, the effects of certain macronutrients on hunger and satiety, and the interactions of exercise, eating behavior, and central mediating mechanisms. The function of bingeing in the regulation of mood and psychological state has been another important area of advancement in our understanding of eating disorders. The role of symptoms in "self-regulation" in bulimia nervosa has been clearly developed and extended by Johnson and Connors in this volume.

A tremendous amount has been learned in a relatively short time about the complications of bulimia nervosa. It is essential for the practicing clinician to be aware of these because some are life-threatening. Others are of interest because they alter the patient's psychological state and thus may interfere with psychotherapy. Many of the sequelae of bulimia nervosa are ameliorated by normalization of eating and weight, but the long-term effects of the disorder are unknown.

Perhaps the greatest advancements have occurred in the area of psychotherapy for bulimia nervosa. Despite divergent theories of etiology, there has been a growing convergence regarding elements of treatment. We have seen a healthy trend toward the integration of different therapeutic modalities with the recognition that no single therapy will suit the needs of every patient. Group therapists appreciate the need for individual treatment, and those who prefer individual therapy have become convinced of the merits of the group approach. Psychodynamic therapists have recognized the importance of self-monitoring along with attention to food, weight, and behavioral control of the cycle of bingeing and vomiting. Cognitive and behavioral theorists have begun to address developmental themes related to separation, identity formation, self concept, and the therapeutic relationship. Most have recognized the value of family therapy for some cases. These accommodations do not necessarily reflect a weakening of theoretical premises, but rather a systematic evolution within each ideological camp toward addressing recurrent themes in treatment. This is not to be confused with the unsystematic application of multicomponent treatment packages that fail to take into account the manifold needs of different patients.

The multifaceted approach recommended by Johnson and Connors is an outstanding example of eclecticism at its very best. Their clinical descriptions vividly portray the experiences of different subgroups of patients. From these careful observations have come a range of therapeutic interventions based on years of experience with bulimic patients. Although they rely heavily on modern psychoanalytic thinking, they have integrated powerful clinical strategies from various treatment orientations. The result is not only an effective approach to bulimia nervosa but also a model for psychotherapy that may be applied to other adolescent disorders. Their recognition of the role of biological and cultural predisposing factors has led to practical suggestions that go well beyond the orthodox analytic views expressed by some. The sections on "Techniques for Symptom

Management" and "Special Treatment Issues" are rich with suggestions essential for all clinicians who treat eating-disordered patients, regardless of their theoretical orientation.

The review of treatment studies in this volume strikingly reveals that various treatments have had statistically and clinically significant effects on the frequency of bingeing and vomiting. This is true of studies using different forms of psychotherapy as well as drug treatments. However, the general optimism about the effectiveness of treatment must be tempered by the high dropout rates in some studies and the relatively small number of patients who remain symptom-free at follow-up. Moreover, the follow-up period is inadequate in most studies; thus, the long-term efficacy of treatment remains to be seen. It is hoped that in the future, studies will be better controlled and better able to identify specific subgroups of patients who might respond to different psychological or pharmacological approaches. In this volume, Johnson and Connors have demonstrated remarkable skill in articulating treatment principles which will undoubtedly become the standard for some time to come.

DAVID M. GARNER, Ph.D.
Professor of Psychiatry
University of Toronto

PAUL E. GARFINKEL, M.D.
Professor of Psychiatry
University of Toronto

PREFACE AND ACKNOWLEDGMENTS

The phenomenon of bulimia first captured our attention in the late 1970s. As part of our general work with adolescent patients, we became aware of the increasing incidence of bulimic behavior, predominantly among young women. As we explored further, it became clear that the emergence of the syndrome offered a unique opportunity to investigate the multidimensional nature of psychopathology. Consensus has begun to emerge that bulimia is a paradigmatic psychosomatic disorder in which biological, familial, and sociocultural factors interact in a way that predisposes some individuals to develop bulimic symptoms. Our task in this book has been to present our current understanding of this interaction as well as its treatment implications.

In part I of the book we articulate the controversies that have arisen about definitional criteria and review existing findings regarding clinical characteristics, personality factors, family environments, and biological vulnerabilities. This part ends with our multidetermined conceptualization of the etiology of bulimia.

Part II explores a wide range of treatment issues, including assessment; selective use of individual, family, group, and psychopharmacological interventions; and detailed strategies for symptom management. Special issues such as treatment of character-disordered and therapy-resistant patients are also discussed. Overall, these chapters represent a blend of psychodynamic and cognitive-behavioral conceptualizations. This theoretical integration provides guidelines for the delicate therapeutic task of simultaneously managing symptoms and exploring underlying intrapsychic and interpersonal dynamics.

This has been a difficult book to write, largely because the data base has been increasing geometrically year by year. Unfortunately, the burgeoning literature raises more questions than it answers. Nevertheless, it has been an exciting task to review, synthesize, and speculate on the basis of the current literature and our clinical experience.

This book would not have been possible without the help of many people. We would like to thank Susan Love, Ph.D.; Steve Stern, Psy.D.; George and Tina Barr; Michael Tansey, Ph.D.; Karen Maddi, M.A.; Laura Humphrey, Ph.D.; Becky Bohn, R.N.; Linda D. Lewis, Ph.D.; Bill Swift,

M.D.; John Gillilan, M.D.; Phil McCullough, M.D.; Jennifer Hagman, M.D.; Sheryl Jones, R.D.; Lyn Marshall, R.N.; Marilyn Stuckey, Ph.D.; Darryl Pure, Ph.D.; Patricia Buckley, Ph.D.; Roger Thomson, Ph.D.; Dan Zimbroff, M.D.; David Garner, Ph.D.; Michael Strober, Ph.D.; and Paul Garfinkel, M.D. We would also like to thank our editor, Jo Ann Miller, for her patience and support throughout the entire process of writing this book. Finally, we wish to thank our patients, for allowing us to understand them and helping us learn how to treat them.

CRAIG JOHNSON, Ph.D.
MARY E. CONNORS, Ph.D.

A NOTE TO THE READER

In an effort to avoid grammatical awkwardness, we use feminine pronouns throughout this book to refer to bulimics. This also reflects the fact that bulimia is a disorder that predominantly affects women. However, we do not mean to imply that men cannot also suffer from bulimia.

In the process of writing this book we have had to deal with the fact that psychiatric nomenclature is in a period of transition. The disorder called Bulimia in the third edition of the *Diagnostic and Statistical Manual of Mental Disorders* will almost certainly be more scrupulously defined and referred to as Bulimia Nervosa in the future. Our title thus reflects this change.

PART I

DESCRIPTION OF THE SYNDROME

The case histories in this book are based on actual situations and accurately portray the problems presented by bulimia nervosa. However, all names and identifying characteristics mentioned in the book have been changed, and the case histories represent composites rather than the stories of any specific individuals.

History and Definition
of the Disorder

During the last two decades there has been a proliferation of reports in the psychological literature and the popular press describing pathological eating behavior. The term bulimia, virtually unknown several years ago, has become familiar both to professionals and to the public. With the increased familiarity of the term has come a rapidly burgeoning body of basic research. While this early research has facilitated our understanding of the disorder, it has also spawned confusion and controversy over nomenclature, criteria for diagnosis, etiology, and treatment. In this chapter we provide some historical perspective on the emergence of the syndrome of bulimia, with specific emphasis on some of the confusion regarding nomenclature and definitional issues.

Bulimic Behavior

EARLY REPORTS

Early case reports of bulimic behavior date back to the late 1800s when anorexia nervosa was first described (Gull, 1874). While these early case studies dealt largely with bulimic symptoms such as binge eating (consuming a large quantity of food in a short period of time) in relation to anorexia nervosa, bulimic behavior was also observed in diabetes mellitis (Osler, 1892), malaria (Soltman, 1894), and among young girls who lived away from their families in boarding schools (Soltman, 1894). However, in a historical review of the syndrome, Regina Casper (1983) suggests that detailed reports of bulimic symptoms began to appear around 1940.

Ludwig Binswanger's report is perhaps the earliest and most detailed account of bulimic behavior. In 1944 Binswanger described the case of Ellen West, a pseudonym for a woman who had been treated some thirty years earlier. She was given various diagnoses at the time, including schizophrenia and severe obsessive neurosis; today we would consider her to have had anorexia nervosa with bulimic features. At the age of twenty, Ellen gained weight and was teased by her friends. In order to reduce her weight, she began to fast and to take long hikes. She wrote in her journal: "two things torture me: first hunger, second, the dread of getting fatter." A few years later the dread of fat began to be accompanied by intense longings for food, especially sweets. She started taking numerous thyroid tablets daily and continued the fasting and hiking. Ellen became emaciated, reducing to 92 pounds from a high of 165, and felt "spiritually satisfied" because she was thin. Laxatives were added to her regimen; in her journal she wrote: "my thoughts are exclusively concerned with my body, my eating, my laxatives."

The bingeing behaviors became very prominent. Binswanger noted that she ate foods which she thought were not fattening with great greed and haste:

> Often on the way home she eats up things she has bought for her household and upbraids herself severely for it. Ellen leaves out entire meals, to throw herself indiscriminately with all the greater greed on any foods which may happen to be at hand. Each day she consumes several pounds of tomatoes and 20 oranges. (p. 252)

Ellen's obsession increased, and by age thirty she was taking so many laxatives that she was vomiting nightly and had constant diarrhea. She confessed to her husband that she was living her life with a view only toward remaining thin and that she was subordinating all actions to this end. She became depressed as she continued to struggle with her wish to be thinner and her constant craving for food. She wrote: "this is the horrible part of my life; it is filled with dread. Dread of eating, dread of hunger, dread of the dread. I am in prison and cannot get out." She sought psychoanalytic treatment and hospitalized herself several times for help with severe depression, suicidal thoughts, and her relentless preoccupation with food and weight. However, she obtained no real relief. She wrote: "I am perishing in the struggle against my nature. Fate wanted to have me fat and strong, but I wanted to be thin and delicate." Finally, after a thirteen-year struggle that had left her ever more enmeshed in her obsession, she took a lethal dose of poison.

The case of Ellen West describes in detail the tormented struggle experienced by an eating-disordered woman some seventy years ago. It is illustrative of the depression, obsessiveness about food, and the adversarial relationship with one's body that is seen in our patients today.

Other reports describing the symptoms of compulsive overeating and purging behavior among anorexia nervosa patients appeared at about the same time as Binswanger's work (Bond, 1949; Nemiah, 1950; Nicolle, 1939; Rahman, Richardson, and Ripley, 1939). While most of these reports describe bulimic behavior in relation to anorexia nervosa, as the earlier case reports had, Selling and Ferraro (1945) commented on the appearance of bulimic behavior among a nonanorexic population. They observed that gorging behavior was common among refugee children brought to the United States between 1933 and 1939, and they emphasized the relationship between psychological insecurity and binge eating. According to this report, the children quickly relinquished the gorging behavior once they were placed in foster homes that offered security but would resume the behavior when separated from their new foster parents. These early observations regarding the relationship between separation and binge eating are particularly interesting in light of the findings that many current bulimic patients initially begin binge eating at eighteen years of age. For most, this is the time of their first separation from their families.

BULIMIA AMONG THE OBESE

In the 1950s bulimic behavior among obese individuals was also observed. Hamburger (1951) described a type of hyperphagia among an obese sample that was characterized by a compulsive craving for food. Likening this food craving to alcohol addiction, he observed that these patients constantly craved food, especially sweets, and that they would engage in compulsive eating jags which often involved stealing food or money for food.

Albert Stunkard (1959) was the first to use the term binge eating to characterize a type of pathological eating behavior among obese patients. He observed that these obese binge eaters would consume as many as twenty thousand calories in an extended binge and that there was often an orgiastic quality to the episode. He further noted that the episodes tended to be precipitated by upsetting life events and that the binges were followed by self-condemnation. Later Kornhaber (1970) coined the term stuffing syndrome to describe and elaborate upon the phenomenon of binge eating among obese individuals. More recently, Loro and Orleans (1981) and Gormally, Black, Daston, and Rardin (1982) have found that a relatively high percentage of obese patients report binge eating. Although the symptoms of bulimia continued to appear in studies of weight-disordered patients (those with anorexia nervosa and obesity), it was not until the mid-1970s that reports of bulimic behavior among normal-weight populations began to emerge.

New Nomenclature

BULIMAREXIA

Marlene Boskind-Lodahl (1976) was one of the first investigators to identify the symptoms of bulimia among a predominantly normal-weight population of young adult women; she coined the term *bulimarexia* to describe the group. Boskind-Lodahl received over one hundred replies in response to an advertisement she placed in a campus newspaper for women caught in a "cycle of gorging on food and then purging by habitual forced vomiting, severe fasting, laxative or amphetamine abuse" (1978, p. 90). In her description of the sample she noted that despite the fact that most respondents were of normal weight, they were attitudinally very similar to anorexia nervosa patients in that they felt helpless, had distorted body images, and were extremely fearful of being fat. Boskind-Lodahl noted, however, that these individuals did not appear to be as psychologically disturbed as anorexia nervosa patients. Unlike anorexics, they were able to continue demanding university work, did not require hospitalization, and were sufficiently insightful about their eating problems to seek treatment.

BULIMIA NERVOSA

Following Boskind-Lodahl's observations, in 1979 Gerald Russell published a classic article in which he coined the term *bulimia nervosa* to describe a clinical population of thirty patients who presented with symptoms of bulimia. In addition to presenting detailed clinical descriptions of the group, Russell offered speculations regarding etiology and suggested criteria for the diagnosis. These criteria included: (1) the patients suffer from powerful and intractable urges to overeat; (2) they seek to avoid the fattening effects of food by inducing vomiting or abusing purgatives or both; and (3) they have a morbid fear of becoming fat (p. 445). Although Russell's landmark paper was a valuable contribution to the emerging literature on bulimia, it also created confusion and sparked controversy, part of which revolved around the fact that twenty-four of the thirty patients in his sample had previous histories of anorexia nervosa, although they were currently at normal weight. This aspect of the sample as well as his proposed criteria began to focus questions on how the phenomenon of bulimia should be defined.

TABLE 1.1
DSM-III Criteria for Bulimia

A. Recurrent episodes of binge eating (rapid consumption of a large amount of food in a discrete period of time, usually less than two hours).
B. At least three of the following:
    (1) consumption of high-caloric, easily ingested food during a binge
    (2) inconspicuous eating during a binge
    (3) termination of such eating episodes by abdominal pain, sleep, social interruption, or self-induced vomiting
    (4) repeated attempts to lose weight by severely restrictive diets, self-induced vomiting, or use of cathartics or diuretics
    (5) frequent weight fluctuations greater than ten pounds due to alternating binges and fasts
C. Awareness that the eating pattern is abnormal and fear of not being able to stop eating voluntarily.
D. Depressed mood and self-depreciating thoughts following eating binges.
E. The bulimic episodes are not due to Anorexia Nervosa or any known physical disorder.

NOTE: Reproduced with permission of the publisher, from the *Diagnostic and Statistical Manual of Mental Disorders* (3rd ed.), American Psychiatric Association, copyright 1980, pp. 70–71.

BULIMIA AS A DISTINCT SYNDROME

Shortly after Russell's description and proposed criteria for bulimia nervosa appeared, the American Psychiatric Association published criteria for the diagnosis of bulimia (see table 1.1), which was now considered a distinct syndrome, in the third edition of the *Diagnostic and Statistical Manual of Mental Disorders* (DSM-III, 1980). Several descriptive reports soon followed. Richard Pyle, James Mitchell, and Elke Eckert (1981) reported on a clinical population of thirty-four patients without previous histories of anorexia nervosa who were experiencing significant psychological distress as a result of bulimia. A pair of unusual reports also appeared simultaneously in the United States and Great Britain (Fairburn and Cooper, 1982b; Johnson, Stuckey, Lewis, and Schwartz, 1982). Using large mail samples from readers of popular women's magazines, these studies provided the first data-based indications that bulimic behavior was highly prevalent among adolescent and young adult women.

Other studies also appeared that described the symptoms of bulimia among predominantly normal-weight individuals. Robert Palmer (1979) coined the term *dietary chaos syndrome* to refer to this group; Arthur Crisp (1981) labeled it the *abnormal normal weight control syndrome.*

In summary, prior to the 1940s bulimic behavior was reported as occurring primarily in the context of anorexia nervosa. During the 1950s the phenomenon of binge eating was described among obese populations. It was not until the last decade, however, that the prevalence of bulimic behavior among individuals without significant histories of weight disorder became apparent.

As could be expected with any newly emerging area of conceptual

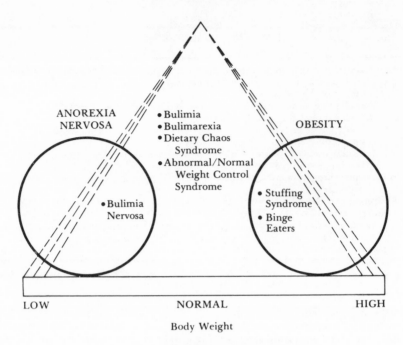

FIGURE 1.1
Spectrum of Bulimic Symptoms

interest, a variety of labels were suggested in an attempt to differentiate the groups. Figure 1.1 indicates which subgroups the labels describe. The figure assumes that the symptoms of bulimia occur across the spectrum of weight disorders, bounded on one end by anorexia nervosa and obesity on the other. The overlapping areas are points where bulimic symptoms merge with the syndromes of anorexia nervosa (bulimia nervosa) and obesity (stuffing syndrome). As depicted, the term bulimia has generally been reserved for patients without weight disorder. Obviously the different labels reflect different definitions of the phenomenon. Consequently, controversy has arisen over the validity of the different definitions.

Definitional Controversies

The criteria that appeared in DSM-III were the first to be officially sanctioned, and it is important to note that they were clinically rather than empirically derived. Consequently, although DSM-III offered an elaborate description of bulimic behavior, significant controversy arose regarding the importance or validity of any of the initial criteria.

This controversy has focused primarily on two issues: What is the relationship of bulimia to weight disorders, most notably anorexia nervosa? And do the current DSM-III criteria adequately differentiate a group who are clinically impaired?

RELATIONSHIP TO WEIGHT DISORDERS

The fifth DSM-III criterion for bulimia states that "the bulimic episodes are not due to Anorexia Nervosa or any known physical disorder." This has generally been interpreted to mean that a current or past history of anorexia nervosa precludes the diagnosis of bulimia. Confusion about this criterion has arisen for several reasons.

As mentioned earlier, Russell's original paper essentially described how the symptoms of bulimia were manifested among individuals who had histories of anorexia nervosa. A number of studies then began to appear that indicated a prevalence of bulimic symptoms among anorexia nervosa patients and that the presence of bulimic symptoms had important clinical implications (Beumont, George, and Smart, 1976; Bruch, 1973; Casper et al., 1980; Garfinkel, Moldofsky, and Garner, 1980; Sours, 1980).

Among these early studies there appeared to be three somewhat consistent clinical characteristics that differentiated anorexics with bulimic symptoms (bulimic anorexics) from anorexics without such symptoms (restricting anorexics). The bulimic anorexics had: (1) a greater frequency of higher premorbid body weights, (2) significant affective instability resulting in various impulse dominated behaviors, and (3) a tendency toward more severe life impairment resulting in less improvement over time.

Several studies have demonstrated that bulimic anorexics have higher premorbid body weights than restricting anorexics. Paul Garfinkel and David Garner (1984) reported that in their sample of 335 anorexics, the bulimic anorexics had a significantly higher incidence of premorbid obesity than the restricting anorexics and that there was a higher incidence of obesity among mothers of bulimic anorexics (47 percent versus 30 percent). Michael Strober (1981) similarly reported that the incidence of premorbid obesity was three times higher among bulimic anorexics (45 percent) than restricting anorexics (15 percent). These findings imply that the biological and psychological consequences of losing and attempting to maintain a low body weight may be quite different for bulimic versus restricting anorexics. Essentially, emaciation may particularly predispose individuals who have higher natural body weights to impulsive binge eating and subsequent purging behavior (see chapter 7).

A highly consistent finding that differentiates the two groups is that bulimics manifest greater affective instability. This instability is characterized by persistently low and yet highly variable mood states often resulting in significant suicidal ideation (Casper et al., 1980; Garfinkel et al., 1980; Russell, 1979; Strober, 1981). A high incidence of impulsive behavior such as shoplifting, self-mutilation, sexual acting out, and substance abuse appears to also accompany the mood difficulty (Bruch, 1973; Casper et al., 1980; Dally and Gomez, 1979; Garfinkel et al., 1980; Strober, 1981). A number of studies have also found a significantly higher incidence of affective disorders and alcoholism among the relatives of bulimic anorexics (Hudson, Pope, Jonas, and Yurgelun-Todd, 1983; Strober, Salkin, Burroughs, and Morrell, 1982). These findings have raised questions about whether individuals who present with bulimic symptoms suffer from a biologically mediated affective disorder.

Finally, several early studies demonstrated that the presence of bulimic symptoms among anorexics indicated a more chronic outcome. Hsu, Crisp, and Harding (1979) followed up one hundred anorexics from four to eight years after their initial presentation for treatment. Bulimia was an indication of poorer outcome and correlated significantly with longer duration of illness. Casper and associates (1980) reported that although their bulimic anorexics were older, there were no significant differences in time of onset of the disorder, suggesting chronicity. Garfinkel and Garner (1982) reported, however, that duration of illness was not significantly different between bulimic and restricting anorexics.

These early studies suggested that the presence of bulimic behavior among anorexics seemed to differentiate a subgroup who had somewhat distinct biological and psychological profiles. Subsequent studies focusing on the importance of weight variables versus the presence or absence of bulimic symptoms found that the presence of bulimic symptoms appeared to have greater clinical significance than history of low weight.

In a well-controlled study, Garner, Garfinkel, and O'Shaughnessy (1983) compared anorexia nervosa patients with no history of bulimic episodes (restrictors) to ones with bulimic episodes (bulimic anorexics) and to patients with no history of anorexia nervosa but who reported significant difficulty with bulimic behavior. The patients completed a variety of personality and family tests. The results indicated that the groups reporting bulimic symptoms resembled each other on most variables and were more similar to each other than to the anorexic group who did not experience bulimic episodes.

Similarly, Norman and Herzog (1983) demonstrated using the Minnesota Multiphasic Personality Inventory that bulimic anorexics and normal-weight bulimics were more similar to each other than to restricting anorexics. Thus these studies indicated that the presence of bulimic symptoms more powerfully differentiated psychobiological differences between groups than current or previous history of low weight.

The confusion around the relationship of weight history to bulimia has been further exacerbated by recent work of Garner and his colleagues.

Garner (1985) has argued that the term normal weight may be inappropriate for a sizable portion of bulimic patients who present with body weights that are normal according to standardized weight tables. Among a clinical sample of 186 patients who were at normal weight "according to standardized norms," one-third of the sample reported a highest weight greater than 110 percent of the matched population weight. Furthermore, the mean lowest adult weight reported in the sample was more than 30 percent below the mean highest adult weight. This indicated that, on the average, this group had a weight loss of over 30 percent at some point.

These findings imply that even though the bulimic patients are at normal weights according to standardized norms, they may be well below what is a normal weight for them as individuals. Consequently, although they may not be visibly emaciated, as are anorexics who are 25 percent below weight norms, bulimic patients may have reduced their body weight to a comparable degree and could be experiencing similar psychological and biological side effects from semistarvation.

The emerging consensus among researchers is that weight status should not be included in the diagnostic criteria for bulimia. Preliminary research indicates that the style of eating behavior—bulimic versus restricting—appears to be a more clinically informative distinction than weight status. Therefore, decisions regarding primary diagnosis (bulimia versus anorexia nervosa) should be based on attitudes and style of eating behavior rather than weight status.

RELATIONSHIP TO LIFE IMPAIRMENT

If we are to focus on attitudes and style of eating behaviors as key diagnostic variables, then it is incumbent upon investigators to clarify which aspects of the phenomenon of bulimia are associated with or predictive of psychopathology. As depicted in figure 1.2, a wide range of bulimic behavior exists in today's culture. Binge eating, dieting, and body dissatisfaction are common among adolescent and young adult women (Halmi, Falk, and Schwartz, 1981; Johnson, Stuckey, Lewis, and Schwartz, 1983; Pyle, Mitchell, Eckert, and Halvorson, 1983). It would be foolish to assume that all individuals who reported episodes of binge eating or body dissatisfaction should be recommended for treatment. Consequently, controversy has emerged regarding the type of symptoms that are necessary to identify psychopathology.

Russell's proposed criteria for diagnosis emphasize psychological and attitudinal factors but do not offer very specific descriptions of the behavior, nor do they indicate at what point these features are pathological. Conversely, DSM-III criteria are much more behaviorally specific but do not attend to attitudinal factors thought to underlie or motivate the disturbed eating behavior. The specificity of the DSM-III criteria has also raised significant questions. The limitations of these criteria are numerous—there is no frequency stipulation; there is no provision for individuals

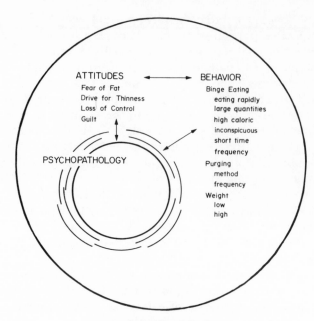

FIGURE 1.2
Domain of Bulimic Attitudes and Behavior

who vomit without bingeing or for those who do not consume large amounts of food but who nonetheless feel out of control, or for how central a role purging should play in making the diagnosis; and there is also confusion regarding the relationship to weight status.

Craig Johnson and Susan Love (1985) made a preliminary data-based attempt to identify which bulimic symptoms would be predictive of psychopathology. Their nonclinical community sample of 510 women reported having difficulty with episodes of binge eating ranging from once per month to several times per day. Thus the sample was a heterogeneous group reporting varying frequencies of bulimic behavior.

A life impairment index was developed and a stepwise multiple regression was used to investigate which variables were associated with life impairment. Independent variables included: (1) behaviors during binge eating (eating rapidly, eating large amounts of foods, and feeling out of control when binge eating); (2) feelings after binge eating, such as helplessness, guilt, and disgust; (3) frequency of binge eating and/or purging; (4) current weight, or previous low weight; (5) age of onset; (6) duration of binge-eating behaviors; and (7) alcohol use. Results indicated that feelings of being out of control, frequency of laxative abuse, frequency of binge eating and vomiting, feelings of guilt, early age of onset, and previous history of low weight accounted for the maximum amount of variance of severity. Nonpredictors included current weight, eating large amounts of food, eating rapidly, feeling helpless or disgusted, duration of illness, and frequency of alcohol use.

TABLE 1.2
Proposed Diagnostic Criteria for Inclusion in DSM-III R

Bulimic Disorder

A. Recurrent episodes of binge-eating (rapid consumption of a large amount of food in a discrete period of time, usually less than two hours).
B. During the eating binges there is a feeling of lack of control over the eating behavior.
C. The individual regularly engages in either self-induced vomiting, use of laxatives, or rigorous dieting or fasting in order to counteract the effects of the binge-eating.
D. A minimum average of two binge-eating episodes per week for at least three months.

Eating Disorders NOS

This is a residual category for disorder of eating that does not meet the criteria for a specific Eating Disorder.

Examples include:

(1) An individual of average weight who does not have binge-eating episodes, but frequently engages in self-induced vomiting for fear of gaining weight.
(2) All of the features of Anorexia Nervosa in a female except for absence of menses.
(3) All of the features of Bulimic Disorder except for the frequency or duration of binge-eating episodes.

These preliminary findings indicate that both attitudinal and behavioral criteria are important indicators of psychopathology. While the study did not include attitudinal factors such as fear of fat and drive for thinness, it was clear that the individuals' subjective experience of dyscontrol and guilt were highly predictive of impairment. Likewise, it is apparent that a frequency criteria for the binge eating and purging behaviors should be included in revision of the DSM-III criteria.

The lack of empirical clarification regarding which, and to what extent, various bulimic attitudes and behaviors are necessary to result in life impairment has made it difficult to know how prevalent clinically significant levels of bulimia are in the population. In figure 1.2, the dotted lines around the area labeled psychopathology are meant to indicate that, at present, we are uncertain as to the amount of psychopathology that exists within the domain of bulimic attitudes and behaviors.

DSM-III R

Just before this book went to press a special subcommittee proposed revisions for the DSM-III criteria for bulimia (see table 1.2). The revisions have remedied some of the problems discussed. The issue of weight disorder has been eliminated by avoiding any criteria related to weight. Most important, the frequency of binge-eating episodes is stipulated. As research continues to accumulate, we hope that the criteria will become increasingly more specific.

2

Epidemiology

In the last chapter we traced the evolution of our awareness of bulimic behavior. Currently we know that it appears to be highly prevalent, particularly among adolescent and young adult women in westernized cultures. Controversy exists regarding the actual incidence, with estimates ranging from 5 to 20 percent. This chapter reviews the data-based studies regarding prevalence, explores the controversies, and attempts to draw some preliminary conclusions.

Epidemiological studies are necessary to generate information about prevalence rates and variation of these rates in different populations, and to identify risk factors that increase the likelihood of developing a disorder. This information is vital for planning treatment and prevention strategies to meet the needs of the affected or at-risk population. However, the information is all predicated on the ability to define what constitutes a "case" of the disorder and to distinguish clearly between "cases" and "normals." With psychiatric disorders, which seem to exist on a continuum of severity, this poses a significant problem. Identifying cases of bulimia is akin to delineating cases of depression, where it is commonly agreed that some individuals have depressive symptoms that are not of sufficient intensity to warrant a clinical diagnosis (Boyd and Weissman, 1982).

This problem of case definition requires that precise operational definitions be used in identifying the disorder in question. Fletcher and Oldham (1959) have suggested three criteria for a good definition: first, it must be appropriate to the current study so that observable behaviors rather than underlying theoretical premises comprise the definition; second, the terms of the definition must be so precise that one is clearly aware of features which must be present and which must be absent for positive case identification; and third, there must be some artificial boundary or threshold of severity for operational purposes should the disorder exist on a continuum.

The data obtained from epidemiological studies are only as good as the case definitions used. As will be seen, a variety of binge eating and bulimia definitions have been used in the prevalence research, and none are without problems. The DSM-III criteria were constructed to provide a focus on observable behaviors; they meet Fletcher and Oldham's first objective well. However, these criteria are not precise and do not specify a severity threshold. Most definitions employed in prevalence studies are equally deficient in this regard. In the following review of the literature, these definitional issues and other problems of epidemiological research will be explored.

A number of reports on the prevalence of bulimia and bulimic behaviors have appeared in the last several years (see table 2.1). Various studies have investigated the prevalence of binge eating and the use of purging techniques. Others have attempted to assess the prevalence of bulimia by operationalizing the DSM-III criteria and, in some cases, narrowing the definition by imposing a frequency stipulation. In addition to bingeing and purging behaviors, the DSM-III criteria for bulimia also mention behaviors such as restrictive dieting and weight fluctuations. Thus a group of studies investigating dieting behaviors and related attitudes will also be reviewed.

Prevalence of Binge Eating and Purging Behaviors

The nineteen studies to be reviewed here have reported widely differing estimates of the prevalence of bulimic behaviors. Estimates of the prevalence of binge eating in females have ranged from a low of 24 percent in a family-practice adult sample (Zincand, Cadoret, and Widman, 1984) to a high of 90 percent in a population of college females (Hawkins and Clement, 1980). Estimates of binge eating in males have ranged from 8 percent (Halmi, Falk, and Schwartz, 1981) to 64 percent (Hawkins and Clement, 1980).

Estimates of the prevalence of vomiting are less disparate across studies. They range from 3 percent of females in a college sample (Chernyk, 1981) to 16 percent in a female high-school population (Johnson et al., 1984). Vomiting in males has been assessed in only a few studies, with estimates ranging from 1 percent (Chernyk, 1981; Lizdas and Abramson, 1984) to 6 percent (Halmi, Falk, and Schwartz, 1981).

Studies that have used questionnaires operationalizing the DSM-III criteria for bulimia have reported prevalence estimates ranging from 5 percent of college females in a clinical sample (Stangler and Printz, 1980) to 20 percent of female college seniors (Pope, Hudson, Yurgelun-Todd, and Hudson, 1984). Bulimia in males has been reported as ranging from 0 percent (Pope, Hudson, Yurgelun-Todd, and Hudson, 1984) to 5 per-

TABLE 2.1
Prevalence of Bulimia and Bulimic Behaviors

Reference	Subjects	N	Males	Females	Response Rate (%)	Bingeing Males (%)	Bingeing Females (%)	Vomiting Males (%)	Vomiting Females (%)	DSM-III Criteria Males (%)	DSM-III Criteria Females (%)	Other
Ondercin, 1979	College females	279	0	279	—	N/A	78	—[a]	—	—	—	—
Stangler and Printz, 1980	College students	500	182	318	100	—	—	—	—	1	5.3	—
Hawkins and Clement, 1980	College students	710	41	231 161 277	—	64	85 90 85	4	7 9 5	—	—	weekly bingeing females 28% 22% 32%, males 13%
Chernyk, 1981	College students	213	72	141	—	27.9	33.6	1.3	2.9	—	—	35% of females and 22% of males binged between once per week and once per month
Halmi, Falk, and Schwartz, 1981	College students, av. age 25	355/639	119 (29 sex unknown)	207	66	7.8	35	6.1	11.9	5	19	1.7% vomiting weekly or more
Collins, Kreisberg, Pertschuk, and Fager, 1982	College females	100/270[b]	0	100	88	N/A	—	—	—	—	9	—

TABLE 2.1 (continued)
Prevalence of Bulimia and Bulimic Behaviors

Reference	Subjects	N	Males	Females	Response Rate (%)	Bingeing Males (%)	Bingeing Females (%)	Vomiting Males (%)	Vomiting Females (%)	DSM-III Criteria Males (%)	DSM-III Criteria Females (%)	Other
Pyle, Mitchell, Eckert, and Halverson, 1983	College students	1355/1379	780	575	98.3	42	61	—	—	1.4	7.8	weekly binge/vomiting: 0.3% males; 1% females weekly binge: 0.4% males; 4.5% females
Cooper and Fairburn, 1983	British family planning clinic females, av. age 24.1	369	0	369	96.1	N/A	26.4 ever; 20.9 in last 2 months	N/A	6.5 ever; 2.9 in last 2 months	—	1.9 fit bulimia nervosa	7.3% bingeing weekly or more; 1% vomiting weekly or more
Johnson et al., 1984	High-school females ages 13–18	1268/1292	0	1268	98.1	N/A	57	—	16	—	8.3	weekly or more bingeing: 21%; weekly or more bingeing plus DSM-III: 4.9%; weekly or more vomiting: 4%; weekly or more binge/vomiting: 1%

TABLE 2.1 (continued)

Prevalence of Bulimia and Bulimic Behaviors

Reference	Subjects	N	Males	Females	Response Rate (%)	Bingeing		Vomiting		DSM-III Criteria		Other
						Males (%)	Females (%)	Males (%)	Females (%)	Males (%)	Females (%)	
Pope, Hudson, Yurgelun-Todd, and Hudson, 1984	Female shoppers	300/304	0	300	98.7	N/A	—	—	—	—	10.3	weekly binge/vomiting: 3%
Pope, Hudson, Yurgelun-Todd, and Hudson, 1984	Students: female college seniors;	287/450	0	287	64	N/A	—	—	—	—	14.7	weekly bingeing; females 10%
	male and female college seniors;	149/300	47	102	50	—	—	—	—	0	19.6	females 12.9%
	male and female high school seniors;	262	107	155	85	—	—	—	—	0	8.4	females 5.6%
Nagelberg, Hale, and Ware, 1984	College females, av. age 18.3	244	0	244	—	N/A	78.7	—	8.2	—	—	weekly or more bingeing: 31.2%
Lizdas and Abramson, 1984	College students	380/1000	137	243	38	—	—	1.5	9.1	2.2	11.9	—
Katzman et al., 1984	College students	812 (105)[b]	327	485	100 (of 105)	38	56	—	—	—	3.9 of 105 female "bingers"	—

TABLE 2.1 (continued)
Prevalence of Bulimia and Bulimic Behaviors

						Bingeing		Vomiting		DSM-III Criteria		
Reference	Subjects	N	Males	Females	Response Rate (%)	Males (%)	Females (%)	Males (%)	Females (%)	Males (%)	Females (%)	Other
Nevo, 1985	College females, av. age 20	689 (505)[b]	0	505	90	N/A	42	N/A	11	N/A	14	—
Zincand, Cadoret, and Widman, 1984	Family practice pop., age range 14–42	176	40	136	95	10	24	—	—	—	10.9 of total population	—
Crowther, Post, and Zaynor, 1985	High-school females	363	0	363	48	N/A	46	N/A	11	N/A	7.7	weekly or more bingeing: 24% DSM-III plus weekly bingeing: 5%; weekly or more B/P: 3%
Gray and Ford, 1985	College students	339	119	220	54	43	63	3	9	4	13	
Healy, Conroy, and Walsh, 1985	Irish students, 17–25	1063	361	701	95	18	37	N/A	N/A	0	3	
										(>1 episode per week)		

— means missing data.
[b] means analyzed in detail.

cent (Halmi, Falk, and Schwartz, 1981) of college males. Peter Cooper and Christopher Fairburn (1983), using Russell's (1979) criteria for bulimia nervosa, found that 2 percent of an adult female sample met these criteria, with close to an additional 2 percent reporting binge eating and laxative abuse without vomiting. Studies that have imposed more narrow criteria involving frequency stipulations have reported that between 5 percent (Pyle, Mitchell, Eckert, and Halvorson, 1983) and 32 percent (Hawkins and Clement, 1980) of females sampled binge eat at least weekly. Weekly binge eating in males has been reported to range between less than 1 percent (Pyle, Mitchell, Eckert, and Halvorson, 1983) to 13 percent (Hawkins and Clement, 1980). Weekly vomiting among females has been estimated at between 1 percent (Cooper and Fairburn, 1983) and 4 percent (Johnson et al., 1984). Weekly binge eating followed by vomiting has been reported to range from 1 percent (Johnson et al., 1984; Pyle, Mitchell, Eckert, and Halvorson, 1983) to 3 percent (Pyle, Mitchell, Eckert, and Halvorson, 1983).

Sampling Issues

Numerous factors may account for the discrepancies in prevalence estimates found in these studies. There may be significant differences among the subjects sampled, in that they include college students; high-school students; patients at various clinics for family planning, medical issues, or psychological problems; and women interviewed while shopping. Even among a supposedly more homogeneous college population, there could be significant differences among samples on such variables as socioeconomic status, racial composition, and age; for example, Halmi, Falk, and Schwartz's college sample (1981) had a mean age of twenty-five, while Nagelberg, Hale, and Ware's student sample (1984) had a mean age of eighteen. Factors such as a school's geographical location, size, and social climate in terms of pressure to achieve, conform, appear a certain way, and so on may create variability among samples that is as yet unexplored.

Few studies report detailed demographic data, and the importance of various elements, with the exception of sex, is not completely clear. All the studies involving male and female subjects have shown clear sex differences, with females showing significantly higher rates of bulimic behaviors and bulimia. This finding is so robust that a number of studies have investigated only female subjects.

The importance of age as a variable is somewhat less clear. Data from clinical samples have indicated that the average age of onset of bulimia is around eighteen (Johnson, Stuckey, Lewis, and Schwartz, 1982; Pyle, Mitchell, Eckert, and Halvorson, 1981), so that one might expect more bulimia in older samples. The Halmi, Falk, and Schwartz study, with its high prevalence rates among a sample of older students, might be interpreted in this light. However, the three high-school samples (Crowther, Post, and Zaynor, 1985; Johnson et al., 1984; Pope, Hudson, Yurgelun-Todd, and Hudson, 1984) also reported relatively high percentages of bulimic behaviors and bulimia. Additionally, the three nonstudent adult populations with wider age ranges do not report higher prevalence rates, despite the fact that subjects had more years in which to develop bulimic behaviors; in fact, they report some of the lowest estimates of binge eating (Cooper and Fairburn, 1983; Zincand, Cadoret, and Widman, 1984). Harrison Pope, James Hudson, and Deborah Yurgelun-Todd (1984) reported that in their sample of female shoppers a lifetime history of bulimia was most prevalent among their youngest age group and progressively less common in their older age group, with a highly significant difference between subjects who were between thirteen and twenty and those who were thirty-one and older. Thus membership in a young adolescent cohort may correlate with prevalence rates equal to or perhaps greater than those of college students, which in turn seem to be higher than those of older adults.

These prevalence studies provide little information on differences that might be attributable to race, ethnicity, or religion. Only Nevo's study (1985) specifically explored racial and cultural differences in her comparison of Caucasian and Asian subjects. She found that less than 3 percent of the Asian women could be labeled bulimic on the basis of modified DSM-III criteria, compared with 14 percent of Caucasian females. No study has compared large enough samples of black and white subjects to be able to address thoroughly the issue of possible racial issues in prevalence statistics. Also, of the nineteen studies reviewed, all but two (Cooper and Fairburn, 1983; Healy, Conroy, and Walsh, 1985) were conducted in the United States. Cooper and Fairburn's British study also employed criteria for bulimia nervosa rather than bulimia, which makes cross-sample comparisons problematic. The dearth of prevalence studies in countries other than the United States severely limits the ability to generalize.

The issue of random selection in the studies must be considered. Studies with relatively low return rates on questionnaires, such as 66 percent in the Halmi, Falk, and Schwartz (1981) study or 38 percent in the Lizdas and Abramson (1984) report, present significant problems. It is unclear who was noncompliant and why: embarrassed binge eaters may have failed to return their questionnaires for fear of exposure, but so may have normal eaters who simply found the questions irrelevant and didn't want to bother with them. Since no study sought out noncompliant subjects to explore this, any generalizing from reports with low response rates must be done with great caution.

Methodological Issues

All but one of the studies evaluated subjects by means of self-report questionnaires (Stangler and Printz, 1980, used interviews). The difficulties inherent in the exclusive use of self-report measures are well known. Several new questionnaires were pioneered in these studies, and reliability and validity data on them are lacking. Diagnosing a clinical entity on the basis of a self-report measure of unknown validity is questionable unless other assessment devices such as interviews are also employed. The typical procedure for case identification in large-scale studies is a two-step process: a screening instrument is followed by a more intensive examination where suspected cases can be confirmed or rejected. While interviews may present problems for some subjects who are concerned about confidentiality, there is no other way to determine a measure's ability to detect true cases of a disorder and reject false positives. The fact that detailed clinical interviews have not been used in bulimia prevalence research is an indication that this work is still in its beginning stages.

Two studies (Pope, Hudson, Yurgelun-Todd, and Hudson, 1984; Pyle, Mitchell, Eckert, and Halvorson, 1983) have administered their questionnaires to a clinical sample of bulimics as a validity check. Pyle and associates found that all thirty-seven bulimic patients responded positively to their three inclusion criteria for a label of bulimia. Used on a control group of eighty-five, the questionnaire identified eighteen out of twenty bulimics in the clinical sample and none of the controls. The authors thus suggest that their study has a low rate of identifying false positives and that their questionnaire probably slightly underestimates actual prevalence rates. Unfortunately, the other studies lack these validity data.

The studies differ in the time period considered in the assessment. Some questionnaires inquire only about current behavior (Hawkins and Clement, 1980); some ask about the last month or two (Cooper and Fairburn, 1983; Katzman and Wolchik, 1984); some about behavior in the last few years (Chernyk, 1981); and some about behavior ever performed in one's life (Johnson et al., 1984; Pope, Hudson, and Yurgelun-Todd, 1984; Pope, Hudson, Yurgelun-Todd, and Hudson, 1984). Because of these differences, studies that include current frequency statistics may be compared most meaningfully.

As mentioned previously, the studies employed different definitional criteria, which probably explains a good deal of the variance. In the Hawkins and Clement study (1980), binge eating was not defined at all; students were asked "Do you ever binge eat?" and were then asked about frequency. The students must have defined binge eating very broadly, as evidenced by a 90 percent affirmative response in one female sample. Others studies have employed the DSM-III definition of a binge (Halmi,

Falk, and Schwartz, 1981; Johnson et al., 1984; Pyle, Mitchell, Eckert, and Halvorson, 1983), inquiring if subjects consume large or enormous quantities of food within a short time period. Other researchers have attempted to operationalize these rather vague criteria by specifying calorie and time totals; Chernyk (1981) defined a binge as the consumption of 4,000 or more calories in two hours or less; Katzman and Wolchik (1984) required 1,200 calories per binge and defined DSM-III's "recurrent" as "eight binges last month"; Nevo (1984) defined bingeing as consuming at least 1,000 calories at one time at least once per month. Studies using the more restrictive definitional criteria have reported somewhat lower rates of bulimia and bulimic behaviors.

Despite attempts to quantify what constitutes a binge, some subjectivity is inevitable. One person's bedtime snack is another's "enormous quantity." Similar problems are encountered in studies that specify calorie minimums, for not all individuals are aware of calorie counts of various foods, and bulimics have been known to give very unreliable estimates of calories consumed during a binge. Probably a number of factors are involved in whether one labels one's own behavior as bingeing. Katzman and Wolchik (1984) found that 56 percent of the females and 38 percent of the males in their college sample replied affirmatively when asked "Do you binge eat?" When the same subjects were asked whether they frequently consumed large quantities of food other than at meals, 37 percent of the females and 43 percent of the males responded affirmatively. Sixty percent of males and 83 percent of females who responded yes to that question also said that they binged. Thus there was a significant sex difference, with females being more likely to label their behavior as bingeing. It is interesting to speculate about what the term bingeing meant to the nearly 20 percent of females who stated that they binged but did not consume much food other than at mealtimes.

Social desirability factors might be involved in whether or not an individual admits to binge eating and other bulimic behaviors. A number of the studies required students to fill out questionnaires in class. The "mindset" students had as they answered questions may have had impact: perhaps they feared that they would be embarrassed in front of peers and teachers by their disclosures, or that they would be in a small minority admitting to this behavior. Alternatively, binge eating could be regarded as a normal and pleasurable collegiate activity for individuals who brag to friends about the quantities of beer and pizza they can consume. In some circles the ability to win an "eating contest" or get one's money's worth at an "all-you-can-eat" restaurant might be admired.

The point at which eating becomes bingeing may be considered in terms of several different characteristics of the eating: amount consumed, frequency and speed of eating, whether it is done alone or with companions, affective state during and after the eating, and whether some type of purging or undoing of the behavior occurs. However, because so little is known about the eating habits of normal eaters, it is difficult to draw conclusions about the first three characteristics. Klesges and associates (1984) found that individuals eating together in cafeterias and restaurants ate more than those eating alone, suggesting that eating larger quantities can be a shared social phenomenon for normal eaters. Much "bingeing" might be this type, where individuals might later shake their heads over how much they ate but would experience no real distress.

The subjective experience of distress would seem to be an important variable in distinguishing between normal overeating and problematic behavior. The DSM-III criteria specify that depressed mood and self-deprecating thoughts following binges are important for the diagnosis of bulimia. Chernyk's study (1981) illustrates some differences between "binges" that caused varying degrees of concern to the students involved. She found that females were more likely to report emotionally upsetting experiences as triggers for binges, to binge on "junk food," and to feel angry, disgusted, and guilty after a binge. Males were more likely to report that binge episodes were associated with events such as physical exertion or being in a good mood and feeling hungry, that they ate protein during a binge, and that they felt happy after the binge. The males' behavior seems to exemplify a type of "bingeing" that involves consuming large amounts without particular concern about one's behavior. The females' experience more closely resembles that of clinical samples of bulimics (Johnson and Larson, 1982; Johnson, Stuckey, Lewis, and Schwartz, 1982; Pyle, Mitchell, and Eckert, 1981).

While the sampling issues and methodological issues mentioned here relate to all nineteen studies, some are much more seriously flawed than others. The best studies have large sample sizes with demographic information reported, a very high return rate, validity checks, clear definitions of bingeing and of bulimia, and have collected information on bingeing and purging that includes frequency variables. The studies of Pyle, Mitchell, Eckert, and Halvorson (1984), Johnson and associates (1984), Pope, Hudson, and Yurgelun-Todd (1984), and Cooper and Fairburn (1983) provide the most useful information. The work of Chernyk (1981) and Nevo (1984) and the high-school study by Pope, Yurgelun-Todd, and Hudson (1984) also merit consideration.

By giving the most serious consideration to the best studies, the wide prevalence estimates reported earlier across all studies may be narrowed. The best estimate of the prevalence of binge eating among females is probably between 26 percent (Cooper and Fairburn, 1983) and 61 percent (Chernyk, 1981). Binge eating in males ranges between 28 percent (Chernyk, 1981) and 42 percent (Pyle, Mitchell, Eckert, and Halvorson, 1983), although it must be remembered that smaller numbers of males have been investigated and that males might define binge eating differently from females.

Because definitional issues are so much clearer, the data on vomiting are significantly less variable across samples. For females the better studies report a range from 3 percent (Chernyk, 1981) to 16 percent (Johnson et al., 1984). The best estimates of vomiting among males range between 1 percent (Chernyk, 1981) and 4 percent (Hawkins and Clement, 1980).

The best studies operationalizing the DSM-III criteria for bulimia cite about 8 percent as the prevalence rate for females (Johnson et al., 1984; Pope, Hudson, Yurgelun-Todd, and Hudson, 1984; Pyle, Mitchell, Eckert, and Halvorson, 1983). Bulimia among males seems to have a prevalence rate of around 1 percent (Pyle, Mitchell, Eckert, and Halvorson, 1983; Stangler and Printz, 1980). Weekly binge eating among females seems to range between 5 percent (Pyle, Mitchell, Eckert, and Halvorson, 1983) and 21 percent (Johnson et al., 1984) and 24 percent (Crowther, Post, and Zaynor, 1985). Weekly vomiting seems to have a very small range, from 1 percent (Cooper and Fairburn, 1983) to 4 percent of females (Johnson et al., 1984). Weekly bingeing followed by vomiting among females also has a very small range, from 1 percent (Pyle, Mitchell, Eckert, and Halvorson, 1983; Johnson et al., 1984) to 3 percent (Crowther, Post, and Zaynor, 1985; Pope, Hudson, and Yurgelun-Todd, 1984).

Thus binge eating is a highly prevalent behavior for males as well as females, although females endorse it more often than do males. The use of purging techniques is much less common, with extremely low rates for males. Around 8 percent of females and 1 percent of males seem to fit the DSM-III criteria for bulimia, and only between 1 percent and 3 percent of females engage in binge eating followed by vomiting at least weekly. However, these data leave many questions unanswered about the point at which various bulimic behaviors cause significant distress to those who engage in them and which aspects of these behaviors are associated with impaired life adjustment.

Prevalence of Dieting Attitudes and Behaviors

Several studies have assessed food-related behaviors that involve voluntary restriction of food intake rather than binge eating as well as the attitudes toward the body that accompany this behavior. While the literature on binge eating deals primarily with behaviors, the dieting literature has explored attitudes as well. Again, we shall review the literature in order to determine which of a group of widely prevalent attitudes and behaviors are associated with a clinically significant problem.

A relatively early study was that of Deisher and Mills (1963), who administered a questionnaire to 690 high-school students ages thirteen to nineteen concerning a variety of issues related to their own health and medical care. Forty-eight percent of the girls and 28 percent of the boys felt they had a weight problem, although this was not specified further.

A later study (Huenemann, Shapiro, Hampton, and Mitchell, 1966) focused more exclusively on weight-related issues. The authors administered several questionnaires and gathered anthropomorphic data from approximately 1,000 California teenagers. According to the data, about 25 percent of both boys and girls were classified as obese or somewhat obese. However, 43 percent of the ninth-grade girls, 49 percent of the tenth-grade girls, and 56 percent of the twelfth-grade girls described themselves as fat, while less than 25 percent of the boys at each grade level did so. Seventy-five percent of the girls said that they were extremely or fairly concerned about being overweight, while a similar percentage of boys expressed concern about being underweight. Between 63 percent and 70 percent of girls wanted to lose weight (exceeding the percentages who described themselves as fat), while more than half the boys wanted to gain, presumably in the form of muscles. In the ninth grade 50 percent of boys and 65 percent of girls said they were trying to do something about their weight, but three times as many girls as boys mentioned diet. By twelfth grade efforts had decreased to 34 percent of boys and 55 percent of girls, with five girls to one boy now mentioning diet.

Nylander (1971) investigated dieting and feelings of being fat in a school population in Sweden. He administered questionnaires to a representative group of 2,370 students ages fourteen to nineteen, most of whom were of normal weight. Among girls, there was a progressive increase in ever having felt fat, from 47 percent at age fourteen to 73 percent at age eighteen. Twenty-six percent of the fourteen-year-old girls and 50 percent of the eighteen-year-old girls reported currently feeling fat. Many had dieted; while dieting was rare before age fourteen, 8 percent of the fourteen-year-old girls had dieted, and dieting peaked at eighteen, with 44 percent of the eighteen-year-old girls having dieted. Not surprisingly, the girls who were above the mean in weight were more than twice as likely to have dieted; of the eighteen-year-old girls whose weight was above the mean for their height, 76 percent were on a diet. Feeling fat and dieting were rare among the boys, with only 7 percent of the eighteen-year-old males reporting feeling fat, and between 3 percent and 4 percent dieting.

Similarly, in a sample of British schoolgirls ages twelve to twenty, Crisp (1981) found that the majority were concerned about being fat and were dieting. He noted that dieting concern increased with menarche, with 27 percent of the girls being concerned about fatness prior to reaching menarche and 48 percent concerned afterward.

The study by Pyle, Mitchell, Eckert, and Halvorson (1983) mentioned earlier also assessed dieting behavior. Of the female subjects, 530 were considered nonbulimic and 45 considered bulimic. Forty-seven percent of the nonbulimics admitted to attempts to control their weight (by a general category including vomiting, laxative abuse, diuretics, enemas, or fasting). Thirty-five percent of the 530 admitted having gone on twenty-four-hour fasts, with 4 percent endorsing this behavior at least weekly. One hundred percent of the students considered bulimic admitted to fasting. Likewise, Kagan and Squires (1983) investigated fasting in a sample of 405 male and female high-school students and found that 12 percent of the females would go on a twenty-four-hour fast at least monthly, and 19 percent of them would do so at least weekly. Among males, 4 percent and 8 percent, respectively, fasted at these frequencies. A 1985 study by Crowther, Post, and Zaynor found that 36 percent of their female high-school students reported fasting for a day or more.

The Johnson and associates (1984) study of 1,268 high-school females cited previously also explored dieting behaviors and attitudes. Students were divided into bulimic and nonbulimic groups; to be placed in the first group, students had to meet the DSM-III criteria for bulimia plus at least weekly bingeing. The two groups did not differ on body weight, but the bulimic group was more likely to see itself as overweight. The bulimic group scored significantly higher on the Body Dissatisfaction and Drive for Thinness subscales of the Eating Disorders Inventory (EDI; Garner, Olmsted, and Polivy, 1983) than the nonbulimic students.

Dieting was defined in this study as "an actual change in eating behavior for the purpose of losing weight." Results indicated a significant relationship between dieting and bulimic behaviors. Of the bulimic group, 68 percent reported that they were currently dieting, compared to 35 percent of the nonbulimic group. There was a significant relationship between frequency of dieting and endorsement of bulimic behaviors: 33 percent of the bulimic group reported that they were always dieting, compared to only 6 percent of the nonbulimic group, and 14 percent of the bulimic group reported dieting more than ten times in the last year, compared to 3 percent of the nonbulimic group. Therefore, 47 percent of the bulimic students could be regarded as chronic dieters in contrast to 9 percent of the nonbulimic students.

Three studies have explored dieting behaviors and attitudes through using the EDI or its earlier version, the Eating Attitudes Test (EAT; Garner and Garfinkel, 1979). Although all three studies relate extreme dieting behaviors to anorexia nervosa rather than to bulimia, they are relevant here to an investigation of the variety of behaviors that may be considered bulimic as well. Button and Whitehouse (1981) administered the EAT to 578 students (446 females and 132 males) at a British college of technology. A 99 percent compliance rate was obtained. A sample of fourteen anorexics also received the questionnaire. High-scoring students (scores greater than 32) were interviewed, as was a random sample of low scorers. The most noticeable difference between the high and low scorers was that the former had a lower minimum weight since puberty. The authors noted that the twenty-eight high scorers formed a heterogeneous group and that they could be divided into three subgroups: normal dieters, those who had an abnormal preoccupation with weight and food, and those who were vomiters and purgers. Thirty-nine percent of the high-scoring group had engaged in vomiting.

Michael Thompson and Donald Schwartz (1982) also used the EAT with a sample of twenty-six anorexic females, twenty-five normal-weight college students whose EAT scores were 25 or more, and twenty-six normal controls (EAT scores 10 or less). They found that binge eating was widespread, with 58 percent of the anorexics, 52 percent of the high-EAT group, and 23 percent of the controls reporting severe or moderate bingeing. Vomiting was reported by 50 percent of the anorexics and 52 percent of the high-EAT group. Fifty-four percent of the anorexics had abused laxatives, as had 20 percent of the high-EAT group. Dieting was extremely widespread, with virtually all of the high-EAT group and many of the controls stating that they were always dieting.

In terms of psychological functioning, the high-EAT group was not significantly different from the controls on the Weissman Social Adjustment Scale (Weissman et al., 1978). Both of the student groups were significantly better than the anorexics, and both appeared to have considerable satisfaction in work, social life, and family interaction, in contrast to the anorexics. Similar to the findings of Button and Whitehouse (1981), the high-EAT group was heterogeneous. The authors described it as comprising a mixture of potential anorexics, clinically depressed women, women under some sort of stress, former models and athletes, and women with an unattainable body ideal. The majority were in a period of stressful development. The authors concluded that women can evidence relatively high levels of "anorexic" symptomatology—that is, extreme dieting attitudes and behaviors—without adverse affects on their life adjustment. The high-EAT scorers had somewhat higher levels of anxiety and depression, but their overall symptom distress was mild.

A recent study (Garner, Olmsted, Polivy, and Garfinkel, 1984) extended and refined this earlier work on a continuum of dieting behavior. Three groups of female subjects were given the EDI: a group of 237 college females, a group of 66 ballet students, and 50 anorexic patients (27 restrictors and 23 bulimic anorexics). The college and ballet students were divided into two groups on the basis of their scores on the EDI's Drive for Thinness subscale. Middle scorers were eliminated to form a Weight Preoccupied (WP) and a Not Weight Preoccupied (NWP) group. The results indicated that dieting behavior and body dissatisfaction were similar for the anorexic and WP groups, while the NWP group scored low on both. On all other subscales, the anorexics scored significantly higher, and were most clearly differentiated from the WP group on Ineffectiveness, Interpersonal Distrust, and lack of Interoceptive Awareness. Again, the WP group was shown to be heterogeneous. Using cluster analysis, a group of women who had elevated scores on all EDI subscales was found. This group had significant psychopathology and perhaps could be considered to have a subclinical variant of anorexia nervosa. Another group was found to be without significant pathology; the authors equated these women with the "normal dieters" of Button and Whitehouse (1981). Thus, while some women who are preoccupied with weight and dieting closely resemble anorexics in eating and other pathology, another group exists that is weight preoccupied without other impairment. Clinical interviews of subsamples of both WP and NWP groups confirmed these impressions. The authors caution against drawing conclusions about weight-preoccupied women on the basis of their eating attitudes alone, in that from such information one might falsely conclude that they are very similar to anorexics.

It is apparent that in the female population body dissatisfaction, the perception of oneself as fat, and dieting behaviors are extremely widespread. There is some evidence that these characteristics have been increasing and that a younger population has been affected; while Nylander (1971) found that dieting was rare before age fourteen, Johnson and associates (1983) found that 52 percent of their adolescents had begun dieting before age fourteen. Like binge eating, dieting attitudes and behaviors are ubiquitous, so much so that nondieters can constitute a minority in a particular peer group. Thus questions must be raised concerning what differentiates normal dieting from a preoccupation with food and weight that interferes with life adjustment. The studies reviewed clearly show that weight preoccupation affects a heterogeneous group of women, ranging from a well-adjusted group to severely impaired anorexics.

Summary

The data reviewed suggest that binge eating, body dissatisfaction, and dieting are highly prevalent behaviors, particularly among young women. These attitudes and behaviors are endorsed by a very heterogeneous group of individuals. Although such attitudes and behaviors are associated with the syndrome of bulimia, only a small minority of these individuals fit the DSM-III criteria for bulimia. Using current criteria, approximately 8 percent of females and 1 percent of males would be diagnosed as bulimic. As we discussed in the first chapter, these criteria may not identify individuals suffering from a clinically significant disorder that results in life impairment. According to more stringent criteria involving frequency stipulations and the involvement of purging, between 1 percent and 3 percent of females engage in binge eating followed by vomiting at least weekly. Based on the very small amount of available data, it appears that less than 0.5 percent of males binge and vomit this frequently.

3

Demographic and Clinical Characteristics

Demographic Information

This chapter presents a comprehensive review of the demographic profile and clinical characteristics of bulimic patients. The data is drawn from two series of reports that include both clinical populations and large, broad-based community samples.

Normally, the presentation of demographic information can be quite boring. While readers may find that to be the case here as well, we found ourselves interested and amazed at the remarkable consistency in findings that emerged between samples. Independent researchers in different continents reported on virtually identical samples within two years of each other. Prior to these reports, which began in 1976, there were no large-sample descriptive reports regarding the symptoms of bulimia. Certainly there had not been any clustering of reports that documented bulimic behavior among such a homogeneous cohort.

Of particular interest in the review are reports from two large-community samples: one we developed in the United States (1982), the other developed by Fairburn and Cooper (1982) in England. Both samples utilized mail surveys to investigate demographic and clinical features of bulimic behavior among individuals who identified themselves as having difficulty with specified symptoms. Subjects responded to invitations to write to the two research projects after media presentations (in magazines and newspapers) on bulimia. Both projects received several thousand responses of which only subsamples were analyzed.

SEX

As depicted in table 3.1, females are highly overrepresented in the samples. While there is consensus that bulimia appears to affect primarily females, many researchers suspect that these findings underrepresent the

TABLE 3.1

Sex Distribution in Clinical and Community Samples

	Males (%)	Females (%)
Clinical Samples		
Russell, 1979	7	93
Pyle, Mitchell, and Eckert, 1981		100
Herzog, 1982	3	97
Fairburn and Cooper, 1984b		100
Mitchell, Davis, and Goff, 1985		100
Community Samples		
Johnson, Stuckey, Lewis, and Schwartz, 1982	1	99
Fairburn and Cooper, 1982		100
Fairburn and Cooper, 1984a		100

incidence of bulimia among males. The labeling in most early research of bulimia as a predominantly female disorder has likely discouraged men from acknowledging distress with the problem.

AGE

As depicted in table 3.2, there is remarkable consistency between both the clinical and the community samples regarding the ages of the individuals at the point of initial contact. The average age across all samples was 23.9 years, with a range from fifteen to fifty-one years of age. There is also striking consistency regarding the relative distribution of ages between samples, with 86 percent of the individuals falling between the ages of fifteen and thirty.

AGE OF ONSET

The average age of onset for both the clinical and community samples was approximately eighteen years old, with a range from nine to forty-five years old. (See table 3.3.) Community samples accounted for more younger ages of onset—12 percent under fifteen—compared to 6 percent under fifteen in the clinical samples. The clinical samples also appeared to have more patients with an older age of onset (11 percent over thirty) than the community sample (3.2 percent over thirty). It is also interesting to note that among all the studies, purging behavior was consistently reported to begin approximately one year after the onset of binge eating.

DURATION OF ILLNESS

Duration of illness was similar between samples, with the average being approximately five years (see table 3.4). The distributions were identical between both the clinical and community samples, with 65 percent of the sample reporting a duration of five years or less.

TABLE 3.2

Age Distribution in Clinical and Community Samples

	Mean Age	Range
Clinical Samples		
Russell, 1979	22.8	16–36
Pyle, Mitchell, and Eckert, 1981	24	19–51
Herzog, 1982	25.3	15–42
Fairburn and Cooper, 1984b	23.5	18–35
Mitchell, Davis, and Goff, 1985	24.8	18–48
Community Samples		
Johnson, Stuckey, Lewis, and Schwartz, 1982	23.7	15–44
Fairburn and Cooper, 1982	23.8	15–35
Fairburn and Cooper, 1984a	28.1	N/A

	Age Distribution (%)				
	15–19	*20–24*	*25–29*	*30–34*	*35+*
Clinical Samples					
Russell, 1979 (N = 30)	30	40	17	3	10
Pyle, Mitchell, and Eckert, 1981 (N = 34)	6	50	26	12	6
MEAN	17	45	22	8	8
Community Samples					
Johnson, Stuckey, Lewis, and Schwartz, 1982 (N = 316)	22	43	22	7	6
Fairburn and Cooper, 1982 (N = 499)	20	46	22	8	5
MEAN	21	45	22	8	6

Other Demographics

All the samples indicated that the patient population was predominantly Caucasian and that the distribution of religious affiliations was similar to population norms (see table 3.6). Most patients were also unmarried (see table 3.5).

Several studies investigated socioeconomic status. In their community sample, Johnson, Stuckey, Lewis, and Schwartz (1982) found (using the Hollingshead method, 1957) patients to cluster in Categories I (graduate-level education and holding high administrative or professional positions), III (administrative personnel, small independent business owners and semiprofessionals), and IV (clerical and sales workers; technicians).

In the clinical samples, Lacey (1982) reported that among a series of twenty bulimic patients, fourteen fathers came from Social Classes IV and V (semiskilled—unskilled), whereas thirteen of the patients would be classified as Social Class I and II. These findings are significant in that

TABLE 3.3
Ages of Onset in Clinical and Community Samples

	Mean Age	Range
Clinical Samples		
Russell, 1979	21.2	13–37
Pyle, Mitchell, and Eckert, 1981	18	11–45
Herzog, 1982	N/A	N/A
Fairburn and Cooper, 1984b	19.7	5–37
Mitchell, Davis, and Goff, 1985	<u>17.7</u>	
MEAN	19.2	
Community Samples		
Johnson, Stuckey, Lewis, and Schwartz, 1982	18	9–36
Fairburn and Cooper, 1982	18	10–35
Fairburn and Cooper, 1984a	<u>20.2</u>	N/A
MEAN	18.7	

	Age Distribution for Age of Onset (%)					
	<15	*15–19*	*20–24*	*25–29*	*30–34*	*35+*
Clinical Samples						
Russell, 1979 (N = 30)	0	53	27	3	9	6
Pyle, Mitchell, and Eckert, 1981 (N = 34)	<u>12</u>	<u>59</u>	<u>15</u>	<u>9</u>	<u>3</u>	<u>3</u>
MEAN	6	56	21	6	6	5
Community Samples						
Johnson, Stuckey, Lewis, and Schwartz, 1982 (N = 316)	12	62	16	6	3	1
Fairburn and Cooper, 1982 (N = 499)	<u>12</u>	<u>58</u>	<u>23</u>	<u>4</u>	<u>1</u>	<u>1</u>
MEAN	12	60	20	5	2	1

they reflect a greater heterogeneity of socioeconomic status than is typically cited for individuals with anorexia nervosa. They also suggest the tendency of bulimics to move up in social class through education.

Family demographics indicate that the birth order of the identified patient was equally divided, with 30 percent being firstborn, 30 percent being middle children, and 35 percent being the youngest sibling (Johnson, Stuckey, Lewis, and Schwartz, 1982). Of the subjects, 2.4 percent were only children and 1.2 percent had a twin sibling. Divorce occurred in 27 percent of the families, 63 percent remained married, and 10 percent were widowed (Herzog, 1982).

TABLE 3.4
Duration of Illness in Clinical and Community Samples

	Mean Years	*Range*
Clinical Samples		
Russell, 1979	4	1–11
Pyle, Mitchell, and Eckert, 1981	4	1–26
Herzog, 1982	N/A	N/A
Fairburn and Cooper, 1984b	3.8	N/A
Mitchell, Davis, and Goff, 1985	7	N/A
MEAN	4.7	
Community Samples		
Johnson, Stuckey, Lewis, and Schwartz, 1982	5.4	1–18
Fairburn and Cooper, 1982	5.2	N/A
Fairburn and Cooper, 1984a	7.9	N/A
MEAN	6.2	

	Duration of Illness (%)			
	≤1 year	*2–5 years*	*6–10 years*	*>10 years*
Clinical Samples				
Russell, 1979	23	53	23	0
Pyle, Mitchell, and Eckert, 1981	18	35	38	9
MEAN	21	44	31	4
Community Sample				
Johnson, Stuckey, Lewis, and Schwartz, 1982	14	51	22	13

WEIGHT STATUS

Current and past weights of bulimic subjects provide somewhat inconsistent information, although trends do emerge. Based on the actuarial tables of the Metropolitan Life Insurance Company (1959), or the matched population mean weight figures, the majority of bulimic women studied were of normal weight for their height at the time weight data was collected. As mentioned in chapter 1, however, the use of the term normal weight may be a misnomer for many bulimic patients.

CURRENT WEIGHT

Among Pyle, Mitchell, and Eckert's sample (1981) of thirty-four patients, 74 percent weighed below the median weight for their height given in the Metropolitan Life Insurance Tables (a medium frame is used as the basis for all statistics). Thirty-five percent weighed below the minimum acceptable weight, although all were less than 15 percent below this weight (mean of 3.45 kg below, range 1.4 to 7.5 kg). Seven patients weighed less

TABLE 3.5

Marital Status in Clinical and Community Samples

	Single (%)	Married (%)	Divorced (%)
Clinical Samples			
Russell, 1979	N/A	N/A	N/A
Pyle, Mitchell, and Eckert, 1981	65	18	18
Herzog, 1982	73	20	7
Fairburn and Cooper, 1984b	71	20	9
Mitchell, Davis, and Goff, 1985	N/A	N/A	N/A
MEAN	70	19.3	11.2
Community Samples			
Johnson, Stuckey, Lewis, and Schwartz, 1982	70.6	18.3	10.2
Fairburn and Cooper, 1982	70.3	20.7	9
Fairburn and Cooper, 1984a	N/A	N/A	N/A
MEAN	70.5	19.5	9.6

than 5 kg above and only two patients weighed more than 5 kg above the median weight for their height.

Results of a larger, subsequent clinical sample reported by the Minnesota group (Mitchell, Hatsukami, Eckert, and Pyle, 1985) indicated that none of their sample was 25 percent below expected body weight; 27.2 percent were 10 to 24 percent below that weight; and 30 percent were 10 percent below that weight; 21.7 percent were 1 to 9 percent above expected weight; 15.7 percent were 10 to 24 percent overweight; and 4.5 percent were more than 25 percent overweight. Fairburn and Cooper's clinical sample (1984b) from England was similar: none of their sample was below 25 percent of expected weight; 5.7 percent were 15 to

TABLE 3.6

Religious Affiliation in Clinical and Community Samples

	Protestant (%)	Catholic (%)	Jewish (%)	Other/None (%)
Clinical Samples				
Russell, 1979	N/A	N/A	N/A	N/A
Pyle, Mitchell, and Eckert, 1981	21	35	9	35
Herzog, 1982	37	27	37	—
Fairburn and Cooper, 1984b	N/A	N/A	N/A	N/A
Mitchell, Davis, and Goff, 1985	N/A	N/A	N/A	N/A
Community Samples				
Johnson et al., 1982	41	34.2	9	15.8
Fairburn and Cooper, 1982	N/A	N/A	N/A	N/A
Fairburn and Cooper, 1984a				

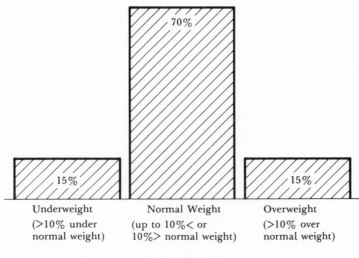

FIGURE 3.1
Current Weight

25 percent underweight; 65.7 percent were 1 to 15 percent underweight; 22.9 percent were 1 to 15 percent overweight; and 5.7 percent were greater than 15 percent overweight.

Among the community samples, Johnson, Stuckey, Lewis, and Schwartz (1982) found that 1 percent were below 25 percent expected weight; 20 percent were 10 to 25 percent below weight; 61.6 percent were between 10 percent below and 10 percent above expected weight; and 17.5 percent were greater than 10 percent overweight. Fairburn and Cooper's findings (1982) among the British community sample were similar: none were below 25 percent expected weight; 2.1 percent were 15 to 25 percent below weight; 86 percent were found within a range of 15 percent below to 15 percent above, and 6.6 percent were greater than 15 percent overweight.

Consequently, as figure 3.1 depicts (combining the data from the clinical and community samples), approximately 70 percent of the samples were within a normal weight range, 15 percent would be considered underweight, and 15 percent overweight.

Previous Weight

HIGH WEIGHT

Pyle, Mitchell, and Eckert (1981) reported that among their clinical sample, 17.6 percent weighed more than the maximum acceptable weight for their height at some point in their life. In contrast, the Minnesota group (Mitchell, Hatsukami, Eckert, and Pyle, 1985) reported several years later that among their larger clinical series, 56 percent of the sample were 10 percent or more overweight at some time since age eighteen (33 percent were between 10 and 25 percent overweight; and 23 percent were 25 percent or more overweight). Among Fairburn and Cooper's British clinical sample (1984b), 54 percent were also found to have been 15 percent or more overweight at some time since menarche. Fairburn and Cooper (1982) reported that 25 percent of their community sample had histories of being more than 15 percent overweight since menarche.

LOW WEIGHT

Previous low weight is interesting because it is a potential indicator of the subgroup of bulimic patients who may have had episodes of anorexia nervosa. Among Russell's sample (1979) of thirty clinical patients, 57 percent had a history of less than 25 percent expected body weight with accompanying prolonged amenorrhea. Pyle, Mitchell, and Eckert (1981) reported that 29 percent of their sample had severe weight loss and associated symptoms that met DSM-III criteria for anorexia nervosa. Mitchell, Hatsukami, Eckert, and Pyle (1985) reported that 14 percent of their clinical sample had histories of being more than 25 percent below expected weight, and Fairburn and Cooper (1984b) found that 25.7 percent of their sample had previously met criteria for the diagnosis of anorexia nervosa.

The incidence of low weight associated with anorexia nervosa was lower among the community samples. Johnson, Stuckey, Lewis, and Schwartz (1982) reported that approximately 6 percent of their sample had previous histories of anorexia nervosa. Fairburn and Cooper (1982) found that approximately 12 percent of their sample had histories of weight loss below 75 percent of expected body weight.

Thus the data from both clinical samples and community studies suggest that while most bulimics are of relatively normal weight when they present for treatment, over half appear to have histories of being overweight. Furthermore it appears that approximately one quarter of the bulimics have been 25 percent underweight at some time.

Overall, both clinical and community samples found that over 90 percent of the bulimic individuals were females; 86 percent of all cases were between the ages of fifteen and thirty. They were predominantly single, upwardly mobile, college-educated individuals from predominantly intact families of more than one child. Sixty-seven percent of the individuals across samples had begun to binge just prior to age nineteen, with average duration of illness at the time of assessment of 5.4 years. Seventy percent of all cases were within a normal weight range at the time of assessment, with 15 percent being significantly underweight and 15 percent being overweight. Roughly one-third to one-half of the individuals appeared to have been overweight at some point. Approximately 10 percent of the community samples and 30 percent of the clinical samples had a probable previous history of anorexia nervosa.

Bulimia Among Males

A small amount of data has recently begun to appear regarding bulimia among males. Fairburn and Cooper (1984a) noted that forty-five males (of a total of 1,391 respondents) returned their questionnaires. Two were anorexic; of the remaining forty-three, eight fulfilled the criteria for bulimia. The authors reported that these men closely resembled the bulimic women demographically. Mitchell and Goff (1984) reported on a series of twelve adult males. These cases included all the males seen for outpatient diagnostic evaluation at the University of Minnesota Eating Disorders Clinic over a three-year period. The mean age at evaluation was twenty-five, the mean age of onset of bulimia was nineteen, and the average duration of illness before treatment was 5.7 years. All twelve patients were Caucasian and all but one were single. Three were students, and all were employed, with a wide diversity of occupations.

Too little data are currently available to draw conclusions regarding the similarities and differences between male and female bulimics. At present, it appears that clinically they are quite similar. It is unclear, however, whether the pathway to the symptomatic behavior is similar between groups.

TABLE 3.7

Frequency of Binge Eating

	More than Once a Day (%)	More than Once a Week (%)	Less than Once a Week (%)
Clinical Samples			
Russell, 1979	N/A	N/A	N/A
Pyle, Mitchell, and Eckert, 1981	56	35	9
Herzog, 1982	N/A	N/A	N/A
Fairburn and Cooper, 1984b[a]	48	51	N/A
Mitchell, Davis, and Goff, 1985	82	16	2
MEAN	62	34	6
Community Samples			
Johnson, Stuckey, Lewis, and Schwartz, 1982	50	42	8
Fairburn and Cooper, 1982	27	33	40
Fairburn and Cooper, 1984a	33	38	29
MEAN	36	38	26

[a] Weekly or greater frequency criteria.

Symptomatic Food-Related Behavior

FREQUENCY OF BINGE EATING

In reviewing the data on frequency of binge eating, several interesting findings emerged. Combining both the clinical and community samples, it appears that, overall, approximately 50 percent of the individuals report binge eating daily or more often, 35 percent have difficulty weekly or greater, and about 15 percent report binge eating less than weekly (see table 3.7). It is interesting to note that the severity of frequency has increased dramatically (56 percent to 82 percent) from 1981 to 1985 in the Minnesota clinical sample. It is also noteworthy that the U.S. community sample reported greater severity of binge eating; 92 percent of the American sample reported weekly or more episodes compared to 60 percent of the British sample.

FREQUENCY OF PURGING

Self-induced vomiting is clearly the preferred mechanism for evacuation, with approximately 50 percent of the individuals in all samples reporting vomiting at least daily and an additional 25 percent reporting vomiting weekly or greater (see table 3.8). Across all samples, approximately 35 percent of the respondents reported using laxatives at least weekly (see table 3.9).

TABLE 3.8

Frequency of Vomiting

	More than Once a Day (%)	More than Once a Week (%)	Less than Once a Week (%)	Never (%)
Clinical Samples				
Russell, 1979	N/A	N/A	N/A	N/A
Pyle, Mitchell, and Eckert, 1981	47	41	6	6
Herzog, 1982	N/A	N/A	N/A	N/A
Fairburn and Cooper, 1984b[a]	74	25	N/A	N/A
Mitchell, Davis, and Goff, 1985	72	12	4	12
MEAN	64	26	5	9
Community Samples				
Johnson, Stuckey, Lewis, and Schwartz, 1982	36	22	9	23
Fairburn and Cooper, 1982	56	16	N/A	N/A
Fairburn and Cooper, 1984a	47	23	N/A	N/A
MEAN	46	20	—	—

[a] Weekly or greater inclusion criteria.

BINGE-EATING BEHAVIOR

In an attempt to gather more precise information about binge eating, Mitchell, Pyle, and Eckert (1981) collected data on the duration and frequency of binge eating and vomiting episodes among forty bulimic patients. This group, who kept careful records for a week prior to beginning

TABLE 3.9

Frequency of Laxative Use

	More than Once a Day (%)	More than Once a Week (%)	Less than Once a Week (%)	Never (%)
Clinical Samples				
Russell, 1979	N/A	N/A	N/A	N/A
Pyle, Mitchell, and Eckert, 1981	3	12	38	47
Herzog, 1982	N/A	N/A	N/A	N/A
Fairburn and Cooper, 1984b	N/A	N/A	N/A	N/A
Mitchell, Davis, and Goff, 1985	20	28	12	40
	12	20	25	44
Community Samples				
Johnson, Stuckey, Lewis, and Schwartz, 1982	14	19	27	40
Fairburn and Cooper, 1982	N/A	N/A	N/A	N/A
Fairburn and Cooper, 1984a	N/A	N/A	N/A	N/A

a group therapy program, reported an average of 11.7 binge-eating episodes per week, with a range of one to forty-six episodes. The mean duration of each episode was reported to be 1.18 hours, with a range from fifteen minutes to eight hours. Among this group, the most common pattern was for the individual to binge eat at least once each day, spending on the average 13.7 hours each week binge eating, with a range from 30 minutes to 43 hours. Of the forty patients, thirty-seven vomited as part of the syndrome; their mean frequency of vomiting episodes was 11.7 per week.

Susan Abraham and Peter Beumont (1982b) asked thirty-two patients who presented to an eating disorders clinic complaining of episodes of overeating to describe their experiences. Patients described the length of binge episodes as ranging from fifteen minutes to three weeks in duration. Some patients, especially those with more recent onset of the behavior, viewed their bulimia as occurring in discrete episodes, up to six in one day. Other patients, often those with long histories of binge eating, described a continuous urge to binge with episodes lasting for days and weeks.

A number of authors* have reported that binge-eating episodes are most likely to occur when patients are alone, primarily during evening hours.

Most binges appear to consist of sweets or salty carbohydrates. These are foods that the patients generally regard as "forbidden." The caloric intake during a binge is difficult to assess. Patients in Mitchell, Hatsukami, Eckert, and Pyle's sample (1981) estimated that during an average binge episode, they consumed 3,415 calories (range 1,200 to 11,500). Abraham and Beumont (1982b) reported that the calorie content of food eaten on what a patient would describe as a "bad day" of binge eating ranged from three to twenty-seven times the recommended daily energy allowance as given by the Australian Food Composition Tables (Thomas and Corden, 1970).

PRECIPITANTS OF THE SYNDROME

Research has indicated that the onset of bulimic symptoms often follows a period of restrictive dieting. This was the case for 88 percent of the thirty-four patients in Pyle, Mitchell, and Eckert's clinical sample (1981), and for 34 percent of the Johnson, Stuckey, Lewis, and Schwartz (1982) sample. In Fairburn and Cooper's clinical sample (1984b), having adopted a rigid diet was cited as the most common precipitating factor. Similarly, Abraham and Beumont (1982) reported that onset of bingeing in their sample followed a period of increased concern about body weight

* See Abraham and Beumont, 1982b; Carroll and Leon, 1981; Johnson, Stuckey, Lewis, and Schwartz, 1982; Mitchell, Hatsukami, Eckert, and Pyle, 1985; and Pyle, Mitchell, and Eckert, 1981.

TABLE 3.10
Precipitants of Binge Eating on the Diagnostic Survey
for Eating Disorders

Precipitating Event	Percent
Prolonged period of dieting	59
Family problems	58
Teasing about appearance	56
Problems in romantic relationship	55
Leaving home	42
Failure at school or work	42
Work transition	23
Difficult sexual experience	21
Illness or injury to self	14
Illness or injury to family member or significant other	13
Death of significant other	10
Pregnancy	4

NOTE: Patients were instructed to check as many items as were applicable.

resulting in dieting. They further noted that this concern with dieting was often associated with a developing interest in the opposite sex.

Eighty-eight percent of the thirty-four patients in Pyle, Mitchell, and Eckert's sample reported traumatic events such as loss or separation from a significant person in their lives as associated with the onset of bulimic behavior. Feelings about sexual changes or arguments with significant others were each cited by 15 percent of patients as related to onset. Carroll and Leon (1981) found that 86 percent of a sample of bulimic women they studied could recall a specific event coinciding with the onset of bingeing. The most frequently mentioned events were losses and separations or important life transitions.

Johnson, Stuckey, Lewis, and Schwartz (1982) reported that 40 percent of their sample attributed the onset of bulimia to difficulty in handling specific emotions, especially depression, loneliness, boredom, and anger. Loss or separation from friends, family, or work were cited by 7 percent, and an additional 7 percent reported interpersonal conflicts as precipitating factors.

Table 3.10 represents recent findings from our clinical sample of bulimic patients. Individuals were asked to identify events they felt preceded or coincided with the onset of their bulimia. Once again, a prolonged period of dieting and difficulty in interpersonal relationships appear to be the most common precipitants.

Among the studies there is striking consensus that prolonged dieting is a central precipitant to the onset of bulimia. The physiological and psychological deprivation induced by dieting, coupled with the occurrence of a stressful life event (separation, interpersonal conflict), may be sufficient to provoke binge-eating behavior among certain individuals. In chapter 7 we elaborate on how biological, familial, and characterological factors may work together to predispose certain individuals to develop bulimia.

The Phenomenological Experience of Binge Eating/Purging

Several studies have attempted to investigate bulimic patients' experiential state before, during, and after a binge/purge episode. These studies have relied on two different techniques to assess the patient's experience. One group of studies simply asked patients how they usually feel before, during, and after an episode (Abraham and Beumont, 1982; Carroll and Leon, 1981; Mitchell, Hatsukami, Eckert, and Pyle, 1985). The other group utilized time-sampling techniques where patients carry diaries over a period of time and report on their thoughts and feelings before and after an episode.

Abraham and Beumont (1982b) asked patients to describe the factors they viewed as precipitating episodes of bulimia. According to the patients, these included tension (91 percent), eating something (84 percent), being alone (78 percent), craving specific foods (78 percent), thinking of food (75 percent), going home (72 percent), feeling bored and lonely (59 percent), feeling hungry (44 percent), drinking alcohol (44 percent), going out with a member of the opposite sex (25 percent), eating out (22 percent), and going to parties (22 percent). Eighty percent of patients described physical concomitants of anxiety before a binge (for example, palpitations, sweating), and feelings of depersonalization and derealization were reported by 79 percent.

Thirty-four percent described relief from anxiety during the binge, and sixty-six percent described freedom from anxiety at the conclusion of a binge. Seventy-two percent reported that they were free of negative mood states while bingeing, while forty-four percent reported frequently having negative feelings after a binge. It appears that the induction of vomiting after a binge influenced the quality of the postbinge mood, with those patients who refrained from vomiting more likely to report anxiety and negative moods. Five patients specifically associated relief with vomiting rather than binge eating.

Carroll and Leon (1981) reported that almost 70 percent of their subjects felt that people in their environment could trigger bingeing, with the mother most commonly identified. Three-fourths of the sample reported that the most frequent affective states preceding a binge were anger, anxiety, rejection, or loneliness.

Mitchell, Hatsukami, Eckert, and Pyle (1985) asked patients to give reasons for their binge eating. The most commonly endorsed items were feeling tense and anxious (83 percent), craving certain foods (70 percent), feeling unhappy (67 percent), not being able to control appetite (59 percent), feeling hungry (40 percent), and inability to sleep (22 percent). Most patients endorsed several items. The authors noted that approximately one patient in five indicated used bingeing and purging as a relaxation method, to induce sleep. Strikingly, both these authors and Abraham and Beumont found that feeling tense and anxious was the single item almost universally endorsed as a precipitant.

Patients reported predominantly negative feelings after a binge episode in the Mitchell, Hatsukami, Eckert, and Pyle sample. They included feeling guilty (87 percent), too full (64 percent), worried (53 percent), and still hungry (23 percent). A minority of patients reported feeling relaxed (23 percent) or satisfied (15 percent).

Figure 3.2 presents findings from our clinical population of seventy-three bulimic patients. Patients were asked to rate how intensely they experienced these different affects on a five-point scale. The most substantial changes occur around the affects calm, excited, bored, panicked, and relieved. Overall, it appears that for most patients the prebinge state is one of agitation, including feelings of boredom, frustration, and loneliness. The process of vomiting appears to result primarily in feelings of calmness and relief. The tension-regulating function of the binge/purge sequence has been further explored through the use of microanalytic techniques.

Johnson and Larson (1982) investigated aspects of bulimics' daily lives through a sampling technique involving subjects' carrying electronic pagers and filling out self-report diaries in response to signals occurring at random times during the course of a day. The sampling data provided a microanalysis of bulimics' prebinge, binge, and postbinge behavior (see figure 3.3). The prebinge reports indicated a disruption in the women's baseline experience characterized by increased appetite and feelings of inadequacy and lack of control. Reports during the binge itself showed that except for a lessening of hunger, negative states were exacerbated during this time. The greatest shift occurred during the purge, when anger declined sharply, alertness increased, and feelings of adequacy and control began to return to baseline. Johnson and Larson concluded that the actual bingeing behavior was no longer relieving but was related to patients' feeling worse. They obtained relief in the purge, however, experiencing a restored sense of control, adequacy, alertness, and a decline in anger. The authors suggested that a transformation may occur over time; the purging behavior rather than the bingeing may become the primary means of tension reduction. They speculated that many women may be bingeing in order to purge, and that the clinical focus should perhaps be on the function of the purging in the maintenance of the binge/purge cycle. This view and its ramifications will be discussed in later chapters.

Davis, Freeman, and Solyom (1985) used similar sampling techniques to investigate both normal eating and bingeing in a group of bulimic subjects and controls. Subjects monitored themselves and wrote down hourly statements about food consumed and whether the food was considered a snack, meal, or binge, and rated hunger and mood on a scale

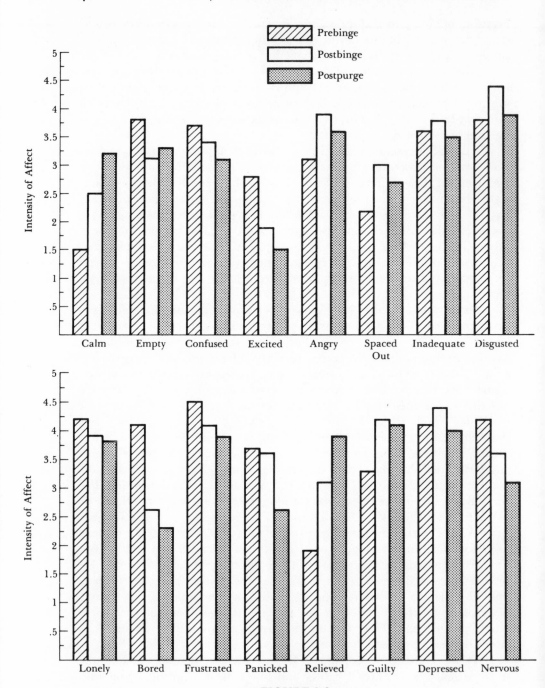

FIGURE 3.2
*Intensity of Affect on the Diagnostic Survey of Eating Disorders (DSED-R)—
Prebinge, Postbinge, and Postpurge*

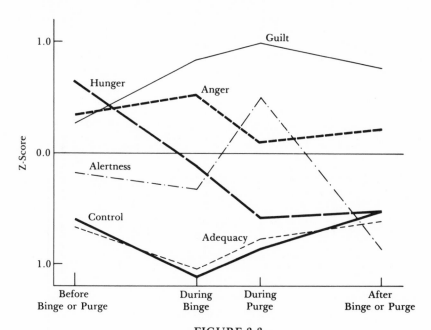

FIGURE 3.3
Reconstruction of the Binge-Purge Sequence

from 1 to 100. Subjects also marked whether and when they were experiencing various unpleasant events. Results indicated that the bulimic subjects experienced more unpleasant events and consumed more snacks but fewer meals compared to controls. Bulimics reported improved mood before and after snacks and meals, while comparison subjects reported improved mood only after snacks and meals.

Bulimics experienced a significant decrease in mood in the hour preceding bulimic episodes and an even greater deterioration in mood in the hour after an episode. Further, bulimics were more likely to be alone prior to and during bulimic episodes, and were more likely to have begun eating or handling food in the hour prior to a bulimic episode. The authors concluded that positive mood, food abstinence combined with hunger, and being in the company of another person facilitates normal eating in bulimics, while negative mood, recent eating, and solitude predisposes them toward bulimic episodes. Davis, Freeman, and Solyom supported data reported by Johnson and Larson (1982) in suggesting that bulimics experience more negative moods than controls and that while they tend to experience negative feelings prior to a binge, they may feel even worse following a bulimic episode.

Eating normal meals is problematic for most bulimic individuals. The majority of the Pyle, Mitchell, and Eckert's sample (1981) reported difficulty in eating normal meals when they were not bingeing, and fasting

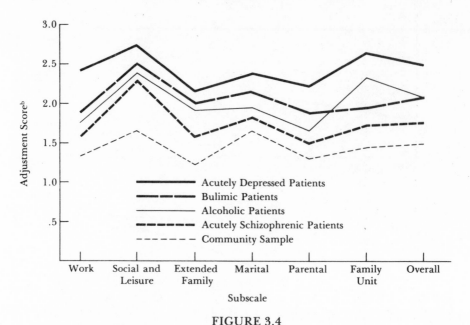

FIGURE 3.4

Social Adjustment Scale Scores of Bulimic, Acutely Depressed, Alcoholic, and Acutely Schizophrenic Women and of Women in a Normal Community Sample[a]

[a] The scores of the depressed, alcoholic, and schizophrenic patients and the community sample are from a study by Weissman and associates. See M. M. Weissman et al., "Social adjustment by self report in a community sample and in psychiatric outpatients," *Journal of Nervous and Mental Diseases* 166 (1978): 317–26, copyright 1978 by Williams and Wilkins.
[b] A lower score indicates better adjustment.

between binges was common. Similarly, Carroll and Leon's study (1981) reported that patients tended to skip meals and severely restrict food intake when not bingeing. In the Mitchell, Hatsukami, Eckert, and Pyle (1985) sample of 275, patients were asked how often they ate "normal meals" (this was not defined further). Only 21 percent reported that they ate two or more normal meals a day. An additional 19 percent indicated that they usually ate one normal meal daily, 39 percent stated that they ate a normal meal between once and several times per week, and 21 percent reported that they ate normal meals less than once a week or not at all. When patients were asked what feelings they usually experienced after eating a normal meal, the item most commonly endorsed was "worried" (44 percent). Others reported feeling hungry (39 percent), guilty (31 percent), or too full (29 percent), suggesting that bulimic patients tend to regard even "normal" eating as an aversive or unsatisfying experience akin to bingeing.

LIFE ADJUSTMENT

One of the more sobering findings in the early studies on bulimic patients is the extent of life impairment among the group. Johnson and Berndt (1983) investigated the functioning of eighty bulimic women in the areas of work, social/leisure, and familial relations using the Social Adjustment Scale (Weissman et al., 1978). The bulimic women had significantly poorer life adjustment in all areas compared to a community sample described by Weissman and associates. (See figure 3.4.) Although the bulimic women were less impaired than an acutely depressed comparison group, they showed more impairment than schizophrenic and alcoholic patients. In general, their pattern was most comparable to that of the alcoholic sample.

Norman and Herzog (1984) also used the Social Adjustment Scale with a sample of forty bulimic women. The scale was administered at the time of their initial evaluation at an outpatient eating disorders clinic and at follow-up nine to fourteen months later. Eighty-one percent of the patients received some form of therapy during this time, with a mean duration of treatment of 40.6 weeks for pharmacotherapy, individual, group, and/or family therapy and a mean duration of 12.4 weeks for nutritional counseling. Scores for the bulimic women both pre- and post-treatment were significantly higher in all areas than those reported for normal women by Weissman and associates and were similar to those obtained by Johnson and Berndt. Moreover, t-tests comparing subjects at the time of evaluation and at follow-up showed no marked differences except for a significant improvement on the work subscale. The follow-up work scale score was still significantly higher, however, than that of the normal comparison group. Similar to the findings of Johnson and Berndt, the bulimic women in this study had significantly better overall adjustment than those in the severely depressed sample, were less well adjusted overall than the schizophrenic sample, and were not significantly different from the alcoholic sample. Norman and Herzog noted that their study confirms social maladjustment as one of the important symptom constellations associated with bulimia, and commented on its persistence despite the fact that most patients had received treatment.

Johnson, Stuckey, Lewis, and Schwartz (1982) asked their community sample of 316 bulimic women to rate how much their eating problems had affected various aspects of their lives. The great majority reported that their thoughts and feelings about themselves were "totally" or "very much" influenced by their eating difficulties (90 percent and 94 percent, respectively). The majority also reported that their eating problems significantly affected their interpersonal relationships (68 percent) and daily activities (65 percent). Work appeared to be the area least influenced by the binge/purge behavior, although 38 percent reported significant interference in their work lives as well.

Mitchell, Hatsukami, Eckert, and Pyle (1985) asked their sample of 275 outpatients whether they experienced any disruption or impairment in social functioning related to their bulimia. Seventy percent reported disruption of intimate or interpersonal relationships: 61 percent indicated family problems, 53 percent reported financial problems, and 50 percent reported work impairment.

We used data obtained from the Diagnostic Survey for Eating Disorders (DSED; Johnson, 1984) to investigate the quality of bulimics patients' relationships and how much their eating problems had interfered with other aspects of their life on a five-point scale. Thirty-seven percent reported their relationship with their mother was poor or fair, while 60 percent said it was good to excellent. Sixty-seven percent rated their relationship with their father as terrible, poor, or fair, while 41 percent rated it as good or excellent. Relationships with husbands, male friends, female friends, and children were all rated more positively than negatively. The eating problems interfered sometimes, often, or always in various areas in the following percentages: work, 58 percent; other daily activities, 88 percent; thoughts, 93 percent; feelings about oneself, 97 percent; and personal relationships, 88 percent.

Social isolation often seems to be another concomitant of bulimia. In the Johnson and Larson (1982) study mentioned earlier, the responses of the bulimic patients were compared to those of normal controls. Beepers were used to monitor the subjects and gather data on how they typically spent their time, thus providing a measure of their social isolation. The average bulimic woman reported being alone for about half (49 percent) of the time she was signaled by the beeper. The average normal control was alone for only one-third of the time (32 percent), a difference that was statistically significant. The bulimic women spent a greater proportion of their time alone and spent much of this time thinking about, preparing, or eating food; in fact, their rate of food-related behavior was well over twice that of the controls. A number of women reported that social withdrawal was a concomitant of their increased involvement with food, and that as time went on they were more likely to stay home and binge instead of engaging in social activities. The bulimics reported their lowest mood states when alone at home, the context in which their symptomatic behavior usually takes place. Further, those who reported the worst experiences in this context were the ones showing the most severe behavioral and affective manifestations of the disorder.

These early findings consistently indicate that individuals with bulimia report significant impairment in all areas of their lives. Although it is unclear to what extent the distress predated the onset of their eating difficulties, it appears that as the disorder progresses it increasingly results in social isolation and life adjustment problems.

Sexual Functioning

Several reports have indicated that bulimic anorexics are more sexually active than their restricting counterparts (Abraham and Beumont, 1982a; Garfinkel, Moldofsky, and Garner, 1980; Russell, 1979), but little work has explored the sexual functioning of normal-weight bulimics.

Abraham and associates (1985) compared the psychosexual histories of twenty bulimic females and twenty matched controls. They found that the two groups were very similar in most aspects of sexual attitudes and behaviors, including mean age at first intercourse (nineteen years) and number of sexual partners. Controls were more likely to experience orgasm with intercourse, while the bulimics were more orgasmic via masturbation, leading the authors to speculate that control issues were important for bulimics. They also noted that the bulimics tended to withdraw from social and sexual activity when at a higher weight and feeling unattractive.

Hazard (1985) compared the sexual functioning of twenty-three bulimic females at a university with that of an age-matched control group of twenty-four non–eating-disordered university females. The bulimic group tended to be more sexually experienced than the control group, with 17 percent of the bulimics never having experienced intercourse compared to 42 percent of the normal controls. None of the differences were significant, however. Despite more sexual activity in the bulimic group, these women were less satisfied with their bodies. The author suggested that these bulimic women appeared similar to an anorexic group described by Abraham and Beumont (1982a), who tended to be sexually active but unresponsive. This "passive sexuality" group appeared to be dependent on men and to crave relationships, but longed more to be held than to have sexual intercourse.

In our clinical sample of seventy-three bulimics, 83 percent had engaged in sexual intercourse, with a mean age for first intercourse of 17.6

TABLE 3.11
Sexual Preferences of the Bulimic and Normal Samples

	Bulimics (%)	Normals (%)
Exclusive heterosexuality	91	89
Heterosexuality with some homosexuality	0	4
Homosexuality with some heterosexuality	3	0
Bisexuality	0	7
Exclusive homosexuality	0	0
Asexuality (no sexual preference)	3	0
Autosexuality (preferring masturbation to sexual relations with others)	3	0

years (mean age of the sample was twenty-four). This was comparable to an age-matched normal control sample, where 93 percent reported having engaged in intercourse by age eighteen (mean age of first intercourse was eighteen). Seventy-two percent of the bulimic sample reported engaging in masturbation, beginning at a mean age of fourteen. This was also similar to the normal control sample, where 72 percent also reported engaging in masturbation, beginning at a mean age of 13.5 years.

Patients were asked to indicate their interest in sex before the onset of bulimia and whether there had been a change after the development of the eating problem. Nineteen percent stated that after onset they were much less interested, 19 percent were somewhat more interested, and 8 percent were much more interested. When asked how satisfied they were with the quality of their sexual activity, 8 percent were extremely satisfied, 17 percent were very satisfied, 5 percent were satisfied, 27 percent were somewhat satisfied, and 27 percent were not at all satisfied.

Patients were also asked about their sexual preferences. Table 3.11 indicates that the bulimic sample was not significantly different from normal controls.

The small amount of existing data on the sexual functioning of bulimics suggests that they tend to be far more sexually active than restricting anorexics but not dissimilar to age-matched controls. Reported degree of satisfaction with sexual activity ranges widely, and there is no clear indication of how the onset of bulimia affects sexual interest. Overall, 40 percent of the patients in our clinical sample reported less interest in sex after onset and 27 percent reported greater interest. Clearly more research needs to be conducted exploring bulimics' sexual experiences, satisfaction, preference, and the relationship of sexual behavior to other aspects of their lives.

Medical Complications*

Long-term outcome studies on bulimia are not currently available. Data have been accumulating, however, that suggest that a number of physical complications may arise as a result of the disorder; some are quite serious. The medical complications and physical discomfort experienced by the bulimic patient are often a result of the evacuation method used following a binge. Furthermore, the consequences of rapid ingestion of large amounts of food, combined with purging, periodic fasting, or excessive exercise, can cause physiological problems, including a chronic state of malnutrition. Overall, though, it appears that many of the physical symp-

---

* We wish to thank Jennifer Hagman, M.D., for her assistance with this section.

toms observed in these patients' behavior are side effects from the disordered eating or purging behavior.

MEDICAL COMPLICATIONS OF BINGE EATING

The rapid consumption of large amounts of food can lead to acute gastric dilatation with consequent pain, nausea, and vomiting (Mitchell, Pyle, and Miner, 1982), and has been reported in several cases to cause gastric rupture and even death (Matikainen, 1979; Saul, Dekker, and Watson, 1981). Pancreatitis, with severe abdominal pain, abdominal distention, fever, and increased heart rate, may result from abrupt pancreatic stimulation during frequent binge eating (Harris, 1983). Nutritional deficiencies resulting from bizarre food selection can be associated with hair loss, brittle nails, fatigue, insomnia, weakness, and mood changes. Dental cavities and erosion of tooth enamel associated with frequent ingestion of high-carbohydrate foods and the regurgitation of gastric acid are also complications of binge eating (Brady, 1980).

CONSEQUENCES OF METHODS EMPLOYED FOR WEIGHT CONTROL

Most bulimic patients vomit after binge eating in an attempt to remove the ingested food from their stomach before the calories can be absorbed. In vomiting, they remove some of the ingested food and also deplete the stomach acids and electrolytes (Harris, 1983; Mitchell et al., 1983). These electrolytes are important in maintaining the integrity of many systems in the body. The imbalances resulting from loss of potassium, sodium, and chloride can lead to cardiac arrhythmias (Garfinkel and Garner, 1982), muscle weakness, tiredness, constipation, and depression (Webb and Gehi, 1981).

Vomiting also results in fluid loss and dehydration. The body responds by retaining excessive water; edema results (Fairburn, 1982). Patients may also experience excessive thirst, decreased urinary output, and dizziness. Lacerations on the fingers or in the mouth may result from using the finger or other instruments to mechanically induce vomiting (Russell, 1979).

Another frequently used purgative method is laxative abuse. Reports indicate that 38 to 75 percent of eating-disordered patients abuse laxatives as a method of weight control (Abraham and Beumont, 1982b; Mitchell et al., 1983; Pyle, Mitchell, and Eckert, 1981). Laxatives, however, are a relatively ineffective method of avoiding calorie absorption as they primarily affect the large bowel (colon), whereas most nutrients and caloric content of foods are absorbed in the small intestine (duodenum, jejenum, and ileum). Fluid absorption takes place in the large intestine. In a study of laxative abuse in bulimia, Lacey and Gibson (1985) found that vomiters ate significantly more yet weighed less, and laxative abusers ate less but weighed more. The laxative abusers achieved weight control primarily through dietary restraint rather than through the pharmacological action of laxatives. Another metabolic study showed that purgation with laxatives produced a decrease in energy absorption of only 12 percent of intake (Bo-Linn, Santa Ana, Morowski, and Fordtran, 1983).

The gastrointestinal system is, of course, affected by frequent vomiting. Esophagitis and ulceration of the esophagus may result from frequent exposure to the acidic stomach contents contained in the vomitus (Goode, 1985). Loss of the gag reflex from frequent mechanical stimulation may result, as well as lower esophageal relaxation and subsequent reflex regurgitation (Garner et al., 1985). Patients may also be at risk for choking on the instruments they use to induce vomiting.

As was mentioned earlier, bulimic patients usually experience erosion of tooth enamel, tooth discoloration, and increased dental cavities. Dental consultation is essential to prevent further periodontal disease (Brady, 1980). These patients may also complain of painless salivary gland enlargement, most often of the parotid gland (Levin, Falks, and Dixon, 1980). This is probably secondary to frequent stimulation from binge eating and vomiting. The swollen appearance of the cheeks is often distressing to the patient, but usually causes no severe medical problems.

Patients who are unable to self-induce vomiting may turn to emetic agents. Those using syrup of Ipecac to induce vomiting are at great risk for developing cardiac arrest and sudden death due to the active emetics in Ipecac (Adler, Walinsky, Krall, and Cho, 1980). These patients may also complain of progressive muscle weakness (Brotman, Forbath, Garfinkel, and Humphrey, 1981).

Most laxatives may be bought over-the-counter. Patients frequently report using Ex-Lax or Correctol, almost always in amounts that far exceed the recommended therapeutic dose. Fluid shifts, dehydration, malabsorption, abdominal cramping, electrolyte imbalances, and muscle cramps are some of the side effects of laxative abuse (Goode, 1985). Finger swelling or clubbing has been observed in several cases as a result of chronic laxative abuse, but this gradually remediates when laxatives are discontinued (Malmquist et al., 1980). Chronic laxative use may cause patients to lose normal bowel reactivity, and patients may become addicted to the laxative, precipitating constipation and withdrawal reactions when laxative use is discontinued (Russell, 1979). Normal bowel function usually returns when the patient stops using laxatives and maintains normal weight and eating behavior (Garner et al., 1985).

Some patients use diuretics to avoid "water weight" gain. Many diuretics must be obtained by prescription, but a few may be purchased without prescription. When inappropriately used, diuretics can have severe consequences on renal function and fluid and electrolyte balance.

In an effort to reduce hunger and maintain energy without eating, bulimic patients often turn to stimulants and "diet pills." Diet pills can be easily purchased over-the-counter and are frequently taken in amounts that exceed therapeutic recommendations. Side effects of daily use include rebound fatigue and hyperphagia, insomnia, mood changes, irritability, and, in extremely large doses, psychosis.

ENDOCRINE AND NEUROLOGICAL CHANGES

The origin and significance of the neuroendocrine changes found in patients with bulimia who maintain a normal weight remain controversial. Evidence for hypothalamic-pituitary-adrenal (HPA) axis involvement is found in dexamethasone suppression test (DST) nonsuppression in up to 67 percent of bulimic patients (Gwirtsman, Roy-Byrne, Yager, and Gerner, 1983). Amenorrhea is observed in more than 20 percent of these women; 50.7 percent exhibit menstrual irregularity (Johnson, 1983). Abnormalities of growth hormone regulation have also been cited (Mitchell and Bantle, 1983). It is important to note, however, that frequent weight fluctuations, fasting, and poor nutrition can have a significant impact on neuroendocrine functioning. A recent starvation study of normal-weight, non–eating-disordered females demonstrated that weight loss, reduced caloric intake, and catabolic state have a very powerful influence on the HPA axis and other endocrine systems (Fichter and Pirke, 1984). Thus the endocrine changes seen in patients with eating disorders are probably directly related to their eating behavior.

Again, in underweight and anorexic bulimic patients, these neuroendocrine changes are more persistent and often more severe. Measurable abnormalities are found in plasma luteinizing hormone and follicle stimulating hormone (Weiner, 1983). With weight gain, some of these parameters return to normal values, but the long-term effects have not been determined.

Neurological changes have also been reported in patients with bulimia and anorexia nervosa. In the central nervous system EEG abnormalities have been studied (Rau and Green, 1975; Wermuth, Davis, Hollister, and Stunkard, 1977), although their significance in eating disorders is not understood. Katz and associates (1984) reported early onset of rapid-eye-movement (REM) stage sleep in bulimic patients as a possible biological marker of depression. Peripheral nervous system changes have been observed, including muscular spasms (tetany) and tingling sensations (peripheral paresthesias) (Fairburn, 1982; Russell, 1979). The role of nutritional status and electrolyte disturbances in these neurological abnormalities requires further investigation.

Many of the medical complications cited in the literature exist as single case reports, but surveys of clinical populations of bulimics have obtained data on the patient's perceived health difficulties since the onset of the binge/purge behavior. In Johnson, Stuckey, Lewis, and Schwartz's community study (1982) of 316 bulimic females, 70 percent reported some change in physical health. Tiredness was most commonly cited (31 percent); stomach problems (16 percent) and dry skin/hair or hair breakage (6 percent) were also mentioned. Abraham and Beumont (1982b) reported that of their thirty-two patients with a probable diagnosis of bulimia, 69 percent complained of swelling of the hands and feet, 47 percent reported fatigue, and 38 percent indicated headaches. In Mitchell, Hatsukami, Eckert, and Pyle's sample (1985) of 275, the following symptoms were reported: weakness (84 percent), a bloated feeling (75 percent), stomach pain (63 percent), sore throat (54 percent), puffy cheeks (50 percent), dental problems (37 percent), and finger callouses (27 percent).

MENSTRUAL DIFFICULTIES

It is well known that amenorrhea is associated with anorexia nervosa, but several reports suggest that menstrual irregularities are also common with bulimic patients. Johnson, Stuckey, Lewis, and Schwartz (1982) reported that 20 percent of their community sample were amenorrheic following the onset of their eating problems, and 51 percent reported current menstrual irregularities. In Fairburn and Cooper's community sample (1982), 40 percent indicated menstrual irregularity and 7 percent reported amenorrhea. Abraham and Beumont (1982) indicated that 77 percent of their bulimic sample reported at least one episode of amenorrhea of three months or longer. The episodes were invariably associated with weight-losing behavior but not necessarily severe weight loss. In our clinical sample, while 47 percent of our respondents reported regular menstruation before the onset of the eating problem, only 32 percent menstruated regularly after onset. Percentages for those who were somewhat irregular or very irregular are not terribly dissimilar pre- and post-onset (24 percent compared to 22 percent; 17 percent compared to 22 percent). Prior to onset 2 percent reported never menstruating; after onset, 17 percent ceased to menstruate.

While patients in treatment often report noticing a relationship between their menstrual cycle and their binge eating, little data document this relationship. In our clinical sample, 38 percent of our patients reported feeling there is such a relationship. Thirty-one percent stated that they felt most vulnerable to binge eating one to two days prior to menstruation; 31 percent seven to ten days prior; 19 percent three to six days prior; 12 percent eleven to fourteen days prior; 6 percent after menstruation; and 0 percent during menstruation.

Leon, Phelan, Kelly, and Patten (1984) explored the relationship between binge eating and the menstrual cycle. A group of forty-five women diagnosed as bulimic kept daily records of eating behavior, moods, physical condition, and other information for nine weeks. Subjects were blind to the study's hypotheses. Eight women were identified as having a premenstrual pattern, which included mood changes and physical complaints. However, no relationship between menstrual cycle and change in eating behavior was discovered either for this group or for those subjects who did not evince a premenstrual pattern.

The relationship of binge-eating episodes to menstrual cycle may be one of the most interesting areas of research to emerge in the future. At this time, however, it is unclear as to how they are related.

IMPULSE CONTROL AND SUBSTANCE ABUSE DIFFICULTIES

The literature consistently reports that bulimic anorexics have greater difficulties with impulse control than restricting anorexics. Garfinkel, Moldofsky, and Garner (1980) reported that their bulimic anorexics had a history of more stealing, more alcohol use, and greater use of street drugs than restrictors. Casper and coworkers (1980) found that bulimic anorexics had significantly more incidents of compulsive stealing than restrictors. Russell (1979) found that eleven of thirty bulimia nervosa patients (the majority of whom had a history of anorexia) had made at least one suicide attempt. Garfinkel, Moldofsky, and Garner (1980) also found that suicide attempts and self-inflicted injuries were more common among bulimic anorexics than restrictors.

Normal-weight bulimics seem to exhibit similar difficulties with impulse control. Pyle, Mitchell, and Eckert (1981) found that stealing was common in their sample of thirty-four bulimics. Fifty-three percent began a pattern of stealing after onset of the eating disorder. Twenty-six percent reported stealing prior to onset, and 12 percent continued to steal after onset. Overall, 65 percent of the sample were actively stealing. Food was the usual item stolen, although several also stole clothing, cosmetics, and jewelry. Carroll and Leon (1981) reported that 50 percent of their sample of thirty-seven admitted to shoplifting, particularly food. Weiss and Ebert (1983) compared fifteen bulimics to fifteen normal controls; 67 percent of the bulimics admitted to stealing, compared to 13 percent of the controls. Fairburn and Cooper (1984b) reported that one-third of their sample of thirty-five outpatients admitted to having shoplifted food in the past, although only 6 percent stated that they were currently stealing.

Some researchers have noted substance abuse problems among their subjects. Pyle, Mitchell, and Eckert (1981) reported that 24 percent of their bulimic patients had significant chemical dependency problems. At the time of evaluation, 41 percent were using alcohol at least several times a week and 18 percent were using it daily. Twenty-one percent reported intermittent amphetamine abuse, while 12 percent admitted to daily use. Fifty percent of their patients reported alcoholism in at least one first-degree family member, and 21 percent reported having an alcoholic father.

Carroll and Leon (1981) investigated the substance abuse histories for thirty-seven bulimics and their families. Sixty-one percent of subjects stated that they had used alcohol excessively, and 46 percent had used drugs to excess. Fathers who had drug or alcohol problems were reported by 49 percent of the sample, while 14 percent of the mothers, 20 percent of the sisters, and 26 percent of the brothers were so described. Fifty-one percent of the sample had at least one first-degree relative diagnosed as chemically dependent. The authors commented that their data suggested a generalized substance abuse pattern.

Weiss and Ebert (1983) reported that significantly more bulimics than normal controls used marijuana, cocaine, amphetamines, and barbiturates. While not statistically significant, there were consistently more users of other substances including phencyclidine (PCP), LSD, glue, and alcohol in the bulimic group. However, frequencies of use were not specified, so that alcohol abuse or dependence versus normal social drinking could not be assessed.

Mitchell, Hatsukami, Eckert, and Pyle (1985) reported that 20 percent of their sample of 275 admitted to using alcohol several times a week or more prior to the onset of bulimia, and 49 percent reported this pattern after onset. Thirty-four percent indicated that they had a history of "problems" with alcohol (defined as a period of six months of regularly drinking to excess or having problems with family, work, finances, or police due to drinking) and other drugs. Eighteen percent indicated a prior history of chemical dependency treatment.

Another class of impulsive behaviors reported in conjunction with bulimia are suicide attempts and self-mutilation. Abraham and Beumont (1982b) reported that nine out of thirty-two patients (28 percent) had made a suicide attempt. Johnson, Stuckey, Lewis, and Schwartz (1982) reported that 14 percent of their sample of 316 had made a gesture or a "plea for help," while 5 percent had made a serious attempt. In the study by Weiss and Ebert (1983) comparing bulimics to normal controls, six out of fifteen bulimics (40 percent) had made a suicide attempt, compared to none of the control women.

The data from several studies, particularly those involving outpatients rather than the community samples, suggest that bulimics experience a variety of impulse control difficulties, including stealing, substance abuse, and suicidal behavior. Family histories of substance abuse have also been noted.

Bulimia and Affective Disorders

Over the last several years an increasing body of literature has emerged suggesting that bulimia may be a symptom expression of a biologically mediated affective disorder. Several converging pieces of evidence have been offered in support of this hypothesis (Pope and Hudson, 1983).

The first line of evidence is related to preliminary findings that have indicated that a large number of bulimic patients report symptoms characteristic of unipolar and bipolar illness. These symptoms include a persistence of low and highly variable mood states, low frustration tolerance, anxiety, substance abuse, and suicidal ideation (Carroll and Leon, 1981; Johnson and Larson, 1982; Pyle, Mitchell, and Eckert, 1981; Russell, 1979). Although these early reports suggest that bulimic patients present with vegetative symptoms similar to patients with major depression, the etiology of the depressive symptoms may be physiological side effects from weight loss or fluctuations in nutritional status or psychological side effects from repeated exposure to a pattern of thoughts and behaviors that results in feelings of helplessness, shame, guilt, and ineffectiveness.

There is very little evidence available to help resolve these questions. Strober, Salkin, Burroughs, and Morrell (1982) reported that parents of bulimic anorexics described their children during childhood as being clingy, ritualistic, and argumentative. Parental descriptions of restricting anorexics' childhood were much more benign. These data suggest that those patients manifesting bulimic symptoms appear to have premorbid histories of affective instability. Tim Walsh and associates (1984) also reported that 65 percent of a sample of bulimic outpatients reported that the symptoms of depression predated the onset of the eating difficulty.

The most compelling evidence for the biological depression hypothesis comes from family studies that indicate a high incidence of major affective disorder among first- and second-degree relatives of bulimic patients. Using the family history method among a sample of seventy-five patients with bulimia, Hudson and his colleagues (Hudson, Laffer, and Pope, 1982; Hudson, Pope, Jonas, and Yurgelun-Todd, 1983) found that 53 percent had first-degree relatives with major affective disorder. Likewise, substance abuse disorder was found to be highly prevalent (45 of 350 relatives). Results further indicated that the morbid risk factor for affective disorder in relatives was 28 percent, which was similar to that found in families of patients with bipolar disorder. Strober and his colleagues (Strober, 1981; Strober, Salkin, Burroughs, and Morrell, 1982) found similar rates of affective disorder among anorexic patients who manifested bulimic symptoms. They compared these patients to restricting anorexics. Overall, the familial prevalence for affective disorder, considering both first- and second-degree relatives, was 13 percent for bulimic anorexics and 6 percent for restricting anorexics. Maternal affective disorder was also found to be far more prevalent for the bulimic anorexics. The raw prevalences were equivalent to morbid risk for affective disorder of 20 percent in the bulimic anorexic families compared with 9 percent in the restrictor anorexic families. (The estimated morbid risk factor in the general population is 6 percent.) When bipolar illness could be identified, it occurred more frequently in the relative of a bulimic anorexic patient. Histories of alcoholism also differentiated the two groups. Pooling across first- and second-degree relatives, the overall rate of alcoholism among relatives of bulimic anorexics was 18 percent compared to 8 percent in relatives of restrictor anorexics. Alcoholism was three times more prevalent in fathers of bulimic than restrictor anorexics.

There has also been a preliminary attempt to identify biological markers associated with depression and bulimia. Although consistent markers predictive of affective disorder have not been isolated, two that are under consideration are suggestive of major depression among bulimic patients.

The DST and the thyroid releasing hormone stimulating test have been found positive in bulimic patients with the same frequency as in patients with major depression and much more frequently than would be expected in normal control populations (Gwirtsman, Roy-Byrne, Yager, and Gerner, 1983; Hudson, Laffer, and Pope, 1982). Sleep architecture studies have also recently indicated that a subgroup of normal-weight bulimics (with previous histories of anorexia nervosa) displayed sleep disturbance (shortened REM latency) characteristic of patients with affective disorders (Katz et al., 1984).

Finally, early findings regarding the effectiveness of antidepressant pharmacotherapy increases support for the depression hypothesis. Both open trials and double-blind placebo studies of tricyclic and monoamine oxidase inhibitor treatment has resulted in significant improvement in bulimic symptoms (Hughes, Wells, Cunningman, and Ilstrip, 1986; Pope and Hudson, 1982; Pope, Hudson, Jonas, and Yurgelun-Todd, 1983; Walsh et al., 1982). (For extended review see chapter 9.)

Although further research is necessary to substantiate the prevalence of affective disorders among bulimic patients, it is clear that, overall, they experience significant affective instability that may predate the onset of their bulimic symptoms. To what extent the depressive symptoms are biologically mediated remains controversial.

4

Personality Profile

Over the years several observations have been made regarding the psychopathological characteristics of eating-disordered patients. These characteristics include: low self-esteem, self-regulatory deficits, body-image disturbance, separation/individuation fears, mood disorder, cognitive distortions, boundary disturbance, and a tendency to be perfectionistic, compliant, and distrustful. In this chapter we review the findings regarding personality characteristics of bulimic individuals as well as anorexic subjects in those studies that allow for direct comparison with bulimic populations.

Our understanding of the psychological characteristics of eating-disordered patients has been significantly advanced recently by the development of the EDI (Garner, Olmsted, and Polivy, 1983). Garner and his colleagues translated the clinical observations of several early theorists into quantifiable scales. The EDI contains eight subscales, including interoceptive awareness, body dissatisfaction, ineffectiveness, interpersonal distrust, drive for thinness, maturity fears, perfectionism, and bulimia.

The EDI can be used to answer some of the common questions regarding similarities and differences between subtypes of eating-disordered patients and other clinical and normal populations. We use the subscales of the EDI as an organizing schema to present some of the current findings regarding the psychological characteristics of these different groups.

Interoceptive Awareness

Hilde Bruch (1962, 1973, 1978) originally identified three primary features of anorexia nervosa: interoceptive awareness disturbances, body-image distortion, and profound feelings of ineffectiveness. The centerpiece of Bruch's conceptualization was the proposed disturbance in interoceptive awareness.

Interoceptive awareness refers to an individual's ability to accurately identify and articulate a variety of internal states such as hunger, satiety, and affects. This is quite similar to the term alexithymia, which has been used to describe this deficit in other psychosomatic disorders (Sifneos, 1973). Bruch felt that this type of deficit resulted from specific early disruptions in the mother-child interaction (see chapter 5).

Most of the work exploring interoceptive awareness deficits among eating-disordered patients has focused on cues related to hunger and satiety. Garfinkel and Garner (1982) reviewed a number of articles indicating both anorexic and obese patients are less accurate than normals in perceiving the amounts of food directly introduced into their stomachs (see, for example, Coddington and Bruch, 1970). Obese individuals have also been found to be less able to respond appropriately to internal satiety cues and are more influenced by external cues such as food availability, salience, and palatability (Nisbett, 1972; Schachter, 1971; Schachter and Rodin, 1974). Findings with anorexic patients indicate disturbed sensations of satiety including bloating, absence of stomach sensations, nausea, and aches and pains. They are also less responsive to internal cues related to nutritional requirements as measured by the satiety-aversion to sucrose test (Garfinkel, Moldofsky, and Garner, 1979; Garfinkel et al., 1978). Garfinkel and Garner concluded that "anorexics appear to have disturbed interoceptive experiences and specifically misperceive stimuli that lead to satiety in normal subjects. Their perceptions of satiety appear to be less influenced by internal states than by their cognitive expectations related to food intake" (p. 153).

The interoceptive awareness subscale of the EDI was designed to further assess this proposed psychological characteristic of eating-disordered patients. The subscale is composed of such questions as: "I get confused about what emotion I am feeling," "I get confused as to whether I am hungry or not," and "I have feelings I can't quite identify."

As seen in figure 4.1, all three of the anorexic and bulimic groups scored significantly higher than obese and normal controls. Interestingly, the scores of both bulimic groups were comparable and significantly higher than the restricting anorexic group. Further research has indicated that interoceptive awareness disturbance is highly correlated with body-image distortion and that high scores on the ineffectiveness, interoceptive awareness, and interpersonal distrust EDI subscales differentiate anorexics from weight-preoccupied individuals (Garner, Olmsted, Polivy, and Garfinkel, 1984).

Unfortunately, sophisticated investigations similar to those conducted with anorexic and obese individuals have not appeared with bulimics. The preliminary indications are, however, that patients with bulimic symptoms (regardless of weight history) report more difficulty with interoceptive awareness than restricting anorexics. This is probably a reflection of bulimics' greater overall intrapsychic disorganization compared

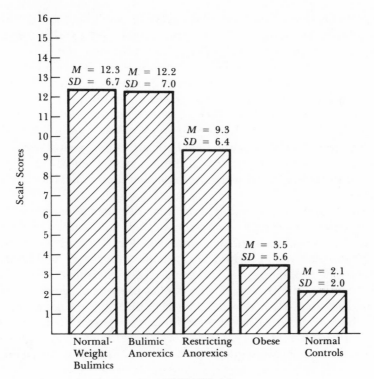

FIGURE 4.1
Interoceptive Awareness

NOTE: We wish to thank Joann Hendelman, M.A., for providing the obesity sample used in this figure and in figures 4.2, 4.4, 4.5, 4.6, 4.7, 4.8, and 4.9.

to restricting anorexics. It appears that interoceptive awareness difficulties are a significant pathognomonic indicator for all three eating-disordered groups. Furthermore, these difficulties appear to be closely related to the symptoms of ineffectiveness and body-image disturbance.

Body Dissatisfaction

Body-image disturbance has long been regarded as one of the central features of anorexia nervosa. Anorexics typically overestimate their body size, and the persistence of this overestimation has been associated with poor outcome (Garfinkel and Garner, 1982).

The body-image construct has been troubling for theorists because the term has been used in a variety of ways. Bruch's original thinking regarding "disturbed size awareness" among anorexics was that the phenomenon was related to, or a side effect of, the problems of interoceptive awareness. Essentially, disturbed size awareness would be one aspect of a more global difficulty with accurately perceiving internal states. Currently body-image disturbance is regarded as consisting of both perceptual and cognitive-affective components. The perceptual component refers to the individual's ability to accurately estimate her size; the cognitive-affective component refers to the patient's beliefs or attitudes toward her body. In the latter component, patients may accurately assess their size but report extreme dissatisfaction and distortions regarding their beliefs about their size.

Empirical studies investigating perceptual estimates of body size have found that anorexics generally overestimate their body size compared to normal controls, a characteristic that is associated with lower pretreatment weight, greater denial and resistance to treatment, greater likelihood of relapse following hospitalization, and more severe psychopathology (Garfinkel and Garner, 1982). Virtually no studies have appeared comparing bulimic patients to other eating-disordered populations using perceptual indices of body-size distortion. In a preliminary report utilizing the distorting photograph technique, Garner, Garfinkel, and O'Shaughnessy (1985) found that normal-weight bulimics demonstrated perceptual body-size distortions similar to both restricting and bulimic anorexics.

Recently, more emphasis has been placed on investigating the attitudinal rather than the perceptual aspects of body-image disturbance. Findings indicate that, overall, body-size dissatisfaction is highly correlated with low self-esteem, feelings of inadequacy, depression, anxiety, interpersonal sensitivity, external locus of control, and poor ego strength.

There also appears to be a significant male-female difference in the body-dissatisfaction literature, with women overestimating their size and reporting substantially more dissatisfaction with their body size than men (Fallon and Rozin, 1985; Gray, 1977; Huenemann, Shapiro, Hampton, and Mitchell, 1966). This body dissatisfaction also appears to result in females weighing themselves more often (Dwyer, Feldman, Seltzer, and Mayer, 1969), and dieting more frequently (Gray, 1977).

Several different instruments have been used to assess body dissatisfaction among eating-disordered patients. The body-dissatisfaction subscale of the EDI is composed of such questions as: "I think my stomach is too big," "I think my thighs are too large," and "I feel satisfied with the shape of my body." As seen in figure 4.2, all three eating-disordered groups and the obese individuals reported substantially more body dissatisfaction than normal controls. Also, for most eating-disturbed patients, the focus of the dissatisfaction is on the stomach and thighs (see figure 4.3). Interestingly, both bulimic groups and the obese individuals reported more body dissatisfaction than the restricting anorexics. It appears, how-

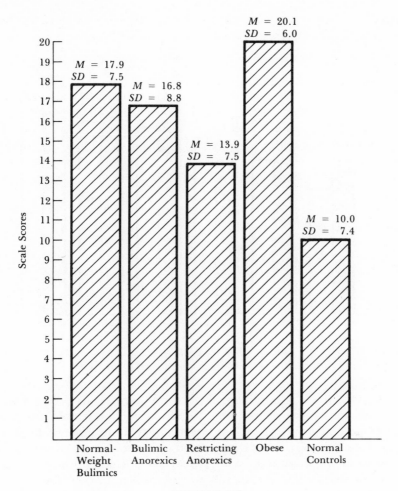

FIGURE 4.2
Body Dissatisfaction

ever, that for obese individuals, body dissatisfaction is not as intimately related to interoceptive awareness difficulties or profound feelings of ineffectiveness. The differences between both bulimic groups and the restricting anorexics is probably a function of the latter group feeling more in control with their eating behavior.

Body dissatisfaction appears to be a fairly prevalent phenomenon among contemporary young women from westernized countries. The compelling question regarding bulimia is whether there are qualitative differences regarding body-image disturbance that have clinical or etiological significance. Essentially, can we identify different groups where the body-image disturbance reflects specific intrapsychic deficits? For ex-

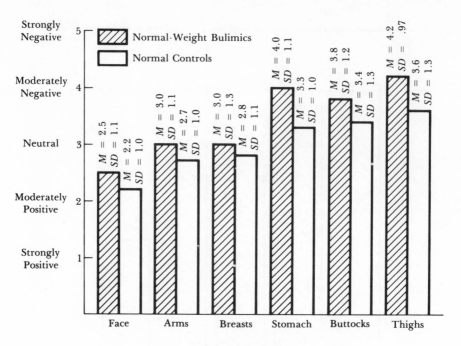

FIGURE 4.3
Body Image Perceptions from the DSED-R

ample, as with the obese individuals, is there a group of bulimics who report high body dissatisfaction, but the dissatisfaction is not a function of an intrapsychic difficulty such as interoceptive awareness? In contrast, what are the characteristics of the group in which body-image disturbance is severe, resulting in significant life impairment? Among this group, can we more specifically differentiate subgroups in which the body disturbance reflects different defensive adaptations, cognitive style, and ego strength? It is our opinion that among the subgroup of restricting anorexics who are highly treatment resistant, the body-image disturbance reflects a more delusional psychological organization with substantial paranoid features (high interpersonal distrust). For another subgroup, the body-image disturbance may be predominantly a reflection of intense fears of psycho-biological maturation (high maturity fears). These patients may develop an adversarial relationship with their bodies because various bodily aspects, such as secondary sexual characteristics, become symbolic representations of impending separation expectations. The presence of body-image dissatisfaction and distortion among eating-disordered patients has been established. The focus should now shift to identifying clusters for whom the body-image disturbance has unique meaning or serves a specific, psychologically adaptive function. Pursuing this line of inquiry should enhance the specificity and effectiveness of our treatment interventions.

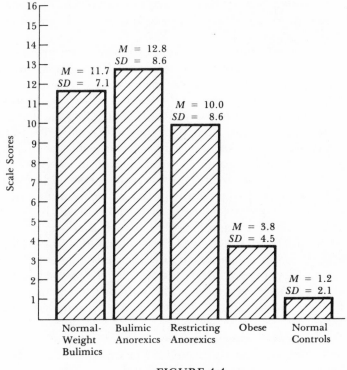

FIGURE 4.4
Ineffectiveness

Ineffectiveness

According to Bruch, a final cardinal feature of anorexia nervosa is a paralyzing sense of ineffectiveness. Numerous studies using a variety of different tests have indeed found that anorexics and bulimics report significantly lower self-esteem than normals. The self-esteem problems appear to include high self-expectations, self-criticalness and guilt, high needs for approval from others, external locus of control, low assertiveness, and interpersonal sensitivity (Connors, Johnson, and Stuckey, 1984; Katzman and Wolchik, 1984; Love, Ollendick, Johnson, and Schlesinger, 1985; Nagelberg, Hale, and Ware, 1984).

The ineffectiveness subscale of the EDI attempts to assess these clinical observations through such questions as: "I feel ineffective as a person," "I feel generally in control of things in my life," and "I feel that I can achieve my standards." As depicted in figure 4.4, it appears that there is little difference among the eating-disordered groups; all three report substantially more ineffectiveness than normal or obese controls. Profound feelings of ineffectiveness do indeed appear to be highly characteristic of eating-disordered patients.

A number of interesting clinical questions arise regarding the relationship among the interoceptive awareness, ineffectiveness, and body dissatisfaction subscales. If changes occur in an individual's ability to identify and articulate internal states, will the feelings of ineffectiveness and body dissatisfaction automatically improve? If controlling the body is initially an adaptive effect to gain control of the feelings of ineffectiveness, then would restricting anorexics in the early stages of self-starvation report lower ineffectiveness scores because of the control and discipline they were exercising? Finally, can feelings of ineffectiveness and body dissatisfaction change without changes in the interoceptive awareness deficits?

These three characteristics appear to be intrapsychically linked. If an individual is psychologically undifferentiated such that she cannot tell how or what she feels, then it is likely she will feel out of control and inadequate. It is also understandable how the body might become an arena in which a variety of psychological issues might be focused, especially issues of control and differentiation. The body is the leading edge or primary interface with the world. It is a concrete representation of the boundary between "me" and "not me" or "self" and "other." It is the container that houses our internal states and the object that is presented to the world as a representation of "self." Consequently, it can become a stage where a variety of intrapsychic and interpersonal control issues are constantly enacted.

Interpersonal Distrust

Clinicians have consistently reported anorexic patients to be highly defensive and quite resistant to therapeutic involvement. The quality of the resistance often takes on paranoidlike features, with potential caretakers being experienced as hostile and malevolent intruders. This is in contrast to findings among bulimic patients; while they are quite rejection-sensitive, they often willingly seek help from others. As seen in figure 4.5, the subscale interpersonal distrust, which is composed of such questions as "I trust others," "I have close relationships," and "I need to keep people at a certain distance," appears to differentiate both anorexic groups from the normal-weight bulimics, obese, and normal controls. Similar to the body-image disturbance findings, as research unfolds we may find that the construct of interpersonal distrust may have very different meanings

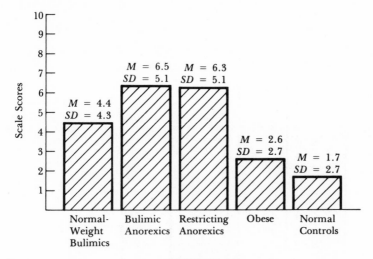

FIGURE 4.5
Interpersonal Distrust

that differentiate groups and suggest different treatment nuances. For example, among the restricting anorexic group, the distrust of others may reflect a fear of intrusive overinvolvement from others. Consequently, a therapist would want to be alert to overinvolvement issues with a patient. In contrast, for the bulimic group interpersonal distrust might reflect a fear of underinvolvement or rejection. If this is the case, a therapist would want to be alert to a patient's fear of rejection, abandonment, disengagement, and so forth. (For a more detailed explanation see chapter 9.)

Drive for Thinness

The drive for thinness subscale measures excessive preoccupation with dieting, weight gain, and the pursuit of thinness. Some of the questions on the EDI include: "I am preoccupied with the desire to be thinner," "I think about dieting," and "I am terrified of gaining weight." Both bulimic groups report substantially greater preoccupation with thinness than restricting anorexics, and all three eating-disordered groups report substantially more preoccupation than obese and normal controls. These findings seem to offer some interesting insights into relationships between perceived control and the drive for thinness (see figure 4.6).

If the pursuit of thinness (self-starvation) is regarded as a defense

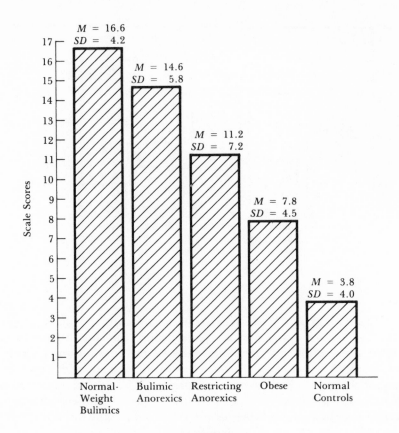

FIGURE 4.6
Drive for Thinness

against feelings of being out of control and if bulimic behavior is experienced as a loss of control, then patients who experience bulimic episodes
would experience more inadequacy and perhaps be more preoccupied
with trying to achieve the fragile defense of thinness through food restriction. Essentially they would be more preoccupied with achieving thinness and more fearful of weight gain because their eating behavior is
more out of control.

Maturity Fears

A number of investigators have observed that the drive for thinness among
anorexia nervosa patients may be an adaptive effort to avoid the psychobiological demands of puberty (Crisp, 1980). They suggest that the severe

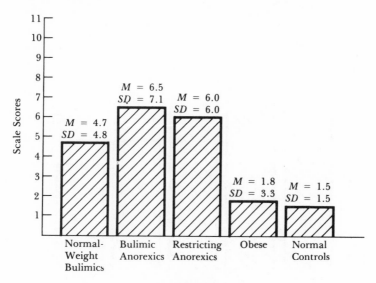

FIGURE 4.7
Maturity Fears

emaciation which accompanies self-starvation simultaneously returns the individual biologically to a prepubertal state and minimizes expectations for psychological separation. The maturity fears subscale of the EDI was designed to assess this dimension and includes such questions as: "I wish I could return to the security of childhood," "The demands of adulthood are too great," and "I wish I could be younger."

Findings on the subscale indicate that both anorexic groups score higher than the bulimics at normal weight and normal and obese controls (see figure 4.7). It is interesting to note that this was one of the few subscales in which scores for restricting and bulimic anorexics were almost identical. It would seem that, on this subscale, differences in weight were more important than the presence or absence of bulimic behavior. Consequently, it would appear that there may indeed be an important relationship between severe weight loss and fears of psychobiological maturation. Furthermore, this subscale may identify the adaptive function of a specific behavior (weight loss) that is unique to one group of eating-disordered patients.

Perfectionism

The perfectionism subscale of the EDI represents an attempt to measure high achievement expectations and strivings thought to be characteristic of eating-disordered patients (Bruch, 1973, 1978; Dally, 1969; Garner,

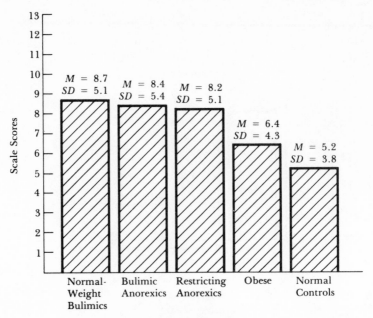

FIGURE 4.8
Perfectionism

Garfinkel, and Bemis, 1982; Kalucy, Crisp, and Harding, 1977). The scale consists of such questions as: "I hate being less than best at things," "I have extremely high goals," and "I feel that I must do things perfectly or not at all." This subscale appears to be the weakest discriminator among the different subscales. All three eating-disordered groups score higher than normal controls, and there is little difference between eating-disordered groups (see figure 4.8). Apparently, while eating-disordered patients report a high degree of perfectionistic strivings, normal and obese controls do as well.

Bulimia

The bulimia subscale of the EDI assesses the extent of bulimic behavior through such questions as: "I stuff myself with food," "I think about bingeing," and "I have gone on eating binges where I feel that I could not stop." As expected, both bulimic anorexics and normal-weight bulimics score significantly higher than restricting anorexics and normal controls (see figure 4.9).

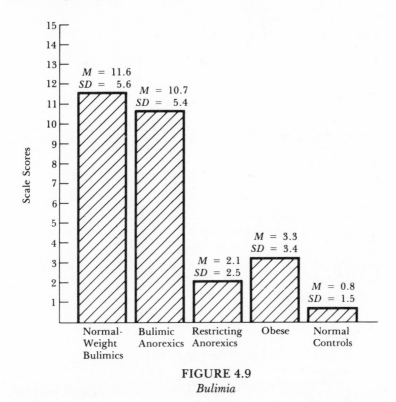

FIGURE 4.9
Bulimia

The EDI has provided a preliminary tool to test prevailing clinical observations and assess thoughts and behavior that may be unique to eating-disordered patients. Obviously, additional work needs to be done. Comparisons between other psychologically disordered groups will be important to determine if any of these findings are unique to eating-disordered individuals. Increased sample sizes will allow for cluster analyses to determine if there are important subtypes. It is hoped that the use of the EDI will also shed light on whether changes on these different dimensions are in any way associated with treatment outcome.

Standard Measures of Psychiatric Symptoms

MINNESOTA MULTIPHASIC PERSONALITY INVENTORY

Several studies have used the Minnesota Multiphasic Personality Inventory (MMPI) to evaluate the level and type of psychopathology found among eating-disordered patients. Rybicki, Lepkowsky, and Arndt (in

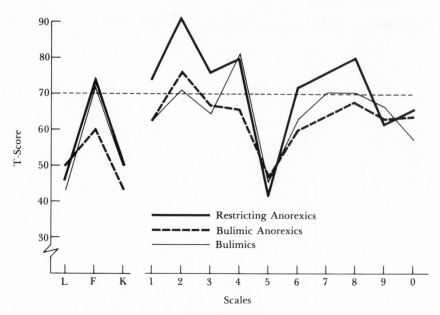

FIGURE 4.10

Mean MMPI Profile[a] for Normal-Weight Bulimic, Restricting Anorexic, and Bulimic Anorexic Patients

[a] The MMPI scales L, F, and K are for validity and 1–0 are the clinical scales. 1 = Hypochondriasis, 2 = Depression, 3 = Hysteria, 4 = Psychopathic Deviate, 5 = Masculinity-Femininity, 6 = Paranoia, 7 = Psychasthenia, 8 = Schizophrenia, 9 = Hypomania, and 0 = Social Introversion. A T-score greater than 70 is indicative of elevated symptomatology.

NOTE: Reprinted from D. K. Norman and D. B. Herzog, "Bulimia, anorexia nervosa, and anorexia nervosa with bulimia: A comparative analysis of MMPI profiles," *International Journal of Eating Disorders* 2 (1983): 43–52. Copyright © 1983 by John Wiley and Sons, Inc. Reprinted by permission of John Wiley and Sons, Inc.

press) and Pyle, Mitchell, and Eckert (1981) compared normal-weight bulimics to normal controls and found, as expected, that the former group had significantly more overall psychopathology. In both studies bulimics peaked on scales 4 (Psychopathic Deviance) and 2 (Depression), with Psychasthenia and Schizophrenia also above 70. The peak 4/2 profile indicates that bulimics experience chronic depression, exaggerated guilt, poor impulse control, and low frustration tolerance. The high Psychasthenia and Schizophrenia subscales also suggest that bulimics tend to be rigid and meticulous, worrisome, apprehensive, and dissatisfied with social relationships. In addition, they indicate that bulimics are vulnerable to seclusiveness and manifest some disturbance in clarity of thought and communication.

Recent studies have also compared normal-weight bulimics to both restricting and bulimic anorexics. Norman and Herzog (1983) compared MMPI profiles of these three groups; their normal-weight bulimics had no history of anorexia nervosa. As depicted in figure 4.10, overall, the bulimic anorexics reported the most symptomatology; the restricting anorexics reported the least. The Psychopathic Deviance (PD) subscale was the only scale to vary significantly by diagnosis. Both bulimic groups had higher PD scores than restricting anorexics, probably reflecting their greater vulnerability to impulse-dominated behavior.

The peak profile code of restricting anorexics (287) indicated withdrawal, depression, anxiety, alienation and agitation, avoidance of close interpersonal relationships, and fear of loss of impulse control. These findings were consistent with those reported by Small and associates (1980), with restricting anorexics.

The peak code profile of bulimic anorexics (248) indicated irritability, alienation, underachievement, unpredictability, suicidal thoughts, sexual conflicts, and overall poor adjustment. These patients also tended to be suspicious and distrustful, but concomitantly had high needs for affection. The peak code profile of normal-weight bulimics (428) indicated poor impulse control, acting-out behavior, troubled family relations, poor insight, egocentricism, shallow interpersonal relationships, chronic depression, and a vulnerability to addictive behaviors. Norman and Herzog also noted that both bulimic groups had high 4, low 5 profiles, which are associated with hostility and anger, coupled with an inability to express these feelings directly and stereotypic conventional views of femininity.

In summary, the bulimic anorexic appears to be most disturbed, with scores on seven of nine MMPI subscales in a pathological range. This is consistent with findings that this patient group has the poorest prognosis (Casper et al., 1980; Garfinkel, Moldofsky, and Garner, 1980; Strober, Salkin, Burroughs, and Morrell, 1982). The bulimics at normal weight, although less pathological overall, were most like the bulimic anorexics in their vulnerability to impulsivity. In contrast, restricting anorexics appear to be more depressed, showing signs of character disorder and more vulnerability to psychosis. All groups reported significant mood disorder characterized by chronic depression, irritability, and alienation.

Hatsukami, Owen, Pyle, and Mitchell (1982) explored further the similarities between bulimics and other addictive populations. They compared female bulimics, screened for no history of alcohol or drug abuse (36 percent of the sample was excluded because of problems with substance abuse) to female inpatient substance abusers. Results indicated that modal profiles were quite similar between the two groups and consistent with the previous MMPI findings for bulimics at normal weight. Compared to the substance abusers, the bulimics did show a tendency toward more obsessive-compulsive symptoms, such as anxiety, ruminative thinking, and difficulty making decisions. These findings suggest that the nature of the self-regulatory difficulties bulimics experience is quite similar to those in substance abuse populations. Consequently, some treatment methods that have been useful with substance abuse populations may also be useful with bulimic patients.

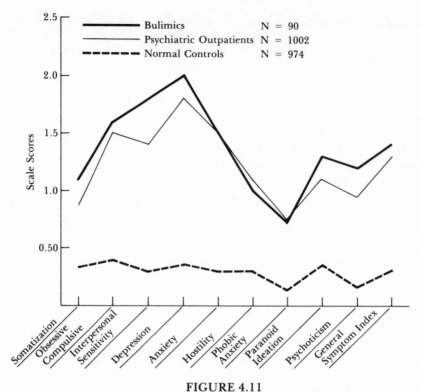

FIGURE 4.11
Findings in a Clinical Population Given the Symptom Checklist 90-Revised

SCL-90r

Figure 4.11 presents findings from our clinical population of bulimic patients on the Symptom Checklist 90-revised (SCL-90r) compared to norms provided by Derogatis and Cleary (1977) for general psychiatric outpatients and normal controls. The findings indicate that the bulimic patients report levels of symptomatic distress comparable to those reported by general psychiatric outpatients. Their specific symptom profile is characteristic of depressed individuals who are quite rejection-sensitive and self-depreciating.

Sex-Role Orientation

In the last several years there has been considerable interest in the sex-role orientation of bulimic women. Boskind-Lodahl (1976) proposed that women who manifest bulimic symptoms are "hyperfeminine" in that they demonstrate an overcompliance to currently prescribed ideals for femininity. She suggested that because of the current cultural value placed on thinness as the ideal female body shape, these women are at greater risk for pursuing thinness through extreme dieting or evacuation techniques.

Several studies have attempted to explore this hypothesis. Dunn and Ondercin (1981) used the Bem Sex Role Inventory (BSRI; Bem, 1974) to investigate whether a sample of women who ate compulsively would be either more masculine or more feminine in self-concept than a normal control group. Their results indicated that the two groups did not differ on either the masculine or feminine subscales.

Originally, the BSRI yielded only two subscales, masculinity and femininity. Test refinements, however, have resulted in the addition of two subscales, titled androgeny and undifferentiated (Spence, Helmreich, and Stapp, 1975). With the new scoring individuals could continue to score simply as high masculine or high feminine; but if they score high on both the masculine and feminine subscales, they are classified as having an androgenous identification, which has been found to be associated with high self-esteem among women. Conversely, if individuals score low on both the masculinity and femininity subscales, they are classified as "undifferentiated," indicating they do not have a clear sense of sex-role identity.

Lewis and Johnson (1985) utilized the new scoring technique to compare normal-weight bulimics to normal controls. The results indicated that significantly more bulimics fell into the undifferentiated category. The findings led to an interesting discussion of what constituted hyperfemininity. The authors concluded that scoring in the undifferentiated category may indicate a form of hyperfemininity that places this group at high risk for psychological impairment, given the current cultural climate for women.

They cited evidence that, traditionally, women more than men have been socialized away from self-definition (Block and Van der Lippe, 1973) and that an undifferentiated identity among women may have had adaptive significance in the maintenance of the nuclear family. The change in role expectations for women over the last two decades, with its emphasis on increased self-definition, may have particularly stressed this group and made them vulnerable to seeking new norms for self-definition. The prevailing cultural emphasis on thinness, particularly for women, may have provided these women an opportunity to define themselves by achieving a culturally valued body shape.

The crucial point of Lewis and Johnson's discussion, however, was that the group at risk for developing bulimia were not women who strongly endorsed items indicating what is traditionally thought of as highly feminine sex-role identification. Instead, the group at risk appears to be those who do *not* strongly endorse any sex-role identification.

Intrapsychic Factors

Much speculation has occurred regarding the intrapsychic world of eating-disordered patients. Although comprehensive and systematic investigations of this dimension have not been conducted, preliminary reports are beginning to appear. In a well-controlled study, Laura Humphrey (in press) utilized the Structural Analysis of Social Behavior (SASB; Benjamin, 1974) to compare restricting anorexics, bulimic anorexics, bulimics at normal weight, and normal controls. The intrapsychic dimension of the SASB yields eight clusters: spontaneous self; self-accepting and exploring; self-nourishing and cherishing; self-protecting and enhancing; self-monitoring and restraining; self-indicating and oppressing; self-rejecting and destroying; daydreaming and neglectful of self. The results indicated that, overall, the introjects of the eating-disordered groups were significantly less friendly and more hostile than those of controls. This was manifested in their being less spontaneous, self-accepting and exploring, self-nourishing and cherishing, and self-protecting and enhancing than normal controls. Conversely, the three eating-disordered groups were more self-indicting and oppressing, self-rejecting and destroying, and daydreaming and neglectful of self.

Further analysis indicated that the bulimic subtypes were significantly less self-nourishing and cherishing and self-protecting and enhancing than either restricting anorexics or normal controls. Bulimic anorexics consistently had the most self-destructive introjects.

These results demonstrate that a preponderance of self-hating rather than self-loving introjects is a general characteristic in both anorexia nervosa and bulimia. Consistent with earlier MMPI findings, the bulimic anorexic group appeared to report the most severe disturbance. Also similar to previous findings, normal-weight bulimics, although slightly less disturbed than the bulimic anorexics, appear to be more similar to them than to either restricting anorexics or normal controls.

Rorschach

It has been suggested that both anorexics and bulimics manifest a wide range of ego deficits. The Rorschach has been the test used most to measure ego strength. In a thorough review of its use with eating-disordered patients, Small (1984) reported that a variety of variables have been examined with anorexic patients; these include cognitive-perceptual factors (Palazzoli, 1971; Rowland, 1970; Small et al., 1982; Strober and Goldenberg, 1981; and Sugarman, Quinlan, and Devenis, 1982); content and dynamic factors (Luyckx and de Aguilar, 1972–73; Moron and Bruno, 1972–73); personality traits (Palmer, Mensch, and Matarazzo, 1952; Wagner and Wagner, 1978); and defensive style (Thielgaard, 1965).

According to Small, studies investigating the conceptual and perceptual dimensions appear to have offered the most information regarding ego strength. Strober and Goldenberg (1981) studied ego-boundary disturbances among twenty anorexic patients. Using five indices related to boundary disturbance on the Rorschach (affect elaboration, overspecificity, incongruence, fabulized combinations, barrier, and penetration), these researchers found that anorexics exhibited higher levels of overspecificity (that is, the degree to which descriptive elaboration of response is excessive or idiosyncratic) and affective elaboration compared to a control group of depressed adolescent females. They concluded that these findings were evidence of boundary disturbances. Furthermore, they established that the disturbances were not a function of weight loss and malnutrition. The authors also noted that heightened barrier scores were found, suggesting a rigid overdefinition of boundaries. They theorized that this overdefinition of boundaries aided the individual in defending against intrusiveness by others.

Also using the Rorschach, Sugarman, Quinlan, and Devenis (1982) studied boundary disturbance in twelve anorexics. In comparison with a control group of hospitalized females, anorexics produced more contamination responses. This type of response reflects condensation of thought and a breakdown in self-other boundaries. Thus, like Strober and Goldenberg (1981), these authors too provide empirical support for ego impairment. The other boundary measures, fabulized combination (serious and regular) and confabulation responses, did not differentiate the two groups. No difference was found in drive-dominated ideation, which suggests that there is an empirical basis for deemphasizing psychosexual formulations. In contrast to Strober and Goldenberg's results (1981), less affective elaboration was found among anorexics.

Rowland (1970) studied twenty-three anorexics using projective techniques. His findings indicated strong depressive trends, body-image disturbances, psychotic trends, poor ego control, poor reality testing, and strong feelings of isolation. Palazzoli (1971) studied twenty-four anorexics on the Rorschach and found two types: one group showed clear thinking disturbances and another group did not. Those who achieved complete recovery belonged to the second group, while fatal outcomes were found only in the group with thinking disturbances.

Small and associates (1982) compared twenty-seven primary anorexics with eighteen female schizophrenics, all of whom were hospitalized. Generally, the anorexics had intact Wechsler Intelligence Profiles but poor Rorschach records. Schizophrenics showed lowered IQs and a poor Rorschach protocol. While anorexics demonstrated greater integrating and organizing capacity than schizophrenics did, their delta index score (a measure of pathological thinking that includes contamination, confabulation, and combination responses) fell in the disordered range. Statistically the anorexics' scores did not differ from those of the schizophrenics, but scores of the latter group were higher.

Very little systematic work has been done to test bulimic patients with the Rorschach. Kaufer and Katz (1983) compared twenty anorexics (ten with bulimic symptoms) to twenty normal controls. The results were consistent with previous findings. Over one-half of the anorexic patients displayed high levels of disturbances in thinking and frequent presence of primary process material. Interestingly, there were no differences between the bulimic and restricting anorexics in any of the scoring categories.

Thus in reviewing the Rorschach findings, there appears to be a striking consensus that anorexic patients, both restricting and bulimic, manifest significant ego impairments, including boundary disturbance, disturbed reality sense, fragile defenses, poor affect management, and thinking disturbances. Furthermore, the specific degree and quality of the ego impairment appear to be most similar to patients with borderline personality organizations.

Bulimia and Borderline Personality Organization

"Borderline" is a complex concept, which has been described in various ways by different authors (Grinker, Werble, and Drye, 1968; Gunderson and Singer, 1975; Kernberg, 1975; Masterson, 1976). Despite the different emphases of these authors, the borderline concept has been developed into a diagnostic category that identifies a group of individuals who share common characterological features. Patients who meet the criteria for borderline personality organization manifest distinct symptoms that appear to be the result of early developmental difficulties. These patients generally have significantly impaired ego resources. Intrapsychically, they are diffuse and undifferentiated, with fragile self-other and inner-outer boundaries, resulting in a vulnerability to breakdown in defenses (de-differentiation) during stress. These self-regulatory deficits result in affective instability, which fluctuates between rageful agitation to an anaclitic, empty depression. A variety of impulse-dominated behaviors are present (self-mutilation, bulimia, promiscuity, substance abuse, shoplifting), representing defensive efforts to self-regulate. Generally the borderline cognitive style is concrete and egocentric. The thinking of these patients can be quite dichotomous, superstitious, and magical. Interpersonally, their relationships are chaotic and undifferentiated. In an effort to compensate for their impoverished ego resources, they will frantically seek relationships in which they are highly dependent on the other for need gratification or self-regulation.

Data-based reports on the incidence of borderline phenomena among bulimic patients are scarce. Hudson and his colleagues (1983) reported that among a sample of forty-nine patients with bulimia, eight (16 percent) also met rigorous criteria for borderline personality organizations. They also found that there were no significant differences in the prevalence of borderline personality organization between active or remitted bulimics or an age-matched comparison group of outpatient subjects with major depression.

In a more elaborate study, Bigman (1985) found that among a sample of twenty-nine eating-disordered patients, eight (28 percent) met DSM-III criteria for Borderline Personality Organization on Axis II. Analysis comparing the borderline and nonborderline eating-disordered patients on the SCL-90 indicated that the former group was more severely symptomatic on all indices than the latter group. Furthermore, on the EDI the borderline group manifested greater maturity fears and interpersonal distrust than the nonborderline group. Finally, a member of the borderline group was more likely to be related to someone with alcohol or drug problems, to have a history of prior treatment for emotional difficulties, and to have greater life impairment as a result of her eating problems.

The relationship of borderline phenomena to eating disorders is perhaps one of the most interesting research questions that has arisen. Preliminary indications are that from one-quarter to one-third of the patient population manifests ego deficits and symptoms characteristic of borderline character disorders. Further research on the relationship between treatment responsiveness and presence or absence of character pathology should yield information on the use of different treatment strategies within the eating-disordered population (see chapter 5). In chapter 12, a review of the literature indicates that roughly one-third of the eating-disordered patients show little change in response to different treatments. It is possible that this more refractory group of patients has a higher incidence of severe character pathology that makes relatively brief interventions less useful to them.

Cognitive Characteristics

Beck and his coworkers (Beck, 1967; Beck, Rush, Shaw, and Emery, 1979) have identified patterns of cognitive distortions that characterize depression. Garner, Garfinkel, and Bemis (1982) and Garner and Bemis (1984) have reported on these distorted thinking patterns as they apply to anorexic patients. These cognitive distortions are also extremely useful in describing a bulimic group. After the onset of bulimia, many of these distortions become centered on the symptom itself. However, these cognitive patterns probably contribute to the development of bulimia, although they may become even more entrenched after symptom onset. Our views on the cognitive distortions found in bulimics are derived from our clinical experience rather than from data-based studies. Nonetheless, we feel that these conceptualizations are important in describing a bulimic population since a complete model of personality must be understood as involving the individual's affects, cognitions, and behaviors. In addition, these cognitive characteristics play an integral role in our treatment of bulimia.

Dichotomous thinking is characteristic of the bulimic cognitive schema. The self and the world are viewed in terms of extremes; one is all good or all bad, with no middle ground. (This could also be termed all-or-none or black-or-white thinking.) If one is not perfect, then the only other alternative is being a total failure. Extremely high expectations for performance are not tempered with realistic self-appraisal. Because the spectre of absolute and humiliating failure looms in any new venture, bulimics have difficulty engaging in the process of experimentation, which is necessary in order to obtain understanding of what one really likes and is good at. When the expectation is that one must be perfect at everything or catastrophe will ensue, procrastination and paralysis are often the result. The self is generally viewed as deficient, and the bulimic's relationship with food provides her with daily "evidence" that this is the case. Different foods are viewed as good (low calorie) or bad (high-calorie sweets and "junk" foods). Bulimics consider themselves totally good and in control when they are dieting stringently and avoiding "bad" foods. Yet often one bite of a "bad" food is enough for bulimics to conclude that they have "blown it" and that they are all bad. Frequently this conclusion triggers a binge; since one has already failed, one might as well "go all the way," get rid of all the "bad" food by bingeing on it, and then purge. The syllogism "Food is bad—I eat food—I am bad" illustrates the negative self-evaluation based on eating behavior. Because the bulimic's standards as she views herself are so polarized, it could take as little as one bite or a one-pound weight gain to cross the line from all good (thin, in control) to all bad (fat, weak, loathsome). Consequently, the self-estimation of the typical bulimic is predominantly negative.

While no measures that accurately assess the nature and scope of a patient's cognitive distortions have been developed yet, clinical experience suggests that distortions such as dichotomous thinking exist on a continuum. More high-functioning neurotic patients seem to have relatively circumscribed areas of dichotomous thinking, perhaps confined primarily to food-related behaviors or perfectionistic attitudes concerning school or job performance. We have also observed dichotomous thinking in narcissistic patients, who are quite grandiose in their self-expectations; for example, one patient stated her conviction that if one couldn't win the Nobel Prize for literature one was an utter failure as a writer and should not continue this fruitless activity. Finally, on the lower end of the continuum, patients with more borderline personality organizations tend to use splitting, which might be regarded as the most primitive form of dichotomous thinking. Splitting is used defensively in an effort to protect a positive view of oneself or another from the intrusion of negative affects; it also represents a developmental failure in the ability to integrate different feelings and tolerate ambivalence. For example, a patient might say to her therapist, "I can't be angry with you because I need you," or "My parents are totally wonderful—it's all my fault that I'm so terrible."

Another cognitive distortion typical of the bulimic group is faulty attribution of control. Bulimics tend to regard the self as externally controlled and helpless. This is particularly apparent in a bulimic's stance toward her food-related behavior, where comments such as these are typical: "My bingeing is totally out of my control, so that when I'm overwhelmed by the urge I just do it," or "Once I ate one cookie I simply couldn't stop eating until the whole box was gone." The bulimic imbues the inanimate object—food—with power and control over her rather than experiencing herself as able to make decisions concerning eating.

This sense of oneself as controlled by external events and circumstances often extends beyond the realm of food, as Beck (1967) has noted with his depressed patients. This ties in with bulimics' higher than normal scores on the ineffectiveness subscale of the EDI. Patients have commented "success in life is all a matter of luck and timing, and I have neither." The ramifications of this helpless stance will be discussed further in a later section.

Paradoxically, while bulimics generally view themselves as externally controlled and helpless, they also tend to subscribe to the belief that one has personal control and responsibility for the happiness of others. They often lack a sense of the legitimacy of their own needs and wishes, coupled with the belief that they must be responsive to the feelings of others at all times. Often these patients seem to have been used by narcissistic parents as their caretaker, in a reversal of the usual parent-child roles. Bulimic patients view their own emotions as potentially overwhelming and destructive, and keep them to themselves so that others will not be harmed. They relinquish responsibility for their own feelings and busy themselves attempting to protect others from painful affects. The frustration and deprivation that result remain unexpressed and contribute to additional feelings of helplessness. Comments such as "I tend to feel responsible when someone close to me is upset," "There is nothing more important than making sure all the people you are close to are happy," and "Whenever anything goes wrong I can't help thinking it must be my fault" are not uncommon. Again, it is likely that both types of these control fallacies exist on a continuum of severity and will vary in terms of how circumscribed they are, how rigidly they are adhered to in the face of alternative perspectives, and from which specific developmental stages they evolved. The narcissistic grandiosity of believing oneself to be the source of all difficulties and to possess the power to change others' emotions whether or not one was involved in causing them is particularly striking.

Magnification, or the tendency to exaggerate the meaning or significance of a particular event, is another cognitive distortion seen in bulimics. This commonly relates to the overvaluation of thinness, which is regarded as the most important thing in the world and the key to all success and beauty. "Nothing else in life counts for anything unless you're thin" and "Unless I'm as thin as I want to be, I am a complete failure" are frequently heard.

Another cognitive distortion, personalization or self-reference, is often seen in conjunction with this overvaluation of thinness. In personalization, patients make egocentric interpretations of impersonal events. For example, they may state that "I can't go out on the street because everyone will notice my stomach sticking out" or "I can't eat in public because everyone will be thinking I'm such a fat pig I should not be eating anything." Again, grandiosity is involved in the assumption that they will be the center of attention, and in some more disturbed patients the personalization assumes a paranoid quality.

Bulimics, like depressives, are noted for their minimization or discounting of all of the positive aspects of a situation while exaggerating the negative details. This is particularly true in their own self-evaluations. A bulimic is more likely to view herself as a fat, worthless slob than as a bright, talented account executive. They overlook or strongly negate positive aspects of their identity and behavior. This is strikingly true in their attitude toward their own improvement; for example, a patient will say "what does it matter that I binged less this week, since I still binged?" Discounting and dichotomous thinking may relate closely to one another.

Overgeneralization is another cognitive distortion in which unwarranted conclusions are drawn on the basis of little evidence. Often a single incident is cited as proof that similar events will inevitably continue to occur. Patients will make such statements as "I binged again today and I was really trying not to, so I know I'll never get well." In non–food-related realms, a patient will conclude that since a man she recently met did not call her, she will never find a satisfying relationship.

The cognitive distortion of magical thinking may include several dimensions, ranging from illogical thought patterns based on unquestioned misinformation to more blatant examples of primary process infantile wishes. Bulimic patients often hold to a variety of misconceptions concerning food, such as "Everything you eat after 6 P.M. turns directly to fat" or "I know I'll gain ten pounds immediately if I eat this meal without purging." In non–food-related areas, patients with narcissistic and borderline characters often manifest merger fantasies, such as "I resent having to tell my partner how I feel because he should just *know*." We have also observed what we have come to describe as transformational fantasies, wherein the patient wishes for a change in a certain area of her life and then believes that instant and dramatic modifications will occur far beyond the realm where the change may actually take place. This is most commonly seen in the areas of weight and relationships; we have heard such comments as "I know my life would be totally different if I could lose that ten pounds," or "If only I had a good relationship all my other problems would disappear."

Beck (1967) has identified what he calls a general cognitive deficiency, in which there is disregard for an important aspect of a life situation such that the patient will ignore, fail to integrate, or not utilize information derived from experience. Only the current activity, rather than its long-term consequences, is concentrated on. This is typical of the bulimic pattern of thinking, where patients focus only on the binge while it is occurring and then determine to start afresh the next day by fasting. Despite the fact that a day's deprivation usually triggers another binge the following night, patients may go through this cycle day after day for years. Each night's vows for perfection are broken the next day without patients learning from their experiences.

Beck (1967) suggested that these sorts of cognitive distortions generate feelings of depression and low self-esteem. Bulimic patients likely are already depressed by the time they develop the symptom. In part, the symptom represents an effort to deal with these painful affects that cannot be expressed verbally. However, we believe that as bulimia progresses, the depression and low self-esteem actually worsen.

The cognitive world of the bulimic may be described in terms of Bandura's self-efficacy model (1977). Bandura proposed that two types of expectations mediate behavior change: outcome expectancies, defined as an individual's estimate that a particular behavior will lead to certain outcomes, and efficacy expectancies, defined as the conviction that one can successfully perform the behavior necessary to produce the outcome. The bulimic's cognitive schema typically includes a gross overestimation of the importance of thinness as the key to all personal and interpersonal success, so that the outcome expectancy is very high. The efficacy expectancy, however, is very low; the bulimic interprets every experience of hunger as evidence that she is completely out of control of her eating and that only purging prevents her from becoming extremely obese. Seligman's revised learned helplessness theory (Abramson, Seligman, and Teasdale, 1978) suggests that the combination of very high outcome expectancies and very low efficacy expectations may lead individuals to adopt a learned helplessness pattern of responding.

Learned helplessness theory provides a conceptualization of the low self-esteem and depression characteristic of bulimics. According to the theory, the individual's low self-esteem is associated with the belief that desired outcomes are not contingent upon acts in his or her own behavioral repertoire, but that for other people outcomes *are* contingent upon their actions. For example, the bulimic feels that she herself cannot eat normally and achieve her ideal weight but that other women can. The theory also suggests that the intensity of the self-esteem loss and affective changes will increase with the certainty and importance of the event the individual is helpless about. The bulimic is typically in a constant state of physiological and psychological deprivation, starving herself or keeping down only small portions of low-calorie foods. The experience of hunger will be constant if one is starving oneself all day, but when everything but diet soda and cottage cheese becomes forbidden, hunger cues are signals for feeling frighteningly out of control. Several times a day the bulimic is involved in an experience that results in lowered self-esteem and the deepened conviction that food is dangerous, hunger is dangerous, and the self is not to be trusted. (For more details see chapter 7.)

The dimensions of stability, externality, and specificity are crucial to understanding the helplessness deficit. Bulimic patients attribute their unattainable outcome to lack of ability, a stable and internal factor. It is also more global than specific, affecting a wide variety of outcomes. The Seligman group suggests that depressives often make internal, stable, and global attributions for failure and may make external, specific, and perhaps less stable attributions for their successes. Depression will be most far reaching when the estimated probability of a positive outcome is low, when the outcome is highly positive and perceived as uncontrollable, and when the attribution for this uncontrollability is to a global, stable, and internal factor. This is an accurate portrayal of the inner experience of bulimic patients; they feel that they are not able to achieve mastery of their body, that it is due to their personal weakness, and yet that this mastery is the prerequisite for everything in life worth having.

Summary

In reviewing the personality literature for bulimia, it seems clear that it is too early to draw firm conclusions regarding all aspects of bulimics' characteristics. Too little research has been done. Those reports that do exist are based on small sample sizes and generally have not been replicated. Despite the preliminary nature of the findings, however, some consistent trends are emerging.

Overall, bulimics appear to have significant problems identifying and articulating their internal states. One consistent finding regarding their internal states is that they appear to have moods that are highly variable and fluctuate from persistent fatigue and depression to feelings of agitation accompanied by impulsive behaviors. Their depression and low self-esteem may also be related to their cognitive distortions.

Their experience of themselves appears to be one of self-doubt, uncertainty, and ineffectiveness. They have high self-expectations and are very harsh, critical, and punitive in their evaluations of themselves. They are self-conscious in the presence of others and are highly sensitive to signs of rejection or disapproval. Despite this sensitivity, however, they generally seek interpersonal relationships.

While little data document their ego resources, the suggestion is that at least a subgroup are vulnerable to intrapsychic difficulties (boundary lapses) similar to patients with various character disorders. In chapter 5, we rely more on clinical observations in an attempt to elaborate on the nature of these intrapsychic deficits.

5

Developmental Considerations

The nature and degree of psychological impairment among patients presenting with eating disorders are best understood within a developmental context. Psychodynamic theory, despite its sometimes tedious emphasis on metapsychology, offers the most comprehensive framework to understand the spectrum of eating-related symptoms among psychiatric patients.

Psychodynamic conceptualizations of eating disorders have paralleled the evolution of psychoanalytic thought. Freud's final model of the mind consisted of three interrelated agencies: the id, ego, and superego. The id was the seat of libidinal drives or impulses; the ego was the center for executive functions, such as organizing the self-maintenance and goal-directed activity of the organism; and the superego was the conscience or moral agency of the individual. This was eventually referred to as the drive-conflict model because it focused on conflict that occurred among these different agencies. Early drive-conflict theories of anorexia nervosa and bulimia regarded self-starvation as a defense against a variety of conflicts. These included sexual fantasies or oral impregnation fears (Moulton, 1942; Rowland, 1970), a reaction formation against oral incorporative wishes (Masserman, 1941) and a defense against ambivalent oral sadistic and cannibalistic fantasies (Blitzer, Rollins, and Blackwell, 1961). The bulimic's binge eating and vomiting was viewed as an expression of rage toward the ambivalently held maternal object (Benedek, 1936; Guiora, 1967).

Eventually psychoanalytic theory began to focus on the functions of the ego and its adaptive ability (Hartmann, 1958; Rapaport, 1967). This model was appropriately referred to as the ego psychological model. Bruch (1973) focused on the ego weaknesses and interpersonal disturbances of eating-disordered patients. She identified specific deficits, such as in-

teroceptive awareness, and highlighted the paralyzing sense of ineffectiveness most of these patients experienced.

More recently in the psychoanalytic literature, self-psychology (Kohut,
1971) and object relations theory (Kernberg, 1976; Mahler, Pine, and
Bergman, 1975; Masterson, 1977) have emerged. They represent an in-
tegrative confluence within a developmental framework of attachment
theory (Bowlby, 1969), cognitive psychology (Piaget, 1954), and traditional ego psychology (Hartmann, 1958; Rapaport, 1967). This new orientation has been facilitated by the elaboration of an empirically based,
dynamically oriented developmental theory (Mahler, 1971; Mahler, Pine,
and Bergman, 1975).

Mahler and her colleagues detailed the sequence of interactions that
occur between the infant and primary caretaker which either facilitates
or impedes the child's separation and individuation. In the following pages,
we present a brief overview of Mahler's developmental stages. We then
comment on the developmental deficits that have been proposed to exist
among eating-disordered patients.

Stages of Separation-Individuation

Mahler, through careful laboratory studies, observed that normal psychological separation-individuation* unfolds in a somewhat consistent and
predictable manner which culminates with the internalization of the ability
to self-regulate (see figure 5.1).

Throughout this chapter we use the term capacity for self-regulation,
which implies the developmental achievement of being able to accurately
identify needs and effectively organize adaptive need-gratifying responses.
It also implies sufficient internal resources to manage impulses/drives,
delay gratification, tolerate frustration, and to soothe dysphoric affects,
such as anxiety and depression. The attainment of this function/structure
occurs as a result of recurrent interactions of the child with a "good-
enough" mother (primary caretaker, primary love object). In good-enough
mothering, the primary caretaker develops a holding environment that
consistently and empathically allows development to occur in doses
that neither overwhelm nor stifle the child. The recurrent experience of
good-enough mothering results in the progressive internalization of this

---

* Mahler differentiated between two intrapsychic developmental tracks, which she clarified as being intertwined but not always commensurate or proportionately progressing.
Individuation is identified as the evolution of intrapsychic autonomy, perception, memory,
cognition, and reality testing. Separation refers to the intrapsychic development of differentiation, distancing, boundary formation, and disengagement from the mother.

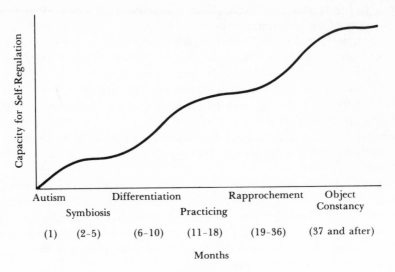

FIGURE 5.1
Stages of Psychological Growth

experience until, ultimately, the individual can perform this function in the absence of immediate contact with the primary caretaker. The attainment of this capacity could also be referred to as developing a cohesive sense of self, object constancy, self-esteem, and perhaps even identity.

According to Mahler's stage theory, an infant proceeds from an initial state of normal psychological autism to an intense symbiotic attachment (symbiotic phase). From within the symbiotic matrix, the child begins the gradual process of separation-individuation, which takes place in four subphases: differentiation, practicing, rapprochement, and on the road to object constancy.

AUTISM

The autism period encompasses the month immediately after birth. It has been characterized as a time when sleeplike states prevail and the infant strives primarily for physiological homeostasis. It is believed that the infant is psychologically in a state of primitive hallucinatory disorientation and at this point has not specifically attached to a primary caretaker. Since attachment is nonspecific in the early stage, good-enough mothering involves attending to the infant's basic physiological needs. Obviously the infant's capacity for self-regulation is virtually nonexistent.

SYMBIOTIC PHASE

Attachment to the mother is the principal task of the symbiotic phase, which lasts from one month to four or five months. From the second month on, a dim awareness emerges in the child of a specific significant other that is need-satisfying. During this phase, the infant behaves and functions as though he or she and the mother were an omnipotent system—a dual unity within one common boundary. The infant is completely dependent upon the mother for need gratification or internal regulation. It is during this stage that a complex pattern of mutual cueing between mother and child unfolds, which results in the "infant becoming the child of this particular mother" (Lichtenstein, 1964). During the symbiotic stage the good-enough mother is able to allow attachment to occur without threat to her own boundaries, to decode the child's early efforts to communicate his or her need states, and to organize a response that attends to that need. The concept of mutual cueing has specific developmental importance for the eating-disordered population because of its significance in the learning of interoceptive awareness.

SEPARATION-INDIVIDUATION

If during the symbiotic phase the child develops a sense of confident expectation that the mother is capable of attending to his or her needs, the process of separation-individuation, which begins at four to five months and lasts till three years, will begin to unfold. According to Mahler, this process of separation-individuation has several nodal points that can be behaviorally observed and seem to reflect some specific cognitive and affective changes in the infant.

Differentiation. At about four to five months the gradual ontogenetic evolution of the sensorium allows the infant to be more permanently alert when awake. Attention, which has been primarily directed inward, gradually expands outward.

> The more the symbiotic partner has helped the infant to become ready to hatch from the symbiotic orbit smoothly and gradually—that is, without undue strain on his own resources—the better equipped has the child become to separate out and to differentiate his self representations from the hitherto fused symbiotic self-plus-object representations. (Mahler, 1968, p. 181)

At about six months the infant engages in tentative experimentation of differentiating self from others. This behavior includes exploring mother's body and clothing and scanning for her in the environment. From seven to eight months a behavioral pattern termed *checking back to mother* emerges that signals the increased somatopsychic differentiation. This is a process of comparing the unique characteristics of one's specific mother to others. This increased differentiation of mother from others culminates around nine months with the sometimes observed phenomenon of "stranger anxiety."

Practicing. The practicing subphase begins approximately at ten months and lasts to about sixteen to eighteen months. Increasing locomotor maturation allows the infant to *physically* separate from the mother and to proceed with the development of autonomous ego apparatus.

> Expanding locomotor capacity during the early practicing subphase widens the child's world; not only does he have a more active role in determining closeness and distance to mother, but the modalities up to now that were used to explore the relatively familiar environment suddenly expose him to a wider segment of reality; there is more to see, more to hear, more to touch. How this new world is experienced seems to be suddenly related to mother who still is the center of the child's universe from which he only gradually moves out into ever-widening circles. (Mahler, Pine, and Bergman, 1975, p. 66)

Psychologically this developmental stage is described as the time when the child has a "love-affair with the world." If the mother and child have established her as a safe anchor, then the child increasingly distances him- or herself from her and becomes enamored with practicing motor skills and exploring the "other-than-mother world." During this time the child is usually impervious to knocks and falls and familiar adults can more easily substitute for the mother. During exploration it is important for the mother to be in close proximity so that the child can quickly return and "emotionally refuel."

Good-enough mothering during this period involves accepting the gradual separation of the toddler and encouraging his or her interest in exploring the other-than-mother world. Of crucial importance, however, is the ability of the good-enough mother to be emotionally available for refueling, according to the child's needs.

Rapprochement. The rapprochement subphase begins around eighteen months and extends to roughly twenty-four months. Mahler and her associates labeled this subphase the rapprochement period to capture the ambivalent and often contradictory behavior of the child during this time.

Toddlers' increased locomotor and cognitive development allow them to increasingly separate and individuate. Accompanying this increased ability is an increased awareness that separation means losing the feeling of parental omnipotence and "oceanic oneness" that has been experienced in the symbiotic dual unity. The observed reaction to this awareness of loss is increased separation anxiety. In contrast to the practicing subphase, where infants were often impervious to frustration and relatively unconcerned about the mother's presence, during this phase toddlers become somewhat preoccupied with the mother's whereabouts and begin to actively approach her to participate with them in the acquisition of new

skills. This is a turbulent time for infant and mother. The child ambivalently struggles with wishes for symbiotic reunion with the love object
and yet fears being reengulfed in the symbiosis. Behaviorally this is acted
out by rapidly alternating sequences where the child will shadow the
mother in a clingy fashion and then dart away and reject active holding.

During the latter part of the rapprochement phase, the child's predominant fear shifts from a fear of loss of the other to a fear of loss of
love of the other. These are the harbingers of superego development
where fear of rejection, disappointment, and shame become internal
experiences.

During this subphase the good-enough mother needs to strike a delicate balance between "holding and releasing" and "being there and not
there." Essentially the task becomes to comfort the child's fear of object
loss by being available for emotional refueling and simultaneously being
able to relieve the fear of engulfment by allowing the child to increasingly
separate according to his or her needs.

One noteworthy dimension of the rapprochement phase is the emergence of the use of transitional objects. Children invest these objects with
the power to soothe and comfort them. The transitional object becomes
a concrete, symbolic representation of the mother's function of soothing
and comforting. It is not the mother, but it has the symbolic power to
function like the mother, and, most important, it is something the child
can concretely take with him or her and have control over in the physical
absence of the mother. Given the fact that the child lacks adequate internal
structure for self-regulation, the external object becomes invested with
the ability to regulate tensions. With good-enough mothering, the self-
regulating function that the transitional object serves increasingly becomes
internalized. The transitional object is, therefore, a way-station between
externally controlled and internally controlled self-regulation.

The concept of transitional objects, and the implied underlying developmental issues, has important clinical implications for some patients
with bulimia. For some of these patients, food or their act of binge eating
appears to serve a function very similar to that of a transitional object.
This will be discussed more thoroughly in part II. It is most important to
note, however, that the adult's reliance on a concrete object (such as food)
for tension regulation implies a self-regulatory vulnerability associated
with the rapprochement phase.

On the Road to Object Constancy. The fourth subphase, which occurs
around thirty-six months, is characterized by the unfolding of complex
cognitive functions. These include verbal communication, fantasy, reality
testing, the stabilization of self and other boundaries that allow for a sense
of individuality, and, finally, the consolidation of object constancy. Object
constancy refers to the child's ability to evoke an image or intrapsychic
representation of mother that is comforting in her physical absence. According to Mahler:

The slow establishment of emotional object constancy is a complex and multi-determined process involving all aspects of psychic development. Essential prior determinants are 1) trust and confidence through the regularly occurring relief of need tension provided by the need satisfying agency as early as the symbiotic phase. In the course of the subphase of the separation-individuation process, this relief of need tension is gradually attributed to the need satisfying whole object (the mother) and is then transferred by means of internalization to the intrapsychic representation of the mother; and 2) the cognitive acquisition of the symbolic inner representation of the permanent object (in Piaget's sense) in our instance to the unique love object: the mother. Numerous other factors are involved such as innate drive endowment and maturation, neutralization of drive energy, reality testing, tolerance for frustration and anxiety and so forth. (Mahler, Pine, and Bergman, 1975, p. 110)

During this phase the child is generally able to accept separation from the mother once again (similar to the practicing period) and can once again play independently.

Once the fundamental separation and individuation occur, the child enters latency, which is a period of consolidation and relative quiesence. With the emergence of adolescence, however, separation and individuation issues are once again revived, but at a substantially different level from childhood.

Separation-individuation conflicts take on different dimensions with the psychobiological maturity of the child. Early developmental deficits or conflicts, which may have been obscured during latency, are rather quickly exposed under the impact of the second separation period (Blos, 1967). While Mahler's detailed, stage-specific observations do not extend to adolescence, there have been numerous observations regarding the developmental tasks of this life stage, which is the period when anorexia nervosa and bulimia most commonly begin. Foremost among these tasks is the renewed demand for separation.

In this culture, age fifteen to eighteen is considered a time when a child is basically expected to move beyond the nuclear family and become a member of the larger and more diverse society. The onset of puberty also forces an integration of issues such as adult strength, mobility, and sexuality. Finally, the adolescent must consolidate a sense of self (identity) that he or she can rely upon to navigate the demands of independent living.

Our intent in presenting the normal developmental model was to establish what average, expectable tasks confront an individual during the period of risk for developing eating disorders. The reason for the more specific focus on infant development is that most investigators feel that, for at least a majority of eating-disordered individuals, disruptions that occur during the separation-individuation phase place a person at risk for problems with subsequent developmental stages, particularly adolescence.

In the next section we integrate our understanding of how specific psychopathological adaptations related to eating disturbance might emerge during development.

Developmental Deficits and Eating Disorders

It is important to note that the feeding interaction between mother and child is one of the first and primary arenas in which communication occurs. The nonverbal, presymbolic transaction that occurs lays the groundwork for neurophysiological and intrapsychic schemas that will organize the infant's experience. Nourishing others and being nourished is an emotionally charged event. There is great opportunity for pathological expression of psychological conflicts, or deficits, from mother to infant in this early transactional process. It is also understandable how food becomes endowed with complex values and elaborate ideologies, religious beliefs, and prestige systems.

The complexity of the interaction between mother and child during the feeding process has been written about extensively (Charone, 1982). What is of interest here is whether the emergence of the symptomatic behavior of anorexia nervosa and bulimia as adaptations to early developmental difficulties can be identified.

It is important to note that the response styles of primary caretakers are as variable as any other human behavior and undoubtedly reflect each individual's unique physiological and psychological makeup. Not surprisingly, transgenerational research has demonstrated that how we care for others is largely a function as how we were cared for. For example, abused children often become abusing parents, and children who were reared by chaotic and undifferentiated caretakers become chaotic and undifferentiated caretakers themselves. Assuming that the child is simply a *tabula rasa* upon which a script is imposed from the outside is an error that must be avoided, however. Research has also indicated that children do not simply incorporate the parents' response style wholesale. Instead, infants are active participants; their unique reactive style affects not only how they experience being cared for but also how they *will* be cared for. For example, colicky babies may experience more frustration around receiving comfort, not so much as a function of deficits in the caretaker but as a side effect from a physiological state that makes an adequate response difficult. Given this scenario, one could imagine how, with time, the child's persistent physiological problems would lower the caretaker's frustration tolerance, thus establishing an early pattern of frustration between caretaker and child. In contrast, some children seem particularly resilient and emerge relatively unscathed from very disturbed holding environments. Considering that the feeding process is the initial arena in which these interactions occur, the potential for the action sequence of eating to become disturbed is staggering.

Several prominent theorists have attempted to determine the specific disruption in the early holding environment that would lead to subsequent problems such as anorexia nervosa or bulimia. Bruch (1962) suggested that the symptomatic behavior of anorexia nervosa was an adaptation to early developmental disruptions that occurred in the late symbiotic or early differentiation subphase of separation-individuation. Earlier we reviewed Bruch's observations that the central issues for anorexia nervosa patients revolve around difficulties with interoceptive awareness, body-size distortion, and a paralyzing sense of ineffectiveness. We mentioned the importance of the construct of interoceptive awareness to body distortion and feelings of ineffectiveness. Bruch recognized the centrality of this difficulty and elaborated a formulation of how a child would develop this type of difficulty when interacting with a particular type of caretaker.

According to Bruch, the ability to identify or articulate internal states, including hunger and satiety, are learned behaviors. She believed that the acquisition of this ability is a function of early mother-child interactions around need states and need gratifications, and proposed a model for normal development of interoceptive awareness (see figure 5.2).

Children are active participants in their development. Their participation involves emitting a signal related to some need state that they initially experience as diffuse and undifferentiated. The caretaker must decode the signal and organize a response. The child's increasing ability to appropriately differentiate his or her internal states will be facilitated or interfered with according to the caretaker's ability to accurately decode and respond to the child's cues.

> Appropriate responses to cues coming from the infant, in the biological field as well as the intellectual, social and emotional field, are necessary for the child to organize the significant building stones for the development of self-awareness and self-effectiveness. If confirmation and reinforcement of his own and initially rather undifferentiated needs and impulses have been absent, or have been contradictory or inaccurate, then the child will grow up perplexed when trying to differentiate between disturbances in his biological field and emotional interpersonal experiences, and would be apt to misinterpret deformities in his self-body concept as externally induced. Thus he will become an individual deficient in his sense of separateness, with diffuse ego boundaries, and feel helpless under the influence of external forces. (Bruch, 1973, p. 56)

Bruch further elaborated on how faulty decoding by the primary caretaker results in confusion and lack of differentiation of internal states, particularly related to the experience of hunger (see figure 5.3).

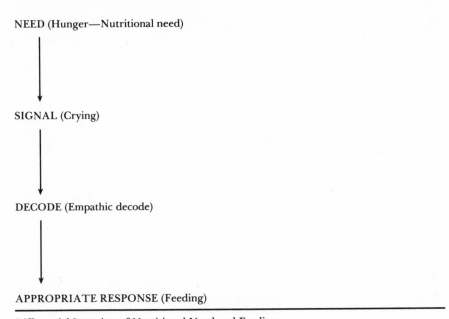

NEED (Hunger—Nutritional need)

SIGNAL (Crying)

DECODE (Empathic decode)

APPROPRIATE RESPONSE (Feeding)

Differential Learning of Nutritional Need and Feeding

FIGURE 5.2
Normal Development of Interoceptive Awareness

When a mother offers food in response to signals indicating nutritional needs, the infant will gradually develop the engram of hunger as a sensation distinct from other tensions or needs. If, on the other hand, a mother's reaction is continuously inappropriate, be it neglectful, over solicitous, inhibiting or indiscriminantly permissive, the outcome for the child will be perplexing and confusing. When he is older he will not be able to discriminate between being hungry or satiated, or between nutritional need and some other discomfort or tension. (Bruch, 1973, p. 56)

Since both restricting anorexics and bulimics appear to manifest substantial difficulty with interoceptive awareness, perhaps specific differences in the mother-child interaction predispose patients more toward a restricting versus a bulimic adaptation to the interoceptive difficulties. In the following sections we will argue that both maternal over- and under-involvement result in unempathic decoding and would predispose children to the type of self-regulatory difficulties observed in restricting anorexics and bulimics. Furthermore, we also believe that restricting behavior is a specific adaptation to maternal overinvolvement and that the bulimic behavior reflects an adaptive response to maternal underinvolvement.

It is important to note that this early attempt to differentiate restricting and bulimic individuals according to specific developmental disruptions is quite speculative. As depicted in figure 5.4, we are talking about a

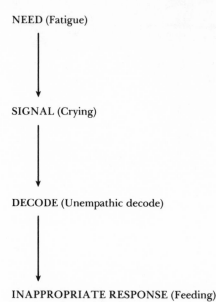

NEED (Fatigue)

SIGNAL (Crying)

DECODE (Unempathic decode)

INAPPROPRIATE RESPONSE (Feeding)

Interoceptive Awareness Difficulties; Confusion Around the Relationship Between Nutritional Need, Fatigue, and Feeding

FIGURE 5.3
Abnormal Development of Interoceptive Awareness

normal distribution of maternal responsiveness within both groups, but with clustering along the continuum of maternal involvement. The rationale for attempting this differentiation is that if the differences in the nature of maternal responsiveness are accurate, then it may well suggest different treatment strategies for the two groups.

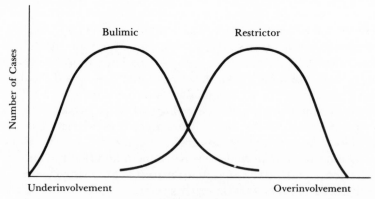

FIGURE 5.4
Disruptions in Maternal Preoccupation

MATERNAL OVERINVOLVEMENT AND THE RESTRICTING STANCE

A number of investigators have observed that mothers of classic restricting anorexia nervosa patients are domineering, intrusive, over-protective, and overtly or more subtly discouraging of separation-individuation. They encourage enmeshment and often respond to the child according to their own needs rather than those of the child. This enmeshment prevents the child from acquiring a firm, independent, co-hesive sense of self and leaves him or her dependent on the primary caretaker for self-regulation. During childhood and latency there is min-imal developmental pressure to disrupt the symbiotic attachment between mother and child. The beginning of adolescence, however, with its new demands for separation and individuation, can potentially disrupt the relationship. It is at this point that self-starvation serves a variety of adap-tive functions.

Bruch originally suggested that the anorexics' relentless pursuit of thinness and defiant defense of that behavior was an adaptive effort to take charge of their selves. Control of their selves was concretely repre-sented by controlling their bodies, and the measure of control was con-tinued weight loss. The persistent pursuit of thinness then would serve a dual function of undoing feelings of ineffectiveness by successfully achiev-ing body control (thinness) and by engaging in an oppositional behavior that, at least at a superficial level, disrupts the symbiotic relationship with the mother.

Palazzoli (1974) suggested a slightly different adaptation in the an-orexic stance. Like Bruch, Palazzoli observed that anorexic patients ex-perience significant self-definition and self-regulatory difficulties as a result of enmeshed symbiotic relationships with overcontrolling mothers. How-ever, Palazzoli argued that the changes that occur during puberty, when the girl's body begins to change and become more like her mother's, are overwhelming and engulfing to these patients. According to Palazzoli (1974), "Because of the development of breast and other feminine curves, the body is experienced concretely as the maternal object, from which the ego wishes to separate itself at all costs. . . . The patient considers and experiences her body as one great incorporated object which overpowers her and forces a passive role upon her" (p. 90).

Palazzoli concluded that anorexia is a form of intrapersonal paranoia that should be classified somewhere between schizophrenia and depres-sion. The anorexic experiences food intake as an increase to a monstrous thing (the body at the expense of the central ego). The anorexic stance then becomes a desperate attempt to live, by overcoming the all-powerful, bad body that is the embodiment of the bad internal object.

Another group of observers, probably best represented by Crisp (1980) and his colleagues, have emphasized that the severe weight loss among restricting anorexic patients protects them from the psychological and biological demands that accompany puberty. The emaciation that accompanies the starvation biologically returns the individual to a prepubertal physical state. Endocrine changes that are directly related to weight loss, or percentage reduction of adipose tissue, eliminate secondary sexual characteristics (breast and hip development, menstruation, and so forth). This basically relieves the pressure of biological maturation and the attendant demands around sexuality and separation. Interestingly, the manipulation of body weight essentially allows the patient to control the timing and pace of puberty. Psychologically, the severe emaciation minimizes separation demands. Also, paradoxically, the debilitating side effects and fragility associated with severe emaciation ensure further enmeshment and symbiotic attachment to the primary caretaker. It is important to note that the adaptive function of the weight loss is to protect the ego-impaired patient from developmental demands for which she is unprepared. The anorexic behavior appears to allow the patient to make a self-assertive statement while simultaneously ensuring that separation expectations will be minimized.

The common denominator among these different theories is that the restricting anorexic child reaches puberty with developmental vulnerabilities around self-awareness, self-definition, and self-regulation. Furthermore, the vulnerabilities are precipitated by some degree of maternal overinvolvement. The self-starvation is a desperate attempt to assert some autonomy, defend the fragile self against further maternal intrusiveness, and protect the fragile ego from the psychobiological demands of adulthood. We would also like to suggest that the predominant defensive style of restrictors is paranoid in nature. They attempt to establish and maintain boundaries by utilizing rigid, overdetermined, avoidant defenses. They differentiate a sharp inner/outer, self/other border and then utilize the paranoid defenses to protect the boundary from intrusive invasion. As we will show, this behavior contrasts with that of bulimics, who appear to rely more upon hysterical defenses in an effort to compensate for self-regulatory deficits arising from an experience of underinvolvement with the primary caretaker.

MATERNAL UNDERINVOLVEMENT AND THE BULIMIC STANCE

According to Mahler's developmental model, those children that negotiate separation and individuation most easily are the ones who have developed a sense of consistent and predictable security during the symbiotic phase and who are encouraged to separate during the practicing/rapprochement phases. We believe that the developmental histories of bulimic patients reflect a pattern of underinvolvement with the primary caretaker that interferes with the separation-individuation process.

In contrast to mothers of restricting anorexics, mothers of bulimic patients have been described as passive, rejecting, and disengaged (see chapter 6). It is important to emphasize that they usually are not blatantly neglectful caretakers; on the contrary, superficially they appear to adequately attend to their child's primary needs. The underinvolvement or disengagement appears to be more subtly manifested as a type of emotional unavailability. The quality of the caretaking could be characterized as form without substance. Although the primary needs are attended to, there is no warmth in the holding experience or mutually enjoyable mirroring (gleam in the eye) that facilitates the capacity for self-soothing. These mothers generally have intrapsychic deficits themselves that result in affect-regulation problems. The child's infantile needs appear to overwhelm the caretaker or provoke rageful resentment.

The primary caretaker's emotional unavailability sends the child into the differentiation phase with a very tenuous bond to her. The child's experience is one of insecure footing from which to launch. Under these circumstances the child might become tentative and even clingy. The clinginess, particularly through the rapprochement phase, further taxes the mother's limited resources and may provoke increased rejection of the child's needs to be soothed and comforted. Under these circumstances there are a number of substitutes that the child might use. There is a strong likelihood that since soothing is unavailable from the mother, the child will begin to seek self-regulatory tools outside the mother/child unit. Since food has such powerful symbolic associations, it is likely to be adopted by the child as a self-regulatory tool. The function that the food serves could be conceptualized as being similar to that of a transitional object. In essence, it becomes something the child invests with the ability to comfort her and, more important, that she has control over.

In summary, both maternal over- and underinvolvement can result in impairment in the child's ability to self-regulate (obtain object constancy, a cohesive self, and positive self-regard). For the restrictor, self-starvation may be an adaptive effort to defend against self-regulatory deficits resulting from maternal overinvolvement. In contrast, the bulimic's chaotic eating behavior may reflect a desperate attempt to compensate for an "empty experience" resulting from maternal underinvolvement. In a sense, the fundamental difference between the restricting and bulimic mode could be thought of as the bulimic's search for something to take in compared to the restricting anorexic's attempt to keep something out.

Since most bulimic patients regard themselves as failed restrictors, what prevents them from relying on the restricting defense? Self-starvation is a highly depriving behavior that is motivated by intense commitment or fear. Ascetics and zealots experience a spiritual purity or fanatical commitment in response to self-starvation. The deprivation enhances their sense of strength. For classic restricting anorexics, the self-starvation (control of body) may serve to defend them against the threat of maternal intrusiveness. The sense of protection allows them to feel strong and safe.

Among the bulimics, however, we have found that deprivation associated with self-starvation is unbearable over time because it exacerbates the fundamental deficit in the holding environment, which is emptiness resulting from parental detachment.

Consequently, in the absence of being able to sustain more paranoid/avoidant defenses, the bulimic is pushed toward a defensive adaptation that involves efforts to take in things to compensate for feelings of emptiness or dysphoria. This pursuit of emotional supplies is often frantic, diffuse, and chaotic, reflecting perhaps a more primitive hysterical defensive style.

The Spectrum of Eating Disorders

Because of the immense transactional importance of the early feeding interaction, it is important to note that feeding disturbances are often part of the symptomatic expression of a wide range of psychopathologies (Bruch, 1973; Swift and Stern, 1982). One difficulty in working in the area of eating disorders at this time is avoiding the tendency to take a sign-oriented approach to diagnosing bulimia. More specifically, we believe that there is an increasing tendency to overdiagnose bulimia, when in fact we are often dealing with a wide range of ego deficits that involve food-related problems as one of several adaptations.

Figure 5.5 is an attempt to depict the relative distribution of bulimic patients along a developmental continuum. Although bulimic symptoms undoubtedly appear in individuals who have very primitive ego strength as well as those who have relatively high ego strength, the former cases are atypical. Most patients with clinically significant cases of bulimia appear to manifest ego deficits that would be associated with difficulties during the differentiation phase of separation-individuation, resulting in character disorder.

PSYCHOTIC DISORDERS

As suggested in figure 5.5 one population of patients presenting with bulimic symptoms have extremely primitive ego resources. These patients are often schizophrenic or severely schizoid. The function the bulimic behavior serves and the cognitions that attend the symptoms are different from more typical cases. More specifically, psychotic patients with bulimic symptoms most often do not express a drive for thinness, morbid fear of fat, or self-depreciating thoughts following a binge episode. If they do

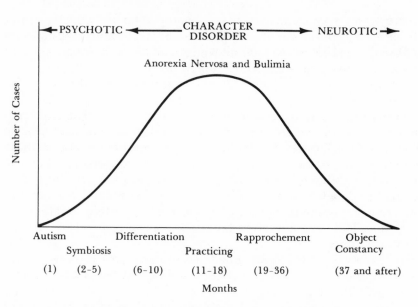

FIGURE 5.5
Range of Psychopathology for Anorexia Nervosa and Bulimia Patients

express distorted thinking regarding food or their bodies, it is part of a larger psychotic organization and is not circumscribed as with most anorexic and bulimic patients.

It is often apparent in the histories of schizophrenic patients that the early feeding interaction was chaotic. Primary caretakers who are psychologically disorganized or undifferentiated are likely to transmit the disorganization to the infant, and, as mentioned, the feeding interaction is a prime arena for this transmission. If the caretaker is not able to progressively and differentially decode the infant's signal of different need states and then consistently offer an accurate response, the child will most likely develop a deficit in her own ability to differentiate and accurately respond to needs. For example, if a child is crying (signal) because she is tired (need), and 30 percent of the time mother responds by changing her diaper, 30 percent of the time feeding her, and 30 percent of the time by having her nap, it is likely that the child will not learn how to differentiate needs. Consequently, responses will often be inappropriate, random, and ungratifying.

CASE: PSYCHOTIC BULIMIC

Carol. Eighteen-year-old Carol, the only child of an unmarried schizophrenic mother, was brought to a residential treatment center when it was apparent that neither she nor her mother could attend to her needs.

The presenting complaint from mother and patient was Carol's uncontrollable eating episodes and sporadic abuse of laxatives and self-induced vomiting. Clinical interviews indicated that Carol was actively hallucinating and was cognitively disoriented. Although her weight was high normal, she manifested no body-size distortion or dissatisfaction and no drive for thinness.

During the course of treatment, it became apparent that Carol was profoundly undifferentiated. She felt a great deal of confusion around different bodily processes, need states, and appropriate responses to these different states. Data gathered from the mother indicated that because of her own undifferentiated ego resources, she was not very helpful in teaching her daughter how to differentiate need states and organize appropriate responses to them. From the mother's report, it was also clear that feeding had been a multipurpose tool used to respond to virtually all of Carol's needs.

Predictably, food and feeding had become a singular response to any disruption in Carol's mood state. She would become particularly symptomatic with her binge eating when she was more actively hallucinating. The binge eating was clearly an effort to distract her from the auditory hallucinations, and she experienced no guilt or self-depreciating thoughts following a binge episode.

CHARACTER DISORDERS

As suggested earlier, we and many others* believe that patients who present with clinically significant levels of eating disorders have ego deficits that are characteristic of patients who have character disorders. Furthermore, these ego deficits reflect disruptions in the early interactions between the parental holding environment and the child (late symbiotic phase through rapprochement).

In the next sections we attempt to differentiate between eating-disordered patients who present with borderline characteristics and false self/narcissistic characteristics. We also attempt to identify how restrictors and bulimics differ within these two character-disordered groups (see table 5.1).

Borderline Personality. Earlier we reviewed data that indicated a substantial number of eating-disordered patients manifest symptoms characteristic of borderline personality organization. These patients usually have significant ego impairments that result in self-regulatory difficulties. They are quite vulnerable to temporary episodes of de-differentiation (breakdown of self/other or inner/outer boundaries). Phenomenologically, patients experience this as a fragmentation of self or depersonal-

---

* See Bruch, 1973; Goodsitt, 1984; Lerner, 1983; Sours, 1980; Sugarman and Kurash, 1982; Swift and Letven, 1984; Swift and Stern, 1982; and Wilson, 1983.

TABLE 5.1

Variations in Character Pathology for Anorexic and Bulimic Patients

	Borderline Malevolent	False Self/Narcissistic Non-malevolent
Restrictor Overinvolvement	Malevolent Intrusiveness (Intentional) Attachment—Hostile, controlling enmeshment Separation—Retaliation by other, injury to self Self—Repeatedly overwhelmed, in danger Other—Punitive, controlling, harsh, critical Defenses—Paranoid defenses used to establish and protect boundaries—splitting	Non-malevolent Intrusiveness (Unintentional) Attachment—Controlling but less hostile and punitive enmeshment Separation—Depletion of both self and other, injury to other Self—Extension of other, without identity, ineffective, reactive Other—Fragile Defenses—Less paranoid, more obsessive, phobic
Bulimic Underinvolvement	Malevolent neglect (Intentional) Attachment—Hostile disengagement resulting in clingy dependence Separation—Abandonment, emptiness, fragmentation Self—Worthless, unlovable Other—Withholding, punitive Defenses—Hysterical/ impulsive used in effort to introject, projective identification	Non-malevolent Neglect (Unintentional) Attachment—Less hostile disengagement; wish for intimacy versus fear of disappointment, discovery, rejection; injury to other Separation—Protective of self and other, pseudoautonomy, distant closeness Self—Fraud, inadequate, destructively needy Other—Incapable of adequate holding Defenses—Schizoid defenses, avoidance, denial, isolation of affect, intellectualization, suppression

ization. During these regressions, affects can become quite labile, ranging from rageful agitation to an empty, anacliticlike depression (Blatt, 1974; Lidz, 1976). Borderline patients' experience of self and other is often laced with a sense of aggression or malevolence that results in sadistic and masochistic interactions with self and other.

These patients appear to adapt a variety of different defense mechanisms. Two styles seem to have particular relevance to the distinctions between restrictors and bulimics that we have begun to make. Some borderline patients appear to become more paranoid during ego regressions. They attempt to protect the endangered and fragile self by projecting or externalizing any threat outside the overdetermined boundary. Generally, the more rigid the patient's overdetermination, the more vulnerable she feels to boundary failure or disintegration.

In contrast to the paranoid defense, another group of borderline patients appear to have more chaotic, diffuse, hysterical defensive styles. For these patients the ego regression provokes a frantic search outside the self for something that will distract, soothe, or orient them away from the mounting disorganization. Unlike the paranoid borderline, the defensive adaptation is to bring something in (introject) that will relieve the panic, anxiety, or dysphoria they are feeling. As depicted in table 5.1, individuals who are relying predominantly on restricting behavior are attempting to utilize a paranoid defense against overinvolvement, while those who manifest bulimic symptoms have more diffuse, chaotic hysterical defenses that are responses to experiences of underinvolvement. As different treatment approaches are necessary for these two groups, we now shall further articulate some of the clinical differences between restricting and bulimic borderline patients.

RESTRICTING BORDERLINE PATIENTS

The key feature among restricting borderline patients is that they have experienced parental overinvolvement as *malevolently* intrusive. The caretaker has attempted *intentionally* to enmesh the child in a hostile dependent relationship. These patients perceive that their efforts to separate or differentiate will result in active punishment or retaliation. Attachment for these patients means enmeshment in a controlling, hostile, intrusive relationship. The experience of the self is one of repeatedly being overwhelmed by another who does not have the child's best interest at heart. These patients desperately erect paranoid defenses in an effort to protect the fragile self from being overwhelmed.

Body-image distortion among these patients is a central feature to their psychological adaptation. Earlier we suggested that there were both quantitative and qualitative differences between eating-disordered patients regarding body-image disturbance and that patients who persisted in their body-image distortion had the poorest outcome. It has been our clinical experience that those patients who are most treatment resistant (poorest outcome) fall into this category of restrictor borderline personality.

In an effort to protect the fragile self from intrusiveness that is experienced as malevolent, the restricting borderline patient has essentially created a paranoid system in which fat becomes the symbolic focus of the paranoid defense. While these patients are not grossly psychotic, in moments of perceived threat their thinking, particularly regarding their bodies, can become somewhat delusional.

These patients do not have a schizophrenic psychological system. Rather they are more similar to paranoid state patients, who develop elaborate defenses to protect themselves from a perceived threat. The defense of the self against the threat then provides a mechanism for structuring one's life. But the paranoid structure can be maintained only as long as the central belief or distortion is preserved. The patient must cling to the one central distorted belief, because if that belief is not true, then all subsequent behavior does not make sense. The delusional belief regarding the perceived threat and the psychological organization erected against the threat are circumscribed, however, and often do not result in complete psychological debilitation.

The restricting borderline patient initially attempts to establish a sense of self by taking charge of her body (body equals self). Fat becomes a concrete symbol of a feared feeling of hostile invasion and control. It then becomes a paranoid object that has many distortions associated with it, including an attribution of volition (fat has a mind of its own, goes where it is unwanted, will take over, and so forth). The patient can then mobilize her defenses against this threat and achieve a sense of control and safety, which is highly reinforcing.

The distorted body image allows the patient to develop an autonomous, self-derived belief system that is organized around a central perceived threat (fat). The defense of the self against the perceived threat (fat) gives the patient a sense of *purpose* (goal), and the fear associated with the perceived threat (fat) provides *motivation* to the individual in order to avoid the threat. The accomplishment of thinness (avoidance of fat) then results in a profound sense of control. If she acknowledges her thinness (no fat), however, then purpose and motivation are lost. She would also experience cognitive dissonance if she did not cling to the body distortion. Emaciated individuals do not intentionally starve themselves unless they are crazy (out of control). Consequently, she must change the perception/belief about her degree of fatness in order to avoid the dissonance and preserve the psychological system. The tenacity of the patient's protection of the distorted body image is an indication of the degree of intrapsychic brittleness or fragility. It is crucial for therapists to understand that, for these patients, the disturbed belief about their bodies is a necessary distortion that allows a psychological organization to exist, which gives the patients autonomy, control, and a sense of purpose and motivation.

Treatment of these patients is difficult and usually requires years of consistent and caring involvement. The predominant transference themes usually revolve around issues of control and autonomy. These patients are usually attentive to any indication that therapists are trying to assert their will upon them. They are highly distrustful and quick to assume that therapists are intentionally attempting to enmesh them in a relationship where they will ultimately be punished for autonomous behavior. The therapists' task is to create a therapeutic holding environment where patients learn they can engage in an interdependent relationship without the aggressive-punitive control issues they are familiar with. This is often a highly complicated task since the adaptation these patients have made (pursuit of thinness) can place them at serious medical risk due to their low weight. The low weight can provoke intrusive behavior from the staff that a patient experiences as aggressive and punitive. Given this dilemma, we have found it useful to use a split management treatment model with this subpopulation of patients. Therapists are not primarily responsible for behavioral management issues. While they need to be aligned for the most part with the treatment team, it is also important that the therapist be viewed by both patient and staff as the primary advocate for the patient.

Treatment of these patients can be similar to treatment of paranoid characters. Their delusional systems (fat) can become quite calcified over time and resistant to outside influence. Often they achieve a certain level of life adjustment. Despite maintaining chronically subnormal body weights, they will often return to work but lead relatively isolated social lives.

CASE: RESTRICTING ANOREXIC BORDERLINE

Rita B. Twenty-year-old Rita was brought to treatment by her mother. At the time of the consultation, she was five feet seven inches tall and weighed ninety-two pounds, had been amenorrheic for five years, and insisted that nothing was wrong with her. Rita had a five-year history of recurrent episodes of anorexia nervosa. She had seen three therapists during this time and had been briefly hospitalized for weight restoration. She presented as a suspicious, angry, defiant young woman.

The onset of Rita's anorexia began during the summer preceding her transition to high school. She began dieting in preparation for her sister's wedding, which was to occur during the summer. She began to severely restrict her food intake, particularly avoiding red meat (which she concretely visualized as filled with fat). She also began a ritual of strenuous exercise that occupied several hours each day.

One year before the onset of Rita's anorexia, her father had experienced what he termed a "heart attack," which left him virtually housebound for one year. Rita's father was an emotionally unavailable man, who has marked obsessional and phobic tendencies and was vulnerable to rage outbursts. The details of his heart attack were unclear. The cardiologist felt that he had experienced a major anxiety attack and was treating him with imipramine. Following his heart attack, Mr. B. had become phobic about being outside the house and had become very preoccupied with and vigilant to changes in his bodily functioning. Rita experienced her father as emotionally unavailable but affectively volatile. She felt that any interaction that occurred between them was usually in the context of a rage outburst.

Mrs. B. presented as an angry, depressed woman who had always been overwhelmed by the emotional demands of marriage and child rearing.

There appeared to be at least three generations of mother/daughter enmeshment. Mrs. B. still had contact with her own mother several times per day, and commented that if she did not maintain the contact her mother would "murder her." Mrs. B. experienced her own mother as oppressive and tyrannical and felt powerless to do anything about it. She had married young in an unsuccessful attempt to escape the enmeshment.

Rita experienced her mother as overwhelmed, needy, angry, hypercritical, intrusive, and vindictive. Over the course of treatment, Rita offered countless stories of her mother's intrusiveness and vindictiveness. She recalled how her mother would rummage through her personal items in her room and listen in on phone conversations. Whenever Rita would begin to develop a close peer relationship, the mother would actively sabotage it, usually by betraying some of the information Rita had shared with her. Mrs. B. would also complain to Rita about the emptiness she felt in her marriage, always ending by telling Rita she did not know what she would do without her. These intimate discussions would usually alternate with episodes of Mrs. B. exploding at Rita for some mistake she made, accusing her of being incompetent, worthless, a bad person, and incapable of caring for herself. When Rita began to starve herself, her mother became increasingly intrusive by demanding information concerning food intake and bodily functioning. At one point Rita protested that it was her body and she would treat it as she pleased. This provoked a tirade from her mother where she screamed that Rita's body was her body; she had given her the body and what Rita did to her body she was doing to her.

Rita established fat as a paranoid object and mobilized her life to defend against any malevolent invasion by it. Fat had essentially become a concrete manifestation of the maternal intrusiveness. It was something that she could control. When Rita would have an ego regression, her thinking about fat (what it is, how it occurs, what affects it) would become increasingly distorted, often bordering on being psychotically delusional. It is important to note that thinness for Rita was not an aesthetically pleasing experience or a competitive achievement. She was not exhibitionistic about her thinness. Instead it offered a sense of safety.

Several interesting twists in Rita's treatment are worth mentioning. Rita required hospitalization where intensive individual, family, and milieu treatment could be conducted. Hospitalization was difficult for her. After her arrival we learned that she had never spent an evening away from home, except for the previous brief hospitalization (a one-week hospitalization on a medical unit for weight restoration). Predictably, she was very resistant to treatment interventions, particularly weight restoration. An interesting series of behaviors developed over the course of her rather lengthy hospitalization (seven months). As she began to gain weight, she began to complain of intense facial numbness. According to her, she experienced any chewing as debilitatingly painful; neurological examinations ruled out a range of possible organic difficulties. She claimed she could not eat until the problem of her facial numbness was "cured." This problem was accompanied by preoccupation with environmental toxins and possible allergic responses. In a sense, these environmental toxins became the new paranoid object. Gradually the focus of her concern shifted from fat to the numbness. With the shift in focus, she was able to tolerate some weight gain. At one point she began carrying around a washcloth and even named it her "nana." She continued to use the washcloth to soothe herself throughout the hospitalization and after discharge. After leaving the hospital, Rita returned home with plans to move into a structured living situation. She and her family continue to be seen regularly in intensive outpatient treatment.

BULIMIC BORDERLINE PATIENTS

In contrast to the restricting borderline, the key feature for bulimic borderline patients is parental underinvolvement that is experienced as *malevolent* neglect. Most often the primary caretakers, for a variety of intrapsychic reasons, have had difficulty being emotionally available for their children. For some, the child's neediness or dependency overwhelms their own poor ego resources and threatens boundary disintegration, or the attention given the infant provokes regressive longing and resentment over injuries they themselves have sustained developmentally. Whatever vulnerability the infant triggers, the result is that the caretaker emotionally disengages from the child. This leaves the child without external help to regulate her internal states. Particularly for borderline patients, this disengagement or withholding has an aggressive or intentional quality that contributes to the patients' more sadomasochistic tendencies.

These patients often internalize the emotional unavailability of the caretaker as evidence that they are unlovable, worthless, and deserving of punishment. They will then mutilate themselves in an effort to punish themselves, with the body once again becoming a concrete representation of self. Interpersonally, they are repeatedly involved in sadomasochistic relationships. Attachments are marked by clingy neediness that alternates with rageful, paranoid withdrawal. Separation is terrifying because it results in profound emptiness, feelings of abandonment, and ego fragmentation. Self-mutilation often appears not only as an effort to punish the unlovable self but as an effort to avoid depersonalization.

Bulimic borderline patients often attempt to utilize a restricting-paranoid defense. The experience of deprivation inherent in starvation is unbearable, however, because it exacerbates the prevailing feelings of emptiness. Self-starvation may also be an effort at self-punishment or an effort to starve out the bad self. Ultimately, though, the bulimic borderline patients are unable to sustain the paranoid stance and must rely on more frantic efforts to take in things from the outside (introject) to relieve the chaos and dysphoria.

In contrast to the controlled, obsessivelike treatment demands of restricting patients, work with bulimic borderline patients is much more active and stormy. The disorganization and franticness of these patients creates chaos in treatment; both patient and therapist are constantly vulnerable to acting out this franticness.

The primary transference themes usually revolve around whether the patient is capable of being loved and whether the therapist is committed, durable, and able to help her contain and organize her thoughts and behaviors. These patients will usually repeatedly test to see if the therapist will reject or abandon them, which would thus confirm their beliefs that they are unlovable. They will also test to see if the therapist can consistently soothe or organize them when they become distraught.

Since the principal dynamic of bulimic borderline patients centers on issues of underinvolvement, therapists should be much more actively involved with these patients' management than with restricting patients. The therapist should become actively involved in the patient's day-to-day functioning, erring on the side of overinvolvement rather than underinvolvement. We encourage therapists working with these patients to liberally share of themselves psychologically, within the boundaries of the therapeutic framework.

Attachment, however, is usually not the most demanding part of the treatment. Separation is usually far more complicated. Once these patients find an adequate holding environment, they can become quite demanding about getting their needs met. Their profound neediness and constant vigilance around abandonment issues can be very exhausting for a therapist. Since long-term treatment is usually necessary, we generally recommend a team approach. In contrast to the split management model used with the restricting borderline group, for these patients the individual therapist should be primarily responsible for case management. The availability of other team members to the patient is usually reassuring to both patient and therapist. Basically, when the therapist begins to feel exhausted, other team members can become more available to the patient. This relieves the therapist and helps reassure the patient that care will continue.

Although long-term outcome data are not available for these patients, it is our clinical impression that improvement does occur, but very slowly. Chaos remains a part of their lives. With time and a consistent treatment relationship, however, they develop better psychological tools to manage their chaos. Many of these patients continue the binge/purge behavior, but the degree to which it interferes with their lives markedly decreases, and other self-destructive behaviors such as substance abuse and self-mutilation disappear. Although they are able to work and engage in interpersonal relationships, both aspects of their lives are episodically in turmoil.

Regina T. Eighteen-year-old Regina was brought to treatment by her parents at the insistence of her school—her parents had been reluctant to acknowledge that anything was wrong with her. At presentation Regina was five feet five inches tall and weighed seventy-three pounds; she had been near this weight for more than nine months.

Regina appeared disheveled and exhausted. From the beginning of the consultation, it was clear that she had a long history of developmental difficulties. Her mother remembered her as a clingy, demanding child prone to temper tantrums. She was a behavior problem throughout school and has been prone to a variety of illnesses, including allergies and gastrointestinal difficulties. Regina had always been a chaotic eater and had experienced recurrent weight fluctuations. At sixteen years old, she had become very active sexually. She sought out brief relationships that were primarily sexual. She also began smoking cigarettes and abusing drugs, with cocaine and amphetamines her favorites. She began losing weight after a criticism from one of her sexual partners concerning the size of her thighs. She attempted to starve herself, but found it too demanding. Consequently, she began vomiting and abusing laxatives. The introduction of purging behavior also made her aware that she could eat without consequence, so she began binge eating, often simply as a prelude to the vomiting or laxative use. Regina was immediately hospitalized and individual and family therapy were initiated.

Regina's hospitalization was stormy. The restrictions placed on her provoked her into rageful tirades. She felt that we were trying to kill her by withholding things that allowed her to feel good or calm. She would become so agitated that the staff would literally have to hold her. The agitation would often cycle with periods of extreme depression, where she reported feeling empty and as though she did not exist. At these times she would often become agitated and seek to take in anything that would distract or calm her.

Family therapy revealed that the family was quite disengaged, chaotic, and that an air of hostile dependency prevailed. Mrs. T. presented as an exhausted alcoholic woman who had progressively deteriorated over the years. Although she had not been physically abusive to the children, it was clear that she would have difficulty attending to their emotional needs. Mr. T. had inherited a business, which occupied his time. He dressed eccentrically and appeared rather disorganized. Sitting with the father was a somewhat disconcerting experience. His thinking was quite tangential and he had a tendency to digress into lengthy lectures. One theme that he was particularly interested in was "survival of the fittest." He regarded himself as a Darwinian and was preoccupied with "gene pools," which we later learned had enormous relevance in the family system.

After several months of family treatment, the parents disclosed a significant family secret. Regina had a brother who was one and one-half years older and sister who was six months older. All three children had been adopted. We learned, however, that Regina was actually the natural child of Mr. T. After learning that Mrs. T. was unable to have children, Mr. T. proceeded to recruit a woman in the neighborhood to bear an offspring of his (without Mrs. T.'s knowledge). He impregnated the woman and she subsequently gave birth to Regina. Mr. T. then informed Mrs. T. of the birth of the daughter and presented the child to her to be raised with the other two adopted children. Mrs. T. was both injured and outraged by her husband's conduct. But she also felt paralyzed by her own sense of inadequacy about not being able to reproduce. Consequently, with enormous ambivalence, she agreed to raise the child. It was also later learned that the father, who was disappointed with the birth of a daughter, had returned to Regina's natural mother in an attempt to have a son. The woman refused to become impregnated again.

Although Mrs. T. met Regina's basic needs, emotionally she fluctuated between ambivalence to feeling outright hatred toward the girl. The mother even admitted that at times she would intentionally withhold emotional comfort from Regina because she wanted to punish her husband. She also resented Regina because she was a representation of her own inadequacy.

Regina adapted to the withholding by internalizing a self-representation that she was bad. She knew her mother was rejecting her and she assumed that it was because she was such a bad person. It appeared that her various symptomatic behaviors were efforts to soothe a prevailing dysphoria that she routinely felt.

The task of treatment with Regina was to stay with her through thick and thin, so to speak. She constantly expected us to give up on her, thus confirming her belief that she was unlovable. She repeatedly tested the treatment team by trying to provoke a rejection through emotionally demanding or physically acting out behavior, and persistently questioned in her mind whether we would stay with her and whether available human contact could help her contain her feelings. Regina's treatment was quite demanding and required a team of therapists who were in close communication.

FALSE SELF/NARCISSISTIC PATIENTS

Heinz Kohut (1971) and D. W. Winnicott (1965) both described a group of patients who initially present for treatment with neuroticlike life adjustment problems. As treatment progresses, however, it becomes clear that these patients have significant developmental deficits that result in self-regulatory difficulties. Winnicott coined the term *false self* organization to describe a particular adaptation these patients make to disruptions in the early mother-child relationship. According to Winnicott, a true self, or the normal development of a sense of self independent of other, occurs as a result of empathic encouragement by the primary caretaker of the infant's spontaneous (self-generated) gestures. Essentially, the mother encourages, values, and responds to cues emanating from the infant. If these spontaneous gestures continue to be encouraged, they evolve into self-awareness and self-directed behavior. These individuals feel that thoughts, feelings, and action originate from within themselves and there is a sense of connectedness to the events in their lives.

False self organizations emerge when the primary caretaker is unresponsive to or overrides the infant's spontaneous gestures. Unempathic mothering resulting from either over- or underinvolvement disrupts the growth of the capacity for interoceptive awareness, which in turn precludes the possibility of consolidating self-regulatory skills.

The false self adaptation occurs when the individual creates a persona in an effort to compensate for or hide the interoceptive deficits. This persona is usually reactive and accommodating. These individuals usually complain of feelings of nonexistence, fraudulence, and ineffectiveness. They often have a veneer of adequate integration and achievement, because they superficially have good social skills. Unfortunately, they discount or devalue whatever success they have experienced because they feel they are frauds. Consequently, self-esteem can never be enhanced because any successful achievement is negated.

We believe that individuals who present with false self/narcissistic organizations, although they can be quite disturbed, have greater ego resources than borderline patients. They do not generally experience others as having malevolent intent, as with borderline patients, and they are not as vulnerable to the more severe boundary lapses of the borderlines. Individuals with either restricting or bulimic behavior may present with false self organizations. There are specific differences between the two subtypes, and their false self organizations reflect efforts to adapt to different types or disruptions in the holding environment.

RESTRICTING FALSE SELF PATIENTS

The dynamics and clinical presentation of restricting patients who present with false self organizations closely resemble the classic restricting anorexic Bruch and others (Goodsitt, 1984; Story, 1976) have written about for so many years. In fact, one has to be struck with the similarity between Winnicott's formulations regarding "maternal impingement and subsequent false self adaptation" and Bruch's conceptualization of how narcissistic, overcontrolling mothers lead to interoceptive awareness difficulties (see figure 5.3). According to Bruch, the pathway to anorexia nervosa begins during early childhood (differentiation/practicing subphase) when these patients adapt to maternal intrusiveness by becoming compliant "parent pleasers." This adaptation leaves their sense of self and their capacity for self-regulation intricately tied to or dependent on the primary caretaker. Essentially, they become experts at reading cues from others about how to feel and behave. Given the dependence on external resources, they also learn to freely accommodate themselves to others because they would be lost if the relationship were disrupted. The self-starvation, with the attendant resistance to external influence, is an attempt at assertive, independent behavior. It is an effort to establish some sense of competency, control, or identity that is independent of and often in conflict with significant others. In contrast to the borderline restrictor, the restrictor false self group do not experience the intrusiveness as intentionally malevolent or sadistic. The attachment, while controlling, is not laced with the aggression of borderline restrictors. Separation fears do not revolve around fears of retaliation or annihilation. Instead they center more around the side effects of loss, which result in a feeling of depletion in both self and other. These patients often become very concerned about the effect their separation will have on others. They experience themselves as extensions of others without identities and, subsequently, terribly ineffective. There is a substantial discrepancy between how others see them (usually competent) and how they see themselves. They are less paranoid than borderline restrictors and rely more on obsessive-compulsive and phobic defenses.

Treatment with this group is much less complicated than with borderline patients, primarily because they do not view the world as primarily malevolent; consequently they are less paranoid and more engageable in treatment.

The primary transference themes revolve around ambivalence regarding attachments and fears of depletion in both self and other should separation occur. A dynamic tension around attachment is constantly enacted with the therapist. Patients simultaneously feel the need to rely on the significant other psychologically in order to regulate tensions, but when this happens they feel engulfed, without identity, and ineffective. Given this ambivalence around attachment, the therapist's task is to restrain himself or herself from intervening with the patient too quickly, or too actively.

The primary theme regarding separation is that both self and other will not be able to function without the continuance of the enmeshment. In contrast to borderline restrictors, restrictor false self patients fear not rageful retaliation from the significant other for separating but instead that both will experience debilitating depression. Given that these patients have generally relied heavily on others to negotiate life, they are often quite phobic about new situations.

Therapists should generally err in the direction of benign underinvolvement with these patients. The tendency to quickly and actively provide solutions when the patient is struggling with difficult decisions must be carefully avoided. Gentle encouragement of autonomous actions, providing neutral consultation during decision processes, and reassuring the patient that her separation will not provoke disorganization in others (the therapist) are important guidelines for treating these patients. Split management is also very useful with these patients to minimize the risk of intrusive overinvolvement by the therapist.

Effective individual and family treatment usually result in good outcomes with these patients. While treatment may be relatively long, it generally does not require the very long-term commitment as with the borderline patients. This group often fully recovers from anorexia nervosa although throughout their lives they often remain vulnerable to relying too heavily on the thoughts and actions of others.

CASE: RESTRICTING ANOREXIC FALSE SELF

Cristy Y. Sixteen-year-old Cristy was brought to treatment by her parents on the insistence of her pediatrician. Cristy's mother made all the arrangements in a competent and thorough manner. The only difficulty was that we had trouble finding a time when the husband could attend because of his busy schedule. When Cristy arrived for the consultation, she was five feet four inches tall and weighed eighty-two pounds.

During the evaluation, we learned that Cristy was the only child and was born when both parents were in their mid-thirties. We also learned that she was a nationally ranked junior tennis player and a straight-A student. Her early developmental history was unremarkable. She had never been a discipline problem, and there was no history of tantrums or argumentativeness. In fact, she appeared to have been adultlike from an early age. Her mother recalled her as being well mannered, nonexcitable but perhaps somewhat shy. She had no history of dating but did have close girl friends.

Apparently Cristy began dieting when she went away to tennis camp during the summer before her sophomore year in high school. The precipitant for her dieting was a comment by her mother that she might want to lose some weight while at camp. At the time she left she weighed approximately 110 pounds. According to Cristy, there was also a very competitive atmosphere among the other girls at the camp about dieting and weight loss. She lost approximately fifteen pounds while at camp. When she returned to attend school (which included transferring to a new school), she continued to lose weight. At the time of evaluation, her food intake was approximately 500 calories per day of mostly vegetables. Her exercise ritual included running four to five miles a day and doing several hundred sit-ups. Interestingly, she had stopped playing tennis.

Cristy felt particularly good about the way she looked, felt in control, and was angered by people suggesting that she was having difficulty. In fact, she felt that for the first time in her life she was doing something that was all her idea.

Cristy's mother was concerned but confused by her behavior. It was clear in speaking with her that this was the first time Cristy had opposed Mrs. Y., who was a very attractive, well-groomed woman. Over the course of treatment we learned that Mrs. Y. had been a promising tennis player, but apparently never achieved the ranking that was expected of her. She was also the only child of a wealthy family that was appearance and status conscious. Her tennis career ended when she married. Following the marriage, she did not work and reported being quite bored, until Cristy was born several years later.

Mr. Y. was a very ambitious and successful entrepreneur. His work required that he travel extensively, which prevented him from being with the family. He felt that he worked hard and provided a luxurious lifestyle for his wife and daughter, which was all that should be expected of him. As treatment with Cristy and her family unfolded, it became clear that since birth, Cristy had become the source of her mother's emotional supplies. It also became clear that Mrs. Y. had worked very hard to make her daughter over in her own image. She had pushed Cristy toward tennis from an early age, with expensive lessons and coaching from her. She had always coordinated Cristy's wardrobe, often choosing most of her clothes herself. She carefully managed her daughter's diet and was always commenting on how her body tone appeared. (Mrs. Y. had a long history of weight preoccupation, exercised religiously, and was constantly jumping from diet to diet.)

Cristy's recollection of her childhood was marked by ambivalence. She recalled always feeling very close to her mother but was also angered by her mother's control of her. According to her, there were times when she wanted to protest, particularly about playing tennis, but two things stopped her. First, she feared her mother's disappointment and disapproval. Cristy knew how invested her mother was in her life and felt that if she protested or changed, then her mother would be left with nothing. Cristy also knew that if her mother began to falter and perhaps withdraw, she also would be lost. Second, Cristy had become accustomed to the attention, praise, and approval for her behavior from the world in general. She felt that if she quit playing tennis and became noncompliant, people would be angry with her and reject her. She had become dependent on her mother for guidance about how to maintain the image. To protest or change this would risk both the mother's and her own psychological equilibrium. Although Cristy knew that there was a substantial discrepancy between how she saw herself and how the world saw her, there was no compelling reason to change things until she faced the prospect of separation following high school. The separation of tennis camp alerted her that she needed to make an adaptation to the transition that faced her.

Cristy's self-starvation solved several problems simultaneously. It allowed her to pursue a goal that her mother and the general population valued, but doing it to an extreme was unique and totally her idea. Also, the emaciation and attendant concern over her fragility raised serious questions regarding her ability to effectively separate and attend college. Cristy's treatment was characteristic of patients who present with this type of psychological organization. Initially she passively agreed to attend treatment and appeared to comply with the treatment demands, which included weight restoration. As weight gain began to occur, however, she became progressively more upset but would not openly protest the intervention. Instead she attempted to avoid the conflict by cheating on her weigh-ins. While some clinicians see this as sociopathic manipulation, to us it was a desperate attempt to gain our approval without having to sacrifice her self-directed stance. It also protected her from articulating the dilemma she was experiencing. When we made it increasingly difficult to avoid the conflict, she progressively became tearful and enraged. As she became more vocal about her fears, she became less resistant to weight gain. She also became openly defiant and angry toward her parents, particularly her father. The alliance she had developed with the treatment team allowed her to challenge her relationship with her mother without fear that she would be left without any support. Her anger at her father was focused on his unavailability to both her and her mother. She felt that if he had been more emotionally attendant to her mother, she would not have become as enmeshed with her daughter.

It also should be noted that Mrs. Y. attempted to disrupt the treatment when it became clear that Cristy was attaching to the treatment team and was attempting to separate from her. And it is noteworthy that Cristy's anger did not have the paranoid quality of the borderline anorexic. She did not feel out of control with her feelings, nor did she feel self-destructive. Anger was foreign to her and she feared others' disapproval when she felt angry. She did not, however, fear that she would hurt herself.

BULIMIC FALSE SELF/NARCISSISTIC PATIENTS

For bulimic patients, the pathway to the false self organization appears somewhat different, once again reflecting the nature of the holding environment deficits. As with their borderline counterparts, these patients have also experienced some disruption during separation-individuation that has resulted in a disengagement with the primary caretaker. Unlike the borderline bulimic, however, these patients do not experience the caretaker's unavailability as intentional or malevolent. Their ego resources are also more sophisticated so that regressions, lability of affect, and so forth, are less visibly manifested. Instead of the borderline patient's frantic defenses, these patients rely more on avoidance, denial, isolation of affect, and intellectualization. Interacting with them is similar to being with a high-level patient who has schizoid tendencies.

These patients exhibit a unique adaptation to the maternal disengagement. They respond to the unavailability of the caretaker by affecting a pseudomature adaptation. In essence, they have enough ego resources to compensate by prematurely taking responsibility for their own and often others' self-regulation. Unfortunately the caretaker, or the broader family, experiences this premature adaptation system as a relief, which results in the child's receiving positive reinforcement and even a sense of self-esteem for compliant, nondemanding, hyperresponsible behavior.

The prefix "pseudo" is appropriate because while the child has adequate structure to adapt superficially, she does not have adequate structure to accommodate her more infantile needs, such as being comforted and soothed when frightened, angry, anxious, or simply needy. In the absence of the caretaker's ability to respond to these dysphoric and disrupted states, the child splits them off and isolates them. Often these patients interpret these needs as troublesome, a sign of being out of control, and perhaps even destructive. Progressively, these patients feel they are two people: one whom the world sees as competent and in control of things and another who feels desperately needy, which patients experience as being out of control. The discrepancy between the two states results in a self-representation of fraudulence and inadequacy. A self-defeating "Catch-22" emerges in which the patient immediately devalues any compliment or praise for successful achievement because it indicates that the other person has been fooled or is a fool. Consequently, others who offer compliments are discredited as incompetent judges. Attachment or the possibility of intimacy for these patients provokes a wish/fear dilemma, which revolves around their wish for someone to recognize and respond to their needs juxtaposed against their fear of allowing someone to see their neediness. Allowing someone to see this side is frightening because the acknowledgment of having needs might collapse the self-esteem and self-organization that has evolved as a result of the pseudomature behavior. As a result of this fear of discovery, interpersonally these patients maintain what we have labeled a *distant closeness*. In interacting with them, one has the illusion of relating, but over time it becomes apparent that they are desperately protecting a separateness. Unlike the schizoid character where one senses predominantly an intrapsychic vacuousness along with impoverished social skills, with these patients one senses there are a range of feelings that are being actively suppressed.

For these patients, food has often become their safest and most trusted ally. They will allow themselves to behave in the presence of food in a way they would not allow any person to observe or participate in. They also invest food with the ability to regulate different tension states. Some patients will actually anthropomorphize food—attributing to it such humanlike qualities as volition and the ability to relate to them. One patient with some insight into this spoke of "cuddling up to the food." Allowing a person to help with difficult feelings would mean risking too much exposure. It also involves turning to the world of humans, who have been experienced as much less reliable than food.

The primary transference themes with these patients revolve around issues of attachment. Often these patients have two questions in their minds: will the therapist be distracted by their pseudomature behavior, thus neglecting their infantile needs, and, if the therapist recognizes these needs, can he or she demonstrate that the intensity of these needs will not destroy the therapist or result in a shameful loss of the patient's self-esteem?

The therapist's task in the therapeutic relationship is to patiently and carefully encourage dependency. It is crucial, however, that such patients never feel that the therapist needs *them* to function adequately in order to survive or thrive. Overall, the therapist must communicate to patients that he or she recognizes that they have psychological needs and wants to and is capable of responding to those needs.

Establishing and sustaining a therapeutic alliance with these patients is a delicate process. They are ambivalent about intimate involvement and will "bolt" from treatment if the involvement is not paced slowly. Our clinical impression is that these patients improve significantly if a therapeutic relationship is formed and sustained over a period of time.

CASE: BULIMIC FALSE SELF/NARCISSISTIC

Julie. A thirty-year-old, single woman, Julie reported having daily binge/purge episodes for twelve years. She had never been in treatment before, and initially she was very ashamed of and humiliated by acknowledging her difficulty. At the time of the initial consultation, her weight was within normal limits and she did not appear to have a history of significant weight loss. She did, however, report being teased about being overweight as a child. She lived with her family, had never been involved in a significant heterosexual relationship, and had a job as a research analyst for a brokerage firm.

Individual psychotherapy with Julie unfolded slowly and very tentatively. She seemed reluctant to complain about any of her difficulties and often seemed more interested in the state of *my* well-being rather than her own. Gradually I (C.J.) learned that she was the fifth child and only daughter of six children. When she was three-and-a-half years old, her mother had a major stroke while giving birth to her younger brother. She apparently had been in poor health for several years and had been warned of the high risk for stroke if she became pregnant again. The stroke left her extremely debilitated. She was partially paralyzed and had a severe speech impediment, which made her difficult to understand. The father was a very dedicated man. He was quite religious but appeared to maintain an emotional distance. Julie's response to the trauma was to immediately begin to physically and psychologically take care of her father and brothers. No housekeeper was hired, and progressively Julie assumed the household chores. At age seven she was in charge of laundry, much of the food preparation, and cleaning. She would return home early from school to attend to these responsibilities. Julie was regarded by her father and the extended family as a godsend, a saint, and an extraordinary "little adult." It was clear that Julie had become very much accustomed to the approval she received for her adult caretaking behavior. Unfortunately, this pseudomature competency was juxtaposed against a little girl who was desperately needy but fearful to let anyone know. This was evidenced by her admission that as a child, when she was very sad and lonely, she would retreat to her room where she would crawl into a fetal position on the bed and rock herself. She did this frequently, but no one knew of the behavior. In fact, she shamefully admitted that, at present, she would binge eat till she was extremely full, then rock, and finally vomit on a daily basis. Also, she would often drink to mild intoxication before binge eating, so that she could relieve the prohibitions she felt against feeling needy. During the rocking, she would always imagine different members of her family holding her.

Her binge eating began when she was seven or eight years old, and resulted in her being overweight. She painfully remembered being teased by other children about her weight problem. High school was marked by the same routine as grade school, with her devoting most of her time to taking care of the household. Socially, she had virtually no heterosexual relationships and very few girl friends. Her life consisted of taking care of the father and brothers, which she simultaneously valued and felt enraged about. To acknowledge that she was needy and unhappy was unacceptable because it would mean she was not as competent as everyone thought. She would also have felt terribly guilty, since her father appeared to endure the hardship without complaining.

Following high-school graduation, she entered a community college, which allowed her to remain at home. It was at this time she began vomiting, an act that allowed her to reduce her weight, which was in turn socially reinforcing. She began doing it on a daily basis.

When she entered treatment, she had begun working as a support analyst in a brokerage house and was still living at home. Treatment was focused on helping her differentiate herself from the family involvement and recognize and attend to some of her needs in other ways besides binge eating and rocking. Eventually she moved into her own apartment and left her support position to become a senior-level executive. As she became more engaged in the therapeutic relationship, she shifted the function of taking care of herself from the eating and rocking to the therapeutic relationship's holding environment. With the attachment, she spoke more freely of her neediness and fear that both she and others would collapse if its depth was disclosed. She admitted her rage toward the circumstances that affected her childhood and was both sad and angry that others could not see her pain. She struggled a long time with feeling angry toward her mother and father. Neither had intentionally created the circumstances, she knew, but she was still angry that things had turned out as they had. There was a poignant moment in the treatment that seemed to capture some of what she felt as a child. She tearfully reported one day that the evening before she had been waiting in line at the checkout counter of a grocery store. Ahead of her was a father and his young son. As they were standing in line, the father realized that he had forgotten one item. He delegated his son to hold the place in line and watch over the food. Julie noticed the pride that the child felt for having been given the responsibility. After the father left, the line began to move. The food items had been placed on a conveyor belt that barely was within the child's reach. As the belt continued, the food began to pile up behind a divider and become disorganized. The child became panicky and began frantically to try to contain the food. Julie was paralyzed as she watched the young boy fight back tears while trying to remain in control. The father suddenly appeared, took control, and contained the disorganization. With relief, the child broke into tears and Julie had to flee the store. She had initially been angry at the man for the unfair request he made of the child, but then realized that she had been most upset when she saw the comfort and soothing he offered to the child when he was upset.

As Julie became increasingly comfortable and confident that human interaction could help her soothe herself, her involvement with ritualized eating behavior decreased.

NEUROTIC PATIENTS

As represented in figure 5.5, another population of patients who present with anorexic and bulimic symptoms do not manifest the ego impairments associated with the other groups. These patients primarily have more neurotic conflicts. They generally have adequate intrapsychic structures and have become involved in food-related behavior for more specific reasons. There are often clear precipitants for the onset of the behavior, which can be conceptualized as a developmental adjustment reaction. Pursuit of thinness among this group often revolves around identity and achievement issues, or it can be seen as a more transitory adaptation to some trauma. For the bulimics, their behavior may be a compensatory alternative to conflictual drives such as sexuality or aggression, or it may simply be a maladaptive behavior that has developed as a result of misguided information concerning dieting. If depression is observed, it usually revolves around issues of guilt and shame rather than more anaclitic concerns, such as abandonment. Cognitively, this group of patients is very capable of functioning abstractly, and they can understand and interpret their behavior in a symbolic manner. Their interpersonal relationships are differentiated and developmentally appropriate.

CASE: RESTRICTING NEUROTIC

Sue T. Seventeen-year-old Sue came from a middle-class Italian-American family with four children, of whom she was the youngest. She was brought to treatment by her concerned and perplexed parents. At presentation she was five feet seven inches tall and ninety-five pounds (premorbid weight was 125 to 130 pounds).

Sue's developmental history was quite normal. She had done well in school, had close female friends, had been athletic, and had no obvious mood disturbance. Sue's family was very close-knit but not pathologically enmeshed. Mrs. T. appeared to be a caring woman. She was quick to admit that she and her husband had been somewhat overprotective with their daughter. Mr. T., likewise, appeared to be a caring man who was attentive to his wife and children. Two brothers were both attending school out of state, and the older sister had married and moved several houses away from the family. She and her husband spent a lot of time with the family.

There did not appear to be a clear precipitant to the self-starvation. Sue simply quit eating during the summer of her junior year in high school. She lost weight very quickly over one month. The only thing that her parents noticed was that she had become withdrawn, sullen, and appeared frightened several weeks prior to her starvation. Efforts to investigate what she was experiencing were met with increased withdrawal.

While Sue was not opposed to treatment, she seemed frightened of it. She was compliant with treatment expectations around weight restoration until her weight approached her premorbid menstrual weight (110 pounds). At this point she became quite panicky. After several months of individual psychotherapy, we learned what was so frightening about approaching her menstrual threshold.

During the summer of her junior year, Sue was spending a great deal of time, including nights, at her sister's home. Apparently, as she spent more time there, her brother-in-law began to pay a lot of attention to her. Eventually he began to become sexually aggressive with her. Sue felt trapped: she was terrified to alert the family and simultaneously felt ashamed that she in some way had provoked the pursuit. She was also fearful that if she disclosed the problem, the family would be thrown in turmoil. A solution became apparent to her after she was sick with the flu near the time of her brother-in-law's molestation. She was quite pale and had lost weight during her brief illness, and her brother-in-law seemed less interested in her. She presumed that it was because she appeared thin and frail. Feeling that emaciation would protect her from his sexual advances, she began to pursue thinness more aggressively. The strategy worked, particularly as she began to lose her secondary sexual characteristics.

Once Sue felt secure enough in the therapeutic relationship to disclose this, work then proceeded on alternative strategies for dealing with the dilemma she was in. As she felt safer with her ability to control her brother-in-law, she offered minimal resistance to weight restoration.

CASE: BULIMIC NEUROTIC

Amy A. Amy, twenty-one years old, was the middle child of three female siblings in an upper-class, intact family. When Amy presented for treatment she had been bingeing and vomiting on a daily basis for three years, and was within a normal weight range.

During the initial evaluation, Amy's developmental history appeared normal. She attended school easily, was socially active, a good student, and basically enjoyed her childhood and adolescence. There were some difficulties in the family. Mrs. A. has recently entered treatment for depression. Mr. A. appeared concerned, but emotionally distant and preoccupied with his work.

Amy's trouble had begun during her freshman year of college at an elite southwestern school she had enrolled in at her mother's suggestion. Amy had a history of dissatisfaction with her body size. Although her weight was within a reasonable limit, her body style was short and more rounded. She particularly felt she should be ten pounds thinner and had an ideal image of herself as more angular. She weighed herself daily, was upset if her weight fluctuated upward, and had dieted chronically since early adolescence.

Within several months after arriving at school, she gained approximately ten pounds, due both to the change in eating habits at school and to episodes of binge eating. These episodes originally began as group events among several female friends that they referred to as "pigging out." In the second semester, Amy pledged a highly competitive and appearance-conscious sorority. She began to feel very fat and ugly in comparison to many of her sorority sisters. While living in the sorority house, Amy became aware of the practice of self-induced vomiting as a mechanism for weight control; she was introduced to it by several of her sorority sisters. With vomiting, she found that she could eat chaotically and still maintain or even lose weight. Eventually she was vomiting whenever she felt she had overeaten. While the weight loss that Amy achieved by vomiting increased her self-esteem and made her more confident socially, particularly with men, it had the unfortunate effect of greatly reinforcing her bulimic behavior.

When Amy entered treatment, she was highly motivated to change. A short-term treatment program that focused on the sociocultural pressures she was feeling to be thin, how to normalize her food intake, self-monitoring of her affective states, and the challenging of various cognitive distortions was effective in eliminating her bingeing and vomiting within two months. It is also important to note that as Amy became nonsymptomatic about her eating behavior, we learned that she had a long history of bladder discontrol since childhood. She had been through extensive neurological workups. The diagnosis offered was "nervous bladder" and no treatment was recommended. In exploring the circumstances that led to the incidents where she lost bladder control, it became evident that the behavior appeared to be anxiety related. We began a trial of 150 mg of imipramine, and she became symptom-free within several weeks. Two-year follow-up indicated that she remained symptom-free of her bladder difficulties and that she very rarely had difficulty with binge eating or vomiting.

Summary

The symptoms of anorexia nervosa and bulimia can reflect a range of developmental deficits. A majority of patients presenting with these syndromes manifest deficits characteristic of individuals who have character disorders. Clinical speculations were offered regarding the different adaptations that restricting and bulimic behavior might serve for individuals who specifically present with borderline features or false self/narcissistic organizations. Finally, treatment implications were discussed and case illustrations were presented.

6

Family Factors

In recent years the role of family variables in the pathogenesis of anorexia nervosa and bulimia has received increasing attention. In a thorough review of the literature, Kog and Vandereycken (1985) emphasized, however, that well-controlled, data-based research demonstrating family psychopathology is quite limited. In this chapter we review the literature on the family characteristics of both anorexia nervosa and bulimic patients.

Demographics and General Findings

Demographically, anorexic and bulimic patients appear to come from predominantly higher social class families. Bulimic patients, however, cluster more in the lower-middle-class range. Family size, the patient's birth order, and the incidence of broken homes among both patient groups do not differ significantly from the general population.

Findings about psychopathology among family members are mixed. Weiss and Ebert (1983) found no difference in the number of hospitalizations for psychiatric disorders between normal-weight bulimics and normal-weight controls. Likewise, Garfinkel and associates (1983) and Crisp, Harding, and McGuinness (1974) could not establish any significant difference between parents of normal-weight bulimics and restricting anorexics on a series of psychological tests. Strober, Salkin, Burroughs, and Morrell (1982), however, found significant psychological differences between parents of restricting anorexics and of bulimic anorexics. They found that fathers of bulimics scored significantly higher on MMPI scales measuring general maladjustment, impulsivity, low frustration tolerance, and hostility. In contrast, fathers of restricting anorexics scored higher on scales associated with emotional sensitivity, passivity, submissiveness, and withdrawal from social interactions. Mothers of bulimic anorexics were also distinguished from mothers of restricting anorexics. Mothers of bulimics scored significantly higher on scales measuring psychosomatic preoccupation and depression, while scores of mothers of restrictors indicated that they were more socially introverted and phobic. Both parents of bulimics scored significantly higher on scales indicating greater intrafamilial disturbance and a lesser degree of inner control. When a multiple regression analysis was performed, maternal depression and paternal impulse disturbance and depression were found to be predictive of greater severity of bulimia among the patients.

While it is not clear to what extent parents of eating-disordered patients exhibit personality disturbances, a greater incidence of affective disorder and substance abuse (primarily alcoholism) among first- and second-degree relatives of bulimic patients compared to the general population and compared to restricting anorexia nervosa patients has been consistently found (see the section entitled "Bulimia and Affective Disorders" in chapter 3).

Recently a number of researchers have begun studying the incidence of eating and weight disorders among family members. Gershon and associates (1983) found significantly more eating disorders among first-degree relatives of patients with anorexia nervosa or bulimia when compared to a control group of medical patients. Garfinkel and coworkers (1983) found no difference among restricting anorexics, bulimic anorexics, and normal controls on parents' actual weights, body-size estimates, and body satisfaction. Several studies, however, have found a higher incidence of maternal obesity among the bulimic subgroups compared to the restricting anorexics (Garfinkel, Moldofsky, and Garner, 1980; Herzog, 1982; Strober, 1981).

The extent of general ill health among eating-disordered families has also been investigated. Sperling and Massing (1970) found significant differences in chronic illness between fathers of anorexics (25 percent) compared to normal controls (2.4 percent). Weiss and Ebert (1983), however, found no differences between normal-weight bulimics and normal-weight controls in the number of hospitalizations for physical disorders or for the incidence of allergic disorder or asthma. Strober (1981) found that gastrointestinal illness was more prevalent among parents of bulimics compared to restricting anorexics (14 percent versus 5 percent in the mothers and 32 percent versus 14 percent in fathers). Herzog (1982) found at least one parent of 50 percent of bulimic patients have had serious morbidity or mortality due to a physical illness, versus 23 percent for the anorexics.

The Nature of the Family Environment

ANOREXIA NERVOSA

As discussed in chapter 5, early impressions were that patients with anorexia nervosa came from enmeshed families with demanding and overcontrolling parents who superimposed their own needs onto their daughters, thus interfering with strivings for autonomy and individuation. Bruch (1970) examined the early development of sixty patients with anorexia nervosa and concluded that while the children had been well cared for, self-expression and autonomous functioning were not encouraged. She characterized the parents as follows:

> The parents may be described as over-protective, over-concerned and over-ambitious. They over-value their children and expect obedience and superior performance in return. As long as the children comply, they fulfill their parents' dreams of their own ideals by growing and behaving exactly as the parents had planned and expected. With approaching adolescence, conditions change and the child starts to make justifiable claims for independence. This is unacceptable to the parents and the illness begins as an expression of struggle that is not being acknowledged. (Bruch, 1977, pp. 2–3)

Palazzoli's observations (1978) of the family were similar to Bruch's regarding the nature of the family environment. She wrote:

> With very few, if any exceptions, the conspicuous figure in the home of anorexic girls is the mother; the father is usually an emotional absentee, generally overshadowed, and secretly or openly belittled, by his wife. . . . The girls became the model children of a domineering, intolerant and hypercritical woman, who prevents them from standing their own ground and stunts emotional development. (p. 39)

Palazzoli later adopted a family systems perspective. She observed that the anorexic families could be characterized as having a strong collective sense of the family for which individuality and autonomy was required to be sacrificed and any form of self-interest must be abandoned. Open alliances between family members were forbidden, but frequently covert coalitions between a parent and a child or a parent and his or her own parent could be found. Thus generational boundaries were not clearly established. Selvini-Palazzoli saw the problem of covert coalition as "the central and most serious problem facing families of anorexic patients" (1978, p. 209). Open alliances between two family members would violate the high value the family placed on solidarity and loyalty. Thus disagreements and conflicts were denied rather than openly expressed.

Minuchin, Rosman, and Baker (1978) identified many features that were similar to those described by Selvini-Palazzoli. According to them, the psychosomatic family in general and the anorexic family in particular is characterized by four critieria: enmeshment, overprotectiveness, rigidity, and lack of conflict resolution. In an enmeshed family, autonomy and independence are sacrificed for the sake of loyalty and protection. Communication proceeds in an indirect manner and the open expression of conflict is quickly diffused. The symptom of overprotectiveness is an outgrowth of the enmeshment. Family members seem to be tuned in to each other so that the slightest sign of distress or anxiety is noted and responded to. The intrusive concern by family members curtails the child's autonomy. Furthermore, she cannot challenge the control exerted by the family members since it is done indirectly and under the guise of unselfish concern. Since wishes are not expressed openly, any disagreement is regarded as betrayal. The anorexic's overinvolvement with the family prevents her from developing the necessary skills to deal with the outside world in general. Thus her development in terms of separation and individuation is seriously blocked.

Like Selvini-Palazzoli, Minuchin found that the boundaries within the family were poorly defined, leading to a lack of privacy and independence. Rigidity in anorexic families results in a strong investment in maintaining the status quo. They are not open to necessary change; therefore, issues that threaten familial homeostasis are not allowed to rise to the surface. Since the open expression of potentially conflictual matters is suppressed, conflict resolution is not achieved. Minuchin observed that the symptom of anorexia nervosa can have the function of detouring conflict. Essentially the family is unified by their concern for the sick child.

Few data-based studies that substantiate these observational reports of anorexic families are available. In a well-controlled study Morgan and Russell (1975) reported on the family characteristics and clinical features of forty-one anorexia nervosa patients. They found that in 34 percent of the cases an anomaly of family structure occurred during the patient's childhood, such as separation from or loss of the mother or serious family discord. In 54 percent of the cases the premorbid relationship between the family and the patient was judged to be disturbed. In half of these cases the disturbance consisted of the child's excessive dependence on the mother. In these cases, the mother was found to have a close but dominating and critical attitude toward her daughter. Kalucy, Crisp, and Harding (1977) found similar results in a study of fifty-six families who had children with anorexia nervosa. They found that the anorexic child was characterized by an excessive degree of closeness to the mother in 39 percent of the cases, to the father in 25 percent of the cases, and to both in 13 percent. They were related excessively negatively to their mothers in 11 percent of the cases, to the father in 20 percent, and to both parents in 4 percent of the cases.

Crisp, Harding, and McGuinness (1974) found some support for the systems hypothesis that anorexia nervosa in the child has a protective function which serves to detour conflict and maintain homeostasis within the family. The authors examined the psychoneurotic characteristics of the parents of female anorexia nervosa patients via a standardized measure (Middlesex Hospital Questionnaire, Crown and Crisp, 1966). The control group consisted of a normal population comparable in age, sex, and marital status. Results indicated that the mean psychoneurotic status of the parents at the time of their daughter's admission to the hospital was only slightly elevated. However, following restoration of the patient's weight, the parents' level of psychoneurotic morbidity on the same measure increased. This was especially true for maternal anxiety and maternal depression, which increased significantly after weight restoration if the marital relationship had been judged to be poor. Interestingly, the study found that fathers of bingers and purgers scored significantly higher than fathers of abstainers on anxiety, obsessional, and depressive scales immediately following their daughters' treatment.

In a direct test of their hypothesis regarding the family environment of anorexia nervosa patients, Minuchin, Rosman, and Baker (1978) compared anorexic, asthmatic, and diabetic families to two nonpsychosomatic control groups. Clinical observations of behavioral interventions between groups indicated that the anorexic families were the most enmeshed, overprotective, rigid and conflict avoidant.

Goldstein (1981) compared the family triads of hospitalized anorexics, hospitalized nonanorexics, and preschizophrenic adolescents. He examined parental behavior on measures of dependency/insecurity, interpersonal boundary problems, and cross-generational blurring as manifested in the triadic interaction between mother, father, and index offspring. On all these behavioral features, anorexic family units scored the highest and were significantly different from the disturbed adolescent (outpatient) and nonanorexic (inpatient) groups. When the components of the total score were analyzed separately, scores for a combined index of dependency-insecurity (requests for support, protectiveness of others, tentative speech, and backing down when statements were countered by another) most consistently discriminated families of anorexics from the other groups.

DESCRIPTION OF BULIMIC FAMILIES

Only recently have data-based studies begun to appear on families of normal-weight bulimic patients. Those studies that have appeared show consistent findings. Johnson and Flach (1985) used the Family Environment Scale (FES; Moos, 1981) to compare a sample of 105 outpatient bulimics to a control group of 86 who were screened for bulimic behavior or disturbed eating attitudes. Results indicated that bulimic women perceived their families as being significantly less supportive and helpful (low Cohesiveness) and felt that the families did not encourage assertive, self-sufficient behavior (low Independence). Interestingly, compared to normal controls they viewed their families as experiencing a great deal of conflict and anger (high Conflict), and yet they reported that open, direct expression of feelings was discouraged (low Expressiveness). Furthermore, although achievement expectations were not significantly different between the two groups of families (Achievement Orientation), there was significantly less emphasis in the bulimic families on intellectual and social activities (low Intellectual-Cultural Orientation), ethical and religious issues (low Moral-Religious Emphasis), and participation in recreational activities (low Active-Recreational Orientation). Finally, bulimic families were not found to be significantly different from normal controls in the degree of familial structure (Organization) or the extent to which set rules exist in the family (Control). Although the families of the bulimic subjects were not found to be significantly different from those of normal controls in the degree of familial structure or the extent to which set rules exist in the family (Control and Organization), a regression analysis predicting severity of illness indicated that low familial organization was predictive of severity of illness among the bulimic patients.

Arnold Ordman and Dan Kirschenbaum (1985) found similar results using the FES and Family Adaptability and Cohesion Evaluation Scales (FACES; Olson, Bell, and Portner, 1978) with twenty-five bulimic outpatients and thirty-six normal controls. The bulimics reported less cohesion and expressiveness, more conflict, and less emphasis on independent behavior in their families compared to normal controls.

Both of these studies suggest that bulimic family milieus could be characterized as disengaged but enmeshed, with high conflict and low emphasis on self-expression, particularly of conflictual issues. A high achievement orientation prevails against a backdrop of low emphasis on intellectual and social activities. Finally, while overall the rules and structure within the bulimic families appear comparable to those of normal control families, greater disorganization in the bulimic families results in greater severity of symptoms.

BULIMIC VERSUS RESTRICTING ANOREXICS

Attention has also been directed recently to investigating differences in family environments between restricting and bulimic anorexics. Strober (1981) compared twenty-two bulimic anorexics to twenty-two restricting anorexics on the FES. Results indicated that bulimic anorexic families were characterized as having a higher level of conflictual interactions and expressions of negativity among family members. In contrast, mutual support, concern, and clarity of structure and rules or responsibilities were strongly associated with restrictor families. In addition, parents of bulimic anorexics reported higher marital discord than parents of restrictors. Bulimic anorexics reported feeling more distant from both of their parents (particularly fathers) than restricting anorexics.

Figure 6.1 compares restricting anorexics, bulimic anorexics, normal-weight bulimics, and normal controls on the FES. The family environment of normal-weight bulimic patients seems similar to that of bulimic anorexics. The only apparent differences between the two groups were that families of the normal-weight groups scored substantially lower on expressiveness and conflict and higher on achievement expectations. The restricting anorexic families were perceived as being more cohesive as well as more discouraging of independent behavior than those of the normal-weight bulimic group.

In a similar study, Humphrey (1987) compared fourteen normal-weight bulimics, sixteen bulimic anorexics, and twenty-four normal controls on the FES and FACES. The findings indicated that both normal-weight bulimics and bulimic anorexic families reported more distress in patterns of relating than did normal controls. All members of both groups of bulimic families experienced less involvement and support, greater isolation and nondisclosure, and more detachment among family members than was found in normal families.

Garner, Garfinkel, and O'Shaughnessy (1985) reported similar findings using the Family Assessment Measure (Skinner, Santa-Barbara, and Steinhauer, 1983) to compare the families of fifty-nine normal-weight bulimics, fifty-nine restricting anorexics, and fifty-nine bulimic anorexics. Their findings indicated that bulimic families reported significantly greater overall family pathology than restricting anorexics and that the pattern of scores between bulimic groups were quite similar. Differences between bulimic and restricting patients were most evident on a control subscale, suggesting that impulse-related disturbances found in the bulimic patients may reflect an overall family pattern of self-regulation difficulties.

Kog, Vertommen, and DeGroote (in press) showed similar findings using the Family Projections Questionnaire to compare families of the same three classes. The families of restricting anorexics reported significantly less conflict, more cohesion, and less disorganization than families of bulimic anorexics or normal-weight bulimics. The latter two did not show significant differences.

In a comprehensive and well-controlled study, Humphrey (1987) compared family relationships among restricting anorexics, bulimic anorexics, normal-weight bulimics, and normal families. Seventy-four family triads completed a series of self-report ratings using the SASB (Benjamin, 1974). Results indicated that patients with all three subtypes of eating disorders experienced significant family distress compared to normal controls. The two bulimic subgroups were generally more similar to one another in that both parent/daughter triads reported greater neglect,

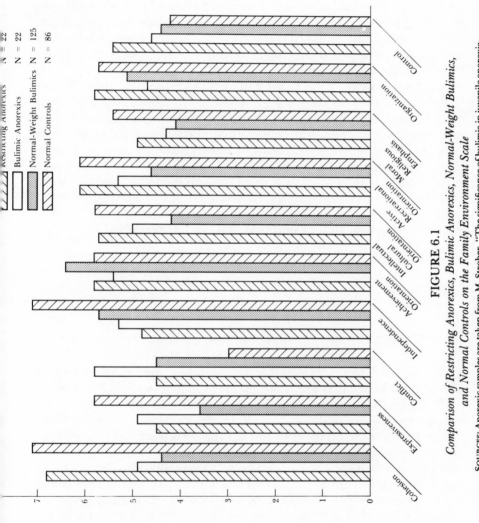

FIGURE 6.1

Comparison of Restricting Anorexics, Bulimic Anorexics, Normal-Weight Bulimics, and Normal Controls on the Family Environment Scale

SOURCES: Anorexic samples are taken from M. Strober, "The significance of bulimia in juvenile anorexia nervosa: an exploration of possible etiological factors," *International Journal of Eating Disorders* 1 (1981): 28–43, copyright © 1981 by John Wiley and Sons, Inc. Reprinted by permission of John Wiley and Sons, Inc. Normal-weight bulimic and normal control samples are from C. Johnson and A. Flach, "Family characteristics of 105 patients with bulimia," *American Journal of Psychiatry* 142 (1985):1321–24.

attack, and blaming toward each other combined with less understanding, nurturance, and support. Thus they experienced more hostile attachment and hostile control, but also less affection and affirmation in the parent/ daughter relationships.

Some unique parent/daughter differences also emerged between the groups. Daughters and fathers from both bulimic groups agreed that their relationships were significantly less friendly and more hostile than were those of normal controls. In contrast to the bulimic groups, the restricting anorexics and their fathers were generally more positive, and comparable to controls. Distress was apparent, however, as the restricting anorexics experienced their fathers as significantly more hostile toward them than did normal controls.

Findings regarding the mother/daughter relationship were similar. Both bulimic subtypes reported greater blame, sulking, attacking, withdrawing, and neglecting and warding off by their mothers than did restricting anorexics and normal controls. Mothers of restricting anorexics were perceived much more positively, comparable to those of normal controls. Humphrey concluded that "families of both bulimic anorexics and normal weight bulimics were more hostilely enmeshed and neglectful of their daughters in contrast to restricting anorexics who appear much more 'pseudo mutual' in that they juxtaposed greater affection with simultaneous control and/or negation of their daughters" (p. 16).

Summary

In reviewing the data, it appears that the family environments of restricting and bulimic individuals are quite different. The families of restrictors could generally be characterized as enmeshed with weak generational boundaries. Covert coalitions among family members prevail, and the mandate within the family is to protect the pseudomutual relationships by denying conflict or difficulty. It also appears that the patients' regressive, anorexic behavior serves to protect a homeostasis in the family by minimizing developmental changes such as separation-individuation. Overall, the restrictor families seem to have a phobic orientation to the world that results in overprotection and overcontrolling behavior by the parents.

In contrast, families of bulimic patients (both anorexic and normal weight) appear to be much more disengaged and chaotic. A great deal of conflict and hostility is apparent in the families, but once again open expression of this conflict is not encouraged. Unlike the restrictor families, however, the conflict does not appear to be denied. Within the bulimic families it seems that the family members have neither the intrapsychic tools nor the energy to deal with the conflicts. Despite their greater detachment and isolation, within the bulimic families there is also a deemphasis on independent/assertive behavior. Consequently, the child is enmeshed in a hostile dependent relationship with a family system that is disengaged, chaotic, and neglectful. Also, in contrast to the restrictor families, which are characterized as phobic, constricted, and overprotective, bulimic families appear to be much more affectively labile and undercontrolling.

7

Etiology: A Biopsychosocial Perspective

Up to this point in the book, we have reviewed data indicating that the incidence of bulimia has appeared to increase over the last several years (see chapters 1 and 2). We have also reviewed findings indicating that the disorder has appeared to affect a relatively homogeneous cohort of adolescent and young adult females who present with a variety of biological, intrapsychic, and familial profiles. In this chapter our aim is to integrate these various findings into a model of etiology, suggesting how biological, familial, and sociocultural factors may have placed this cohort at risk for developing psychiatric symptoms (see figure 7.1). We also describe how the pursuit of thinness and subsequent bulimic behavior may have emerged as an adaptation to the difficulties that are characteristic of these patients. What we are proposing is an early risk factor model for bulimia. Although the data base regarding bulimia is currently too weak to offer a sophisticated conceptualization, we hope this early integration will lend direction to future research regarding the etiology of the disorder.

Biological Factors in the Development of Bulimia

The contribution of biological factors to the onset and perpetuation of bulimia is unclear. Although a wide range of endocrine abnormalities is observed among these patients, the abnormalities appear to be mostly side effects from the behavior and are easily reversible. Exciting research exploring the HPA axis is under way, with special interest in neuropeptides such as cholecystokinin and pancreatic peptides (Crawley and Beinfeld,

1983; Smith, 1980; Morley, 1980). To date, however, nothing compelling has emerged regarding etiology.

The relationship of bulimia to affective disorders has received the most attention. As reviewed earlier, an increasing body of literature has suggested that bulimia may be a symptom expression of a biologically mediated affective disorder. Several lines of evidence have been offered in support of this hypothesis: (1) many bulimic patients report vegetative symptoms that are characteristic of patients who have primary affective disorder; (2) there is a high incidence of affective disorder and substance abuse among first- and second-degree relatives of bulimic patients; (3) DST and thyroid releasing hormone stimulating tests, as well as sleep architecture studies, have indicated disturbance similar to control groups of depressed patients; and finally (4) some patients have responded favorably to antidepressant pharmacotherapy.

Although the relationship remains controversial, there is some consensus among clinicians and researchers that the bulimic population, overall, experiences substantial and frequent affective instability. By affective instability we mean that the group is vulnerable to rapidly fluctuating moods, including irritability, anxiety, fatigue, restlessness, despair, and agitation. We feel safe in suggesting that the group is emotionally reactive, that the emotional reactivity is a longstanding problem predating the onset of the eating disorder, and that biogenetic factors have contributed to this reactivity. Consequently our etiological model begins with a child who may be biologically at risk for experiencing substantial affective instability. If she were placed in a family environment that provided adequate psychological tools to manage the affective vulnerability, then she would be less at risk for developing psychiatric symptoms. However, the nature of bulimic individuals' family environments exacerbate rather than decrease the risk of psychiatric impairment.

Family Factors

As reviewed in chapter 6, the family environment of the bulimic patient can be characterized as disengaged, chaotic, highly conflicted, and neglectful. Family members use indirect and contradictory patterns of communication, are deficient in problem-solving skills, are nonsupportive of independent behavior, and are less intellectually and recreationally oriented than the families of normal controls, despite their higher achievement orientations. These family characteristics generally result in children feeling disorganized, disconnected, insecure, and anxious. It is also important to note that it is the type of family environment one would expect to find if substance abuse, impulse disorder, or affective disorder existed among the parents. Consequently, at this point in the risk factor model, the child who may be struggling with a biological vulnerability to affective instability is living in an unstable family environment. Despite the high risk loading of both biological and familial factors, if the child were able to lean on a consistent and stable structure within the sociocultural milieu she might be able to compensate for the lack of structure within her immediate family. Unfortunately, particularly for young women, the broader sociocultural context simultaneously exacerbates feelings of instability and, ultimately, suggests a pathological adaptation to that instability.

Sociocultural Factors

Obviously biological and familial factors alone could not explain why we are observing an increase in a specific symptom picture among a rather homogeneous cohort (fifteen to twenty-five-year-old, middle- to upper-class, Caucasian, college-educated women in westernized countries). Consequently, the broader sociocultural context must be examined to see if any events occurred during the period of increased incidence that would selectively bias the group at risk as well as the specific symptom expression. Retrospectively it appears that two cultural events that could account for this occurred simultaneously.

ROLE DESTABILIZATION

The mean age of the bulimic patient population indicates they are the first generation of young women raised at the beginning of the feminist movement. Several authors have observed that during these years the sociocultural milieu for young women was in substantial transition, which appears to have contributed to role and identity confusion among at least a subpopulation of this age group (Bardwick, 1971; Lewis and Johnson, 1985; Palazzoli, 1974; Schwartz, Thompson, and Johnson, 1982). Garner, Garfinkel, and Olmsted (1983) review evidence that these shifting cultural norms forced contemporary women to face multiple, ambiguous, and often contradictory role expectations, including accommodating more traditional feminine expectations, such as physical attractiveness and domesticity; incorporating more modern standards for vocational and personal achievement; and taking advantage of increased opportunity for self-definition and autonomy. Garner and his colleagues suggest that "while the wider range of choices made available to contemporary women may have provided personal freedom for those who were psychologically robust, it may have been overwhelming for the field-dependent adolescent who lacked internal structure" (p. 183).

Thus the bulimic population is part of a select group that was being raised at a time when female role expectations were in significant transition. It could be speculated that the destabilization of sex-role norms would be particularly unsettling for a group already predisposed to affective instability.

CULTURAL PREOCCUPATION WITH THINNESS

A second cultural shift emerged concomitantly with the feminist movement that appears to have biased the specific symptom expression of food- and body-related behavior. More specifically, during the mid-1960s an emphasis on thinness for women emerged. Researchers have documented that over the last two decades the preferred body style for women in particular has become progressively slimmer (Garner, Garfinkel, Schwartz, and Thompson, 1980). This emphasis on thinness has been accompanied by a proliferation of diet products. According to market research in the early 1980s, 45 percent of all American households have someone dieting during the year. Furthermore, women are far more likely to diet than men, and their overwhelming reason for dieting is cosmetic rather than concern for health. It is also interesting to note that the drive for thinness among women has occurred at a time when the population averages for weight have progressively trended higher, largely as a result of better nutrition. Furthermore, it appears that the current idealized feminine form (tall, narrow hips, thin thighs) is a body style that may be biogenetically impossible for most women to achieve.

Consequently, amid a milieu of increasing focus on achievement and confusion about how to express the drive to achieve, the pursuit of thinness may have emerged as one vehicle through which young women could compete among themselves and demonstrate self-control. In fact, the accomplishment of thinness has increasingly become a very highly valued achievement that secures envy and respect among women in the current culture.

Conversely, the absence of weight control, leading to even moderate obesity, results culturally in social discrimination, isolation, and low self-esteem. Susan Wooley and Wayne Wooley (1979) reviewed numerous studies that document the stigma of obesity in childhood and adolescence. They assert that the overweight child is regarded by others as "responsible" for the condition and that failure to remediate the situation is viewed as "personal weakness." Both normal-weight and overweight children themselves describe obese silhouettes with such pejorative labels as stupid, lazy, dirty, sloppy, mean, and ugly. Female children add worried, sad, and lonely to the list of adjectives, which suggests that for them obesity carries connotations of social isolation (Allon, 1975; Staffieri, 1967, 1972).

This negative attitude toward endomorphic children prevails for both sexes. In adolescence and adulthood, however, there is increasing evidence that females are more affected than males by this antifat prejudice. Empirical research has shown that obese girls have greatly reduced chances of being admitted to college compared to nonobese applicants (Canning and Mayer, 1966); obese job applicants are less likely to be hired than their slimmer counterparts (Roe and Eickwort, 1976); once hired, their job performance is more likely to be negatively evaluated (Larkin and Pines, 1979); they are less likely to make as much money; and they are less likely to get top spots when promotions are made. Finally, compared to nonobese women, overweight women are much more likely to achieve a lower socioeconomic status than their parents (Goldblatt, Moore, and Stunkard, 1965).

In summary, against the backdrop of confusing cultural expectations and high achievement expectations, the pursuit of thinness (which can be scaled and measured) and avoidance of obesity seem to have emerged as one very concrete activity through which young women could compete and obtain consistently favorable social responses that held the possibility of enhancing self-esteem. Unfortunately, as we shall explain later, the selected goal may have been a particularly bad fit for many young women.

It seems clear that the recent destabilization of norms for young women contributed further to a sense of instability and that the prevailing emphasis on thinness may have biased them to competitively pursue disturbed attitudes and behaviors regarding food and weight. It is extremely important to note, however, that not all young women who were exposed to this cultural milieu developed psychiatric symptoms such as eating disorders. Therefore we must explore more closely the unique personality characteristics that may have predisposed some young women to become symptomatic.

Personality Factors

We noted earlier that the nature and extent of psychological deficits among bulimic patients can be quite varied (see chapter 5). There are, however, several features that are characteristic of the group, as we have reviewed. There is substantial evidence that bulimics experience significant affective instability, which is manifested in depressed and highly variable mood states and various impulsive behaviors. Consequently, these patients have long histories of feeling somewhat out of control and perhaps helpless in relation to their bodily experience. This undoubtedly contributes significantly to another prominent personality trait among bulimics: low self-esteem or profound feelings of ineffectiveness. Although these feelings are commonly associated with any genre of psychopathology, certain features are particularly descriptive of bulimic patients.

As discussed, many bulimic patients have difficulty identifying and articulating internal states (interoceptive awareness). It is likely that this difficulty contributes significantly to feelings of being psychologically undifferentiated and helpless in controlling internal states (self-regulation). Besides the sociocultural factors that might contribute to women feeling dissatisfied with their bodies (imperfect appearance), those who experience difficulty modulating internal states may feel more dissatisfaction, perhaps even rage, at bodies they experience as being defective containers of their affects.

Further exacerbating self-esteem problems are findings that bulimic patients are quite sensitive to rejection, which results in feelings of social discomfort and nonassertive behavior.* Finally, amid these various vulnerabilities, bulimic patients have high expectations of themselves that result in persistent shame, guilt, and self-criticalness over the repeated discrepancy they feel between their actual and ideal selves (Goodsitt, 1984; Kohut, 1971).

The biological, familial, and sociocultural milieus have combined to shape an individual who is at high risk for feeling fundamentally out of control of her internal life. Given these circumstances, it is likely that the person would begin to seek some external adaptation in an attempt to gain control over her internal discomfort. Because of the issues related to bodily experience, it would seem obvious that the adaptation would need to be focused in that arena. But why is food-related or dieting behavior selected rather than any other potential behavior, such as drug abuse, promiscuity, delinquent behavior, or more primitive types of self-mutilating behavior? The following section presents observations on how the pursuit of thinness could emerge for these patients as a viable adaptation to the difficulties that have been reviewed.

* See Boskind-Lodahl, 1976; Connors, Johnson, and Stuckey, 1984; Johnson, Stuckey, Lewis, and Schwartz, 1982; Norman and Herzog, 1983; and Pyle, Mitchell, and Eckert, 1981.

The Pursuit of Thinness as an Adaptation to Self-Regulatory Deficits, Interpersonal Sensitivity, and Achievement Expectations

As discussed, three personality features appear to be consistently characteristic of bulimic patients: (1) pervasive self-regulatory difficulties that result in feelings of ineffectiveness and being out of control, (2) lack of confidence interpersonally, and (3) a drive to successfully compete and achieve goals. In the following paragraphs, we would like to suggest how the accomplishment of thinness could be viewed by bulimic patients as an effective solution to these problems.

SELF/BODY MASTERY

Clinical observations and data-based research have documented that an early and primary source of feelings of mastery for children comes from successful control of bodily functions and movements. Over the last several decades an emphasis has emerged on women taking control of their bodies. Thus a demonstration of being in control of one's body appears to have become, more generally, a demonstration that one is in control of one's life. More specifically, for this group of patients the accomplishment of thinness, or the control of the amount and distribution of fat, has become a demonstration to themselves that they can control the container that houses their affective states. Furthermore, merely weighing themselves serves to provide some external, concrete indicator of their level of control as these patients lack the internal ability to tell whether they are in control or not.

INTERPERSONAL CONFIDENCE

Many bulimic patients lack confidence interpersonally and feel self-conscious and unattractive. The accomplishment of thinness among these women not only enhances self-confidence, but also often results in significant social transformations. Many women report dramatic increases in their social desirability (popularity) as a result of weight loss.

ACHIEVEMENT

Finally, the pursuit of thinness has also become a vehicle to express achievement. As mentioned, one change that has occurred during the years of increased incidence has been an increased emphasis on achievement for young women. Unfortunately, coexisting with this increased emphasis on achievement were relatively few socially valued avenues in which young women could compete directly. The pursuit of thinness seems to have emerged as one way in which young women could compete and demonstrate intrapsychic and interpersonal achievement. Not only did this avenue for achievement and competition appear benign, but it was even socially sanctioned.

Thus there are several reasons why the pursuit of thinness would become a functional adaptation to the personality vulnerabilities mentioned. While it seems clear how the pursuit of thinness and accompanying dieting behavior would increase in incidence, it remains unclear how the bulimic symptoms also increased in incidence. We now turn to a synthesis of how those symptoms might emerge.

The Adaptive Context of Binge Eating

We have argued that over the last two decades a cultural milieu has progressively emerged, particularly for women, that has engendered the belief that if one can control weight (body) and achieve thinness, this will be an intrapsychically and interpersonally reinforcing demonstration of self-control. Thinness, of course, results from extended calorie restriction. Consequently, the increase in the incidence of bulimic behavior occurred during the time when large numbers of adolescent and young adult women were pursuing thinness through highly restrictive dieting.

Research has indicated that the onset of bulimic symptomology is often caused by periods of prolonged calorie deprivation (Johnson, Stuckey, Lewis, and Schwartz, 1982; Pyle, Mitchell, and Eckert, 1981). Over the last several years a growing body of research has documented that both physiological and psychological side effects result from semistarvation, and that counterregulatory behaviors, such as binge eating, also occur in reaction to prolonged states of calorie deprivation.* The physiological side effects reported include gastrointestinal discomfort, decreased need for sleep, dizziness, headaches, hypersensitivity to noise and light, reduced strength, poor motor control, edema, hair loss, decreased tolerance for cold temperatures, visual disturbances, auditory disturbances, and parasthesias. Additional side effects include persistent tiredness, weakness, listlessness, fatigue, and lack of energy. Psychological symptoms include increased depression, irritability, rage outbursts, increased anxiety, social withdrawal, and loss of sexual interest. Specific increases in food-related behavior, which occur from semistarvation states, include an increased

* See Garfinkel and Garner, 1982; Garner et al., 1984; Glucksman and Hirsch, 1969; Herman and Mack, 1975; Herman and Polivy, 1980; Keys et al., 1950; and Rowland, 1970.

obsession with food, food hoarding, prolonged eating behavior during mealtimes, peculiar taste preferences, and hyperconsumption of substances such as coffee and gum.

The explanation offered for the appearance of these side effects is that as the body drops below an individual's minimal biogenetically mediated (set point) range of weight, the body initiates a variety of compensatory behaviors designed to conserve energy and to begin to increase body weight to the internally prescribed weight range (Garner, Olmstead, Polivy, and Garfinkel, 1984; Keesey, 1980, 1983; Mrosovsky and Powley, 1977; Nisbett, 1972). This is particularly true for women, who must maintain approximately 23 percent adipose tissue in order to menstruate (Frisch, 1983). Any time the body fat threatens to drop below this range, a specific biological imperative ensues that involves a persistent and intense drive toward caloric intake. Foremost among the compensatory behaviors that emerge in reaction to caloric deprivation is an increased vulnerability to binge eating (rapid consumption of a large quantity of food in a short period of time).

THE PSYCHOBIOLOGICAL IMPASSE

As figure 7.1 shows, at this point in the etiological model, we have an individual who has attempted to compensate for a variety of self-regulatory and self-esteem deficits by becoming thin. If success in becoming thin causes her weight to drop to near the set-point range (menstrual threshold), a variety of physiological and psychological side effects occur. Foremost among these is that the individual becomes increasingly agitated. Essentially, the person who is already vulnerable to significant affective instability is now engaging in a behavior that will ultimately exacerbate one of the primary problems she was attempting to solve (self/body mastery).

At this point the individual is at what could be referred to as a psychobiological impasse. The psychological adaptation developed is at odds with biology, and the self-esteem developed through the accomplishment of low weight is threatened. In fact, it is likely that the individual experiences the body's relentless drive to consume calories as evidence that the body once again is out of control. As figure 7.2 illustrates, a belief system that is logically consistent could emerge that would result in the individual interpreting the internal experience of hunger as a signal that she was out of control and failing at her appointed task. This guarantees that many times a day she would have an internal experience (hunger) that she would interpret as evidence that she was ineffective and a failure. Paradoxically, then, the effort at compensation results in an exacerbation of many of the original difficulties.

Against this backdrop of heightened affected instability, lowered self-esteem, and semistarvation, any stressful life event would be taxing to

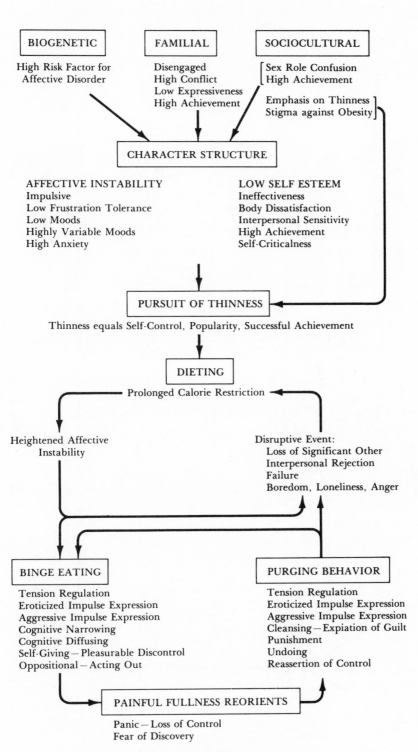

FIGURE 7.1
Factors that Contribute to the Onset of Bulimia

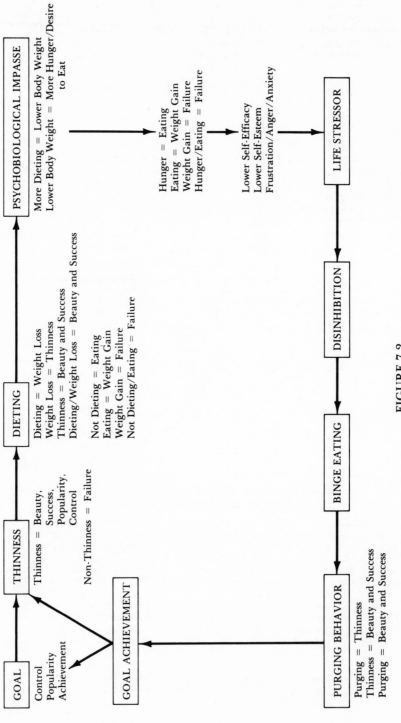

FIGURE 7.2

The Psychobiological Impasse

the failing defensive adaptation (thinness equals control and achievement). Given the semistarved state, if disinhibition occurred, the most likely expression of the breakdown in defenses would be binge eating.

BINGE EATING

By the time most patients reach clinicians, the original reasons for the onset of the bulimic behavior may be obscured. As the binge eating/ purging cycle emerges, these behaviors begin to serve compensatory or adaptive functions for the patient. These behaviors may serve to regulate affect, as impulse expression, as self-nurturance, and to express oppositionality.

Affect Regulation. Given the evidence for affective instability in these patients, it is easy to see how binge eating could emerge as a relatively safe mechanism for regulating different tension states. As noted, research studies have indicated that bulimics often experience a wide range of highly variable mood states that they have difficulty identifying, articulating, and controlling. Throughout the day the variability, range, and seeming unpredictability of the different mood states may become overwhelming and disorganizing for the patient. The concrete and repetitive act of bingeing and purging can serve an integrating function, allowing these patients to reliably create a predictable affective and cognitive state. Essentially, when overwhelmed by confusing and variable mood states, the bingeing and purging becomes both an explanation of the dysphoria ("I am feeling bad because I have binged") and a mechanism for actually helping to regulate the dysphoria ("I feel relieved after I have binged").

Impulse Expression. Bulimic patients are vulnerable to impulsive behavior. Episodic binge eating can be a relatively safe mechanism for being impulsive, since it does not carry significant moral, legal, or medical consequences, as does promiscuity, delinquent behavior, or drug abuse. More specifically, bulimic patients can eroticize the binge-eating episodes, thus offering an alternative response to sexual feelings if they are conflicted about masturbation or sexual activity. Similarly, binge eating and subsequent purging can become an effective mechanism for expressing aggressive feelings that these individuals have difficulty expressing interpersonally.

More obsessive, overcontrolled patients also use binge eating to temporarily be out of control or have the phenomenological experience of letting go or spacing out. These patients create an experience of controlled dyscontrol. They invest food, an inanimate object that has no volition and can have only as much power as they grant it, with the power to overcome them and make them become impulsive. This allows them some relief from an overcontrolled psychological world, without having to take responsibility for the impulsive episodes.

Self-nurturance. Some bulimic patients are tormented by a profound sense of guilt that results in a belief that they should deny themselves pleasurable or self-enhancing activities. They are quite self-sacrificing, and their continuous efforts to care for others often leave them feeling depleted and exhausted. The act of binge eating (with the attendant attribution that the event was externally determined) can serve as a mechanism for briefly feeding themselves.

Along similar lines, the basic mistrust of others some bulimic patients experience prevents them from receiving emotional supplies from the outside. Consequently, they will invest food and the act of binge eating with the ability to soothe, comfort, and gratify them. In this regard, they often project onto the food humanlike qualities that give them the illusion of receiving emotional supplies from a source other than themselves. The fact that food (an inanimate object) can behave only as they desire allows them simultaneously to refuel and yet be protected from potential disappointment in human relationships.

Oppositionality. Binge eating can also serve as a mechanism for expressing oppositionality. For patients who feel that external authority figures have imposed significant restraint on them, binge eating can become an expression of acting out or defiance. This is particularly true of bulimics who were raised in families where weight control and dieting were greatly emphasized by the parents. For these patients the act of binge eating becomes a statement of protest and an expression of autonomy.

Whatever specific adaptation binge eating serves, once an episode has ended, the patients generally feel some combination of guilt, shame, disgust, and fear of being discovered. These feelings become concretely manifested in a sense of panic that they will gain weight, which would be an observable indication that they are out of control, disorganized, undisciplined, and greedy, and so forth. Consequently, the use of evacuation techniques such as self-induced vomiting, laxative abuse, and enemas emerges as a viable mechanism for undoing the binge eating.

PURGING BEHAVIOR

Like binge eating, purging behavior can serve a variety of different adaptive functions, some of which may become more important than the actual act of binge eating in the bulimic's psychic economy. As with binge eating, the act of purging can serve as a mechanism for tension regulation. This is particularly true of aggressive feelings. Self-induced vomiting can be a rather violent act, and the physical process of vomiting can be a real catharsis for aggressive feelings. For patients who feel especially guilty and self-critical about their binge-eating episodes, purging can serve as a self-punishment and an act of undoing or penitence that pays for the crime of impulse expression. For the oppositional patient, it allows her to get away with something without "getting caught" or having to pay the price of overeating.

For more borderline patients, the act of purging (primarily laxative abuse) appears to serve an integrating function similar to other forms of self-mutilating behavior. The intense pain created by the persistent diarrhea appears to make them feel alive and in touch with reality.

Most important, as figure 7.2 depicts, the purging behavior becomes highly reinforcing because it allows individuals to avoid the psychobiological impasse of restrained eating. Essentially, purging allows patients to eat in any compensatory way they desire without the negative consequence of weight gain. Several investigators have noted that the purging behavior can become so highly reinforcing that for some patients a transformation occurs: instead of purging so that they can binge eat they binge eat so that they can purge (Johnson and Larson, 1982; Rosen and Leitenberg, 1982).

Unfortunately, as does the adaptive effort of the pursuit of thinness, the purging adaptation simultaneously creates and solves a problem. In the absence of immediately apparent negative consequences, bingeing and purging progressively increase until patients use the cycle to regulate a variety of affective and cognitive states. Eventually they feel addicted to, and controlled by, the process, which again results in lower self-esteem and heightened affective instability.

Summary

This chapter synthesized our knowledge of how biological, familial, and sociocultural factors predispose predominantly adolescent and young adult women to develop bulimia. Young women who are at risk for developing bulimia appear to have a biological vulnerability to affective instability. This affective instability is exacerbated by both a family environment that is chaotic and conflictual and social role expectations that are confusing because they are in transition. These factors contribute to a personality profile that includes self-esteem and self-regulatory difficulties. The sociocultural milieu suggests to young women that the achievement of thinness would help remedy their self-esteem and self-regulatory problems. Yet, paradoxically, the physiological and psychological side effects of semistarvation and the belief system associated with the pursuit of thinness eventually lead to a psychobiological impasse that actually exacerbates the original difficulties of affective instability and low self-esteem. Binge eating emerged as a counterregulatory reaction to the psychobiological impasse, and the binge/purge sequence eventually serves a variety of psychological adaptations.

PART II

ASSESSMENT AND TREATMENT

8

The Initial Interview

Throughout the book we have emphasized the variety of different adaptations that bulimia may serve for individuals. Given the heterogeneity of these adaptations, effective treatment requires multidimensional and specialized interventions. As depicted in figure 8.1, a comprehensive treatment program for bulimia should have access to family, group, and individual psychotherapy as well as medical and nutritional evaluation services. In addition to full outpatient services, it is useful to have access to an inpatient setting where special protocols for eating-disordered patients can be used.

The centerpiece of our treatment program is the initial consultation. It is our opinion that as the incidence of bulimia continues to rise, it is increasingly important to develop more specific evaluation procedures in order to identify the unique meaning of the disturbed eating behavior to the individual. Once the specific adaptation has been identified, treatment needs to be tailored to each patient's special requirements.

This emphasis on individualization runs counter to a growing trend in some treatment settings to view patients with bulimia as a generic group that should be treated with generic interventions. We have become alarmed recently by the number of treatment settings that are buying "canned" or "packaged" treatment programs for eating-disordered patients. While these programs are often cost-efficient and easier for staff because they offer "rules" for treatment, there are several significant problems with them. Foremost among our concerns is the fact that no long-term or even midterm outcome studies document the effectiveness of any treatment strategy. Therefore it is certainly premature and perhaps presumptuous to concoct (and sell) treatment packages. Second, such treatment programs may offer both staff and patients a false sense of security regarding our degree of knowledge about treating these disorders. This is not to say that we have learned nothing over the last several years; it is more a plea of caution to avoid premature conclusions regarding what constitutes effective treatment.

The field is still young enough that professionals who are doing initial

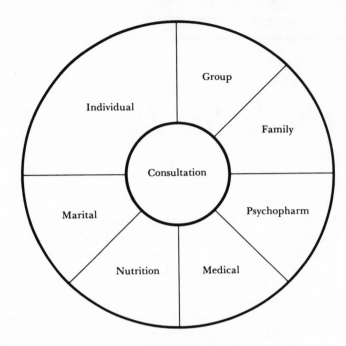

FIGURE 8.1
A Multidimensional Treatment Program for Bulimia

interviews should have broad training across different types of psycho-pathology in order to make a sophisticated differential diagnosis. Additionally, it is incumbent upon treatment programs to construct data bases that will allow us to draw conclusions regarding effective treatment.

The Data Base

Given that our understanding of the diagnosis and treatment of bulimia is relatively new, it is particularly important that treatment settings establish data bases utilizing standardized measures. These data bases should allow us increasingly to identify variables that affect outcome (see chapter 12). Information should be collected in a number of categories. In the next sections we discuss these categories and the standardized instruments that are often used to measure them.

SYMPTOMATIC EATING BEHAVIOR AND ATTITUDES

The Diagnostic Survey for Eating Disorders-Revised (DSED-R; Johnson, 1984; Love and Johnson, 1984). This standardized intake survey focuses on various aspects of anorexia nervosa and bulimia. The questionnaire is divided into twelve sections, which provide information on demographic factors, weight history, body image, dieting behavior, binge-eating behavior, purging behavior, exercise related behaviors, sexual functioning, menstruation, medical and psychiatric history, life adjustment, and family history. The survey can be used as a self-report instrument or as a semi-structured interview guide. (The DSED-R is reproduced at the end of this chapter.)

Eating Disorders Inventory (Garner, Olmsted, and Polivy, 1983). This multiscale measure assesses traits common in anorexia nervosa and bulimia, such as drive for thinness, body dissatisfaction, and perfectionism.

GENERAL SYMPTOMATIC BEHAVIOR

Symptom Checklist-90 (Derogatis and Cleary, 1977). This multidimensional symptom inventory evolved from the Hopkins Symptom Checklist (HSCL). It quantifies psychopathology in terms of such symptom constructs as somatization, anxiety, hostility, and interpersonal sensitivity.

Beck Depression Inventory (BDI; Beck et al., 1961). This instrument assesses the degree of depression and categorizes scores from no depression to severe levels.

LIFE ADJUSTMENT

Social Adjustment Scale (SAS; Weissman, 1975). This scale measures performance over the last two weeks in the areas of work, social activities, relationship with extended family, and roles as spouse, parent, and family member.

FAMILY ENVIRONMENT

Family Environment Scale (Moos, 1974). This instrument measures the social environment characteristics of families in terms of such dimensions as relationship (such as cohesion and conflict), personal growth (such as independence and achievement orientation), and system maintenance (organization and control).

PERSONALITY

Minnesota Multiphasic Personality Inventory. This empirically derived instrument measures symptomatology, including such categories as depression, hypochondriasis, hysteria, paranoia, and hypomania.

Structural Analysis of Social Behavior (Benjamin, 1983). This questionnaire classifies interpersonal transactions in terms of such aspects as affiliation, interdependence, autonomy, attachment, and intimacy.

The Borderline Syndrome Index (BSI; Conte, Plutchik, Karasu, and Jerrett, 1980). This instrument measures characteristics thought to be central
in borderline psychopathology, including poor impulse control, absence
of a consistent self-identity, and impaired object relations.

The First Five Minutes of the Consultation

It has been our experience with eating-disordered patients that the first
several minutes of the consultation are extremely important. We usually
initiate the interview by inquiring how the person is feeling about coming
for the consultation. The purpose of the question is to assess whether the
patient is seeking help voluntarily or because of various degrees of coercion
from friends, family, or the community. Although there are always ex-
ceptions, more bulimic patients present voluntarily than anorexia nervosa
patients.

We then ask if the patient has talked with anyone specifically about
her difficulties with food. Our purpose here is to assess how ego-syntonic
the symptoms are and to attempt to be sensitive to the fact that many
individuals have never acknowledged their difficulties with food and feel
very ashamed and humiliated in doing so. This is particularly true for
patients who present with bulimic symptoms.

If the patient has been in treatment before, we ask what she found
helpful and nonhelpful. We also ask if the previous therapist directly
inquired about food-related behavior. Some patients who were in long-
term treatment never admitted the problem to the therapist or were discouraged from focusing on it.

After these initial questions, we present to the patient the agenda for
the consultation. We mention that we have many questions to ask, some
of which may seem intrusive. Our reason for asking so many questions
so quickly is to assess, in as little time as possible, where the patient is
in the course of the eating disorder so that we can make treatment
recommendations.

Overall, the most important task of the first five minutes is to communicate to the patient, either explicitly or through the spirit of the interview, that we are interested in a collaborative inquiry rather than an inquisition into the events that may have resulted in the onset of her symptoms.

Over the years we have debated the relative merits of structured versus unstructured initial interviews. Based on our experience, we have concluded that structured interviews are preferable. While there appear to be some important advantages in conducting an unstructured interview, we feel the costs outweigh the benefits. Although waiting patiently and quietly for patients to disclose their difficulties can yield important information about their capacity for tension regulation in an unstructured situation, the level of their social skills, and their capacity to articulate internal states without assistance, patients often view such an interview as sadistic withholding or as evidence that the therapist does not have specific knowledge regarding their particular problems. The structured interview allows the therapist to demonstrate an awareness of some of the unique aspects of eating problems through knowledgeable inquiry. It also establishes a common language at the onset. Most eating-disordered patients' lives revolve around food-related thoughts and behavior; consequently, their language reflects this preoccupation. While the treatment task is to provide patients with different ways to organize their lives (or a different language), we have found it helpful in the initial stages of contact to inquire directly about food-related attitudes and behaviors. This is particularly important with patients who have been discouraged from talking specifically about these matters in previous treatment.

The Interview

WEIGHT HISTORY

The structured interview begins with questions regarding the patient's weight history and feelings toward her body. The overall objective here is to investigate how much weight preoccupations and fluctuations have affected the patient's self-esteem and life adjustment.

After obtaining the patient's current height, weight, and ideal weight, we investigate whether there are occupational considerations that affect the patient's attitudes toward her weight. Individuals in the entertainment and fashion industries are high-risk groups because of rigorous and often unrealistic criteria for weight regulation (Druss and Silverman, 1979; Garner and Garfinkel, 1980). These groups are often special treatment problems because their self-esteem and livelihood are unalterably tied to industries that demand a weight maintenance that is debilitatingly subnormal.

We then inquire about the patient's highest and lowest past weights since the age of thirteen. If periods of significant weight fluctuations are mentioned, potential correlations with specific life events, such as major transitions, separations or losses, family problems, recurring illness, and the like, are investigated. This early process of inquiry regarding possible psychological correlates of weight fluctuations can help the patient begin to think psychologically about the relationship of her food, weight, and body-related behavior to events in her life.

During the initial consultation, patients will often see these patterns for the first time. For example, many of our patients realize that when they are rejected in a romantic relationship, they attempt to "start over" or restore a sense of control by dieting or losing weight. It is interesting to note that if this process is repeatedly successful at restoring control and self-esteem (and it often is because our culture responds favorably to weight loss, particularly among women), then initiating weight loss or dieting can eventually become a generalized response to a wide range of traumatic situations.

Information about weight during childhood and early adolescent years is often unreliable. Consequently, we focus on how much emphasis the family and peer milieu placed on such factors as thinness, dieting, and appearance, and what influences this emphasis has had on the patient's self-concept and beliefs about such issues as self-control, social acceptance, and the like. We also inquire very specifically whether the patient has been teased about her weight. It is important to establish the extent of the teasing, the context, the content, who specifically was doing the teasing, and its impact on the patient.

Periods of significant weight loss are important to determine, with particular attention paid to the speed and method used. Recent research indicates important personality and outcome distinctions between patients who lose weight by restricting their food intake and those who utilize purging behavior accompanied by episodes of binge eating (Casper et al., 1980; Garfinkel, Moldofsky, and Garner, 1980).

We also inquire whether amenorrhea developed during the weight loss, and, if so, within what weight range it occurred. This information about the patient's weight threshold for menstruation to occur can be helpful in establishing what is, minimally, a biologically acceptable weight range for her.

BODY IMAGE

Body-image perception among eating-disordered patients ranges from mild distortion or dissatisfaction to severely delusional thoughts regarding body size. Likewise, the degree to which body-image perception affects life adjustment falls along a continuum from mild to severely debilitating. Consequently, the primary task of the second phase of the interview is to assess the level of body-image distortion and what psychological adaptation it may be serving, and to investigate to what extent it is interfering with life adjustment.

While most women do report that they are dissatisfied with the size and shape of their bodies, their dissatisfaction does not necessarily interfere with life functioning. We attempt to investigate how much the patient's self-consciousness about her body affects her life adjustment by inquiring whether the dissatisfaction prevents her from doing certain things, such as dating, becoming sexually involved, exercising, or participating in activities that require some bodily exposure. While investigating this, we also attempt to assess the discrepancy between the patient's perception of her body size and her actual body size. If the body perception is quite distorted, we often ask if others disagree with her perception. Patients with more delusional body-image distortion are threatened by this inquiry and often react with hostile resistance. As reviewed earlier (see chapter 6), patients who present with more delusional perceptions of their body size are often quite paranoid, have fragile and brittle intrapsychic resources, are treatment resistant, and consequently have poorer outcomes.

DIETING BEHAVIOR

The primary purpose of our questions regarding dieting behavior is to assess the length of time the patient has dieted. As reviewed earlier (see chapter 2), early onset and frequent dieting were highly predictive of subsequent bulimic behavior among adolescent females (Johnson, Stuckey, Lewis, and Schwartz, 1982). We also want to assess how much psychological and physiological deprivation is being experienced as well as the cognitive-emotional system that has evolved around the behavior. Overall, we attempt to learn when dieting first began, why, and whether there was a particular source of encouragement.

Of particular interest is how preoccupied other members of the family are with food and weight. As one would suspect, many of our patients have parents who are food- and weight-preoccupied (Kalucy, Crisp, and Harding, 1977). In addition, many parents have a more generalized focus on appearance as being of paramount importance, such as a mother who snapped "Stop crying—you'll get wrinkles!" at her weeping daughter. We are also beginning, like others (Crisp, 1980; Garfinkel and Garner, 1982), to see families that have several children who have had, or are currently having, difficulty with anorexia nervosa or bulimia.

It is also important to assess how much of a psychological system has developed around the concept of dieting. We inquire whether the patient thinks of food as "good" or "bad" and how it affects her to eat either "good" or "bad" foods. We also try to assess how much magical or superstitious thinking is associated with the food-related behavior (Garner and Bemis, 1982) by asking the patient to explain her understanding of what calories are, how food is digested, what the function of fat is, and how most fad diets work.

Finally, we attempt to assess to what extent either psychological or physiological deprivation may be triggering binge eating or specific food cravings. Recent research has indicated that some individuals who chronically restrain their eating are highly vulnerable to counterregulatory episodes of binge eating (see the section entitled "Restraint Theory" in chapter 10). Likewise, research has accumulated over the years indicating that most individuals who are physically starved (calorie deprived) are also highly vulnerable to impulses to binge eat as a result of biological pressures to obtain calories (again, see chapter 10).

SCALE BEHAVIOR AND EXERCISE

Ritualized behavior around body measurement and exercise are common side effects of a chronic preoccupation with dieting. It is important to assess how frequently the patient weighs or measures herself, how ritualized the behavior is, and how minor fluctuations in weight affect self-concept and daily activities.

We also investigate the longest period of time during the past six months that the patient has gone without weighing or measuring herself, and what events correlate with this period of time. So the clinic staff can assess how integral the measurement process is to the patient's psychological homeostasis, we often ask whether she would be willing to temporarily delegate the monitoring of her body size.

Exercise, like weighing behavior, can become highly ritualized and quite debilitating. We investigate what adaptive function the exercise serves in the patient's psychological system. Inquiry into how the patient experiences the absence of exercise often offers clues regarding the adaptive context. Exercise can serve a variety of purposes, including a hypomanic defense against a fear of paralyzing depression, a form of masochistic self-punishment, a goal-oriented pursuit of achievement-serving narcissistic/exhibitionistic concerns, or as a general mechanism for regulating such tension states as anxiety, anger, and depression. We do not mean to imply that exercise always serves a pathological purpose; in fact, pleasurable and noncompulsive exercise can be a great help to patients as they gradually relinquish symptomatic behaviors and become involved in other activities. However, its function for the patient must always be assessed.

BINGE EATING

Our objective during the next phase of the interview is to investigate, at both a macro and a micro level, the adaptive significance of the binge-eating behavior.

Macroassessment. We are interested in determining when the problem eating began, the precipitating circumstances, and whether fluctuations in eating behavior correlate with recurring life events. During the macroassessment it is also useful to inquire about the longest time the patient has been binge-free since the onset of her difficulties, what her life circumstances were during these periods, and what her affective response was to the symptom-free period. Patients often report symptom-free periods that correspond to vacations, leaving home, embarking upon or ending a relationship, or good or difficult times at work. Some patients find symptom-free periods to be frustrating, difficult, anxiety provoking, and depressing, while others report them to be happy, tension-free times. Inquiry into symptom-free periods can also yield important information regarding successful and unsuccessful strategies the patient has employed to cope with the binge eating.

We also investigate whether the patient's episodes of binge eating vary according to her menstrual cycle. Clinical evidence is beginning to suggest that these may be related in some women, especially those prone to premenstrual stress syndrome. These women usually report that their appetite increases just prior to menstruation, especially for sweets and carbohydrates.

Microassessment. The microassessment focuses on the details of the patient's daily routines. We usually begin this inquiry by asking the patient to describe her daily eating pattern. We have her describe in detail the previous day's activities, including meals, binge episodes, and routine events. Initially we are particularly interested in learning when and to what extent she is eating meals. We also want to know what she regards as a reasonable meal and a binge, because many bulimic and anorexic patients have come to interpret any consumption of food as a loss of control.

The microassessment of meals, moods, and binge eating is often facilitated by requesting that the patient carry a time sampling diary (see figure 8.2, which is a form that she fills out several times a day for at least one week).

After describing her daily eating patterns, we have the patient focus more specifically on her binge-eating episodes. We attempt to assess whether there are particular foods, events, times, or emotional states that recurrently trigger the episodes. Research has indicated that most patients have difficulty with food when they are alone in unstructured situations. This is usually during evening hours when they are at home alone (Carroll

FIGURE 8.2
Daily Self Monitoring Form

Date: _____ Time filled out: _____ AM/PM

What were you thinking about? _____

_____

Where were you? _____

_____

What was the **main** thing you were doing? _____

	Not at All	Somewhat	Quite	Very
How much choice did you have in selecting this activity?	+ --- + --- + --- + --- + --- + --- + --- + --- + --- +			
Did you feel in control of your activity?	+ --- + --- + --- + --- + --- + --- + --- + --- + --- +			
How guilty did you feel?	+ --- + --- + --- + --- + --- + --- + --- + --- + --- +			
How vulnerable did you feel?	+ --- + --- + --- + --- + --- + --- + --- + --- + --- +			
How self-conscious were you?	+ --- + --- + --- + --- + --- + --- + --- + --- + --- +			
How much were you concentrating?	+ --- + --- + --- + --- + --- + --- + --- + --- + --- +			
How satisfied did you feel with yourself?	+ --- + --- + --- + --- + --- + --- + --- + --- + --- +			
	0 1 2 3 4 5 6 7 8 9			

Describe your mood:

	Very	Quite	Some	Neither	Some	Quite	Very	
Alert	0	o	·	—	·	o	0	Drowsy
Happy	0	o	·	—	·	o	0	Sad
Irritable	0	o	·	—	·	o	0	Cheerful
Strong	0	o	·	—	·	o	0	Weak
Angry	0	o	·	—	·	o	0	Friendly
Active	0	o	·	—	·	o	0	Passive
Lonely	0	o	·	—	·	o	0	Sociable
Adequate	0	o	·	—	·	o	0	Inadequate
Free	0	o	·	—	·	o	0	Constrained
Excited	0	o	·	—	·	o	0	Bored
Proud	0	o	·	—	·	o	0	Ashamed
Confused	0	o	·	—	·	o	0	Clear
Tense	0	o	·	—	·	o	0	Relaxed
Fat	0	o	·	—	·	o	0	Thin

Describe your physical state:

	None	Slight	Moderate	Severe
Hungry	+ -- + -- + -- + -- + -- + -- + -- + -- + -- + --			
Tired, slowed down	+ -- + -- + -- + -- + -- + -- + -- + -- + -- + --			
Aches and pains	+ -- + -- + -- + -- + -- + -- + -- + -- + -- + --			

FIGURE 8.2 (*continued*)

Who were you with?

( ) Alone
( ) Brother(s), sister(s)
( ) Mother
( ) Father
( ) Strangers
( ) Coworkers

( ) Friend(s):
    Number _____
    ( ) Male
    ( ) Female
    ( ) Other(s): _____

Describe how you feel about one of the persons you are with. (If alone and thinking about someone, describe feelings about that person):

	Very	Middle	Very	
Close to	+ --- + --- + --- + ---	+ --- + ---	+ --- + --- + --- +	Distant from
Inferior to	+ --- + --- + --- + ---	+ --- + ---	+ --- + --- + --- +	Superior to
Friendly toward	+ --- + --- + --- + ---	+ --- + ---	+ --- + --- + --- +	Angry with
In control of	+ --- + --- + --- + ---	+ --- + ---	+ --- + --- + --- +	Controlled by

(Identify the person you are referring to: _____)

	Not at All	Somewhat	Quite	Very
How preoccupied were you with eating?	+ --- + --- + ---	+ --- + --- + ---	+ --- + ---	+ --- +
Do you feel your eating has been out of control since the last report?	+ --- + --- + ---	+ --- + --- + ---	+ --- + ---	+ --- +
How confident did you feel that you could resist the urge to binge eat?	+ --- + --- + ---	+ --- + --- + ---	+ --- + ---	+ --- +
	0 1 2	3 4 5	6 7	8 9

Indicate your food intake since the last report:

Type	Quantity
_____	_____
_____	_____
_____	_____
_____	_____

How many times have you binged since the last report? _____

How many times have you purged since the last report? _____

and Leon, 1981; Johnson, Stuckey, Lewis, and Schwartz, 1982; Pyle, Mitchell, and Eckert, 1981).

Bulimics generally binge on foods they normally deprive themselves of, such as sweets or carbohydrates, which they regard as bad. We have learned that, unfortunately, most of our patients do not eat during the day, the period of time that is most structured, and attempt to eat at night, which is their most unstructured time. These high-risk evening hours are thus made more difficult because the patients are usually calorie-deprived at their most vulnerable period of the day.

PHENOMENOLOGICAL EXPERIENCE

At this point in the interview we investigate the patients' phenomenological experience of binge eating. We are specifically trying to discover what type of tension states they are attempting to regulate or what type of affective release they are seeking through the binge eating. As mentioned earlier, research has suggested that bulimics often experience a wide range of mood states. The act of bingeing and purging may serve a variety of functions for patients, including affect regulation, impulse expression, self-nurturance, oppositionality, and self-punishment (see chapter 7).

It is clear that the act of binge eating carries a unique significance for each patient, and it is incumbent upon the interviewer to try to understand what specific function or functions it serves.

PURGING BEHAVIOR

In this part of the interview we want to determine the onset, precipitants, duration, frequency, and method of purging behavior. Early research has indicated that most bulimic patients use self-induced vomiting as a preferred evacuation technique and that they begin purging approximately one year after the onset of binge eating (Johnson, Stuckey, Lewis, and Schwartz, 1982; Pyle, Mitchell, and Eckert, 1981).

The assessment of purging behavior begins by inquiring if the patient purges and what means of evacuation she uses. While most patients use self-induced vomiting, it is not unusual to see patients who also use laxatives and diuretics at different times or in combination. Each method of purging has potentially serious medical side effects. Vomiting and abuse of laxatives and diuretics have been associated with electrolyte imbalances, cardiac irregularities, and rebound edema once the behavior has stopped (Fairburn, 1982; Garfinkel and Garner, 1982; Mitchell et al., 1983). Laxatives have also been shown to damage the intestinal mucosa, though their effects appear reversible (Curry, 1982). In addition to these difficulties, other problems associated with self-induced vomiting merit inquiry.

Some patients report that after they have used self-induced vomiting for a period of time they have found it increasingly easy to regurgitate, noting that merely the intent to purge or a tightening of their abdominal muscles is enough to result in emesis. Others have said that the sensation of food in their stomach is sufficient to start a gag reflex. Still other patients who have used self-induced vomiting have noted that, with more frequent use, it is increasingly difficult to trigger their gag reflex. Such attenuation of the gag reflex may be dangerous. Not only does it result in patients using increasingly strong stimuli to trigger it, but it may also increase the likelihood of accidental aspiration of food or vomitus.

Given these difficulties, it is clear that a detailed inquiry into the topography of purging is required. Other factors that must be determined include the onset, precipitants, duration, and frequency. Similarly, it is important to ask whether or not every binge is followed by a purge or if each purge is occasioned by a binge. Clinical experience suggests that some patients purge following binges only, while others purge following meals too. Other patients report that only some binges are followed by purges; we attempt to determine why this is so, by identifying any relations that exist between certain binge episodes and purging.

As with binge eating, it is important to determine the antecedents and consequences of purging. To this end, we have found it useful to inquire about the time of day purging occurs; who was present before, during, and after the purge; and what thoughts and feelings the patient had before, during, and after the purge. As we described in chapter 7, purging, like binge eating, can serve a variety of different adaptive functions, particularly regarding tension regulation.

Also as with binge eating, it is important to inquire about the longest period of abstinence from purging, including precipitants, its effect on the bingeing behavior, and the patient's level of discomfort. At the same time, it is useful to inquire about the methods patients have used successfully and unsuccessfully to abstain in the past.

It is also important to explore the patient's understanding of what purging accomplishes. Most bulimics believe that it is necessary to reduce their weight and works by preventing calorie absorption. While this is true of emesis, it is not true of either laxatives or diuretics; laxatives have been shown to be ineffective in controlling calorie absorption (Bo-Linn, Santa Ana, Morowski, and Fordtran, 1983). Many laxative-abusing bulimics have peculiar and idiosyncratic beliefs about the drugs that may reflect more psychoticlike thinking. Similarly, though diuretic abusers seem to understand that the medications do not affect calorie absorption, they often have mistaken notions as to how they work.

PERSONALITY FEATURES

Throughout the inquiry into food-related behavior we are also forming an opinion about the patient's characterological features. There are several main areas to evaluate that are consistent with our formulations in chapters 5 and 7.

Affect Awareness and Regulation. Earlier we reviewed evidence that many bulimic patients have significant difficulty identifying and articulating internal states (interoceptive awareness). We hypothesized that overall problems with self-regulation were side effects of this fundamental difficulty. Given the importance of this concept in the etiology of bulimia, the degree of deficit in interoceptive awareness must be assessed, although it is difficult to do. Primarily interviewers must rely on their clinical observation of how quickly and precisely patients are able to talk about their feelings. While making this assessment, however, it is important to distinguish patients who are conflicted about expressing feelings from those who do not know what they are feeling.

We also hypothesized earlier that affective instability was generally characteristic of bulimic patients and that, for some, there appears to be a biogenetic predisposition to unstable affects. Consequently, it is important to assess the nature of the patient's affective experience.

Generally we have found that bulimics present with symptoms that are characteristic of agitated depression, anxiety disorder, or panic states. These patients report a great deal of mood variability, recurrent anxiety, irritability, restlessness, boredom, difficulty falling asleep, short attention span, and low frustration tolerance. Overall, these patients have an anxious, driven quality that often results in impulsive behavior. Some will actually describe panic attacks that include tachycardia, hyperventilation, and a profound sense of losing control.

A smaller group of bulimic patients present with symptoms more characteristic of vegetative depression. They report chronic low mood, persistent fatigue and lethargy, difficulty awakening and rising in the morning, frequent crying episodes, and lack of motivation. These patients are much less impulse dominated, a fact their food-related behavior reflects. For them binge-eating episodes are usually planned events. Patients will plan a binge, usually late in the evening, and then look forward to it as something to pull them through the day.

In an effort to tease out the extent of biogenetic vulnerability, we inquire if any of the patient's relatives have had difficulty with depression, anxiety, alcohol, or drugs. If there are positive symptom presentations for depression and a positive family history, we strongly consider using antidepressant medication as an adjunct to treatment. We and other workers have found that the tricyclic and monoamine oxidase inhibitor medications to be most helpful with food-related symptoms among patients presenting with agitated depressions, anxiety disorders, or panic states. Although medication is useful in relieving some of the depressive symptoms among the vegetatively depressed group, it seems to have less impact on their food-related behavior (see chapter 12).

We have also found it useful to try to differentiate between patients with anaclitic (Lidz, 1976) and introjective depression (Blatt, 1974). Patients with anaclitic depressions are highly dependent and have an intense need to be directly connected to a need-satisfying object. They feel disorganized and lost when alone, because they lack the internal resources to direct themselves when others are not present. They generally have very fragile boundaries and are quite vulnerable to loss of impulse control and enmeshment in interpersonal relationships. These individuals are usually frightened of being abandoned and present as quite weak and helpless. Their usual significant developmental deficits are also characteristic of borderline patients, described earlier.

In contrast, patients with more introjective depressions present with an obsessive preoccupation with performance, achievement, and perfectionistic strivings. They critically judge all their efforts and report a persistent sense of guilt and shame. They generally feel they have failed to meet expectations and standards, and they usually attempt desperately to gain approval and acceptance through their achievements. Although most bulimic patients will present with some issues around achievement, guilt, and shame, this type of depression reflects a higher level of intrapsychic structure characteristic of false self/narcissistic and neurotic patients.

EXPERIENCE OF SELF AND OTHERS

During the course of the interview it is important to formulate ideas about how the person views herself and others. Bulimic patients will generally report a variety of self-perceptions that reflect low self-esteem. Characteristic feelings include inadequacy, worthlessness, ineffectiveness, self-criticalness, shame, and guilt.

Experience of others seem to be more highly variable. As mentioned earlier, some eating-disordered patients view the world as consisting of others who have malevolent intentions toward them. These patients report others to be intrusive, manipulative, exploitive, abusive, destructive, dangerous, and unreliable. Obviously, for patients who view others as malevolent and dangerous, establishing a trusting therapeutic alliance with these patients is a delicate process. In contrast, some bulimics view others as basically benign or even caring and loving. This is usually juxtaposed against a view of themselves as undeserving of benign or loving care.

In an effort to identify patients with false self organizations, we often ask how others view the patient. A substantial discrepancy between others' opinions (highly adequate) and the patient's (highly inadequate) usually is a preliminary indication of a false self organization.

It is also useful to form an opinion about the quality of the patient's social skills. While some bulimics may have interpersonal difficulties due to social skills deficits, clinical experience suggests that most are knowledgeable about proper interpersonal responses but inhibit themselves. Most bulimics appear to be exquisitely sensitive to the reactions of other people and fear angering them. Rather than risk anger or rejection, bulimics often inhibit their own responses. The end result is that they may avoid other people, often feel dissatisfied with their relationships, and may settle for poor relationships rather than risk assertiveness.

Overall, the initial interview should provide the therapist with some preliminary ideas of how the patient views herself and others and how these perceptions will affect her ability to engage in a therapeutic relationship.

COGNITIVE STYLE AND DEFENSIVE ADAPTATIONS

It is also useful to observe the patient's cognitive style during the interview. How concrete is her thinking? Does she present in an obsessive, ruminative manner, or are her responses impulsive, diffuse, and impressionistic? What is her capacity for introspection? To what extent can she decenter from herself and view her behavior from a broader perspective? In addition to assessing the overall cognitive style, it is also important to evaluate the extent to which the patient has the cognitive distortions characteristic of eating-disordered patients that we reviewed earlier.

Understanding the patient's defensive mode is helpful in anticipating what type of therapeutic strategy will be necessary for her to tolerate and profit from treatment. Defenses should be assessed in four main categories.

Denial. To what extent does the patient acknowledge that there is difficulty in her or the family system? Patients who present with high denial are often in treatment nonvoluntarily and are at high risk for noncompliance and dropping out of treatment.

Avoidance of Affect. Patients who are in conflict or frightened of various affects will utilize a variety of avoidant defenses, which include suppression, repression, disassociation, distraction, splitting, and intellectualization.

Projective Identification. Projective identification (Klein, 1946; Ogden, 1979; Tansey and Burke, 1985) is an interactional process whereby an individual unconsciously communicates her experiential state by eliciting thoughts and feelings within another individual that resemble her own. For example, a patient who is feeling enraged may behave in a way that provokes similarly rageful feelings in the therapist. When working with a patient using this defensive adaptation, therapists must be alert to their own reactions as ways to understand the patient's inner experience.

Oppositionality. To what extent does the patient need to undo, resist, or customize a treatment intervention? It is important to be aware that any intervention, but direct interventions especially, are likely to provoke oppositionality, or the patient will transform the intervention in some unique way that reflects her need to feel in control.

In chapter 5 we defined the differences in characterological features between borderline and false self/narcissistic patients, and restricting and bulimic modes of behaviors within these groups. We suggested that there is a primary difference of paranoid versus hysterical cognitive/defensive style. This is an important distinction to look for during the initial evaluation. Among patients with a predominantly paranoid-obsessive style, suspiciousness, hypervigilance to details, rumination, phobic concerns, projection, and distancing will be observed. Among the patients with hysterical styles, diffuseness, impulsivity, franticness, quick attachment, and idealization will be seen.

FAMILY CHARACTERISTICS

It is important to explore family issues for several reasons. Foremost, it is necessary to rule out whether the patient's symptomatic behavior is serving some adaptive function within the family system. Second, delineation of structural and communication style within the family should influence the treatment approach chosen. For example, more active and directive modes of therapy would be indicated for patients from disengaged and chaotic family milieus, and less active styles of treatment would be indicated for patients from enmeshed and overprotective families.

In general, the quality of relationships among family members should be investigated. This can usually be accomplished by asking the patient to describe her parents and what her family is like. We try to assess the family's cohesiveness, communication style, method of conflict resolution and behavior control, and the patient's role.

Cohesiveness. Cohesiveness refers to the quantity and quality of involvement within the family system. Assessing cohesiveness within the family is important because either under- or overinvolvement of family members can result in self-regulatory deficits.

A crucial factor affecting cohesiveness is the nature of the boundaries that exist among different family members. Boundaries refer to the rules that govern interpersonal issues, such as distance versus intimacy and autonomy versus symbiosis. Weak, porous boundaries among family members usually result in enmeshed family systems, which are characterized by extreme forms of closeness and intensity in family interaction. There is usually a high degree of overprotectiveness, which results in poor differentiation and an incapacity for independent self-regulation. Bulimic patients from enmeshed family systems are often quite phobic and dependent. The food-related behavior is often a desperate attempt to regulate themselves in the absence of external caretakers. Disengaged families represent the opposite end of a continuum of boundaries and cohesiveness. Within disengaged families, boundaries are overdefined and insensitive, which results in a lack of feeling of "connectedness" or meaningful involvement with others. Bulimic patients from disengaged families are often withdrawn and have had to develop autonomy prematurely. The deficits these patients experience in their ability to regulate themselves occur as a result of under- rather than overinvolvement.

Communication Style. Communication style relates to how the family exchanges information. Are messages directly and clearly expressed with appropriate affect, or are they displaced and affectively impoverished?

There are three characteristic communication problems within families of eating-disordered patients that should be investigated during the assessment.

The first problem can be termed disqualification and disconfirmation, which involve patients learning that expression of their thoughts and feelings is inaccurate or not valued. Another problem is incongruence and shifting of focus, which are narcissistically oriented communication styles that result in individuals withdrawing from efforts to communicate because it is an empty or disorganizing experience. The final problem is double-binding, which occurs when a patient is given mutually exclusive messages. This type of communication often results in anxious conflict and feelings of being trapped, paralyzed, and hopeless.

Problems in communication such as these often result in individuals having difficulty identifying and clearly articulating internal states, which, as we have emphasized, is characteristically troublesome for many bulimic patients. Consequently, the extent to which communication style has contributed to the eating disorder should be assessed.

Conflict Resolution. Many eating-disordered patients come from family systems in which they have not been given adequate tools to navigate interpersonal and intrapsychic conflict when it arises. It is important to assess whether patients have learned to openly acknowledge and accurately identify conflicts or whether they have learned to deny, avoid, and displace dysphoric events in an effort to maintain family homeostasis. It is also necessary to assess whether the patient has been criticized, rejected, or personally attacked as a result of expressing conflict. Many bulimic patients feel intimidated by or nonassertive in conflicts and attempt to resolve them through food-related behavior. Once again it is important to assess how the familial style of conflict resolution has affected the patient's feeling of freedom to express conflict.

Behavior Control. It is useful to assess what patterns the family has adopted for rewarding and punishing behavior. More specifically, is the family organized around clearly stated rules and are punishments logical consequences for rules that are broken? Are rules rigidly enforced, thus contributing to a type of all-or-none thinking? Are rules absent and chaotic in a way that perhaps contributes to a patient's impoverished sense of internal control and subsequent vulnerability to impulsive behavior? Finally, does the family system warmly compliment adequate performance, thus facilitating self-esteem, or does it highly criticize all efforts, thus undermining positive self-regard?

Roles. Roles refer to repetitive patterns of behavior by which individuals fulfill family functions. It is important to assess whether the patient serves a specific role within the family and what the demands of the role include. More specifically, is the role developmentally and structurally appropriate, or is it rigid or flexible? Are there demands to be overadequate or underadequate? To what extent does the role mesh with other family members' needs, and how satisfied is the individual with the role?

When assessing roles in the family system, it is especially important to identify what the developmental challenges are for each family member, particularly the identified patient and the parents. It is noteworthy that the age of risk for developing eating disorders is adolescence and young adulthood, a time when most parents are in or approaching midlife issues. Many conflictual issues and pathological resolutions can emerge in the family system at this time (Johnson and Irvin, 1983). Among eating-disordered patients, separation fears that are shared by both parents and child can be resolved by the child's assumption of a "sick role," thus binding her into the family system. Likewise, many eating-disordered patients have been delegated to maintain a certain appearance (thinness) to narcissistically gratify the parents, or to achieve at a high level and thus compensate for parental frustration over their own limited opportunities or successes. This latter role delegation is particularly important to assess because the age group and sex at risk for developing eating disorders— adolescent and young adult females—represent a cohort that has been exposed to multiple and often contradictory role expectations, as discussed in chapter 7.

MEDICAL ISSUES

Medical evaluation should be a routine part of the assessment. Investigating histories of major illness or recurrent illness, such as gastrointestinal problems, allergies, chronic pain, and so forth, can provide useful signals to the interviewer that the patient is more globally psychosomatic. We usually inquire if the patient has experienced any changes in her health since the onset of her eating difficulties. Common complaints include tiredness, weakness, feeling bloated, stomach pains, and dental problems.

GENERAL CONSIDERATIONS

During the evaluation a number of general areas are considered. These areas include life adjustment, capacity to be alone and to have fun, priorities and willingness to change, and motivation.

Life Adjustment. What is the overall quality of the patient's life? To what extent has the symptomatic behavior affected her work, daily activities, and interpersonal relationships?

Capacity to Be Alone. Given that most bulimic patients binge eat when they are alone, it can be quite useful to investigate how they feel about time alone. We have repeatedly observed two different types of difficulty with solitude that appear to reflect different degrees of intrapsychic structure. Among the group of patients with more severe self-regulatory difficulties, being alone is experienced as a highly anxious and disorganizing time when they feel lost, out of control, abandoned, and as though they are falling apart. Binge eating is used to create a predictable structure that is soothing. In contrast, among a group of patients who are obsessive and highly achievement oriented (neurotic), time alone provokes excessive rumination about the things they are supposed to do and the things that they have failed to accomplish. If they are in conflict about doing the task, or are exhausted by the relentless drive to accomplish, binge eating is often used as a mechanism to space out or distract themselves from the obsessive drive to achieve.

A more schizoid or false self group actively pursues time alone. It is seen as a relief from the demands of social intercourse. Binge eating alone becomes a time when patients can behave as they truly feel: needy and out of control.

Capacity to Have Fun. Does the patient have a concept of "fun" or letting go, and if so, what does she do to accomplish it? What is the breadth and quality of her involvement in hobbies or activities that give her pleasure? It has been our experience that many patients have abandoned previously pleasurable activities as they have become more enmeshed in bulimic behavior.

Priorities and Willingness to Change. Sometimes it is useful to ask a patient what her goals are and what is most important to her. This is a challenging and often threatening question for patients. False self and obsessional patients often offer a litany of socially appropriate goals, while patients with more diffuse psychological organizations are at a loss.

One question seems particularly informative regarding bulimics' priorities and willingness to change. We often ask purging patients: "Would you be willing to gain ten pounds in exchange for not having any more difficulty with binge eating, purging, or food preoccupation?" We explain that, in our experience, if the purging behavior is curtailed, binge eating often dramatically decreases in quantity and frequency. Interrupting the purging behavior restores some restraint, because the biological and psychological consequence of unrestrained eating (nausea, painful fullness, weight gain) cannot be avoided. There is, however, a risk of weight gain if the purging is suspended.

One group of patients assures us that they would rather be dead than gain ten pounds—the group who have experienced a Cinderella-like transformation as a result of losing weight. These women have either become upwardly mobile socioeconomically or their romantic-social life has improved significantly as they have achieved thinness. Their weight loss is usually accomplished by highly restrictive dieting, which cannot be maintained over a long period of time. Rather than return to what they experience as a "social isolation," which they feel would occur with weight gain, they begin to use various purging techniques so they can abandon the restrictive diets and yet maintain thinness. They are frightened of change, because they have actually experienced the social discrimination and alienation with which our culture stigmatizes overweight individuals, particularly females. Their dread of gaining ten pounds reflects an entrenched yet fragile psychological integration and is not a favorable prognostic indicator.

Motivation. Some patients are so endogenously depressed that they simply do not have the energy or motivation to challenge their disturbed eating behavior. It is often useful to treat these patients with antidepressant medication. Relief from the depression allows them to engage and respond to interventions aimed at the disturbed eating.

Other patients have developed learned helplessness. Learned helplessness (Seligman, 1975) is a construct that has emerged from work with laboratory animals exposed to repeated shocks without an opportunity for escape. After a prolonged period of time these animals will not use an escape even if it is provided. They develop a type of amotivational syndrome as a result of feeling trapped by their circumstances.

Like these animals, many bulimic patients experience a type of learned helplessness and feel hopelessly enmeshed in the binge/purge cycle. These patients have come to feel that there is little or no chance for escape. One important function the initial consultation can serve is to provide the hope that the symptomatic behavior can be managed, so that it will no longer seriously disrupt the patient's life. Preliminary evidence indicates that this initial intervention provides patients with sufficient motivation to reduce binge-eating episodes by up to 50 percent (Connors, Johnson, and Stuckey, 1984).

Summary

In most comprehensive treatment programs, the initial consultation serves a vital function. It is a delicate task with multiple demands. The clinician must obtain sufficient information to render a diagnosis; make treatment recommendations according to observed distinctions among patients; and quickly establish a therapeutic relationship with the patient that simultaneously challenges, supports, and offers hope. As our ability to accomplish these tasks in the initial consultation improves, so will our treatment effectiveness.

Diagnostic Survey for Eating Disorders—Revised

INSTRUCTIONS: This questionnaire covers several eating problems that may or may not apply to you. You may find it difficult to answer some questions if your eating pattern is irregular or has changed recently. Please read each question carefully and choose the answer that **best** describes your situation **most of the time**. Also, please feel free to write remarks in the margins if this will clarify your answer. Thank you.

Card 1
(Column)

Name

Social Security Number   (1–9)

Current Address

Permanent Address

Telephone   (Day)   (Night)

Date   (10–15)

Code   (16–21)

Identifying and Demographic Information

Card 1
(Column)

Sex   Male _____₁   Female _____₂   (22)

Age _____   (23–24)

Race (check one).

Caucasian _____₁   Black _____₂   Oriental _____₃   Hispanic _____₄

Other (Specify) _____   (25)

Your present religious affiliation (check one).

Protestant _____₁   Catholic _____₂   Jewish _____₃

No Affiliation _____₄   Other (Specify) _____   (26)

Card 1
(Column)

Religious affiliation of your family of origin (check one).

Protestant _____₁   Catholic _____₂   Jewish _____₃

No Affiliation _____₄   Other (Specify) _____   (27)

Marital status (check one).

Single _____₁   Married _____₂   Separated _____₃

Divorced _____₄   Widowed _____₅   (28)

Current occupation _____   (29)

Father's occupation _____   (30)

Mother's occupation _____   (31)

Spouse's occupation _____   (32)

Present primary role (check one).

Wage earner _____₁   Housewife/husband _____₂   Student _____₃

Other (Specify) _____   (33)

Current living arrangement (check one).   (34)

With parents or relatives	_____₁
Dorm or shared apartment with friend	_____₂
Conjugal (intimate relationship with one other person including spouse, boyfriend, girlfriend, etc.)	_____₃
Alone	_____₄

Highest level of education (check one for each person).   (35–38)

	Self	Father	Mother	Spouse
Completed post-graduate training	1 _____	_____	_____	_____
Some post-graduate training	2 _____	_____	_____	_____
Completed college, received four year academic degree	3 _____	_____	_____	_____
Some college, but didn't receive four year academic degree	4 _____	_____	_____	_____

Card 1
(Column)

	Self	Father	Mother	Spouse
Completed high school; may have attended or completed trade school or attended other non-academic training requiring high school completion	5———	———	———	———
Some high school	6———	———	———	———
Some grammar school	7———	———	———	———
No schooling	8———	———	———	———

Is your mother currently living?   Yes ———₁ No ———₂   (39)

Mother's age ———   (40–41)

What category best describes your mother's weight? (Circle one.)   (42)
(If no longer living, best described your mother's weight.)

1	2	3	4	5
very underweight	underweight	normal weight	overweight	very overweight

How preoccupied with food or weight is (was) your mother? (Circle one.)   (43)

1	2	3	4	5
not at all	somewhat	moderately	very much	extremely

Is your father currently living?   Yes ———₁ No ———₂   (44)

Father's age ———   (45–46)

What category best describes your father's weight? (Circle one.)   (47)
(If no longer living, best described your father's weight.)

1	2	3	4	5
very underweight	underweight	normal weight	overweight	very overweight

How preoccupied with food or weight is (was) your father? (Circle one.)   (48)

1	2	3	4	5
not at all	somewhat	moderately	very much	extremely

Number of brothers ———   (49–50)

Number of sisters ———   (51–52)

Do you have a twin brother or sister?   Yes ———₁ No ———₂   (53)

How many of your siblings are overweight?   ———   (54–55)

How many of your siblings are underweight?   ———   (56–57)

Weight History

			Card 1 (Column)
Current weight	___ lbs.		(58–60)
Current height	___ inches		(61–62)
Desired weight	___ lbs.		(63–65)

Adult Years

Highest adult weight since age 18	___ lbs.	at age ___	(66–70)
Lowest adult weight since age 18	___ lbs.	at age ___	(71–75)
How long did you remain at your lowest adult weight?	___ days ___ weeks ___ months		(76–79) (80) = 1 Card 2 (Column)

Adolescent Years

Highest weight between ages 12–18	___ lbs.	at age ___	(22–26)
Lowest weight between ages 12–18	___ lbs.	at age ___ ___ inches	(27–33)

Using the scale below, please select the number which indicates your perception of your weight during the following years:

1	2	3	4	5
extremely thin	somewhat thin	normal weight	somewhat overweight	extremely overweight

6–12 years old ___   (34)

12–18 years old ___   (35)

18–30 years old ___   (36)

30 and over ___   (37)

As a child were you teased about your weight? (Check yes or no.)

Underweight	Yes ___₁	No ___₂	(38)
Overweight	Yes ___₁	No ___₂	(39)
No weight problems as a child	Yes ___₁	No ___₂	(40)

To what extent were you teased? (Circle one.)

1	2	3	4	5	(41)
never	rarely	sometimes	often	always	

Are you in an occupation that requires you to maintain a certain weight?

Yes ___₁   No ___₂   (42)

Card 2
(Column)

Are you in a food-related occupation?   Yes _____₁ No _____₂   (43)

Has there ever been a time when your feelings about yourself or your social
life changed substantially as a result of weight changes? (Check one.)   (44)

Yes, <u>improved</u> when <u>lost</u> weight   _____₁

Yes, <u>improved</u> when <u>gained</u> weight   _____₂

Yes, <u>worse</u> when <u>lost</u> weight   _____₃

Yes, <u>worse</u> when <u>gained</u> weight   _____₄

No change   _____₅

How satisfied are you with the way your body is proportioned? (Check one.)   (45)

1	2	3	4	5
not at all satisfied	slightly satisfied	moderately satisfied	very satisfied	extremely satisfied

Please indicate on the scales below how you feel about the different areas of your body.
(Circle one.)

	Strongly Positive	Moderately Positive	Neutral	Moderately Negative	Strongly Negative	
Face	1	2	3	4	5	(46)
Arms	1	2	3	4	5	(47)
Shoulders	1	2	3	4	5	(48)
Breasts	1	2	3	4	5	(49)
Stomach	1	2	3	4	5	(50)
Buttocks	1	2	3	4	5	(51)
Thighs	1	2	3	4	5	(52)

At your current weight, how fat do you feel? (Circle one.)   (53)

1	2	3	4	5
not at all fat	somewhat fat	moderately fat	very much fat	extremely fat

During the past month, on the average, how many times have you weighed
yourself or measured your body size? _____ number of times/per week.   (54–55)

Using the scale below, please indicate the intensity of your feelings while you   (56–75)
are in the <u>process</u> of <u>gaining</u> weight.   (80) = 2

1	2	3	4	5
not at all	somewhat	moderately	very much	extremely

Independent _____   Confused about my thoughts/
                           feelings _____

Not sexual _____   Calm _____

Being my own person _____ Special _____

Helpless _____   Strong _____

Confused about who I am _____   Unsuccessful _____

Popular _____   Childlike _____

Self-assured _____   Rebellious _____

Sexually appealing _____   In control _____

Alone _____   Living up to others' expectations _____

Abandoned _____   Empty _____

Using the scale below, please indicate the intensity of your feelings while you are in the <u>process</u> of <u>losing</u> weight.

1	2	3	4	5
not at all	somewhat	moderately	very much	extremely

Independent _____   Confused about my thoughts/
                           feelings _____

Not sexual _____   Calm _____

Being my own person _____ Special _____

Helpless _____   Strong _____

Confused about who I am _____   Unsuccessful _____

Popular _____   Childlike _____

Self-assured _____   Empty _____

Abandoned _____   Rebellious _____

Sexually appealing _____   In control _____

Alone _____   Living up to others' expectations _____

Dieting Behavior

Have you ever been on a diet?   (42)

    Yes _____₁   No _____₂

Card 3
(Column)

At what age did you begin to restrict your food intake due to concern over your body size?

(43–44)

_____ years old

In your first year of dieting, how many times did you start a diet?

(45–47)

_____ number of times

Over the last year how often have you begun a diet?

(48–50)

_____ number of times

Using the scale below, please indicate how often you use the following behaviors as a way to diet.

(51–58)

1	2	3	4	5
never	rarely	sometimes	often	always

Skip meals _____   Reduce portions _____

Completely fast _____   Go on fad diets _____

Restrict carbohydrates _____   Reduce calories _____

Restrict fats _____   Diet camps/spas _____

Please indicate which physical symptoms you have experienced since the onset of your eating problems.

(59–73)

(80) = 3

	Yes_1	No_2		Yes_1	No_2
Sore throat	____	____	Water/fluid retention	____	____
Weakness/ tiredness	____	____	Dental problems	____	____
Seizures	____	____	Hair loss	____	____
Feeling bloated	____	____	Growth of fine downy hair	____	____
Stomach pains	____	____	Overly sensitive to noise, light, or touch	____	____
Feeling cold	____	____			
Dizziness	____	____	Muscle spasms	____	____
Redness of eyes	____	____	Other (specify) _____		
Swollen glands (e.g., under jaw)	____	____			

Card 4
(Column)

Using the scale below, please indicate how often the following people have encouraged you to diet.

(22–31)

1	2	3	4	5
never	rarely	sometimes	often	always

Boyfriend _____   Sister _____

Girlfriend _____   Employer _____

Mother _____   Teacher/coach _____

Father _____   Child _____

Brother _____   Doctor _____

Using the scale below, indicate how characteristic the following statement is
of you. "I have an intense fear of becoming fat, which does not lessen as I
lose weight." (Circle one.)   (32)

1	2	3	4	5
not at all characteristic	somewhat characteristic	moderately characteristic	very characteristic	extremely characteristic

---

Binge Eating Behavior

Have you ever had an episode of eating a large amount of food in a short space
of time (an eating binge)?   (33)

Yes _____₁   No _____₂

Please circle on the scales below, how characteristic the following symptoms are of your
eating binge.

	Never	Rarely	Sometimes	Often	Always	
I consume a large amount of food during a binge	1	2	3	4	5	(34)
I eat very rapidly	1	2	3	4	5	(35)
I feel out of control when I eat	1	2	3	4	5	(36)
I feel miserable or annoyed after a binge	1	2	3	4	5	(37)
I get uncontrollable urges to eat and eat until I feel physically ill	1	2	3	4	5	(38)
I binge eat alone	1	2	3	4	5	(39)
I binge eat with others	1	2	3	4	5	(40)

Card 4
(Column)

How long does a binge episode usually last? (Check one.)   (41)

    Less than one hour   ———₁

    1–2 hours   ———₂

    More than 2 hours   ———₃

Using the scale below, please indicate how likely you are to binge eat during these times/at these places.   (42–51)

1	2	3	4	5
never	rarely	sometimes	often	always

8–12 am _____   8–12 midnight _____   Car _____

12–4 pm _____   After midnight _____   Party _____

4–8 pm _____   Work _____   Restaurant _____

    Home _____   Other (specify) _____

How old were you when you began binge eating?   (52–53)

_____ years old

How long did you have a problem with binge eating?   (54–57)

_____ days _____ months _____ years

What is the longest period you have had <u>without binge eating</u> since the onset of the problem?   (58–60)

_____ days _____ months _____ years

Using the scale below, please indicate the degree to which the following circumstances have helped you to <u>not</u> binge eat for that period of time.   (61–72)   (80) = 4

1	2	3	4	5	6
not at all helpful	somewhat helpful	helpful	very helpful	extremely helpful	not applicable

Began dieting _____   Started exercising _____

Sought professional help _____   Began romantic relationship _____

Left romantic relationship _____   Developed illness _____

Left home _____   Divorce _____

Marriage _____   Pregnancy _____

Work _____   Vacation _____

Other: Please specify _____

Using the scale below, please indicate how nervous you feel when eating the following foods.

1	2	3	4	5
never	rarely	sometimes	often	always

Bread/cereal/pasta _____   Eggs _____

Dairy products
(cheese, yogurt) _____   Fruit _____

Meat _____   Snacks _____

Fish _____   Sweets _____

Poultry _____   Vegetables _____

Using the scale below, please indicate how often you eat the following foods when <u>not</u> bingeing.

(32–41)

1	2	3	4	5
never	rarely	sometimes	often	always

Bread/cereal/pasta _____   Eggs _____

Dairy products
(cheese, yogurt) _____   Fruit _____

Meat _____   Snacks _____

Fish _____   Sweets _____

Poultry _____   Vegetables _____

Using the list below, please check which events, either positive or negative, preceded or coincided with the onset of your eating problems. (Check all that apply.)

(42–54)

	Yes₁	No₂		Yes₁	No₂
Death of significant other	___	___	Illness or injury to family member or significant other	___	___
Teasing about appearance	___	___	Problems in romantic relationship	___	___
Marriage	___	___	Family problems	___	___
Leaving home	___	___	Prolonged period of dieting	___	___
Illness or injury to family	___	___	Pregnancy	___	___
Failure at school or work	___	___	Work transition	___	___
Difficult sexual experience	___	___	Other (Please specify)	_____	

Using the scale below, please select the number which indicates the intensity of each of the following feelings <u>before</u> a binge.

(55–70)

(80) = 5

1	2	3	4	5
extremely intense	very intense	moderately intense	slightly intense	not at all intense

Calm _____   Bored _____

Empty _____   Frustrated _____

Confused _____   Panicked _____

Excited _____   Relieved _____

Angry _____   Guilty _____

Spaced out _____   Depressed _____

Inadequate _____   Nervous _____

Disgusted _____   Other (Please specify) _____

Lonely _____

Using the scale below, please state the number which indicates the intensity of each of the following feelings <u>after</u> a binge.

1	2	3	4	5
extremely intense	very intense	moderately intense	slightly intense	not at all intense

Calm _____   Bored _____

Empty _____   Frustrated _____

Confused _____   Panicked _____

Excited _____   Relieved _____

Angry _____   Guilty _____

Spaced out _____   Depressed _____

Inadequate _____   Nervous _____

Disgusted _____   Other (Please specify) _____

Lonely _____

Have you noticed a relationship between the frequency of your binge eating and your menstrual cycle?

(38)

Yes _____₁   No _____₂

If yes, please indicate when during your cycle you feel most vulnerable to binge eat. (Check one.)

(39)

During menstruation   ———1

11–14 days prior to menstruation   ———2

7–10 days prior to menstruation   ———3

3–6 days prior to menstruation   ———4

1–2 days prior to menstruation   ———5

After menstruation   ———6

How uncomfortable are you with your binge eating behavior? (Circle one.)   (40)

1	2	3	4	5
extremely uncomfortable	very uncomfortable	uncomfortable	somewhat uncomfortable	not at all uncomfortable

How willing would you be to gain 10 pounds in exchange for not binge eating anymore? (Circle one.)   (41)

1	2	3	4	5
extremely willing	very willing	willing	somewhat willing	not at all willing

---

Purging Behavior

Have you ever vomited (or spit out food) after eating in order to get rid of the food?

(42)

Yes ———1   No ———2

How old were you when you induced vomiting (or spit out food) for the first time?

(43–44)

——— years old

How long have you been using self-induced vomiting (or spitting out food)?   (45–48)

——— days   ——— months   ——— years

If you have ever tried to induce vomiting (or spitting out food) but decided to discontinue, please indicate the reasons for this.   (49–52)

	Yes₁	No₂
Physically unable to induce vomiting	———	———
Afraid of choking	———	———
Too unpleasant	———	———

Card 6
(Column)

Yes₁   No₂

Concerned about my health   _____ _____

Other (Please specify) _____

Have you ever used laxatives to control your weight or "get rid of food?"   (53)

Yes _____₁ No _____₂

How old were you when you first took laxatives for weight control?   (54–55)

_____ years

How long have you been using laxatives for weight control?   (56–59)

_____ days _____ months _____ years

What is the average number of laxatives that you use?   (60–62)

per day _____ or per week _____

Using the scale below, please select the number which indicates the intensity   (63–78)
of each of the following feelings <u>before</u> a purge.   (80) = 6

1	2	3	4	5
extremely intense	very intense	intense	slightly intense	not at all intense

Calm _____   Bored _____

Empty _____   Frustrated _____

Confused _____   Panicked _____

Excited _____   Relieved _____

Angry _____   Guilty _____

Spaced out _____   Depressed _____

Inadequate _____   Nervous _____

Disgusted _____   Other (Please
                        specify) _____
Lonely _____

Using the scale below, please select the number which indicates the intensity of   Card 7
each of the following feelings <u>after</u> a purge.   (Column)
    (22–37)

1	2	3	4	5
extremely intense	very intense	intense	slightly intense	not at all intense

Calm _____   Bored _____

Empty _____   Frustrated _____

Confused _____   Panicked _____

Excited _____   Relieved _____

Angry _____   Guilty _____

Spaced out _____   Depressed _____

Inadequate _____   Nervous _____

Disgusted _____   Other (Please
                          specify) _____

Lonely _____

Over the last month, what has been the average number of times you have
engaged in the following behaviors per week?

	Average number per week	
Binge eating	_____	(38–40)
Vomiting	_____	(41–43)
Use of laxatives	_____	(44–45)
Use of diet pills	_____	(46–47)
Use of enemas	_____	(48–49)
Fasting (skipping meals for an entire day)	_____	(50–52)

Over the past month, what has been average number of days per week that you have not
engaged in the following behaviors?

	Average number per week	
Binge eating	_____	(53)
Vomiting	_____	(54)
Use of laxatives	_____	(55)
Use of diet pills	_____	(56)
Use of enemas	_____	(57)
Fasting (skipping meals for an entire day)	_____	(58)

Over the past month, on the average, how many times per week have you
been able to eat a regular meal and not compensate in some way (i.e., fasting,
vomiting, using diuretics, laxatives, exercise)?   (59–60)

_____ number of times per week.

Exercise

Card 7
(Column)

How many minutes a day do you currently exercise (including going on walks, riding bicycle, etc.)?   (61–63)

_____ minutes.

Have you ever been involved in serious training in any of the following activities? (Check as many as are applicable.)

	Yes$_1$	No$_2$	
Distance running	____	____	(64)
Weight lifting	____	____	(65)
Dancing	____	____	(66)
Gymnastics	____	____	(67)
Wrestling	____	____	(68)
Swimming	____	____	(69)
Modeling	____	____	(70)
Tennis	____	____	(71)
Other (Specify)			

_____

_____

Other Behavior

Do you feel that you have or have ever had an alcohol or drug abuse problem? (Circle one.)   (72)

1	2	3	4	5
not at all	somewhat	moderate	very much	extremely

Please indicate how frequently you have used the following substances since the onset of your eating problem.

Alcohol (Specify type)	Amount	Daily$_5$	Weekly$_4$	Monthly$_3$	Less than monthly$_2$	Never$_1$	
_____	____	____	____	____	____	____	(73)
Amphetamines (uppers)	____	____	____	____	____	____	(74)
Barbiturates (downers)	____	____	____	____	____	____	(75)
Hallucinogens	____	____	____	____	____	____	(76)

Card 7
(Column)

Marijuana   —— —— —— —— —— —— (77)

Tranquilizers   —— —— —— —— —— —— (78)

Cocaine   —— —— —— —— —— —— (79)

(80) = 7
Card 8
(Column)

Cigarettes none——₁ 0 to ½ pack/day ——₂
1 pack/day ——₃ more than 1 pack/day ——₄   (22)

Have you ever made a suicide attempt? (Check one.)   (23)

No   ——₁

Yes, 1–2 times   ——₂

Yes, 3–5 times   ——₃

Yes, more than 5 times   ——₄

Have you ever tried to physically hurt yourself (i.e., cut yourself, hit yourself
with the intent to hurt, burn yourself with cigarettes)? (Check one.)   (24)

No   ——₁

Yes, 1–2 times   ——₂

Yes, 3–5 times   ——₃

Yes, more than 5 times   ——₄

Have you ever stolen items related to eating or weight (i.e., laxatives, food,
etc.)? (Check one.)   (25)

No   ——₁

Yes, 1–2 times   ——₂

Yes, 3–5 times   ——₃

Yes, more than 5 times   ——₄

Have you ever stolen other types of items? (Check one.)   (26)

No   ——₁

Yes, 1–2 times   ——₂

Yes, 3–5 times   ——₃

Yes, more than 5 times   ——₄

Sexual History

Have you ever engaged in sexual intercourse?   (27)

Yes ——₁ No ——₂

Card 8
(Column)

If your answer is yes, at what age did you first engage in sexual intercourse?   (28–29)

Age _____

Have you ever engaged in masturbation?   (30)

Yes _____₁   No _____₂

If your answer is yes at what age did you first engage in masturbation?   (31–32)

Age _____

Please indicate on the line below your interest in sex before the onset of your
eating problem. (Circle one.)   (33)

1	2	3	4	5
not interested	somewhat interested	interested	very interested	extremely interested

Please indicate on the scale below whether there has been a change in your
sexual interest since the onset of your eating problem. (Circle one.)   (34)

1	2	3	4	5
not interested	somewhat interested	interested	very interested	extremely interested

How satisfied are you with the quality of your current sexual activity?
(Circle one.)   (35)

1	2	3	4	5
not at all satisfied	somewhat satisfied	satisfied	very satisfied	extremely satisfied

Please check your sexual preference. (Check one.)   (36)

Exclusively heterosexual   _____₁

Primarily heterosexual, some
homosexual   _____₂

Bisexual   _____₃

Primarily homosexual, some
heterosexual   _____₄

Exclusively homosexual   _____₅

Asexual (no sexual preference)   _____₆

Autosexual (prefer masturbation to
sexual relations with others)   _____₇

Menstrual History

How old were you when you first started menstruating? (If you have never
had your period, please mark 00.)   (37–38)

_____ years old

Do you have menstrual periods now? (Check one.)   (39)

    Yes, regularly each month   ————₁

    Yes, but I skip a month once in a while   ————₂

    Yes, but not very often (for example, once in six months)   ————₃

    No, I have not had a period in at least the last six months   ————₄

How long has it been since you last menstruated? (If you regularly
menstruate, please mark 00.)   (40–41)

    ————— months

How much did you weigh when you stopped menstruating?   (42–44)

    ————— lbs.

Medical and Psychiatric History

Have you had any serious medical difficulties?   (45)

    Yes ———₁ No ———₂

Are you currently on any medications? Yes ———₁ No ———₂   (46)

    If yes, please identify _____

Have you ever taken psychiatric medications? Yes ———₁ No ———₂ (47)

    If yes, please identify _____

Have you ever been hospitalized for eating or emotional problems?   (48)

    Yes ———₁ No ———₂

If yes, then complete the following:

	Most recent	Second prior	Third prior	Fourth prior	
Date admitted	————	————	————	————	
Date discharged	————	————	————	————	
Duration (months)	————	————	————	————	(49–64)
Age	————	————	————	————	(65–72)
Primary reason for admission*	————	————	————	————	(73–76)

* Use number code: 1 = bulimia; 2 = anorexia nervosa; 3 = chemical dependency;
4 = depression; 5 = psychotic disorder other than depression; 6 = other

Have you ever been treated as an outpatient for eating or emotional problems
(i.e., a logically continuous series of treatments)?   (77)

    Yes ———₁ No ———₂   (80) = 8

If yes, then complete the following:

	Most recent	Second prior	Third prior	Fourth prior	
Date began	———	———	———	———	
Date last visit of series	———	———	———	———	
Duration (months)	———	———	———	———	(22–37)
Age	———	———	———	———	(38–45)
Primary reason for treatment*	———	———	———	———	(46–49)

* Use number code: 1 = bulimia; 2 = anorexia nervosa; 3 = chemical dependency; 4 = depression; 5 = psychotic disorder other than depression; 6 = other.

	Most recent	Second prior	Third prior	Fourth prior	
Please indicate the types of treatment you have been involved in†	———	———	———	———	(50–61)

† Use code number: 1 = individual psychotherapy; 2 = group psychotherapy; 3 = psychiatric medications.

Please circle on the scale below how frequently you experience the following symptoms:

	Never	Rarely	Sometimes	Often	Always	
Extreme sadness	1	2	3	4	5	(62)
Anxiety	1	2	3	4	5	(63)
Difficulty getting up in the morning	1	2	3	4	5	(64)
Crying episodes	1	2	3	4	5	(65)
Irritability	1	2	3	4	5	(66)
Tiredness	1	2	3	4	5	(67)
Difficulty falling asleep	1	2	3	4	5	(68)
Wide mood fluctuation	1	2	3	4	5	(69)

Life Adjustment

Please circle on the scale below the quality of your relationship with each of the following persons:

Card 9
(Column)

	Terrible	Poor	Fair	Good	Excel-lent	Not applicable	
Mother	1	2	3	4	5	9	(70)
Father	1	2	3	4	5	9	(71)
Spouse/significant other	1	2	3	4	5	9	(72)
Male friends	1	2	3	4	5	9	(73)
Female friends	1	2	3	4	5	9	(74)
Children (if applicable)	1	2	3	4	5	9	(75)

(80) = 9
Card 10
(Column)

Please circle on the scale below how much your eating problems interfere with the following areas:

	Never	Rarely	Sometimes	Often	Always	
Work/school	1	2	3	4	5	(22)
Daily activities (other than work)	1	2	3	4	5	(23)
Thoughts	1	2	3	4	5	(24)
Feelings about myself	1	2	3	4	5	(25)
Personal relationships	1	2	3	4	5	(26)

Over the past month, on the average, what percentage of your time each day have you been preoccupied with thoughts of food, weight, and/or eating? (Circle one.)

(27–29)
(79–80) = 10

0%	10%	20%	30%	40%	50%	60%	70%	80%	90%	100%

Not at all   Half the time   All the time

Family History

Have any of your first degree relatives had any of the following problems?   Card 11
(First degree relatives include children, brothers, sisters, parents.)   (Column)

	Number of persons	Relationship to you (e.g. sister)	Require Outpatient Care? (If yes, check below)	Require Hospital- ization? (If yes, check below)	
Ulcers	22–23	24–28	29	30	
Colitis	31–32	33–37	38	39	
Asthma	40–41	42–46	47	48	
Depression	49–50	51–55	56	57	
Manic- depressive	58–59	60–64	65	66	
Schizophrenia	67–68	69–73	74	75	(79–80) = 11
Paranoid thinking	Card 12 22–23	24–28	29	30	
Hallucinations	31–32	33–37	38	39	
Obesity	40–41	42–46	47	48	
Alcohol	49–50	51–55	56	57	
Drug abuse	58–59	60–64	65	66	
Severe anxiety	67–68	69–73	74	75	(79–80) = 12
Phobias	Card 13 22–23	24–28	29	30	
Bulimia	31–32	33–37	38	39	
Anorexia nervosa	40–41	42–46	47	48	
Suicide attempts	49–50	51–55	56	57	(79–80) = 13

NOTE: Johnson, C., "Initial Consultation for Patients with Bulimia and Anorexia Nervosa," in *Handbook of Psychotherapy for Anorexia Nervosa and Bulimia,* ed. D. Garner and P. Garfinkel, New York: Guilford Press, pp. 19–51.

9

Treatment Recommendations

After the initial evaluation the therapist needs to make treatment recommendations. In this chapter we discuss a variety of different treatment modalities. In subsequent chapters we present a detailed review of the outcome studies from various modalities, suggested tools for symptom management, and comments on special treatment issues.

Vulnerability to Overdiagnosis

Over the last several years we have become increasingly concerned about the possibility of overdiagnosing eating disorders. In a culture that has recently been inundated with information about anorexia nervosa and bulimia, we as clinicians must carefully avoid premature labeling of eating difficulties or body-related problems as clinical syndromes of anorexia nervosa or bulimia. We must keep in mind that control issues about eating behaviors, peculiar food preferences, chaotic eating patterns, and body dissatisfaction are often normal developmental occurrences, particularly among adolescents. If therapists prematurely diagnose or label a behavior as a clinical syndrome, they run the risk of treating the person as an eating-disordered patient, thus establishing and consolidating within the individual a particular patient identity.

The vulnerability of anorexia nervosa and bulimia to premature labeling is especially high now. Recent media attention has created significant awareness among parents and the community about these disorders, which have historically been obscure. While increased community awareness certainly facilitates early detection, too much exposure may generate a hyperconcern among parents regarding behaviors that may be normal deviations or transient disturbances.

CASE: *INAPPROPRIATE DIAGNOSIS OF AN EATING DISORDER*

Darlene. Seventeen-year-old Darlene, from a lower-class family, was referred to the Eating Disorders Program at Northwestern Memorial Hospital for evaluation by a medical floor social worker at a nearby children's hospital. The social worker's concern was that Darlene had lost about fifteen pounds over the previous several months (previous weight 105, current weight 90 pounds; height five feet three inches). Six months earlier Darlene had an emergency kidney transplant. She had apparently handled the surgery well and had not begun to lose the weight until four months afterward. The weight loss surprised the staff because she was taking steroids, which usually promote weight gain.

Darlene was brought to the evaluation by both of her parents. She displayed no resistance or unwillingness to attend the consultation. She presented as a somewhat shy but attentive adolescent. It became clear early that Darlene did not manifest the drive for thinness, body distortion, feelings of ineffectiveness, denial of illness, food preoccupation, or social withdrawal that is usually characteristic of anorexia nervosa.

She had obviously been terrified of the surgery despite her brave handling of the situation. When asked what prompted the weight loss, she said that after the surgery, the insertion of the new kidney and the resultant swelling created a bulge on one side of her upper abdomen. The bulge was unsettling to her at both a cosmetic and intrapsychic level. In a somewhat concrete manner she felt that if she ate less the bulge would go away. In talking with her I (C.J.) was surprised that no one had spoken with her about her feelings regarding the intrusion in her body. Since the hospital staff had noticed her weight loss, her mother had begun to push food at her, which annoyed Darlene.

After speaking with Darlene I visited with her parents. Immediately after entering the office the father began to explain in a tearful manner that he was a general contractor who had been out of work over the last several months. He painfully explained that the whole family had lost weight because there had not been enough to eat. It was clear that he was very ashamed of the situation and that he cared a great deal about his family (he had been his daughter's kidney donor). Overall the family appeared intact with reasonably concerned parents.

In this instance the treatment team felt that an eating disorders diagnosis was certainly premature and that therapy in a specialized treatment program was not only unnecessary but contraindicated. One could already begin to sense that with the suggestion by others of eating disturbance (illness), the mother had begun to engage in watchful and managing be-havior that was likely to eventually provoke oppositional behavior in her daughter. The risk that the expression of oppositionality would be food- or body-related was high since that was the area of focus between them.

Our treatment recommendation was that Darlene be followed at the children's hospital, and that her weight should be monitored but that the focus of therapy with her should be her thoughts and feelings about her body since the surgery. We also recommended to the mother that she decrease her concern and vigilance around her daughter's eating and weight-related behavior.

Inpatient Versus Outpatient Treatment

Throughout this book we have emphasized the multidetermined nature of bulimia. Thus comprehensive programs should have access to a variety of treatment modalities, including individual, group, family and marital psychotherapy; pharmacotherapy; nutritional counseling; and medical consultation. While we rely heavily on outpatient intervention, an inpatient unit is also an integral part of our program.

Our inpatient unit consists of ten beds that are used exclusively for eating-disordered patients. The staff has been recruited specifically for work with these patients. The overall focus is milieu treatment with a specific emphasis on tailoring the intervention to the unique needs of each patient.

We are generally slow to hospitalize and try to exhaust all outpatient possibilities before recommending hospitalization. We have found it pref-erable to work with bulimic patients on mastering self-regulatory and life management problems in the actual settings in which they are having difficulty. In our experience, when this patient population is placed in a highly structured and supportive inpatient environment, they immediately do quite well. Unfortunately, many patients quickly relapse when dis-charged to their regular living environment. Consequently, when bulimic patients are hospitalized, we are careful to focus on discharge planning early in the hospital stay. The guidelines we use to recommend hospital-ization include: significant medical difficulty; significant risk of suicide or self-mutilation, or demonstrated inability to provide self-care; inability of family or current living arrangement to provide an adequate psychological environment for improvement to occur; the need to facilitate a complex differential diagnosis; and, on occasion, the need to interrupt the binge/ purge cycle.

Individual Psychotherapy

In our outpatient program, the individual therapist usually serves as team leader for the patient. This means that he or she is responsible for receiving information from different members of the treatment team, integrating the information into some meaningful perspective on the treatment needs of the patient, and then ensuring that the team is informed of the progress of the treatment strategy. We expect the individual therapist to have the broadest perspective on the patient. Although treatment decisions are most often made through a team process in both the inpatient and outpatient settings, in the outpatient clinic the individual therapist is responsible for final decisions. In contrast, final decisions regarding case management on the inpatient service rest with the unit chief. This difference reflects our emphasis on the importance of the milieu factors on treatment in the inpatient setting.

Obviously the individual therapist's task is demanding. While there is no generic way of doing psychotherapy, several important perspectives can help guide therapists. Effective psychotherapy for us means being able to successfully create an interpersonal environment for patients that allows them to make use of a range of different adaptive tools to manage their lives. It is our belief that it is good relationships, not good techniques, that are curative. We also recognize, however, that sophisticated training and understanding of technique facilitates the development of positive therapeutic relationships.

The term technique refers to the particular strategy the therapist adopts to help the patient make use of the therapeutic relationship. Consistent with our thinking throughout this book, any strategy or approach to the patient's problems should evolve through a thorough evaluation of the biological, familial, developmental, and sociocultural factors that have predisposed that individual toward maladaptive relationships and behaviors.

Therapists' initial task is to respond to the patient in a way that communicates that they are invested in learning, along with her, how she experiences the world and what can be done to improve her life. This is particularly true regarding her preoccupation with food, weight, and her body. We teach our therapists a dual perspective. We expect them to have a sophisticated understanding of various behavioral and didactic tools that can be used to manage symptoms (see chapter 10). We also emphasize, however, that the *art* of effective intervention is the constant awareness and processing with patients of how they are experiencing the therapist's actions. The individual psychotherapist should be able to use directive, symptom-focused interventions when indicated and also be able to analyze transference. This contrasts with some psychotherapists' belief that a therapist's active intervention precludes the possibility of analyzing transference. It has been our experience that a concerned offering of tools that have been helpful to other patients facilitates the analysis of transference by more quickly focusing the patient's characteristic responses and resistances to actions in relationships. Once again, the key to effectively balancing symptom management with the analysis of transference is that the therapist maintain the perspective that the action he or she is engaging in with the patient will inevitably, if not immediately, create reactions in the patient. It is the careful and persistent scrutiny of patients' reactions that facilitates the therapeutic alliance and allows "working through" to occur.

Directive interventions the therapist uses include a range of techniques and information, including meal planning, goal setting, self-monitoring, and the exploration of alternative self-regulatory behaviors. In chapter 10 we detail information and different techniques that are useful for therapists and patients to know.

In chapters 5 and 11 we also describe in more detail some common transference and countertransference issues that therapists encounter in their work with eating-disordered patients.

Group Treatment

In our experience, group treatment is extremely useful with bulimic patients. Over the years we have utilized a variety of group formats in both inpatient and outpatient programs. The following sections describe the groups and our experience with them.

BRIEF PSYCHOEDUCATIONAL GROUP TREATMENT

We have reported on brief psychoeducational group treatment before (Connors, Johnson, and Stuckey, 1984; Johnson, Connors, and Stuckey, 1983). We began conducting these groups in 1982, and the format has changed only slightly since that time. Since we knew that issues such as

normalizing eating habits, correcting cognitive distortions, increasing assertiveness, and building self-esteem would be important in therapy, we
decided that two of our main interventions would be self-monitoring, to
increase awareness of the adaptive context of bulimia, and goalsetting to
foster gradual behavior change.

In our first groups all subjects were women who met the DSM-III
criteria for bulimia and were bingeing and purging at least once a week.
The original study involved two groups of ten outpatients, each conducted
by two therapists and using a multiple baseline design. To ensure some
homogeneity among members, we excluded women who were significantly
underweight or overweight and ruled out those who were suicidally depressed or psychotic.

The program consisted of twelve two-hour sessions, with sessions twice
a week for the first three weeks. Prior to the first session all members had
been self-monitoring for a few weeks. They also had to complete a control
scale (Connors, 1983), the Tennessee Self-Concept Scale (Fitts, 1964–
65), the Body Cathexis Scale (Secord and Jourard, 1953), the Assertion
Inventory (Gambrill and Richey, 1975), the Multiscore Depression Inventory (Berndt, Petzel, and Berndt, 1980), and the EDI. The following
is a session-by-session report of interventions in each group meeting.

First Meeting. The first meeting began with introductions. Each member stated her name, talked a bit about her problem (if she wished) and
her hopes and expectations for the group. After some discussion and
questioning of group members by each other, the therapists provided
information on bulimia, starting with the most relevant physical aspects,
such as electrolyte imbalances. Set-point theory was explained and the
women's eating habits were discussed. The therapists also commented on
the sociocultural context that prescribes an obsession with thinness for
women. An article on set-point theory was distributed for discussion next
time, as well as an excerpt from *Such a Pretty Face* (Millman, 1980) entitled
"Being Thin Is the Most Important Thing in My Life." In this article a
woman in her sixties describes her life, which has been devoted solely to
the pursuit of thinness. (The article is reprinted at the end of this chapter.)
Group members expressed their fears and feelings of hopelessness about
ever conquering their eating problems, along with some determination
that they would not allow their entire lives to revolve around being thin.

Second Meeting. The articles handed out at the first meeting were discussed. The therapists stressed that deprivation leads to bingeing, that
group members have to reeducate their bodies in terms of eating in response to hunger, and that they must gradually learn to tolerate the feelings of fullness and possible temporary weight gain associated with more
normal eating. The self-defeating nature of frequent weighing was emphasized. The women began to discuss the more psychological aspects of
bingeing for them, including such issues as competition, fear of success
and/or failure, eating in response to anger or loneliness, and the need

to fill up boring, empty times. The therapists began to give individual feedback to group members concerning the particular feelings that seemed most salient to each woman according to her daily charts.

Third Meeting. Individual feedback was continued in the third meeting. Resistance to filling out the self-monitoring charts was discussed as were cognitive distortions involved in bulimia. Members were asked to talk about their reactions to being in the group so far.

Fourth Meeting. In order to dramatize the idea that the bingeing and purging serves a function, during the fourth meeting the therapists asked the women to fantasize about their lives if they did not have this symptom. Patients shared their feelings of fear and loss, as well as the more positive aspects, with each other. Then they were asked to describe all the techniques they have found helpful in avoiding binges in the past; these were written down and photocopied for distribution during the next meeting. Finally, members were prepared for the next session in which short-term weekly goals would be set.

Fifth Meeting. Written feedback sheets summarizing responses to the daily charts were distributed during the fifth session, along with group members' suggestions for avoiding binges. Then each member set her goal for the week, with much group feedback regarding its feasibility. The therapists encouraged goals such as eating more regular meals, rewarding oneself, engaging in alternative activities, exercising, and so forth as well as ones directly concerned with bingeing and purging. They also emphasized the importance of concentrating on explicit short-term goals rather than the implicit one of "no more binge/purging forever" because for these women, perfectionism was expected to be self-defeating.

Sixth Meeting. In the sixth meeting, members reported progress with goals and accompanying feelings, then set revised goals for the next week. The therapists used some paradoxical techniques, with much reframing and relabeling of "failures" as learning experiences and bad feelings as better than no feelings. Some symptom prescription (Haley, 1963) was used, such as suggestions of every-other-day binges rather than none. Feelings related to the discontinuation of the twice-weekly meetings were discussed.

Seventh Meeting. Progress with the goals was explored and goals for the next week were set in the seventh meeting. Explicit work on assertiveness began (although the issues had come up frequently and had received some discussion earlier). The therapists defined the difference between passive, assertive, and aggressive behavior using material from *Your Perfect Right* (Alberti and Emmons, 1978). Group members then performed an exercise in which they each stated one thing they liked about themselves. First they imagined what their own response might be, then the therapists modeled the response, and finally the members took their turns enacting their responses. Feelings involved in sharing positive feelings about the self were discussed, particularly the fear of being thought conceited. The next exercise involved the same format of covert, modeled, and overt response, but this time each member had to give a compliment to the woman next to her. Feelings about giving and getting compliments were discussed.

Eighth Meeting. Work on goals continued; the emergence of painful feelings no longer anesthetized by the bingeing were discussed. Feelings of neediness, deprivation, rejection, anxiety, and anger were explored, with the therapists continuing to stress that it is a positive change to feel these things and that they can be managed.

Ninth Meeting. Work on goals and painful feelings continued in the ninth meeting. The necessity of finding alternative satisfying outlets for feelings was emphasized.

Tenth Meeting. During the tenth meeting the therapists took the group through a progressive relaxation exercise, suggesting that group members learn to relax rather than binge in response to tension. Copies of different relaxation techniques were distributed. The remainder of the meeting was devoted to progress and resetting goals for the next week.

Eleventh Meeting. Issues of group termination were raised during the eleventh meeting. Work on assertiveness continued, this time focusing on negative feelings about being assertive. Members were asked to describe situations calling for assertiveness in their own lives, and their responses were modified through group feedback and modeling. The link between lack of assertiveness and pent-up feelings that are expressed in binge/purging was repeatedly stressed. The last half of the session focused on goals.

Last Meeting. The first half of the twelfth meeting consisted of "business as usual," with members reporting goal progress. The second half was a discussion of feelings about having been in the group, gains and disappointments, suggestions for the group program, and future plans for treatment, if any. The therapists provided reading lists and descriptions of other treatment resources. Plans were made for individual follow-up interviews two months after this meeting. At the group members' request, a reunion meeting was scheduled then as well.

Improvement in Eating Behavior

Overall, group members reduced their bingeing and purging behavior by 70 percent. The multiple baseline design indicated that the group treatment, as opposed to simple self-monitoring, was producing the results. Improvement rather than total symptom remission was most characteristic.

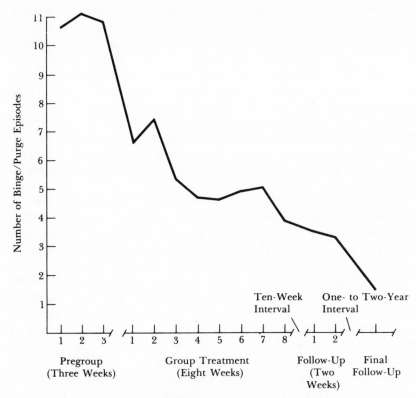

FIGURE 9.1

Mean Number of Binge/Purge Episodes per Week

At a ten-week follow-up 15 percent of the group members had completely remitted; 40 percent had reduced their binge/purge frequency by at least 50 percent; and 45 percent had reduced their frequency by less than 50 percent (see figure 9.1). Further improvement was seen in the one- to two-year follow-up, although it must be noted that many patients received additional treatment during this period.

CORRELATES OF IMPROVEMENT IN EATING BEHAVIOR

Pearson product-moment analyses were conducted to investigate relationships between symptom change and other variables. A significant negative correlation was found between age and reduction in binge/purge episodes; younger age was associated with greater improvement. No significant correlations were obtained between symptom change and history of psychotherapy, marital status, duration of illness, or history of anorexia nervosa. Several significant correlations were obtained between change in eating behavior and improvements on the self-report measures. An increase in perceived control over binge eating as measured by the control scale was associated with actual behavior change. Improvement on the bulimia, interoceptive awareness, drive for thinness, and body dissatisfaction subscales of the EDI correlated with reduced binge eating. There was a trend toward significance in the relationship between improvement on the ineffectiveness subscale and reduced binge eating. Two of the self-esteem measures from the Tennessee Self-Concept Scale showed trends toward significant relationships with behavior change: increases on the positive behavior and personal self subscales were associated with a reduction in binge eating. There was also a trend toward a relationship between high scores on a program adherence checklist and reductions in binge eating.

Specific changes in attitudes and behavior seemed to be related to specific interventions. The educational component of our program explored sociocultural factors relating to women and their bodies, particularly the selective emphasis on thinness for women. Information on dieting, set-point theory, and the role of deprivation in triggering binges helped the women to see how their struggles with food were influenced by certain cultural and biological factors, rather than viewing them as purely personal failures in "willpower." The importance of normalizing eating and of valuing health over thinness was stressed. This information seemed to have an impact on attitudes and behavior. The women ate more normal meals. As measured on the EDI, their drive for thinness and body dissatisfaction improved. The fact that more improvement was seen in the younger group members may indicate that this information had the greatest impact on those whose underlying belief system regarding thinness was less entrenched.

The self-monitoring and goal-setting elements of the program's behavioral component seemed particularly effective. The self-monitoring fostered an increase in interoceptive awareness and a sense of personal choice and control regarding the decision to binge. This sense of control and effectiveness increased as group members experienced success in achieving the goals they had set. In fact, the experience of success was an extremely powerful factor in modifying the eating and purging behavior of those women. Behavioral change through goal setting led to sharp increases in self-esteem and decreases in sadness and learned helplessness. This heightened sense of personal power was reflected in increased comfort with assertiveness.

Group cohesiveness proved to be a vital component of the treatment. The mutual support and understanding of a group were particularly important to these women who had kept their bulimia a secret and expected that others would be disgusted by them. The support of the group seemed to reduce pessimism as members encouraged one another and witnessed each other's successes. While an individual therapist can provide some of the same support functions for patients, group cohesiveness in a homogeneous bulimic group offers a unique holding environment.

Although group treatment was associated with improvement, there were large individual differences in the degree and the maintenance of the response to treatment. Subjects might be divided roughly into three groups: the responders, who improved during the eight weeks of group and showed continued improvement at follow-up; the temporary responders, who progressed during group treatment but did not maintain all the gains after treatment ended; and the nonresponders, who made no substantial gains, or worsened, during the program.

More than half the subjects were responders. Change was associated with program adherence, which suggests that the women who were most highly motivated to comply with various aspects of the program tended to do better. Correlational data also suggested that the younger women with less chronic histories of bulimia had greater success in maintaining their gains from posttreatment to follow-up.

Correlational data provides no clues as to the characteristics of the several temporary responders, other than their tendency to be older. The two nonresponders, who actually increased their number of binge/purge episodes from pretreatment to follow-up, merit close scrutiny. Both were very consistent in their lack of progress during the course of group treatment. One of these subjects had been hospitalized for a schizophrenic break several years prior to group, and she remained rather vague and tangential. She was the only group member to use laxatives and suppositories rather than vomiting. The other nonresponder had had a long history of anorexia nervosa. She was frequently absent from group meetings and rarely spoke when she was present. She described a lonely and isolated existence in which the gratification of bingeing and purging outweighed her motivation to give up the symptom. This subject later became a member of a long-term group for eating-disordered women, where she was reported to be the sole nonresponder.

Patients described the self-monitoring, goal-setting, and assertiveness training exercises as the most helpful components of the treatment. The only component the women cited as not helpful was the progressive relaxation training, which most found very difficult to utilize. These patients were so self-conscious that several said trying to relax in the group setting was actually making them more "hyper."

We have continued to conduct these short-term psychoeducational groups, with a few changes. The relaxation training has been eliminated, although we describe it as a useful intervention and give additional information to those who are interested. We have also attempted to include more group work on these patients' negative body image, which appears to be a crucial treatment component. The initial twice-weekly meetings have been abandoned in favor of twelve weekly sessions.

Our criteria have expanded to include males and binge-restrictors. However, we feel that there should never be just one binge-restrictor in a group consisting primarily of binge-purgers. In one group, a single binge-restrictor who was quite disturbed became a binge-vomiter by the end of the group in her efforts to fit in.

We find that these groups are an effective and efficient "first line" of treatment for many patients. They can produce reduction in the bulimic behavior, increases in self-esteem, and a heightened sense of personal control and effectiveness. Some patients may not need further treatment, but most will. It has been our experience that patients who have made some gains in short-term group treatments are eager for further treatment in the form of individual psychotherapy or long-term group therapy.

RESPONSE-PREVENTION COMPONENT

Recently we have begun to incorporate an exposure-plus-response-prevention (ERP) component into our treatment strategies. The use of response prevention with bulimic patients has been written about extensively by Rosen, Leitenberg, and colleagues (Rosen and Leitenberg, 1982; Rosen and Leitenberg, 1984; Leitenberg, Gross, Peterson, and Rosen, 1984). In their anxiety reduction model of bulimia, they propose that because these patients have a morbid fear of weight gain, eating elicits anxiety, and binge eating elicits it dramatically, while vomiting after eating temporarily reduces the anxiety. These authors suggest that, in bulimia, vomiting serves an anxiety-reducing function similar to checking rituals or compulsive hand washing found in obsessive-compulsive disorders. Once it has been established as an escape response or a negative reinforcer, vomiting sustains the binge eating rather than vice versa. As a result, binge eating will occur only when the patient is anticipating vomiting and will become more severe as the vomiting increases in frequency.

Rosen and colleagues thus propose that the vomiting, rather than the binge eating, should be the target of treatment. They suggest that ERP would be an effective intervention. There are two components to treatment; first, the patient is exposed to the feared stimulus in the presence of the therapist, and second, the escape response of vomiting is prevented. The feared stimulus varies from patient to patient but will include eating certain kinds or quantities of food and then keeping the food down despite anxiety. With repeated exposure, the fear of eating the food should be extinguished.

As these researchers note, this method of treatment is not applicable to all patients meeting DSM-III criteria for bulimia. It seems most indicated for those patients who have formed a very strong link between bingeing and vomiting, such that bingeing would not occur if vomiting were not possible. Patients who binge but do not purge, or those who will keep certain foods down at some times but not others, are not good candidates for ERP.

Response-prevention techniques can be implemented individually or in a group format. Our colleague Patricia Buckley has developed a group treatment program in which patients ate anxiety-provoking foods during group sessions.

These groups met for two hours twice a week for six weeks. Prior to the first meeting patients were asked to complete a questionnaire regarding food preferences and the anxiety associated with various foods. In the first group meeting patients were also asked to rank foods on a five-point scale according to the anxiety each aroused, so that a hierarchy of anxiety-provoking foods could be constructed.

Throughout the six weeks of the group patients self-monitored all eating episodes. This included the food consumed, thoughts and feelings, whether it was considered to be a binge, and level of anxiety on a scale from 0 to 100 percent. Each group meeting began with patients' ratings of their anxiety level and urge to vomit. Then they would eat the particular foods selected for that evening. Over time the group progressed from eating fruit to salty snacks, sweets, foods such as pizza and pasta, and finally full meals in restaurants.

While they ate, the patients were asked to remain silent and focus on the thoughts and feelings provoked by the eating. They rated both their anxiety level and urge to vomit during consumption and every fifteen minutes thereafter. Patients were told to eat until their anxiety and urge to vomit were around 80 percent. After eating, the therapists and group members processed the experience together. The therapists were also able to give each patient individual feedback on the basis of her self-monitoring sheets from the previous session. In the second hour of each group session the therapists gave didactic presentations on restraint theory, the effects of dieting, normalizing eating, relaxation exercises, sociocultural pressures to be thin, nutritional information, and relapse prevention.

Initially the group members experienced great anxiety, ate very little, and kept their heads down rather than attempting interpersonal contact. Over time, however, their anxiety lessened and their food consumption and sociability increased. Although the results of these groups are still being analyzed, preliminary data suggest positive results, with some group members asymptomatic at the end of group and most others experiencing some reduction in binge/purge episodes. It may be that the addition of a response-prevention component to other more typical psychoeducational group techniques constitutes a powerful intervention to which some patients have an extremely positive response.

The basic thrust of these short-term treatment groups is toward understanding the antecedents of the bingeing and purging behavior and developing alternative coping strategies. Patients must be able to think in terms of long-range gains and to delay the immediate gratification involved in the bulimic behavior to some degree. Success in these groups also requires some willingness to relinquish, or at least defer, plans to lose weight by rigid dieting. We have found that these time-limited group formats are excellent for college campuses where individuals may be in the early stages of the disorder. We have also found, however, that the more the patient is character disordered, the less helpful the short-term format is. While the psychoeducational group may be a reasonable starting point for these patients, longer-term treatment is usually required.

SELF-HELP GROUPS

As our treatment program evolved we felt there was a need to develop a forum where eating-disordered patients could meet on a regular basis and receive support from each other. We were interested in exploring the usefulness of a group led by a nonprofessional that was available to individuals at no cost.

We designed a group that met weekly for one and one-half hours. Although it was open to anyone in the community who had difficulty with anorexia nervosa or bulimia, we never advertised the group's existence because we did not want the group to become too large. Over the years group size fluctuated between five and twenty, with a core of eight to ten patients usually attending regularly. All members of the group received a copy of the "group agreement" (see figure 9.2) during the initial visit.

As seen in the group agreement, the self-help/support group was presented to patients as an adjunct to other treatment interventions. The only substantial rule for being able to attend the sessions regularly was that the individual go through the initial evaluation in our program. Our rationale for insisting on this procedure was to ensure that the patient was not unwittingly involved in a support group led by a nonprofessional when other interventions might be more useful to her (for example, medication for depression or anxiety). Most patients viewed this explanation for the criteria as professional and reassuring. Being in treatment in our program was not a prerequisite for being in the group, and after the clinic evaluation some patients attended the group without additional interventions.

The other somewhat unique feature of the group was the leadership structure. Two group members volunteered on a rotating basis for a two-month tenure as group leaders, whose role was as defined in the group agreement. The most important aspect of structuring the leadership in this way was the weekly contact of the leaders with the clinic staff. Essentially, we constructed a support group led by nonprofessionals who were professionally supervised. Professional supervision relieved group leaders of any feeling that they had to be therapists or that they were responsible for managing any disruptive event, such as psychotic or suicidal behavior. Their responsibility was to inform us if group members became seriously

FIGURE 9.2
Group Agreement of the Eating Disorders Program Support Group

---

Group Agreement:
Because of the sensitive nature of the material in the group, participants are asked to not talk about other group members or the content of group discussions outside of the hospital. To insure that prospective group members are receiving appropriate treatment, all members of the group need to have had a consultation with the Eating Disorders Program at Northwestern Memorial Hospital.
To minimize distractions in the group, members are asked to not eat, drink or smoke during the group meetings.

Basic Philosophy:
The group at Northwestern was developed in collaboration with individuals who have struggled with food-related problems. The group was formed to provide a forum for individuals to exchange ideas and feelings concerning their ongoing efforts to lead their lives with a minimum of interference from food-related problems. The group was not designed to solve serious psychological issues, but to serve as an adjunct to other professional treatment interventions.

Group Structure:
The group will meet on Wednesday evenings, 6:30–7:45 P.M. A group Steering Committee will consist of two individuals who volunteer to organize the group for two months. The responsibilities of the Steering Committee are as follows:

1. Commencing and ending the group meeting on time.
2. Meeting on a weekly basis at 6:15 P.M. with a member of the Eating Disorders Clinic who will provide guidance regarding ongoing group issues.
3. Orientating new group members to group format.
4. Obtaining name, address and telephone number of new group members, if they are interested in continuing with the group.

---

distressed. Individuals in the group were likewise reassured by the participation of clinic staff.

Originally we wanted the group to be structured around weekly topics led by group members. The group quickly alerted us that they simply wanted to talk among themselves and that it was unnecessary to have a great deal of structure.

Our experience with this group has been mainly positive. It is very useful to patients to have a sense of community. There are, however, some disadvantages. Many patients with eating difficulties are quite needy and have boundary difficulties. Although we did not prohibit group members from having contact outside the group, we closely monitored the relationships to ensure that individuals were not becoming unwittingly enmeshed in situations that would ultimately create difficulty for them.

The discussions in groups such as these can also become too focused on food, eating, and weight. Supervision can be helpful in monitoring whether the discussions might be actually exacerbating the patients' level of food preoccupation. Finally, support groups that have open attendance can sometimes deteriorate into a collection of individuals who have not been responsive to treatment and who feel hopeless and despairing. This occasionally happens as patients at a higher level of functioning improve and leave the group, resulting in a group that consists predominantly of those who are not improving. In such cases it is often useful to actively recruit new group members who are functioning at a higher level.

LONG-TERM PROCESS GROUPS

Our experience with long-term groups has been mixed. Initially we found that many of our bulimic patients had difficulty sustaining a long-term commitment to a group. This would often result in sporadic attendance, which adversely affected group cohesiveness. As with the non–time-limited self-help support group, we found there is also a tendency in this group to progressively develop a core membership of individuals who do not improve and consequently do not leave the group. Under these circumstances the tone of the group becomes one of hopelessness and despair. We have attempted to solve the commitment issue by building in reevaluation periods at three-month intervals. This allows both the patient and the staff a predictable point where the "goodness of fit" between group and patient, and the usefulness of the group to him or her, would be considered. We have also introduced a prepayment policy for the three-month period. And we have become much more attentive to the need to have an adequate mix of patients with different degrees of severity of character pathology. Consequently we screen much more thoroughly when we are considering introducing new group members. For example, we try to select out patients who have borderline character pathology if a group already has a number of such patients.

Inpatient Group Treatment*

Milieu treatment, composed of a variety of different group interventions, is the primary focus on the inpatient unit at Northwestern Memorial Hospital. The continuously occurring groups include Post Meal Group, Movement Group, Eating Behavior Group, Sunday Supper Group, and Transition Group (see figure 9.3).

* We would like to thank Linda Lewis, Ph.D., and Lyn Marshall, R.N., for the following descriptions of the inpatient groups.

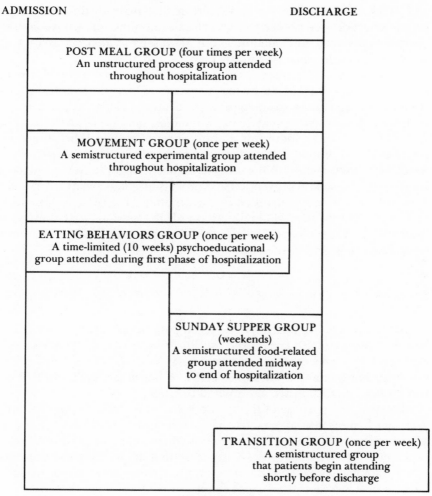

FIGURE 9.3
Inpatient Groups for Bulimics and Anorexics

POST MEAL GROUP

The Post Meal Group is a minimally structured process group attended by all inpatients on the Eating Disorders Unit throughout their hospital stay. As the name implies, this group meets immediately after meals, four times a week. The group leaders are two members of the nursing staff who are supervised weekly by a psychologist.

The two primary goals of this group are to provide an arena for the expression of anxiety and discomfort associated with eating and to help patients increase their awareness of the relationships between anxiety about eating, body size, and emotional states. As the group has evolved, the patients have used this time for three additional purposes: (1) to convey and reinforce the norms for successful involvement on the unit, (2) to handle interpersonal problems that arise on the unit, and (3) to disclose "private" personal information about themselves (such as feelings of neediness) that they had previously experienced as shameful.

These goals and purposes are achieved by leadership involvement that prohibits acting-out behaviors such as purging, which would short-circuit the opportunity to struggle with feelings, reinforces patients' attempts to identify and articulate inner feelings, sensations, and thoughts, and, finally, takes an inquiring, noninterpretive stance. This stance diminishes the likelihood that leaders will react to the patients' dependency needs with intrusiveness and excessive control. This group represents a confluence of response-prevention and process-oriented group techniques. The patients are deeply invested in and committed to these group meetings. Not only do they willingly attend all the sessions, but they have frequently and spontaneously requested additional post-meal groups when crises have emerged on the unit.

THE EATING BEHAVIORS GROUP

All newly admitted eating-disordered patients attend the Eating Behaviors Group, a highly structured psychoeducational group, once a week during the first ten weeks of their hospital stay. Although the group leaders are a psychologist and a nurse, experts in other areas, such as nutrition and internal medicine, are also invited to speak.

The primary purpose of this group is to communicate to the patients that their eating attitudes and behaviors require specific attention and are not viewed by the staff as simply manifestations of psychodynamic problems. The group provides a structure that allows the patients to examine both behavioral and cognitive details of their food-related struggle. This process increases their capacity for self-observation so that they may participate more fully in their own recovery. In addition, the nutritional, medical, familial, and sociocultural material that patients are exposed to broadens their intellectual understanding of the factors related to their disorder.

Group content is divided into discrete units so that all newly admitted patients can become involved immediately. The first three units consist of specific tasks that require each patient to examine his or her own food-related behaviors and attitudes (for example, frequency and time of binge eating and purging, severity of restriction, and so on). Then general principles that can be applied to all patients are derived from the details of these self-observations (for example, restrictive eating, extreme hunger, binge eating or fear of binge eating, dichotomization of food into "good" and "bad" categories). Possible methods of self-intervention are discussed. In subsequent units the focus is on the body, its nutritional needs, its natural biological processes, and its adaptations to disordered eating. In the final units, the focus is on heightening the patients' awareness of social and cultural pressures that may contribute to their eating problem.

While this is an explicitly educational group, it does not employ a lecture format. Relevant information is provided only after the patients have generated questions and issues based on their own experiences. In addition, patients write down their thoughts and feelings during the course of the group; this material is returned to them weekly so that they can have an ongoing record of the thinking that they have done.

The patients' enthusiastic response to this group indicates that they experience it as an empathic response to the food-related concerns that preoccupy them, especially during the first weeks of their hospital stay. Just as important is the evidence that they use the information learned in the group. This becomes apparent when they participate in the Sunday Supper Group where they repeatedly put into practice many ideas that were first discussed in the Eating Behavior Group.

SUNDAY SUPPER GROUP

The members of the Sunday Supper Group meet every weekend to plan, shop for, and prepare a meal that they eat on Sunday evening. Time is set aside for processing this highly provocative experience after cleaning up. To participate in this group, patients must have permission from the staff team responsible for their treatment. As a general rule, patients do not become involved in this group until midway through their hospital stay.

The purpose of this group is to return the control of food-related activities to the patients so that they can experience the challenge of greater freedom within the supportive context of the hospital. In this way they are given the opportunity to practice new behaviors and methods of self-intervention. In addition, as a result of this challenge patients evaluate their therapeutic progress ("I could never have chosen to eat this two months ago") and gain insight into past food-related situations ("When I ate with my family, I never felt free to say what was on my mind").

Each phase of this group stimulates a chance to face the anxieties and fears that have become associated with food. For example, the trip to the grocery store is particularly troublesome for bulimics who have had repeated experiences of lack of control there. Facing these fears with the opportunity to process them as they occur helps the patients feel better prepared for their life after hospital discharge.

The patients are very clear about the helpfulness of this group. They consciously put into practice the new ideas that they were exposed to in the Eating Behavior Group by choosing to prepare foods they had previously considered "dangerous" or "bad," such as pasta and pizza. Despite the anxiety-producing aspects of the group, patients frequently comment on the pleasure derived from preparing and eating a meal together.

THE MOVEMENT GROUP

The Movement Group, which patients attend throughout their hospital stay, meets once per week. While all patients must attend, participation in the activities are optional.

There are three primary goals for this group. First, we wish to increase patients' ability to introspect and to tolerate feelings. Patients are encouraged to distinguish among bodily sensations and to learn how to tolerate powerful affects. Second, we try to improve and build on body image by decreasing perfectionistic performance standards and by increasing confidence and trust in one's own actions. Third, we provide creative and constructive outlets for self-expression by teaching patients how to express genuine and powerful affects through movements.

Music is used extensively. Although 80 percent of the group time is spent in nonverbal activities, verbal interaction is encouraged both at the beginning and the end of each session. At the beginning patients are asked to "focus" attention inwardly so that they might help determine what activities would best suit their needs at that moment. At the end of the session the final wrapup of experiences is also verbal.

The nonverbal movement activities involve both structured activities, such as stretching, yoga, and self-massage, and expressive activities, such as mirroring, use of imaginary objects, and movements to depict an emotion.

The unique characteristic of this group is that because it is primarily nonverbal, patients are less able to utilize certain defenses, such as intellectualization and withdrawal. Furthermore, the experiential nature of this group necessitates a more direct confrontation of body awareness.

Patient response to this group is highly variable. For some it is extremely threatening. For others it offers an opportunity to express and experience themselves that is exciting and new.

TRANSITION GROUP

The Transition Group is a semistructured group designed to support and facilitate the transition from inpatient to outpatient treatment. The constantly shifting membership also necessitates that the group focus on the process of change among its members. All patients begin the group toward the end of their inpatient hospitalization and remain for a maximum of one year following their discharge. The group, which meets once a week in the outpatient clinic, is led by an inpatient nurse and staff psychologist from the outpatient program.

The goals of this group are to maintain the therapeutic gains made during hospitalization by providing continuity between inpatient and outpatient life; to help patients to meet the challenges of general adjustment to outpatient life; and to provide an arena in which patients can continue to increase their understanding of themselves, their relationships with others, and the link between their feelings and their attitudes toward food.

The group time is spent in both structured and unstructured ways. During the unstructured time the focus is on interpersonal relationships both within the group and with others. During the structured time the patients are more task oriented. For example, time is devoted in every group meeting for goal setting, a task that requires patients to identify and carry out steps toward changing problem behaviors, which may or may not be food related. Clearly delineated procedures for handling entry, termination, and irregularity of attendance have been established to mitigate the disruptive effects of fluctuating group membership.

Because this group has both process- and task-oriented components, the therapists must be flexible in their style of leadership. When process issues are salient, the therapists take a nondirective and inquiring stance that facilitates interaction among group members. During the more structured components of the group, the therapists become more directive. For example, with goal setting they actively help the patients assess whether chosen goals are both realistic and challenging.

It has been observed that many patients, especially bulimics, respond extremely well to a highly structured inpatient experience but quickly relapse upon discharge. The Transition Group addresses this problem by continuing with a structure that helps patients with goal setting and relapse management. Furthermore, membership participation during the change from inpatient to outpatient status decreases the sense of abandonment that can be experienced at discharge. And finally, the posthospital involvement of one year gives the patients an extended opportunity for self-evaluation with others who know them well and who are also struggling with reentering the community.

Family Therapy*

When we approach the assessment and potential therapeutic involvement of the bulimic patient's family, we begin with a number of operating principles and assumptions. It has been found that many bulimic women have some degree of developmental conflict between their need to indi-

* This section was written in collaboration with Steven Stern, Psy.D.

viduate and their need to conform to the perceived expectations of their families. Actually, this statement applies to all human beings, but bulimics often display a crippling degree of self-sacrifice that impairs their ability to function effectively in interpersonal relationships. With this in mind, regardless of whether or not we ever treat the patient's family directly, we tend to "think family" from the beginning of assessment. That is, we always ask ourselves such questions as how does the patient's self-denial, self-criticalness, inhibited aggression, or conflicts about sexuality make sense in terms of the implicit rules and expectations that existed and probably still exist in her family? Or, in a later stage of treatment, how does the patient's reluctance to risk change, her fear of success, or her avoidance of a close relationship with the therapist reflect some (perhaps unconscious) loyalty to a family value system that would prohibit such growth from occurring? To put this another way, in treating bulimics, regardless of whether the family is physically present, it is always safest to assume that they are "in the room" affecting the patient's behavior and motivations.

Note that we do not think of the family or, more specifically, the parents as *causing* the patient's problem in any sense that would imply blame on them. We assume that all family members have done their best to fulfill their roles and responsibilities and that the bulimic member's problems represent a symptom of a family-wide, multigenerational developmental impasse. In this sense our thinking parallels that of Skynner (1981), who conceptualized family problems in developmental terms. For example, Skynner might view a bulimic's entire family as developmentally arrested at the level of separation-individuation. Within this framework the ill member's pathological behavior is understood as a necessary component of the entire family's particular adaptive solutions both to developmental pressures from within the family and sociocultural pressures from without.

Despite the potentially pathological interconnectedness between the bulimic patient's behavior and her family, we do not always insist on treating the entire family. To begin with, the family as a whole may not be motivated to change and therefore not interested in treatment. We assume that with families, as with individuals, psychotherapy will probably be ineffective unless there is some impetus to change. Determining who, if any, of the patient's family need to be involved in therapy is a complex assessment and decision-making process. Some of the factors that go into the decision are (1) the patient's age, (2) her degree of dependency on the family, (3) who is motivated to see the patient get help—the patient herself or a family member, and (4) whether the treatment is occurring on an inpatient or outpatient basis. Thus, if the patient is an adolescent still living at home, if she is older but still psychologically dependent, if a parent or spouse rather than the patient herself is manifesting the most concern about her illness, or if the treatment requires an inpatient admission that is traumatic to family functioning, then family therapy of some type is mandatory. However, if the patient is older, more individuated, and motivated for her own therapy, individual and/or group therapy may well be the treatment of choice. Therapists should remain cognizant, however, that much of the focus of the individual work may be on the patient's relationships with her family, and that this work may actually impact upon the family in profound ways. In the course of a patient's individual therapy, some family or marital therapy may be useful, even necessary, to confront and resolve certain issues. As a general rule of thumb in considering who should be involved in treatment, we keep in mind Skynner's recommendation (1981) that in order to effectively treat any psychological problem, a minimal system is needed that includes the *problem*, the *motivation* to do something about it, and the *capacity* (power) to do so. These three elements may be contained in the same person or may be "distributed" among the identified patient and other family members. In the latter case, family therapy is indicated.

Overall, the therapeutic team often needs to function, in certain respects, as "parents" to the family system as a whole. This is not to say that we infantilize the family by taking over responsibility for their decision making, but rather that certain psychological functions which are missing in the family may need to be provided in order for the family to feel adequately contained and understood. Taken together, these functions constitute a kind of therapeutic holding environment (Winnicott, 1965) that enables family members to feel safe to explore their shared problems. Some of the "parental" functions that may be needed with bulimic families are: (1) the provision of external structure and regulation; (2) encouragement of individual initiative within the family; (3) encouragement and tolerance of the expression of affects, including aggression; (4) mediation between conflicting members; (5) tolerance of regression to a more dependent or disorganized state; and (6) reliable availability over time. As Stern and colleagues (1981) have suggested, therapists can expect the families to test them to determine if they can truly provide those functions that are missing in the families. If the therapist cannot, he or she can hardly be expected to be of much help.

USE OF SIGNIFICANT OTHERS

Over the last several years we have become interested in trying to make particular use of specific subsystems within the patient's support network. Enlisting the assistance of a husband, boyfriend, girl friend, or particular family member can be quite useful in select situations. It is important to emphasize, however, that caution and care must be used when actually involving someone who is not professionally trained in a therapeutic endeavor. Therapists who consider involving a significant other in the treatment intervention should feel confident that the person does not have some investment in the patient remaining symptomatic; is not psychiatrically impaired; has the capacity to respond sensitively to intense affects such as anger, anxiety, or depression; and does not have a history of being hypercritical of the patient.

Initially it is always helpful to teach the significant other what the therapist and the patient have learned about the specific functions of the patient's disturbed eating behavior. We also teach the significant other the self-monitoring model that is described in figure 10.1.

Generally we have found that significant others can be especially helpful with two particular aspects of the self-monitoring model: the pre-binge state and the prevention of evacuation. If the patient can tell the significant other that she is feeling vulnerable to a binge episode, the significant other can often help her restore perspective or help her engage in alternative activities that distract her from the increasing drive to eat. We have already described the response-prevention techniques we use to desensitize and demystify food consumption. If the patient is ready to give up evacuation symptoms and if a suitable significant other is found, their working together can be a very powerful experience for both. It is usually feasible only if the patient is bingeing and purging at a particular time of the day, such as evening meals. If so, the patient and significant other would eat that meal together and then remain together for one hour. In preparation for this it is useful to spend time with the patient and significant other and try to anticipate what the patient's feelings might be and how the significant other will react.

This intervention should not be taken lightly. A considerable amount of preparation of the patient and significant other is needed. It must be made clear that the two will have to meet on a routine basis, probably over a period of several weeks, and that they should also meet regularly with the therapist to work through difficulties with the intervention.

Many marital or family issues will often surface by engaging the system in this manner. Therapists generally must be prepared to deal with the systems issues themselves or have quick access to a marital or family therapist.

Psychopharmacological Interventions*

Throughout these chapters we have reviewed data indicating that bulimic patients experience significant affective instability and that, for some, it may be biologically mediated. We have also emphasized the importance

* This section was written in collaboration with Philip McCulough, M.D., and John Gillilan, M.D.

of doing a thorough evaluation in order to identify patient characteristics that might indicate initiating pharmacological treatment.

Before initiating a drug trial, a comprehensive medical evaluation should be performed. A baseline history, physical examination, and laboratory studies, which should include complete blood count, SMA-20 and thyroid functions to rule out dehydration, fluid and electrolyte imbalance, and endocrine abnormalities, are essential before instituting drug treatment. Any abnormalities or other medical complications that surface should be addressed promptly.

It is also helpful to prepare patients psychologically for beginning medication treatment. We make every attempt to inform patients of our rationale for recommending medications. We discuss our understanding of how the medications work and what our experiences have been. Pope and Hudson's book *New Hope for Binge Eaters* (1984) is a useful guide for orienting patients to our rationale for recommending medication treatment.

Many patients have distorted beliefs about psychiatric medications. Some view all as addictive tranquilizers, and others fear that the medications will change their personalities radically. Educating patients directly about how these medications function is often sufficient to counter some of these misguided beliefs.

If a medication trial is recommended after psychotherapy has begun, patients will sometimes feel that they are failing at psychotherapy. We reassure our patients by telling them that as we become more familiar with them, it often becomes clear that an additional treatment tool might be useful. We reemphasize our belief that bulimia is a multidetermined disorder that may serve a variety of different functions and that effective treatment may require using various treatment modalities. Obviously, the therapist must closely attend to what the medication recommendation means to the patient.

One of the most common resistances we encounter from this over-achieving patient population is their belief that medication is simply a "crutch" and that they should be able to "cure" themselves. We often use a diabetes analogy to confront this belief. We ask if patients would be reluctant to take insulin if they had been diagnosed as having diabetes and they knew that their mood and overall life adjustment was being compromised because of the illness. Most patients acknowledge that they would not expect themselves to manage the diabetes through "willpower" and that they would not refer to the insulin pejoratively as a "crutch." We acknowledge that patients may have feelings about their biological vulnerability, but we hope that these feelings would not prevent them from receiving whatever help was available. Certainly, the point could be made that our understanding of diabetes is far more sophisticated than our knowledge of affective disorders. However, when sufficient clinical data is available to suspect a biological contribution to observed affect-regulation problems, the cost-benefit ratio of introducing the medication is quite good.

Interventions with tricyclic antidepressants, second-generation antidepressants, and monoamine oxidase inhibitors (MAOIs) are all promising in the treatment of bulimia (see chapter 12). Tricyclic antidepressants are often the starting point for treatment. As it is well accepted that all tricyclics are approximately equal in effectiveness, the initial choice is primarily based on the symptom picture and side-effect profile. Due to sedative and anticholinergic side effects (particularly constipation), which can be troublesome to a bulimic, it is often wise to choose one of the secondary tricyclics, such as desipramine or nortriptyline, which are more likely to be tolerated by the patient. Treatment is usually instituted at a low dose (for example, 10 mg nortriptyline or 25 mg desipramine) and titrated upward to a therapeutic level over a period of two to three weeks. Serum levels should be checked after the patient has been on a therapeutic dosage for seven to ten days. As poor response is often the result of inadequate serum levels of the medication, the initial trial must be for an adequate duration (usually four to six weeks at the therapeutic serum levels). The actual dosage involved varies greatly from person to person (for example, 50 mg to 300 mg desipramine—or 25 mg to 100 mg nortriptyline—per day). If at this point there has been only a partial response, a second agent, such as lithium carbonate or T_3 (triiodothyronine) or a combination, can be added in a stepwise fashion in an effort to potentiate the tricyclic's effects. Both of these methods are simple, and evaluations can be performed in ten to fourteen days. A 600 to 1,200 mg per-day dose of lithium carbonate will convert some bulimic nonresponders. This may have to do with enhancement of serotinergic transmission and/or stabilization of affective lability. In a similar fashion a subclinical dose of T_3 (25 mcg) may be used to potentiate the tricyclic effect. If no response is achieved after efforts at potentiation are completed, the patient should be taken off the tricyclic and the potentiating drugs. After a drug-free period of approximately two weeks, a trial of MAOIs is indicated.

MAOIs appear to be equally or even more effective in the treatment of bulimia than tricyclics and are particularly helpful in patients who report concomitant symptoms of panic, anxiety, or atypical depressions. A usual starting dosage is 15 mg per day phenelzine, which can be titrated up to a maximum dosage of 90 mg per day over a period of several weeks, or 10 mg per day tranylcypromine up to 30 mg per day. It may produce mild to moderate anticholinergic side effects, which are usually transient. Patient compliance with MAOI therapy is crucial, and for this reason a strong therapeutic relationship is important. Because MAOIs can produce undesirable interactions, it is necessary to educate the patient about which foods, drinks, and medications to avoid. Compliance can be improved significantly by instructing patients as to the nature of the drug-food and drug-drug interactions and providing them with a written list of what is to be avoided. This input will help to eliminate unnecessary fears about hypertensive crises. However, patients also need to be educated about the need for immediate medical treatment if severe headaches, neck stiffness, tachycardia, or other signs of a hypertensive crisis occur.

As with tricyclics, the initial trial needs to be for a long enough time at adequate doses (six to eight weeks) to assess treatment efficacy. Pretreatment and posttreatment inhibition of platelet monoamine oxidase (MAO) may be used as an adjunctive guide. If no response has occurred at this point, the MAOI can be potentiated with T_3 or lithium carbonate in a similar fashion as the tricyclics. If there is still no clinical response, the medication is discontinued, and after a two-week drug-free period a trial of one of the second-generation antidepressants, such as trazodone or maprotiline, may be tried. Experience indicates that 75 to 80 percent of all bulimics have moderate to significant improvement as measured by a reduction in symptoms of bulimia, depression and/or anxiety.

Since many bulimic patients experience significant anxiety, which is sometimes more troublesome than depression, it may be useful to consider anxiolytic medications as well as antidepressants. However, antianxiety agents such as the benzodiazepines render patients quite vulnerable to addiction. Consequently, if the patient presents with an vulnerability to addictive behavior, anxiolytic medications should be avoided or approached very cautiously. We and others in the field have found that it is preferable to utilize antidepressants with anxiolytic effects because they are not addicting and may be taken over longer periods of time. If a patient is not responding to antidepressants after a series have been attempted, or cannot tolerate the side effects, it may be worthwhile to consider the use of a benzodiazepine such as alprazolam. However, the lowest possible effective dosage should be given, preferably for a brief period only. Patients taking these medications need to be monitored carefully.

Assuming a positive treatment response is obtained when this plan is followed, duration of treatment with these agents and monitoring their ongoing use become an important aspect of the treatment. Patients should have regular visits with the physician prescribing medications. This is especially important if psychotherapy is being provided by a different individual. Follow-up visits should include a discussion of the patient's current level of symptomatology as well as any side effects that might be occurring. Blood pressure should be monitored. If lithium carbonate is a part of the treatment, regular serum levels need to be obtained and these patients should have thyroid indices and a creatinine clearance checked at six- to twelve-month intervals.

The goal of maintenance drug therapy is to provide maximal therapeutic relief with the minimum amount of medication consistent with that goal. Often the dosages required to achieve improvement can be reduced somewhat during maintenance.

Overall duration of treatment is controversial. Even for acute major affective disorders, treatment for four to six months is indicated. Since many bulimic patients have been symptomatic for a long time prior to treatment, it is probably wise to continue pharmacological treatment for at least six to twelve months. Even more chronic administration may be necessary, especially if psychotherapy will be continuing for a longer period. If tapering of medication results in an exacerbation of symptomatology, the usual dose should be promptly reinstated. Fortunately, the drugs under discussion can be prescribed safely on a chronic basis.

Medication can be a useful component in a comprehensive treatment approach to bulimic disorders. As noted, a good therapeutic alliance, patience in conducting therapeutic trials of various agents, adequate follow-up visits, and good communication with other members of the treatment team are essential aspects of good care for these patients.

Role of the Nutritionist*

Frequently new patients regard the nutritionist (that is, the registered dietitian) as the only member of the treatment team they need to see, stating that they simply require some nutritional education. Usually this signals the denial and fear of an eating-disordered individual. It also illustrates the emotionally loaded role a nutritionist plays with these patients. The nutritionist is often viewed as an expert in the area of their obsession—food, eating, weight—their potential teacher, advisor, or criticizer in the area where they feel they have failed. Nutritionists working with bulimics must be prepared for the unique role they may play with the patient and with the treatment team.

The nutritionist can gather a recent food recall and diet history most expertly. We use a twenty-four-hour recall and a typical-day format to get an accurate nutritional assessment. We compared this to the patient's food preference and food elimination list. We encourage the patient to distinguish between disliked food and forbidden or "bad" ones on the elimination list. The dietitian's role is to teach patients to view food from a nutritional perspective. The basic food groups form the foundation, with elaboration on eating regularly throughout the day, including protein at every meal, complex carbohydrates versus simple carbohydrates, fats and their function in the diet and body, and the need for variety. The nutritionist restructures and adjusts the patient's eating habits with gradual changes and frequent reiteration of basic points.

The nutritionist plays a distinct role in the eating disorders team. In

* This section was written in collaboration with Sheryl Jones, R.D.

order to provide the most useful information to the team and the patient, the nutritionist must understand the meaning of a patient's behavior and how changes in it can be used to assess the patient's progress. Information on food choices and on the patient's affect and problem-solving ability surrounding these choices are valuable contributions in team meetings and planning conferences. Weight gains and losses may be illuminating, especially with hospitalized patients. Some have difficulty admitting urges or episodes of bingeing and purging, and weight fluctuations can give clues to staff about less communicative patients. Others hover at the lowest end of their weight range and need to be monitored and encouraged not to restrict.

Besides supplying factual information, the dietitian must recognize his or her role not only for the patient but on the team. The nutritionist may have to help team members to refine and broaden their knowledge of nutrition. The patient's obsession makes it vital that misinformation not be passed on to the patient unwittingly. In concentrating on the psychodynamics underlying a patient's preoccupation with food and weight, the team may minimize the importance of the distorted relationship with eating and of the critical roles of information and behavioral techniques in normalizing eating behavior. Thus the eating-disorders nutritionist may need to emphasize his or her skills and potential contributions in these areas as well as serving as the expert in nutrition to the patient and the team.

* * * *

Excerpt from *Such a Pretty Face* by Marcia Millman.

Helen Frank:
Being Thin Is the Most Important
Thing in My Life

When I was fourteen I broke my ankle in summer camp and spent the whole summer being wheeled back and forth in a wheelchair. I gained so much weight that by the time I went home I couldn't fit into any of my clothes. I had to wear the largest male counselor's coat to go home.

My parents were dead, and I lived with an uncle and aunt, and my uncle was horrible to me. When I got home from camp he said I looked pregnant. For a month after that I ate nothing but coffee and gum without sugar—I had a friend chew my gum before I did to take the sugar out. Since then I have been on a rigid diet. The only time in my life I wasn't on a diet was when I was pregnant with my two daughters, and so being pregnant was marvelous.

I was very young when I went to college. I weighed about 140 and my belly stuck out—I was so ashamed I used to wear a coat all the time, even in summer. I was so ashamed of my belly I quit college. I got married then and went to art school.

After we moved to Boston my weight went down to 115 and then 109 (I'm five feet nine inches tall). When we lived in Boston, I would weigh myself five times a day, including after every meal because I didn't want to go over

115 pounds. If I went over it made me feel horrible—it was the biggest thing in my whole life. If I wasn't thin it meant my life wasn't working.

In Boston I would wake up at three or three-thirty every morning and do exercises until six-thirty. I'd do 150 sit-ups in various positions—anything to make my stomach flat. I used to eat a quart of vanilla ice milk every night before I went to bed. It was almost all I ate. My husband pleaded with me to cut it out and eat a hamburger instead, but I wouldn't.

I have two daughters; one of them is naturally thin—she weighs the same as I (she's five-nine and weighs 118)—but she has a flat, flat stomach, which I don't—goddamn it. I'd do anything in the world to have a flat stomach.

My other daughter, Joan, is five-eight and weighs 165, but she's a real athlete and very solid. Still I wish she would weigh 140—she'd be perfect. But she has a successful career, so it doesn't matter so much.

Joan and I are very similar in that we both love to eat. I make wonderful brownies, but I wouldn't eat them. One day I made a batch and went skiing and came back early, and Joan was eating all of them in bed. When I walked in and saw her, her face turned red. I didn't say a word.

When we moved to California my weight went up to 128 and I became very worried, so I stopped eating until it went down to 119 about ten years ago. If I gain two or three pounds I cut out meals and eat only once a day.

My husband would like me to gain a little weight. I weighed 135 when we were married, and he thought that was perfect. I would do almost anything for my husband but my weight comes first and I don't want to weigh over 119. I enjoy living because I keep my weight down.

Even now I do three hours of exercise a day at home and an hour every day in exercise class. It makes me feel good that I do exercises better than some of the twenty-year-olds in the class, even though I'm sixty.

In the winter we ski every weekend—five or six hours a day. When we don't ski we hike—fifty miles during a weekend. We go on scary hikes that I don't enjoy—where it's very rocky. I've had a lot of trouble with my feet—I had a toe taken off one of my feet because it was infected, and the doctor told me I shouldn't hike because I don't have much use from that foot, but we do it anyway.

My diet isn't really good. I eat a lot of sugar, cheese, and fruit. I eat five packages of gum and Life Savers every day because I'm always hungry. For breakfast I eat cottage cheese with cinnamon and a cup of coffee.

For lunch I have half a cantaloupe with cottage cheese or ricotta and coffee. For dinner I have either a hamburger or fish, because of my false teeth, with a little lettuce or a vegetable.

I freeze iced coffee in a tray and eat it during the day while I watch television.

I never drink anything with a meal because it makes my belly stick out. If I drink coffee in the morning my belly sticks out, and then I'm too ashamed to go to exercise class.

On the street I look at people's profiles to see their bellies, not their faces. I think it's remarkable that a person could come out on the street with a big belly. I couldn't do it. In my exercise class I'm amazed at people who come with big bellies.

I always like clothing that makes my stomach look as flat as possible. When

I put on clothes I look in the mirror and if they don't make my stomach look thin I take them off.

In my exercise class everyone kids me and calls me fat Helen. In a way, I know it's neurotic, but I've been quite successful in doing what I wanted to do and that was being thin. It's more important for a woman to be thin. Women are not accepted after fifty. My husband is attractive to a number of women but no one is attracted to me—actually, looking thin makes you look older.

I was very discouraged when I was going to turn sixty, and I thought, "I haven't done a damn thing in my life. I'm just a dumb old housewife with a lot of art around." But then I thought, well, I've stayed thin and still look good in clothes.

NOTE: Reprinted, from *Such a Pretty Face: Being Fat in America,* by Marcia Millman, by permission of W. W. Norton & Company, Inc. Copyright © 1980 (text) by Marcia Millman.

10

Techniques for Symptom Management

Over the years we have found that there is a body of technical information that can be quite useful to both staff and patients. We have also found a range of techniques, including behavioral, cognitive-behavioral, response-prevention, and relapse training, that are helpful in symptom management. We have attempted to synthesize these various techniques and information into a general model of recovery for bulimic patients. The model has been a useful teaching tool for both staff and patients in either individual or group formats. We would like to note, however, that the schema is neither a canned program nor a blueprint for treatment. It is offered as an overall perspective on some goals and strategies for treatment. Furthermore, as discussed in chapter 9, symptom management is often possible only after a solid therapeutic alliance has been accomplished with the patient.

Several assumptions underlie the model. These include observations that most bulimics (1) have difficulty identifying and articulating their affective states, (2) experience significant mood instability, (3) have experienced significant feelings of ineffectiveness regarding their inability to master their internal states, and (4) have ultimately developed maladaptive ways of trying to manage themselves (Johnson and Maddi, 1986).

The four different components of the cognitive-behavioral model address different issues that occur during a binge/purge sequence (see figure 10.1). The task of each component is to interfere with the subsequent link in what could be thought of as a chain behavior or repetition-compulsion.

Prevention

Normalizing food intake
    Physiological deprivation: semistarvation studies
    Psychological deprivation: restraint theory

    Changing eating habits
        Meal plans/portion control
        Timing of eating
        Eating rituals
        Demystification of food groups

    Side effects of meal normalization
    Weight expectations
    Challenging the overvaluation of thinness

Self-monitoring: self-mastery through anticipating difficult situations
    Macro-level: major life repetitions
    Micro-level: daily behaviors

Self-enhancing activities: positive self-investment

Pre-Binge State

Perspective: avoid immediate cognitive lapse
Identify mood state
Common precipitants to a binge episode
Alternative behaviors: "lists" used for delay

Post-Binge State

Commitment to nonpurging: purging reinforces binge/purge cycle
Alternative behaviors: lists used for delay; use of significant others

Post-Binge/Purge Sequence

Episodic disorder: need to recover
Relapse training: beliefs that mediate further episodes
Normal food intake: the best defense against binge eating is to eat

FIGURE 10.1
Strategy for Recovery

Prevention

The overall task of prevention is threefold. First, the therapist wants to encourage patients to develop adaptive routine thoughts and behaviors that allow them to internalize the belief that certain behaviors result in predictable outcomes. Second, the therapist must help patients gain sufficient self-awareness about how certain circumstances affect them so that they can actually develop a sense of self-mastery by being able to predict how they typically respond to these situations. Finally, patients are asked to learn to routinely engage in self-enhancing behaviors that are more adaptive.

Normalizing Food Intake

The first and most logical place to begin symptom-focused work is on trying to establish an adequate and routine feeding schedule. We emphasize to patients that their binges are often caused by a combination of physiological and psychological needs. We present information from semistarvation studies and restraint theory that suggests that prolonged calorie restriction can result in counterregulatory binge eating due to both physical and psychological deprivation.

THE EFFECTS OF SEMISTARVATION ON HUMANS

In 1950 Ansel Keys and his colleagues (Keys et al. 1950) conducted a classic study on the effects of starvation. The experiment involved restricting the calorie intake of thirty-six young and healthy males who were conscientious objectors. In the first three months of the experiment, the men were allowed to eat normally while their behavior was studied. In the next six months the men were restricted to about half of their former calorie intake and lost, on average, about 25 percent of their original body weight. The last phase of the experiment involved three months of refeeding and rehabilitation. The starving men underwent a variety of physical, behavioral, and emotional changes. The changes that were observed are noteworthy because many bulimic patients may be existing in a state of semistarvation.

Metabolic Changes. An overall slowing of the body's physiological processes was noted, including decreases in heart rate, respiration, and body temperature. In addition, by the end of the starvation phase, the basal metabolic rate, which accounts for about two-thirds of the body's total energy needs, had dropped to about 60 percent of normal. Clearly the men's bodies were attempting to tolerate caloric restrictions by simultaneously reducing the need for energy and maximizing the energy from the available calories.

Very interesting changes in the relative portion of fat and muscle tissue were observed during starvation and refeeding. Weight declined by 25 percent, but the percentage of body fat decreased nearly 70 percent and the percentage of muscle fell by 40 percent. Upon refeeding, the greater portion of the regained weight was fat; in the eighth month of refeeding the men were about 110 percent of their original weight but had approximately 140 percent of their original body fat. It took over a year before their body weight and percentage of fat approached the preexperiment levels.

Eating Behavior and Attitudes. The volunteers experienced a tremendous increase in their preoccupation with food as a result of starvation. For most it interfered to the point that concentrating on routine activities became difficult because of intrusive thoughts about food. Talking and daydreaming about food occupied a large portion of the men's time. Eating habits changed drastically as well. Men often ate in total silence, devoting complete attention to their food. They made strange concoctions by mixing foods together and significantly increased their use of salt and spices. By the end of the starvation phase many men would linger over a meal for two hours to prolong it as much as possible. The level of physical activity also dropped as they became more focused on food.

All of the men experienced hunger, but they varied markedly in their ability to tolerate it. Several men were not able to adhere to their diets and had episodes of bulimia followed by self-reproach. During the refeeding phase many of the men ate more or less continually and frequently complained of an increase in hunger immediately after a large meal. Men found it very difficult to stop eating, and some consumed huge numbers of calories. By the fifth month of rehabilitation most men reported some normalization of their eating habits. For some, however, the tremendous overeating continued even beyond the eighth month.

Emotional, Social, and Cognitive Changes. This group of subjects was considered to be emotionally healthy prior to the experiment. Most experienced significant emotional deterioration as a result of starvation. Some of the men's even-temperedness was replaced by irritability and angry outbursts. Anxiety, apathy, and depression also increased among many. Psychological test findings using the MMPI indicated that the starvation resulted in significant increases in depression, hysteria, and hypochondria. These difficulties did not immediately decrease with rehabilitation.

Socially the men grew more withdrawn as the experiment progressed, whereas before the experiment they had been socially outgoing. They reported that contact with others was too troublesome and consequently spent more time alone. Sexual interest reduced dramatically and was slow to return during rehabilitation.

The subjects reported difficulty with concentration, alertness, and judgment during starvation, although they performed normally on standard intellectual tests. It is likely that the impaired concentration reported was related to intrusive preoccupation with food.

The results of the starvation study demonstrate that some of the most common complaints of bulimic patients are also the natural sequelae of semistarvation. Obsessive thoughts about food are to be expected when one is starving; a focus on food at these times would be extremely adaptive. Episodes of binge eating and feelings of affective instability were also found in the normal men following starvation, just as with bulimic patients.

In a recent study of starvation (Fichter and Pirke, 1984), five normal female subjects underwent three to six weeks of complete food abstinence and then were returned to their normal weight. During the starvation period several endocrine disturbances were found, including elevation in plasma cortisol and growth hormone levels and decreases in thyroid stimulating hormone levels. These levels did not return to normal until the original body weight was restored, indicating that even a brief period of severe calorie restriction has significant physiological effects. The data are quite clear that brief starvation or semistarvation significantly disrupts normal functioning.

RESTRAINT THEORY

In addition to the physical and emotional side effects of semistarvation, research over the last decade has demonstrated that, among certain individuals, chronic dieting can provoke psychologically motivated counterregulatory behavior such as binge eating. Herman and Mack (1975) developed a scale that identified a group they labeled restrained eaters. These individuals were habitually concerned with eating, dieting, and weight. They attempted to maintain rigid dietary standards that created significant physiological and psychological stress. This group was also very vulnerable to all-or-none thinking; any violation of their rigid standards of calorie intake provoked binge eating.

Most bulimic patients would unquestionably be regarded as restrained eaters (Ruderman, 1985). Consequently, over the years we have used the literature on restraint theory to emphasize to our patients how setting rigid dietary standards for themselves probably makes them more vulnerable to what they fear most: overeating and subsequent weight gain.

We have found it useful to present two studies to patients. In Herman and Mack's original study (1975), they administered their restraint scale and divided subjects into two groups: those who displayed a great deal of concern around their weight and dieting and those who were unrestrained regarding food intake. Women in each group were given one cup of milkshake, two cups, or none at all. As the subjects were always tested following a meal, those who also drank the milkshakes were likely to be quite full. Next the subjects were asked to participate in a "taste test" and were told to eat as much of the test food (ice cream) as they wished.

The unrestrained eaters behave as one might expect. The more milkshake they drank, the less ice cream they subsequently ate. However, the restrained eaters ate *more* ice cream if they had one cup of milkshake, and even more if they had two cups. The authors concluded that when these restrained eaters felt that they had violated their own dietary restrictions by drinking a milkshake, they abandoned restrained eating for a time. They seemed to feel that since they had already "blown their diets," they might as well go all the way and continue eating foods they typically denied themselves.

The second study conducted by Spencer and Fremouw (1979) demonstrated that subjects' *beliefs* about how many calories they were consuming were more important than the actual amount. These researchers told half their subjects that a preparation they were to drink was very high in calories and the other half that it was very low in calories. Subjects were then invited to eat as much ice cream as they wished. Restrained eaters ate twice as much ice cream when they believed their drink was high calorie as opposed to low calorie. Unrestrained subjects did not show significant differences in the amount eaten. This study suggests that restraint is cognitively mediated. Restrained eaters abandon restraint when they believe they have violated their harsh dietary standards, regardless of calorie intake.

In summary, most bulimic patients have developed a belief that the best way to protect themselves from being out of control with food is to avoid it. It must be pointed out to them that, paradoxically, the more they avoid food, the more preoccupied and compelled to eat they are going to feel. We often, with humor, attempt to establish the perspective with patients that "the best defense against binge eating is to eat."

CHANGING EATING HABITS

Challenging the patient's eating habits will unquestionably provoke substantial resistance. How the resistance is manifested, however, will offer significant clues regarding the adaptive function of the patient's disturbed eating behavior. It will also help clarify the overall extent of the patient's psychopathology.

Our specific approach to normalizing food intake varies according to the patient's unique needs. After obtaining a detailed record of the patients' daily eating habits (see figure 10.2), we begin to recommend changes. We are keenly attentive to how the patient experiences each recommendation. The exploration of her experience of the proposed change is often what allows the patient to effect a change. We also work very hard to present the rationale for our recommended changes in an effort to demonstrate to the patient that we are not acting arbitrarily.

Timing of Eating. Many of our patients attempt to avoid food during the day, when their lives are usually most structured, and then attempt

FIGURE 10.2
Daily Meal Plan

Meal Plan	Food Eaten		
	Day 1	Day 2	Day 3
Breakfast *Food Groups* Egg or meat Bread and starch Fat Milk Fruit			
Snack Midmorning			
Lunch *Food Groups* Meat Vegetable Bread and starch Fat Milk Fruit			
Snack Midafternoon			
Dinner *Food Groups* Meat Vegetable Bread and starch Fat Milk Fruit			
Snack Evening			

to feed themselves when they are at home alone in the evening. Essentially they are trying to handle food when they are at peak hunger in a setting in which they are most vulnerable. We emphasize to patients that we would like them to eat most during the day or whenever their time is most structured.

We focus on the importance of eating breakfast both from a biological and a psychological perspective. Once again we inform patients of how low-calorie intake early in the day can adversely affect their mood states. This is particularly true if they do not eat early in the morning but consume coffee. This combination can destabilize their moods quickly. The psychological advantage of eating breakfast is that the individual begins the day in a nondepriving manner. Generally, it is also an action that challenges patients' routine diet mentality.

Many patients find it easier to eat smaller quantities several times per day. These smaller but more frequent meals protect them from feeling too full at any one time.

Patients will often react to these suggested changes by expressing their fears of losing control of food for the entire day if they begin eating in the morning or during the day. Also, some complain that if they were to eat during the day they would have nothing to look forward to in the evening. We acknowledge their concerns and encourage them to experiment with the changes.

Meal Size and Portion Control. In the early stages of treatment, we feel it is important to err in the direction of being concrete and structured with meal planning. We emphasize to our patients that the meal plans are not "diets" and that the goal of the meal plan is not to lose weight. Rather the goal is to develop a way of eating that they can comfortably rely on throughout their lives.

Bulimic patients frequently ask how much they can eat without gaining weight. We honestly state that there is no precise way of knowing. Weight regulation is affected by a variety of variables, including genetic predisposition to weight gain, amount of exercise, and history of feeding behavior. We suggest, however, that we can offer an "informed guess" about what a reasonable meal plan would be. In negotiating the meal plan with patients, it is important that the therapist assure normal-weight patients that he or she is committed to protecting them from runaway weight gain.

We try to avoid excessive emphasis on calories and instead focus on meeting nutritional needs from the basic food groups. The food diary gives baseline information on types and quantities of food eaten. The task then becomes to patiently negotiate gradual change in both the type and quantity of foods eaten. In the early stages of treatment, working this out on a meal-by-meal basis using the format depicted in figure 10.2 is quite useful.

Since most patients report that they have difficulty stopping eating once they begin, it is useful to develop strategies for controlling portions. Overall, we try to deemphasize weighing food. Instead we rely on food models and visualizaton techniques to help patients learn how average portions look.

It is also our experience that patients will generally eat whatever amount appears before them. Consequently we encourage them to become assertive and take control of the amount of food placed on their plate. In families where the patient does most of the meal preparation, we discourage her from serving family style. Instead we suggest that she portion meals away from the table before sitting down for the meal. When patients are still children in families, we encourage them to serve themselves away from the table and to remove food on the table from their immediate reach.

Portion control in restaurants usually creates significant problems for patients. Since most restaurants serve unreasonably large portions, the prospect of eating in a restaurant is terrifying for most patients. Often they actively avoid eating out, which ultimately interferes with their social lives. We teach patients that when they enter a restaurant, they can casually move bread or other appetizers out of arm's reach in an effort to avoid unwittingly picking at food while they are waiting for their meal. We also have them ask for an extra plate, so that they can serve themselves the portion they feel they can eat comfortably. The rest of the food can be offered to others at the table or removed. The crucial factor is that patients have control over the amount of food that appears on their plate. Despite fear of self-consciousness and embarrassment, mastery of this tool reduces patients' restaurant anxiety and often significantly expands their options for social contact.

Some patients have more difficulty determining proper meal sizes; we encourage them to portion food in separate containers. For example, if they are going to eat cereal each morning, we ask them to divide the large box of cereal into individual portions when they initially bring the cereal home. This is an effort to avoid making difficult decisions around portion size at the moment they are trying to eat, which is usually a high-anxiety time that can affect their perception of the meal size. We have also found gourmet frozen dinners for evening meals to be an excellent alternative to lengthy food preparation during the high-risk evening hours for patients who work during the day and live alone.

Eating Rituals. Patients will often unwittingly establish eating rituals that are counterproductive. Once again we ask patients to detail for us their thoughts and behaviors before, during, and after a meal. After exploring their existing routines, we attempt to formulate new rituals for these times.

Preceding the meal, we want patients to orient themselves before embarking on food preparation or eating. We want them to visualize the entire process of food preparation and eating before they begin. They should not begin the process either impulsively or when they feel hassled or disorganized. Many patients enter their home and reflexively stop in the kitchen, where they quickly "grab" some type of food. This usually triggers more chaotic and impulsive eating. We encourage patients to enter their homes through a different room than the kitchen. We ask that they establish some other entry ritual, such as straightening up, sorting mail, watching television, being with their children, reading the front page of the paper, and so forth. Once they feel that they have transitioned into the home, then they can approach the kitchen.

Food preparation can be a dangerous time because patients often begin to "pick at food." They also can become overwhelmed if too much food is out at one time. We ask that they not eat during food preparation and that they work on one thing at a time. We also ask that they pick up extra food as they go along so that when they begin their meal, food is not visually strewn throughout the kitchen. This also minimizes the amount of food handling necessary after the meal when they may be vulnerable to continuing eating.

During the meal we ask that they sit down in the spot designated as the dinner table. They should avoid eating standing up or in a spot where they characteristically binge eat. We ask patients to minimize watching television or reading during the meal. Such activities distract patients and result in their feeling that they did not eat or that they have lost track of what they have eaten. For patients who eat too quickly, we suggest that they pace themselves by doing things such as putting their fork down between bites. For patients who eat too slowly, we suggest that they put a time limit on their meal.

After the meal, some patients find it helpful to avoid clearing the dishes until later. As a rule of thumb, we encourage patients to engage themselves in some activity then since this is the high-risk time for feeling anxious and vulnerable to purging.

Demystifying Food Groups. Along with issues of timing and portion control, as treatment proceeds the therapist wants to challenge some of the patient's beliefs about different food groups. We have patients identify high- and low-risk foods and try to explore their beliefs about these foods. Some patients simply have bad information, while others have more psychoticlike thoughts regarding different foods. The pace at which one challenges these beliefs obviously depends on the function the belief serves in the patient's overall psychic economy.

Most patients are carbohydrate avoidant and regard this food group as their worst enemy. We routinely take aim at this misconception and attempt to argue that, contrary to their belief, carbohydrates are perhaps their best friends. We explain the difference between simple and complex carbohydrates, how they function in the system, and how they may be particularly helpful in managing hunger.

Although we realize that sweets offer few nutrients, we also feel that suggesting total abstinence from them may paradoxically provoke an attraction to them. Consequently, as patients feel more comfortable with their eating, we encourage them to include "desserts" in their overall scheme for lifetime eating habits.

SIDE EFFECTS OF MEAL NORMALIZATION

Changing patients' eating habits inevitably creates panic about bodily changes. Common complaints include bloating, feeling that food is sitting in their stomachs, and fears about rapid weight gain. These are often predictable side effects from changing eating habits, and it can be very useful for the therapist to acknowledge the possibility of these events occurring. We inform patients that as they decrease their vomiting or laxative use, they may experience rebound edema. We explain that the body has experienced the repeated dehydration from the purging as a drought and that the adaptive response to more fluids becoming available is to retain fluids above the normal level. As the body learns that fluids are consistently available, fluid regulation will normalize. Likewise, the body has experienced the calorie restriction as a famine. The organism's response is to become hypometabolic in order to make effective use of each calorie. When more food is available, initially the body attempts to store reserves. Sometimes this results in a rapid but brief weight gain. As calories are more consistently available, metabolism and weight regulation will normalize. It has been our experience that in the long run, many patients actually lose weight once they stop bingeing and purging. We also explain to patients that if they have repeatedly evacuated over several years, the stomach loses part of its efficiency in digesting food (Dubois, Gross, Ebert, and Castell, 1979). Consequently it may actually take longer for food to digest. Once again, as the stomach becomes more active, the delayed gastric emptying decreases.

WEIGHT EXPECTATIONS

Any effort to normalize eating patterns will quickly focus fears regarding weight gain. The question of what is a reasonable weight expectation for the patient is one of the most delicate that the therapist will confront. We explain to patients our overall perspective on weight expectation and regulation: once calorie intake has been stabilized and reasonable exercise patterns have been established, body weight will normalize in a range that is biogenetically appropriate for them. We emphasize that this is our way of avoiding an arbitrary weight expectation. Likewise, we hope that patients will also learn to avoid choosing weight goals that may be a "bad fit" with their biology and psychology. This perspective generally requires substantial justification because it threatens fundamental beliefs patients have about the importance of weight control and how that is accomplished. We inform patients about what we have learned regarding how the body regulates weight and how much control we seem to have over this process, using set-point theory as an explanatory model (Keesey, 1980; Mrosovsky and Powley, 1977; Nisbett, 1972). Set-point theory suggests that both animals and humans have a biogenetic predisposition to maintain certain levels of body fat. The notion is likened to a thermostat where body fat is expected to remain at a certain level and any deviation from that point induces metabolic changes designed to restore the level of body fat to the prescribed set point. This mechanism is thought to have arisen over millions of years of evolution, enabling our ancestors to survive periods of famine by conserving energy. Polivy and Herman (1983) prefer to use the term natural weight rather than set point, because it connotes a broader range of regulated weight. These researchers suggest what they call a boundary model of weight regulation, in which all individuals naturally operate within an upper and lower limit of biologically defined weights. The span of the boundaries and their upper and lower limits are believed to vary a great deal between individuals. It is also becoming increasingly clear that the amount and distribution of this body fat is genetically prescribed. So as with our height, eye color, skin color, and so forth, the size and shape of our bodies reflects our parentage.

Different studies emphasize this point. In a classic study, Neuman (1902) explored the long-term effect of overeating by systematically increasing his daily calorie intake. For the first year he increased it by 430 calories per day and during the second year by 300 more calories per day. Calculations indicated that he should have gained forty pounds the first year and sixty pounds the second year. Interestingly, he experienced only a slight weight increase. The concept that has evolved to explain this phenomenon is called diet-induced thermogenesis. Essentially the body has the ability to waste calories by raising the basal metabolism. It has also been demonstrated that the body's capacity to burn off excess calories is more pronounced in lean individuals than in obese ones.

A more sophisticated study demonstrated similar results. Sims and his colleagues (1968) attempted to produce obesity in a group of normal-weight male prison inmate volunteers. Over six months, the volunteers attempted to gain between 20 and 25 percent of their original weights. All the men ate approximately twice their usual number of calories daily. While most of them gained the first several pounds easily, the majority found it very difficult to increase their weight significantly despite consuming large numbers of calories. Similar to the starved men's metabolic rates slowing to conserve energy, the overfed men's bodies adapted by increasing metabolic activity. The men complained of an excess of body heat and perspired profusely. Over time they found the task of overeating increasingly unpleasant. After the experiment, with the resumption of more normal eating, the men began losing weight very rapidly and ultimately stabilized their weights very close to their preexperiment weights. Overall, the amount of weight gain accounted for only 25 percent of extra calories consumed.

Likewise, there is significant evidence that when individuals are systematically underfed hypometabolism occurs. The hypometabolism is an adaptive effort to decrease weight loss by using calories more effectively. Our most convincing evidence comes from the literature on the long-term effectiveness of dieting. Stunkard (1978) has reported the striking statistic that only 5 percent of obese individuals maintain a weight loss of at least twenty pounds for two years or more. We emphasize to our patients that it is unlikely that "lack of willpower" among all those who have attempted dieting could account for these poor results. Instead, it appears the body has a strong investment in regulating weight within certain parameters. We also make the commonsense point that if there were any consistent way of losing weight, there would not be so many diet books available. Indeed, there are so many different diet books because no diet works consistently.

We also inform our patients that the more frequently individuals diet, the more difficult it becomes to lose weight. Chronic dieters appear to make increasingly quick metabolic adjustments once caloric restriction begins. Each new time they initiate dieting, the speed and amount of weight they can lose decreases (Garrow, 1974; Wooley and Wooley, 1979).

We recommend several very readable books on this subject to our patients (see the "Recommended Reading" list that appears later in this chapter). These include *The Dieter's Dilemma* (Bennett and Gurin, 1982), *Breaking the Diet Habit* (Polivy and Herman, 1983), and the chapter by Garner and coworkers in the *Handbook of Psychotherapy for Anorexia and Bulimia* (Garner and Garfinkel, 1984) entitled "Psychoeducational Principles in the Treatment of Anorexia Nervosa and Bulimia."

Our overall message is that the chronic pursuit of thinness probably destines these patients to struggle with their own biology in a way that will most likely produce repeated feelings of frustration, failure, chronic food preoccupation, and anxiety. At least at this point, biology does appear to be destiny in terms of weight regulation.

For most bulimics, this is a very despairing conversation because, as we reviewed earlier, many of their premorbid weight histories are above what they consider to be aesthetically appealing. The information we provide suggests that their ideal goals may be unobtainable. This awareness can generate substantial rage, hopelessness, helplessness, depression, and, in some cases, disorganization. We remind our patients, however, that since most of them have had chaotic eating patterns for so long, it is unclear what a biologically reasonable weight for them is. We also inform them that there is some evidence that regular and reasonable amounts of exercise can have an effect on the biological regulation of weight by increasing metabolic efficiency.

CHALLENGING THE OVERVALUATION OF THINNESS

Any attempt to challenge the patient's belief about the importance of dieting may also require that the therapist explore the meaning thinness has for the patient.

Many women have simply internalized the prevailing cultural norm that thinness equals beauty, success, and control (see chapter 7). They have not considered the political and economic implications of their endorsement of the current norm. We have found consciousness-raising material regarding how expectations of women's body size have vacillated historically and how a multibillion-dollar industry is currently exploiting women's preoccupation with thinness to be useful.

Cultural Norms for Thinness. A study by Garner, Garfinkel, Schwartz, and Thompson (1980) illustrates society's recent shift toward more slender shapes for women. These researchers examined statistics on *Playboy* centerfolds and Miss America pageant winners over a twenty-year span (1958–1978). They discovered that both the centerfolds and the pageant contestants have become significantly thinner over the last twenty years. The *Playboy* centerfolds have assumed a more tubular shape, with smaller bust and hip measurements and larger waists. This trend toward a thinner figure in these centerfolds is particularly striking since actual changes in women's bodies over the last twenty-five years have been toward an increase in weight. The Metropolitan Life Insurance weight tables indicate that the expected weight for women under thirty years of age has increased (due to improved nutrition) at about the same rate that the average weight of the centerfolds has decreased. Thus the gap between the real and the ideal has been progressively increasing (see figure 10.3).

Since 1970 the winners of the Miss America pageant have weighed significantly less than the other contestants. Between 1970 and 1978, slightly over 5 percent of female life insurance policyholders between the ages of twenty and twenty-nine were as slim as the average Miss America women. When one considers that *Playboy* centerfolds and Miss America contestants are much more full-figured than the models held up to us by the fashion industry, it is very obvious how few women fit that emaciated but supposedly ideal shape (Garner et al., 1984). In fact, 95 percent of all women do *not* look this way.

We emphasize to patients our belief that it is more important to be healthy than to be thin and stress the consequences of attempting to live below a biologically appropriate weight. The drive for thinness is extremely entrenched in some patients, so much so that we have heard statements like "I'd rather be dead than be fat." It is easy to get into arguments with patients regarding these attitudes. However, a more fruitful approach is to point out that patients can choose to live below their set point, but the consequences will be eternal dieting, unrelenting hunger, and, in all probability, lifelong bingeing and purging.

We have also found an excerpt from *Such a Pretty Face* to be useful

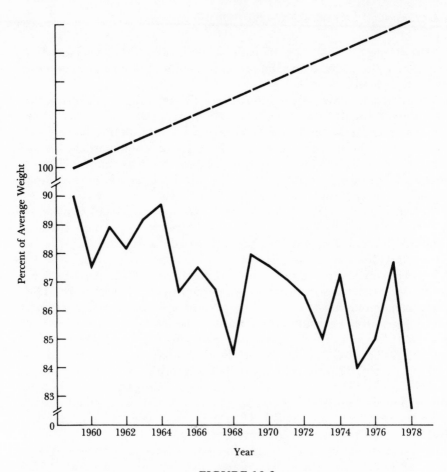

FIGURE 10.3
*Changes in Percent of Average Weight of Centerfolds and Winners of the
Miss America Pageant over a Twenty-Year Period[a]*

NOTE: Adapted from D. M. Garner, P. E. Garfinkel, D. Schwartz, and M. Thompson, "Cultural Expectations of Thinness in Women," *Psychological Reports* 47 (1980): 483-491. Reprinted by permission.
[a] Average weight is based upon the Society of Actuaries' 1959 norms. The broken line represents prorated changes in the average weights for women over the same twenty-year period, based upon the revised Society of Actuaries' 1979 norms.

(Millman, 1980).* This brief autobiographical statement by a woman who accomplished nothing in her life except being thin usually has a powerful impact on patients. They often begin to think seriously about what the future holds if they do not change their behavior.

Most of the cognitive distortions described earlier are seen in patients' overvaluation of thinness. We point out how patients magnify the importance of weight-related issues while minimizing or discounting other

* This excerpt is reprinted at the end of chapter 9.

aspects of their identities. We attempt to have patients focus on things they like about themselves—assets, talents, and other parts of themselves that add to self-esteem rather than destroy it. Frequently we have to intervene with the cognitive distortion of personalization, where patients feel as though all eyes are on them and their fat when they appear in public. We continually emphasize that while patients are overconcerned with these matters, that does not mean that others who view them share their concern. We also point out the magical thinking involved in the fantasy that weight loss will take care of all of life's problems. Group treatment is particularly effective in this regard, as usually there are a few group members who are or have been their desired thin weights and can verify that they still had to cope with all the usual problems in living.

POLITICAL AND ECONOMIC ASPECTS OF DIETING

Susan Brownmiller (1984) has noted that nearly every civilization has sought to impose a uniform shape on the female body, such that some portion of a woman's anatomy was accentuated, rearranged, or reduced. She cites two particularly striking examples: foot binding in China and the wearing of corsets in nineteenth-century America.

Foot binding flourished in China for some eight hundred years. A woman's foot in its natural state was considered to be profoundly ugly and in need of correction. Unbound feet were associated with very low status, while bound feet illustrated the fact that aristocratic women need not stoop to physical labor. The cultural ideal was the "lotus foot," preferably no more than three inches long. This was accomplished by the tight binding of young girls' feet over a period of years, during which time the toes would drop off and the foot would become curved. Needless to say, the resulting excruciating pain and crippling markedly reduced autonomous movement. The lotus foot figured prominently in the pornography of the time and was considered by men to be highly erotic. Generation after generation of mothers taught their daughters to glorify the bound foot, assuring them that the pain was minor compared with the ridicule they would face as women with larger (that is, normal) feet.

Such pain and disfigurement was by no means confined to China. In nineteenth-century America women were taught that their spines and musculature were not strong enough to support the breasts and stomach. Whalebone corsetry extending from the hips to the breasts was the solution. The squeeze of the corset could exert between twenty and eighty pounds of pressure, depending on how tightly the "stays" could be tied. The tiny waist was glorified, and a waist that could not be encircled by a man's hands was unacceptable. For many women the result was constant discomfort and shortness of breath. For some the consequences were more serious: cracked ribs or even death from deformities of lungs and other internal organs.

These examples of painful and debilitating practices to attain a particular cultural ideal are not so different from women's struggles today to attain thinness. The emaciated anorexic and the desperate bulimic represent those whose dedication to the ideal of thinness result in anguish, an obsession that leaves little room for other aspects of life, and potentially life-threatening health problems. Although women who have severe eating disorders experience the most difficulty in their efforts to achieve thinness, most women today express dissatisfaction with their body weight (Rodin, Silberstein, and Striegel-Moore, 1984).

Furthermore, Brownmiller comments that while a variety of preferred standards concerning attractiveness for men have existed (for example, regarding hair length or facial hair), they have not been customs that would result in pain, debilitation, and lessened autonomy, as has been the case for women.

We find it helpful to compare our patients' preoccupation with thinness and the resulting self-destructive behavior to these customs and suggest that patients read Brownmiller's book as well as *The Obsession* (Chernin, 1981). These works can provide patients with a thought-provoking historical and anthropological perspective. These ideas can also generate a healthy anger, as women decide that they need not sacrifice themselves on the altar of thinness in an effort to attain a cultural ideal that is fundamentally antifemale.

All these interventions help a patient to feel that perhaps there is something wrong with current cultural values rather than with her. Discussions of the economics of the diet industry can help women realize how they are being manipulated by promoters of diet books, foods, and other paraphernalia who make billions of dollars per year by convincing women that they are not all right as they are but that they can be by using a particular product. Essentially we attempt to instill in our patients the sense that the diet industry strives to capitalize on their vulnerability and that they need not buy into it. We use humor by discussing some of the more ridiculous diet plans and products, such as a suit that attaches to one's vacuum cleaner, pills that purport to burn fat during sleep, and a diet plan that relies on overconsumption of fruit and the resultant diarrhea for weight loss. We also stress the fact that if any of these diet books and products worked, there would not be a continuous flow of newer products onto the market. However, promoters of these articles know that they essentially have a market that does not "shrink," since people do not achieve weight loss and are willing to try the latest gimmick. Our patients are intelligent women who can become much less vulnerable to marketing strategies when the exploitation of the diet industry is clarified for them.

SELF-MONITORING

Positive self-esteem and feelings of effectiveness occur when one learns how to successfully manage one's life. Feelings of mastery accrue when one repeatedly and successfully navigates challenging life situations. Learning how to anticipate difficult situations and manage one's feeling states in reaction to these events can contribute significantly to an increased sense of mastery.

Patients can be taught a two-tiered model of self-monitoring. At a macroscopic level, the task is to explore and identify global life repetitions. More specifically, the therapist is trying to learn with the patient how she has responded in the past to major life events, such as loss or separation from significant others, major transitions, experiences of failure and rejection, intimate relationships, assuming challenging responsibilities, and so forth. The purpose of the inquiry is to help the patient respond to these circumstances more effectively when they occur.

At a more microscopic level, the task is to help patients learn how to anticipate difficult situations and monitor their internal states daily. It is often useful to have patients fill out monitoring forms (see figure 8.2) several times per day over the course of a week. Patients will often discover recurring patterns of mood fluctuations and disturbed eating behavior related to predictable daily or weekly events. Coming home at night, beginning to prepare food, visiting family, eating in restaurants, food shopping, drinking alcohol, watching television, weighing oneself in the morning, skipping lunch, being alone, and so on are all mundane events that may have predictable effects on the patient. Once again, being able to identify and anticipate vulnerable contexts allows patients to think about developing alternative strategies for coping with these situations, thus facilitating a sense of mastery.

SELF-ENHANCING ACTIVITIES

Many bulimic patients have low self-esteem and have become withdrawn and isolated as a result of food-related behavior. As they become more enmeshed in the binge/purge cycle, their range of involvement with different activities narrows dramatically and too often they quit doing things they once enjoyed. Overall, it seems apparent that the frequency of bulimic episodes is highly correlated with a patient's self-esteem. When bulimics feel better about themselves, they binge less and vice versa. Exploring and encouraging patients to develop or reintroduce self-enhancing activities is extremely important. Since most bulimics are not exercise abusers, we often encourage them to initiate some form of exercise that can help reduce tension and increase self-esteem.

Pre-Binge State

As a result of self-monitoring, most bulimic patients learn to identify situations that make them vulnerable to binge eating. Nonetheless, they will continue to feel the pressure of the impulse to binge eat at times. The overall task of the second phase of the self-monitoring model is to provide the patient with more specific strategies to manage the immediate impulse to binge eat. The primary goal is to introduce mechanisms that will facilitate delay of this impulse.

PERSPECTIVE

Bulimic patients often appear to lapse cognitively under the pressure of strong affects. It is often helpful to suggest a single word that might help patients organize during these times. We use the word perspective to attempt to teach patients to focus away from the immediacy of their affective state. Some striking changes in symptomatic behaviors have been observed as patients begin to rehearse using the word. Apparently, if a therapist uses the word frequently, the patient's later use of the word may evoke a memory of the therapist or the therapeutic holding environment. For character-disordered patients who have difficulty with evocative object recall, the association between the word and the therapeutic holding environment is sometimes sufficient to help soothe them when they feel in danger of losing control. In the early stages of treatment, we often joke with patients that they will probably become sick of hearing the word perspective because we use it so often.

MOOD STATES

We attempt to teach patients that the urge to binge is a signal to them that they need to attend to some internal state. We liken it to how the urge to urinate signals a full or distressed bladder or how a recurring headache is usually a signal of stress or anxiety. The patient's task then is to decode what the signal is indicating specifically. Encouraging the patient to try to be specific in identifying her mood states is important because specifying the mood state is necessary in order to find appropriate and gratifying alternative responses to binge eating. For example, if a patient is feeling depressed and lonely, then withdrawing into her home is an ineffective response to that particular mood state. Likewise, if she is feeling very anxious and agitated, sitting down and attempting to read is also an ineffective response. If a patient, over the course of time, realizes that her urges to binge are related very specifically to a particular affective state, then we will suggest to her, with humor, that she has a built-in barometer for that feeling state. The purpose of this is to demystify the urge to binge. It may even allow the patient to reframe the experience of the urge to binge; rather than indicating that she is about to lose control, the urge is a signal that there is a disruption that must be attended to.

Obviously, the task of specifying what they are feeling is enormously demanding for these patients, who have difficulty identifying and articulating internal states. In fact, for some it will be the essence of treatment. It is important for the therapist to be persistent but patient with this task.

Some patients cannot initially generate labels to describe how they feel. When they attempt to think about how they feel, they become overwhelmed and may become even more confused. Providing these patients with a series of scaled adjectives or a "menu" of potential affective states can be quite helpful in teaching them how to evaluate themselves.

COMMON EMOTIONAL PRECIPITANTS TO A BINGE EPISODE

We have observed that there are a number of recurring emotional themes that make patients particularly vulnerable to a binge episode.

Anger. Anger is a mood state that is frequently troublesome for bulimic patients. For more severely character-disordered patients, the affect can be quite disorganizing and should be approached cautiously. Most bulimic patients, however, avoid expressing anger because they fear the interpersonal consequences, such as disapproval, rejection, or retaliation. They are intimidated interpersonally, which often results in their being exploited. As mentioned earlier, bingeing/purging behavior can emerge as an adaptive effort to cope with this feeling state.

It is our experience that most bulimic patients can benefit from assertiveness training. Frank discussions of their fears that their anger will get out of control and their anxieties about criticism, rejection, and retaliation can help them gain some perspective on their difficulty with this emotion. Direct role playing of difficult social situations, particularly in group treatment settings, can be a very powerful learning experience for them.

We also use Pamela Butler's book *Self Assertion for Women* (1981) as an adjunct to this aspect of therapy. When a patient experiences being appropriately self-assertive, she often finds no need to binge eat. This experience establishes the connection between feelings, behaviors, and binge eating in an extremely salient manner. We tell our patients that the more they express themselves verbally, the less they will experience the urge to manage their feelings by binge eating and purging.

The Capacity to Be Alone. Our research has indicated that the greater a patient's capacity to tolerate solitude, the less likely she is to have trouble with binge eating and purging (Larson and Johnson, 1985). Earlier we discussed our observations regarding two different types of difficulty with solitude that appear to reflect different types of intrapsychic problems (see page 171).

A group of patients with more severe self-regulatory difficulties experience being alone as a highly anxious and disorganizing time when they feel lost, out of control, abandoned, and as if they are falling apart. These patients use binge eating to create a predictable, soothing structure. In contrast, for patients who are obsessive and highly achievement oriented, time alone provokes excessive rumination about the things they are supposed to do and the things they have failed to accomplish. If they are in conflict about doing the task or are exhausted by the relentless drive to accomplish, they often use binge eating as a mechanism to space out or distract themselves.

For patients who become disorganized when alone, we actively attempt to establish rituals other than binge eating that provide structure and may be comforting and soothing. For select patients we might attempt to cultivate a transitional object (see chapter 11) or invite them to call the therapist if they are feeling extremely panicky. Overall, usually these patients will be able to tolerate solitude only after an extended period of consistent and reliable contact with a therapist.

Working with patients who are in conflict about "free time" is much less complicated. Challenging a patient's beliefs about the need to be achieving constantly and giving her permission to be "lazy" at certain times can help minimize the risk of needing to binge eat in order to take a break from all of the responsibility she feels. For some we prescribe blocks of time during the day when they are forbidden from being responsible for achieving. We solicit their most self-indulgent fantasies and challenge them to approximate them. While this may seem like fun to some of us, it is a very demanding request for patients with these conflicts. Often we see the patient attempt to transform the pursuit of self-indulgence into an obligatory task that is accompanied by self-critical evaluation and fear of failure.

Self-Nurturance. Patients who have great difficulty in being self-nurturing or who feel they must always be productive often suggest activities like cleaning or studying as alternatives to bingeing. These patients frequently set up a choice between a disliked activity, such as waxing the kitchen floor, and bingeing. After reaching for the ice cream rather than the mop, they conclude that alternatives will not work for them and that they simply must binge when the urge strikes. The therapist must gently point out that most people would choose an activity which affords some measure of satisfaction over one which is total drudgery. The necessity of giving oneself something pleasurable is stressed, as is the long-term nature of the alternative satisfactions. We state very clearly to our patients that at the moment they wish to binge no other activity will be anywhere near as satisfying, but that new hobbies, social activities, and exercise programs can become so in the long run.

Patients who have been taught to believe that attending to one's own needs (being "selfish") is a capital offense will also have trouble with the whole idea of the legitimacy of doing something nice for themselves. For these patients bulimia represents their only means of self-nurturance, although it is one about which they feel great shame. Often these patients feel so guilty about engaging in enjoyable pursuits just for themselves that it is very difficult for them to utilize alternative activities to bingeing. With these patients we have found it helpful to focus on the cognitive distortion that everyone else's needs take precedence over their own and to point out that their needs should be regarded as equally valid. For patients who have found it impossible to spend even an hour a week doing something enjoyable for themselves, we have resorted to an intermediate tactic: telling them that as long as they are bulimic they are just one more unhappy person who needs help, but that they can be much more effective helpers of others when they feel better. Generally as patients are able to focus a bit more on their own needs without anything catastrophic happening, they are more able to accept the fact that their bulimia was a cry for self-nurturance, and that they must respond in more life-enhancing ways.

Problem Solving. Many patients binge when faced with the need to make a decision. Their perfectionistic and obsessive tendencies can keep them swinging back and forth between alternatives until they become virtually immobilized. Procrastination and paralysis are the result when an individual believes catastrophe will ensue unless she makes the perfect decision. Often patients need to be taught basic problem-solving skills, such as constructing a list of the pros and cons of each possible decision. Because bulimics tend to be such compliant people pleasers, they may need help in trying to figure out what they themselves truly wish to do, apart from the expectations of others. The therapist can also stress that most decisions are not irrevocable and do not influence the entire course of one's life, which may help alleviate some of the pressure to make the "right" decision. The therapist needs to point out that all decisions have their risks and benefits, and that making active choices for oneself is preferable to delaying a decision by choosing the third alternative of bingeing.

Other patients tend to binge when faced with tasks that are experienced as unpleasant and overwhelming—frequently achievement-related projects such as writing papers or reports and studying for exams. Again, paralysis results because of the expectations for perfection. Patients must be taught to break the seemingly overwhelming task into its component parts and approach them one by one. Some patients also need help in setting realistic goals for themselves; for example, one patient believed that she should be able to study for several hours at a stretch without taking any breaks, and we found that she was bingeing in order to take some time off. The notion of rest breaks from study, which were legitimate and deserved, was foreign to her.

Social Supports. Often effective problem solving involves the appropriate use of social supports. A frequent dilemma for bulimics is whether
or not to reveal their problems to those close to them. We have treated
patients who have hidden their bulimia from family members for years,
despite living in the same household. While we do not encourage indiscriminate relevations, we do support our patients in disclosing their difficulties to family members and significant others who could be potential
sources of help. For example, a woman experimenting with eating anxiety-
provoking foods or trying to prevent a binge might be comforted by
having her husband hold her or by being able to share her feelings with
a close friend. Regardless of whether a patient reveals her bulimia to
others, the social isolation that increases with the development of the
syndrome is very troublesome. Patients refuse to see friends because they
feel too fat or too depressed, so they stay home and binge, causing further
isolation. We encourage our patients to push themselves in the direction
of social contact and to set gradual goals regarding calling friends and
arranging get-togethers.

ALTERNATIVES TO BINGE EATING

Once the mood state has been identified, the next step in the model
is to try to engage in an alternative behavior rather than binge eating. It
is crucial that patients experience their adoption of alternative behaviors
as a collaborative effort. Often it is useful for the therapist to actually
write out or tape-record the alternatives with the patient. The concrete
presence of the therapist's handwriting or voice may help the patient
maintain a feeling of connectedness when she is feeling panicky or at risk
of losing control.

The selection of specific alternative behaviors can be an exploratory
process to see what feels better or worse for patients during these high-
risk times. Framing the task as exploratory often helps minimize performance anxiety. As patients become more adept at identifying specific
mood states, the list must be revised to reflect their more sophisticated
ability to discriminate their different moods.

We almost always suggest to patients that they include making contact
with someone as one of their alternative behaviors. If the timing is appropriate in the therapeutic relationship, we encourage our therapists to
invite the patient to contact them. Therapists should extend such invitations cautiously, with full awareness that such contact can become quite
demanding. In general, we teach our therapists not to initiate anything
that they are not prepared to continue throughout the course of treatment.
This often helps prevent impulsive actions. Should a therapist invite contact, patients should be informed that he or she may not be able to respond
to their call immediately but will call back as soon as possible. We have

found certain advantages to using answering machines rather than answering services. The lengthy messages patients often leave feel cathartic to them, and some are simply reassured by the sound of the therapist's voice on the recorded message.

When initially trying to interfere with the binge-eating behavior, patients should not attempt to agree to completely avoid bingeing. Instead the agreement should be that patients will engage in alternative behavior on the list before binge eating. This safeguards against patients feeling they have failed if they binge; it minimizes their psychological feeling of being restrained; and it relieves their potential fear that something is being taken away from them that is necessary for their self-maintenance.

Post-Binge State

No matter how adept patients become at attempting to prevent a binge episode, there will be times when they feel they have eaten too much. After such an episode, the patient once again has an opportunity to interfere with the chain behavior. We encourage our patients to make a central commitment to themselves to stop purging.

COMMITMENT TO NONPURGING

If this patient population adheres to any sort of abstinence model, we feel it should be regarding purging. We mention to patients that while it is impossible for them to abstain from food, it is not physiologicially impossible for them to abstain from purging. For some patients it is useful to explain what we have learned about how the continued use of evacuation techniques fuels the binge/purge cycle. We emphasize that purging is a behavior they can take a stand on; in contrast with overeating versus binge eating, there are no gray zones of interpretation about whether one has purged. If at some point in treatment the therapist feels the need to confront a patient about taking responsibility for her actions, this is a good behavior to focus on. Some patients have been remarkably successful using an abstinence approach. They seem to organize around the commitment to avoid purging. The sense of self-discipline they once derived from starving themselves is shifted to a dogged determination not to purge what they have eaten.

ALTERNATIVES TO PURGING

As with the alternatives to binge eat, it is useful to construct a list that guides the patient during the highly stressful post-binge period. We usually inform patients that if they can avoid purging for forty-five minutes to one hour after the binge or meal, the urge to purge will often abate quickly. Since most patients feel quite agitated during this time, alternative behaviors should be fairly action oriented. The availability of a reliable significant other during this time can be very useful to the patients. Most patients have difficulty being alone when they feel panicky after a meal.

The Post-Binge/Purge Sequence

The overall task of the post-binge/purge phase is to challenge the thoughts and feelings that perpetuate the repetition of the binge/purge cycle once it has occurred. We emphasize to patients that there will be times when they both binge and purge.

We teach our patients that bulimia is an episodic disorder and that the goal of treatment is to minimize the frequency and impact the behavior has on their lives. Since most patients will have bulimic episodes throughout their lives, one very important aspect of treatment is to teach them how to cope with relapses.

RELAPSE TRAINING

Marlatt (1979) and Marlatt and Gordon (1978) have developed a cognitive-behavioral approach to the relapse process. They define relapse as the first reoccurrence of a target behavior after a period of abstinence. Although their work was with addictive behaviors such as alcoholism, drug abuse, and smoking, their model of the relapse process seems applicable to bulimia as well.

Marlatt and Gordon (1978) obtained accounts of relapse episodes from 137 subjects, all of whom had participated in treatment programs for alcoholism, heroin addiction, or smoking. More than three-quarters of all relapse episodes fell into three categories, based on a classification system devised by the authors. Coping with negative emotional states was cited by 37 percent of the sample; with social pressure, by 24 percent; and with interpersonal conflict, by 15 percent.

Marlatt and Gordon suggest that cognitive factors play a primary role in the relapse process. The criterion of total abstinence is the most stringent rule one can adopt, so a single occurrence of the target behavior violates the rule of abstinence. Marlatt has termed the cognitive process by which an individual interprets a relapse the *abstinence violation effect* (AVE). Within Marlatt and Gordon's theoretical framework of the process of relapse, there are three variables: restraint, characterized by strict self-imposed rules, the most stringent of which is the complete abstinence from the behavior; the individual's problem-solving skills, characterized in the relapse process by rigid dichotomous thinking that prevents the individual from utilizing many categories in which to evaluate behavior; and level of self-efficacy, characterized in relapse as the feeling of personal inadequacy and powerlessness due to ineffectual attempts at coping in past high-risk situations.

Winstead (1984), influenced by Marlatt and Gordon's work, investigated a number of cognitive and behavioral factors associated with bulimia. Twenty-five patients who met the DSM-III criteria for bulimia were interviewed regarding periods of abstinence. The range of reported periods of abstinence varied from zero to thirteen years, with an average of 8.8 months. Ninety percent of the relapse situations involved Marlatt's interpersonal category: that is, coping with negative emotional or physical states. Subjects identified anxiety, stress, frustrations, and anger as contributing to their relapse. Weight gain during abstinence, craving certain foods, and loss of self-control were also cited. Twenty-seven percent of relapse episodes included the presence of cognitive factors, including low self-efficacy, perfectionistic attitudes, and irrational beliefs. These subjects were asked about relapse episodes prior to beginning a new treatment. When asked what their expectations were for the current treatment, 72 percent of the group indicated that total abstinence from bingeing and purging was their goal. In terms of Marlatt's model, these subjects have imposed the strictest rule of abstinence upon themselves, and thus the probability of the abstinence violation effect is significant.

Mitchell, Davis, and Goff (1985) investigated relapse in a sample of thirty patients who had been abstinent from bulimic behaviors for at least two months but who later relapsed to active bulimic symptoms. The abstinence was associated with psychotherapy or contact with a self-help group. Relapse was defined as the reoccurrence of bulimic behaviors, including bingeing and purging, with a minimum frequency of several times per week for at least two months. One-third of the patients relapsed within the first month after therapy ended, and an additional 40 percent relapsed between one and three months posttreatment.

When asked what feelings or situations most directly related to their first relapse, 80 percent of the sample mentioned stressful or difficult situations. These included job pressures, exams, and stressful social events. A number of patients mentioned moods such as anxiety, depression, and anger as being directly related to the relapse. Interestingly, no one cited situations associated with food as precipitants, and only one mentioned the involvement of fear concerning weight gain. The authors noted that these patients relapsed into bulimic behaviors in a pattern similar to the usual bulimic behavior; they binged and purged when alone and experiencing stress and negative emotions.

A third study investigating relapse (Freeman, Beach, Davis, and Solyom, 1985) followed up thirty-nine women successfully treated for bulimia nervosa. Six months after treatment five had partially relapsed and eleven had totally relapsed. A stepwise multiple regression equation was performed using data from the EDI and BDI and frequency data. Dissatisfaction with body image was by far the most powerful predictor of relapse. Patients both overestimated their body size and wished to be much thinner.

These three studies assessed the process of relapse in diverse ways, including interviews and the administration of various scales. The first two studies strongly indicate the importance of negative and stressful mood states in precipitating relapse, while the third emphasized body dissatisfaction. Using the same methodology, it is not unlikely that all three of the studies would have produced comparable results. Certainly it has been our clinical experience that both negative mood states and body dissatisfaction are important factors in the relapse process.

Marlatt and Gordon's conceptualization of the relapse process can be very useful in understanding and dealing with it when it occurs in treatment, as well as for teaching patients how to cope with relapse following treatment.

We inform our patients that after a binge/purge episode, bulimics tend to make a variety of statements about themselves that render them vulnerable to further episodes. Some of these statements reflect specific cognitive distortions that are characteristic of patients suffering from a variety of disorders who relapse. Statements that characteristically predispose the patient to further relapse include:

My binge this afternoon has spoiled all of my progress to date—now I have to start over completely.

My binge this afternoon is evidence that I am out of control of all areas of my life.

My binge this afternoon is evidence that I fail at everything.

Since I lost control this morning, the rest of the day is ruined (so I might as well binge again).

Since I could not stop the binge eating today I will never be able to stop.

It is important to teach patients that such statements generally provoke another binge episode because they undermine self-esteem, promote feelings of helplessness, and generate a sense of hopeless despair. Instructing patients to monitor their postepisode statements is the first step to challenging their frame of reference regarding their binge eating. Essentially, the rigid rule of abstinence must be rethought, so that the AVE does not lead to such dichotomous thinking that produces feelings of failure and further relapse.

The first binge episode after a period of abstinence represents a crucial time for patients. When this occurs, the goal to be kept in mind is quick recovery from an episode and avoidance of progression into further days and weeks of bingeing. Therapists can predict for patients that bulimic episodes may recur. This may reassure the patient that all is not lost should bingeing occur, and it can also function paradoxically with the patient doing the opposite of the predicted behavior (Haley, 1963). If the patient does have a binge episode, she needs to be taught to regard it as a cue or signal that she is being stressed in some way and to adopt a problem-solving approach around the stressor.

The patient needs to ask herself what might have triggered a binge episode at this point after a period of being binge-free. Perhaps she has fallen back into the habit of dieting stringently and the binge was triggered by deprivation, as was the case with two of our short-term group patients. Both were hardly bingeing at all by the end of group but went on a liquid protein diet soon after because of persistent body dissatisfaction. At a ten-week follow-up they had resumed their previous high levels of bingeing and purging. Psychological stressors can also provoke relapse, as has been shown in the Winstead and in the Freeman, Beach, Davis, and Solyom studies. It is not unusual to find patients resuming bulimic behaviors following the breakup of a relationship, when feeling overworked, at exam time, and so on.

Patients need to regard these episodes as signals that they must reassess some aspect of their lives and take more constructive action. The cognitive distortions involved in believing oneself to be a total failure may be mitigated by having the patient relabel or reframe the experience for herself as a noncatastrophic learning experience. She could make such soothing statements to herself as: "Just because I binged once doesn't mean I have to keep it up"; "So I slipped—I get to be human and make mistakes"; and "I'm going to learn something from this episode instead of falling back into old behaviors." It is also helpful if a patient can give herself credit for her binge-free time in spite of a lapse, for example, by saying to herself that "I didn't binge for two whole weeks, and no one can take that achievement away from me," or "One binge doesn't mean I'm not making progress." The therapist needs to respond to the binge in an empathic and curious way, and help the patient to do the same. This often involves making soothing statements such as the one just cited so that the patient can later use them to soothe herself.

It is our experience that body dissatisfaction persists long after symptom remission, so that bulimics who have been binge-free for some time remain vulnerable to panic over any weight gain and to the reinstitution of stringent dieting. As mentioned earlier, the deprivation engendered by this may trigger a relapse. Should this occur, it is vital that the patient return to more normalized eating, with the therapist reminding her that the best defense against binge eating is normal eating.

One of the most important, concrete requests we make of patients after a binge/purge episode is that they make themselves eat their next scheduled meal, which many patients will automatically skip. We inform patients that skipping the next meal is an old behavior that can provoke many automatic thoughts and actions. We want patients eventually to realize that skipping meals is the first step in starting the binge/purge cycle, but that by eating again they are committing themselves to new behaviors.

In terms of the relapse process, "forewarned is forearmed." When patients know that they may well have a binge episode following a period of abstinence, they can be prepared to deal with it as an foreseeable learning experience and emerge with further knowledge of their vulnerabilities and the positive experience of problem solving. This can promote feelings of self-efficacy and mastery that could make the next relapse episode (if there is one) easier to cope with.

SETTING GOALS

The presentation of the didactic material and the patient's developing insight into her behavior usually ushers in a new phase of treatment calling for behavior change. After several weeks of treatment, we often use goal setting with patients both in individual and in group therapy. Our group therapy members have cited short-term goal setting as one of the most useful components of their treatment. These patients' all-or-nothing thinking often causes them to expect that unless they immediately cease all bulimic behaviors after beginning treatment, they have failed. We emphasize that instead their goals should be oriented toward small, gradual changes in eating, bingeing and purging, and other areas of their lives. For example, often a patient who is bingeing and purging daily will want to set a goal of getting through the week without a single bulimic episode. We point out that this is a very unreasonable goal given the patient's symptomatic behavior and encourage her to revise it to getting through one day or one typical binge time without bingeing.

A goal should be significant enough to present a challenge to the patient, but not so large that failure to meet it is very likely, particularly early in treatment. Goals should be tailored so that they can provide the patient with success experiences. For a patient who feels helpless and hopeless about her bulimia, even a single experience of observing herself being in control can markedly increase her feelings of competence and effectiveness (Love, Ollendick, Johnson, and Schlesinger, 1985). Bandura

(1977) noted that the experience of personal mastery is the most effective means of promoting a sense of self-efficacy. Setting gradual short-term goals and attaining them can often be a major revelation to the patient, since she previously felt she had to give up her symptomatic behaviors all at once. Success at small goals that ultimately can result in complete cessation of the bulimic behaviors has proven to be a powerful intervention with the patient's dichotomous thinking and a sense of helplessness.

THE ROLE OF EXERCISE

The proper use of exercise can be an extremely important element in a bulimic patient's recovery program, and we often encourage patients to set goals that include exercise. Unlike anorexics, most bulimics do not exercise to excess. Often bulimics entering treatment exercise sporadically or not at all, which further damages self-esteem because of their strong belief that they *should* be exercising daily. Although there is a very positive aspect to the changing cultural norms endorsing fitness and strength for women as well as for men, the "no pain, no gain" message can be taken too far. Many patients believe that unless they rise at 5 A.M. to jog ten miles and then do aerobics, they are not exercising properly. When we suggest a goal related to exercise to sedentary patients, they tend to believe such a regimen is reasonable. In these cases, we emphasize how the patients are setting themselves up to fail by trying to do too much; just as with dieting, their dichotomous thinking leads them to believe they are total failures if they do not accomplish major exercise goals perfectly.

We stress that exercise must be incorporated into each patient's life gradually and that, as with eating, the goal is to establish a routine that can be sustained throughout their life. For a patient who is not exercising at all, taking a half-hour walk one day a week might be a reasonable initial goal. We also emphasize that it is important to find a form of exercise that is enjoyable, which is a new concept for most patients. Often patients will report that they used to jog or swim but cannot seem to get themselves to do it any more. Upon being asked if they enjoy that form of exercise, patients frequently respond that they hate it, expressing surprise that this feeling is considered important. We point out that people in general do not do very well forcing themselves to perform hated activities and encourage our patients to try various forms of exercise until they find one they think they might enjoy.

Regular enjoyable exercise can be beneficial to patients in a number of ways. When they remind themselves that their exercise is helping with weight regulation, it can help to assuage their anxiety about beginning to normalize their eating habits. As mentioned earlier, some evidence suggests that regular aerobic exercise can actually lower the set point and increase metabolic efficiency (Epstein and Wing, 1980; Gwinup, 1975).

When patients find their form of exercise pleasurable, they can use it as a stress reliever and a mood lifter. We also encourage our patients to seek out group exercise activities, such as volleyball and softball. Hopefully, they can learn that exercise can be a fun and social event.

Group Suggestions

As discussed, in our groups we ask patients to share techniques they have used in the past to avoid bingeing. The following is a list of these suggestions; we have found this list so useful that we generally distribute it to patients as they begin treatment. Because the suggestions were contributed by other bulimics, patients generally have a very positive response to them.

> Don't constantly deny yourself your favorite foods or you will wind up feeling deprived and then go overboard. Try to figure out what you really want to eat and allow yourself to have it in moderation.

> Find some form of regular exercise that you can enjoy.

> Get yourself in touch with other people instead of becoming a recluse, even if you really have to push yourself at first.

> Get involved in doing something for someone else; get involved, period!

> Do little things that will make you feel good about yourself.

> If you feel you can't yet control yourself in the presence of certain foods, structure the situation so you can't possibly binge even if you wanted to, such as going out with a friend for *one* dessert.

> If feeling deprived is a big issue for you, you might try the opposite tack and make sure you surround yourself and stock your kitchen with large quantities of your favorite foods; enough so that you're really sure it will be there for you and you won't run out.

> Concentrate on *eating* when you eat; don't try to do bunches of other things at the same time. You have a right to eat and enjoy your food: Savor it! Be conscious of what you're eating instead of running on automatic.

> When you feel the urge to binge, try to think about the negative consequences instead of giving in immediately. Try to figure out what you're feeling and find some alternative activity to satisfy it.

> When you're tired, the solution is to go to bed and sleep, not eat.

You might find that getting really dressed up on occasion can make you feel good about yourself.

Take care of tasks that need doing as they come up and give yourself a pat on the back for your accomplishments instead of using eating to procrastinate. When you are faced with that choice of whether to get something done or binge, envision how good and relieved you'll feel when the chore is no longer hanging over your head, and how much more anxious you'll be later if you binge instead.

When there is a decision to be made, make it. When worried, get into action instead of being paralyzed by indecision.

Deprivation and starvation lead to bingeing. In order not to binge, you must eat regularly, even if very small meals at first. If you do end up bingeing, eat normally at your next meal instead of trying to "make up for it" by not eating and starting the cycle all over again.

Give yourself praise and rewards for your accomplishments. Try to focus some attention on all of your positive attributes (yes, they really are there!) instead of constantly dwelling on everything that seems like a failure.

Problems occur when no planning is done, for instance at lunchtime, so make sure you get organized and make plans for meals, like bringing a lunch to work.

Don't deprive yourself! Bingeing occurs when you're starving from not eating all day, so make sure you eat breakfast, lunch, and dinner. You deserve to eat and to get pleasure from eating!

Remove yourself from situations where you're feeling out of control around food. Get out of the kitchen after dinner until your body has a chance to begin feeling full, *then* go back in and do the dishes.

Avoid shopping situations that make you feel out of control. Don't shop in food stores that display loose bins of food, don't shop when you're hungry, and try to get someone to go with you when you shop.

Avoid similar situations in restaurants, like smorgasbords and all-you-can-eat brunches.

Freeze your leftovers so you won't feel so compelled to finish them off just because they're around.

You might find that acquiring certain food habits will make you feel more secure and cut down on the amount of decision making you have to do concerning food. For instance, eating the same meal in the same restaurant or making the same breakfast every day could make a routine where you could feel legitimate about eating.

It's *okay* to have a bowl of ice cream or those other "bad" foods! You deserve to eat foods you like. Try to pay more attention to exactly what your body is wanting to eat, and then eat it. If you satisfy specific cravings and don't let yourself feel deprived, you'll binge less.

Be aware of what your vulnerable times are, and get into routines where you substitute other activities for bingeing at these times. For instance, take a rest or a bath or do some exercising that you like in order to manage the transition from work to home instead of bingeing. Get into habits like this instead of eating.

Break the habit of using food as your total reward-and-punishment system for yourself. Think of other things you enjoy and learn to reward yourself with buying clothes, going places, allowing yourself to do nothing when you feel lazy, and so forth. Learn to pat yourself on the back, and to forgive yourself too.

Structure the way you purchase and store food, like keeping all your binge foods in one place. It's harder to deny you're really bingeing when you have to go out of your way to get the food.

When you feel horrible about yourself for eating and bingeing, tell yourself it's okay not to be perfect. Make sure you eat breakfast the day after a binge, and don't start the cycle of deprivation/bingeing all over again. Regard your slips as learning experiences and just keep on.

Make a resolution to work on the behaviors that keep the cycle going— vomiting, starving, taking pills to "undo" the effects of overeating make a future binge *more* likely, not less.

Delay the binge and/or the purge; distract yourself with other thoughts or activities. You may find that the urge decreases, or that other things can be satisfying too.

Eat three meals a day. You deserve to eat like everyone else—don't deprive yourself!

Include variety in the foods you eat. Try to break the "diet mentality" of "good" diet food and "bad" binge food.

Exercising promotes a healthy mind and body. By exercising early in the day, you can start the day feeling good about yourself.

Find alternative outlets for feelings that lead to binge eating: call a friend if you're lonely, think about activities you used to enjoy before bingeing took up so much of your time and try them again, pick a new activity you *might* find interesting and try it out.

Go to sleep when you're tired!

Old habits die hard, and your body needs time to readjust. Make changes *gradually*.

Don't weigh yourself so often. As your weight consciousness goes down, so will your self-criticism—and your flexibility will increase!

Counting calories or following a rigid diet may be increasing your obsession. If this is true for you, experiment with greater flexibility.

Identify your vulnerable times and situations. Avoid those situations that you know are sure-fire binge triggers, but force yourself to handle others that have been problematic for you in the past. This way you can build self-confidence and work your way up to handling the really hard times.

Rely upon a spiritual motivator to transcend the difficult moments.

Set daily as well as weekly goals. Remember that one bad meal or one bad day does not determine the future and get back on track!

Write your goals and a list of alternative behaviors to binge eating on cards and carry them with you as a reminder when you're feeling on the verge of losing control.

Confront the negatives—remind yourself of the harm this habit is doing to your body and your emotional well-being and contrast this with the benefits you will get from sticking to your goals.

Remember, *you are not alone* in working on this. Think about other people who understand and are willing to help.

Recommended Reading

It is also our experience that bulimics are often very eager for information about their difficulties, and many patients respond well to recommended reading. Reading about their problem may stir up significant issues, which the therapist needs to be attuned to. In addition, therapists should be familiar with the basic premises of the books they recommend. The following is a list of books we like to recommend to bulimic patients.

BULIMIA AND ANOREXIA NERVOSA: GENERAL ISSUES

Breaking the Diet Habit, by J. Polivy and P. Herman. An excellent book on how to live with your set point, find the boundaries of your natural weight, and normalize eating.

Bulimarexia: The Binge/Purge Cycle, by Marlene Boskind-White and William White. Contains a great deal of useful information on bulimia. The chapters on physical complications of bulimia and the sociocultural context are particularly good. However, it tends to overlook the great difficulties many individuals have in stopping their binge/purge behavior and assumes that giving up the symptoms is merely a matter of motivation. When read with Cauwels's book, it provides more of a range in viewpoints.

Bulimia: The Binge Purge Compulsion, by Janice Cauwels. Presents a detailed overview of bulimia with some directions for getting help. However, it is too focused on severe cases.

The Dieter's Dilemma, by W. Bennett and J. Gurin. The most detailed and informative book on set-point theory. It is a must for anyone who wants a comprehensive picture on the data indicating that all individuals have a biologically determined optimal weight.

Feeding the Hungry Heart and *Breaking Free from Compulsive Eating*, by Geneen Roth. The author, a former compulsive overeater, tells of her own struggles and offers a number of suggestions for others struggling with bingeing. Both books are useful and enjoyable to read, and the latter is particularly helpful.

The Golden Cage, by Hilde Bruch. A classic book on anorexia written by a pioneer in the field.

New Hope for Binge Eaters, by Harrison Pope and James Hudson. Suggests that bulimia is a variant of a biologically mediated affective disorder and recommends treatment with antidepressant medication. While this may be very effective for some people, the conclusions reached by the authors are too narrow.

The Slender Balance, by Susan Squire. Presents some general information and case vignettes on bulimia, anorexia, and obesity. The book is interesting reading, besides being insightful and providing helpful suggestions.

Stop Dieting, Start Living, by Sharon Greene Patton. In this gem of a book, a woman tells of her twenty-five-year struggle with dieting and her decision to stop dieting, after which she finally lost weight. Information on set-point theory and the effects of dieting is presented in a very readable way.

WOMEN AND EATING DISORDERS: SOCIOCULTURAL CONTEXT AND WOMEN'S ROLES

Fat Is a Feminist Issue, volumes 1 and 2, by Susie Orbach. The best books we have seen on the relationship between women's roles, deprivation, and binge eating. Volume 1 presents the theory and volume 2 is more oriented toward suggestions and exercises women can do to break the binge cycle. Most people should disregard the author's theory that women *want* to get fat, which we feel pertains to only a small minority.

The Obsession, by Kim Chernin. A more philosophical approach to eating disorders, suggesting that they represent a search for meaning in women's lives gone awry. It is beautifully written and thought provoking.

SELF-ASSERTION

Self-Assertion for Women, by Pamela Butler. The best book we know on assertiveness training. It is thorough, contains many helpful examples, and is highly readable. This book is a must for most women.

Sweet Suffering: Woman as Victim, by Natalie Shainess. A must for anyone who feels she is a born victim and is unable to stand up for herself. The author discusses the causes of this problem and gives suggestions for recognizing and overcoming it.

COGNITIVE RESTRUCTURING

Talking to Yourself, by Pamela Butler. Another must for most women. The author discusses how to pay attention to what one is saying to oneself and how to identify distorted patterns of thought that then influence moods and behaviors. Although it was written for all women, it is particularly relevant to those struggling with eating disorders.

We have had positive results in discussing various cognitive distortions with our patients. Table 10.1 presents a summary sheet of the various distortions, which may be helpful for patient and therapist alike.

TABLE 10.1
Cognitive Distortions Commonly Found in Bulimics

Control Fallacy or Faulty Attribution

Type A: Viewing the self as externally controlled and helpless; for example: "When I get the urge to binge I'm just helplessly overwhelmed and I just do it," or "Everyone but me seems to have control over my life."

Type B: The assumption of personal control and responsibility for the happiness and well-being of others; for example: "I tend to feel responsible when someone close to me is upset," or "There is nothing more important than making sure the people in your life are happy."

Dichotomous Thinking, All-or-None Thinking, Black-and-White Thinking, Splitting

The self and the world are viewed in terms of extremes: one is all good or all bad; for example: "I'm a complete failure because I ate a bad food today," or "If you can't win the Nobel Prize why even bother to write. You'll be a failure."

Personalization or Self-Reference

Egocentric interpretations of impersonal events, which at their extreme end shade into a paranoid stance. Examples: "I can't go out on the street because everyone will notice how my stomach is sticking out," or "I can't eat in public because everyone will be paying attention to how much I'm eating."

Magnification

The tendency to exaggerate the meaning or significance of a particular event; for example: "Being thin is the key to all success and beauty," or "Nothing else in life counts for anything unless you're thin."

Filtering or Discounting

The tendency to discount all the positive aspects of a situation while magnifying all the negative details; for example: "I'm a fat worthless slob rather than a bright talented executive," or "It doesn't matter that I didn't binge as much as usual last week because I still binged."

Overgeneralization

Drawing unwarranted conclusions on the basis of little evidence; for example: "I binged again today so I know I'll never get well," or "This man I met didn't call me so I know I will never have a satisfying relationship."

TABLE 10.1 (*continued*)

Control Fallacy or Faulty Attribution

Magical Thinking

Illogical, irrational thought patterns based more on infantile wishes and unquestioned misinformation; for example: "Everything you eat after 6 P.M. turns directly to fat." Also appears in the form of merger fantasies; for example: "I resent having to tell my partner how I feel because he should just *know*." Also in the form of transformational fantasies, wherein instant and dramatic changes with implications far beyond the realm where the change takes place are fantasized; for example: "I know my life would be totally different if I could only lose that ten pounds."

General Cognitive Deficiency

Disregard for an important aspect of a life situation, in which the person will ignore, fail to integrate, or not utilize information derived from experience, concentrating only on the present activity rather than the long-term consequences; for example: "I know I binged tonight but I'll fast all day tomorrow and this time I'll really make it."

11

Special Treatment Issues

If a patient is able to take advantage of a symptom-focused approach, much of the symptomatic behavior can change relatively quickly, often over several months. As eating becomes more normalized, the binge/purge episodes are occasional rather than constant, the patient's obsession with food decreases, and she has more energy and motivation to work on other psychological issues. However, a subgroup of patients do not have the intrapsychic resources to be able to take advantage of symptom-focused interventions for some time. In this chapter we discuss some of the unique aspects of working with these difficult patients. We also present our observations concerning common countertransference issues that occur in working with eating-disordered patients.

Resistance Versus Deficit

One advantage of a treatment that begins with a focus on the symptom is that the requisite self-monitoring places significant demands on the patient, which may quickly reveal the strength of her ego resources. Although some patients enjoy monitoring themselves and keep detailed records that function both as personal journals and letters to the therapist, other patients "forget" to fill out their records or do a cursory and uninformative job. In our experience patients who fail to comply with the self-monitoring early in treatment are much less able to make use of psychoeducational treatment than compliant patients (Connors, Johnson, and Stuckey, 1984). When patients do not keep useful records, it must be determined whether they are capable of so doing. If they are, we would conceptualize the difficulty as resistance, implying ambivalence and intrapsychic conflict, but relatively intact ego functioning. If a patient truly is not able to monitor herself, we would classify her as having the severe

self-regulatory deficits, disorganization, and lack of psychic structure
found among character-disordered patients.

Any resistance displayed by a relatively high-functioning patient must
become the focus of treatment. The patient must be confronted with the
discrepancy between her presenting for treatment and her failure to perform actions that have proven helpful in symptom reduction. There are
various causes for this resistance. Some patients are so frightened of their
feelings that self-monitoring is an unpleasant and threatening chore. Many
are terrified of relinquishing their symptom because it feels like their only
source of gratification. With these patients, we stress building in alternative
means of self-nurturing gradually as they experiment with relinquishing
their symptoms. Finally, the fear of weight gain if bulimia ceases is a
universal concern.

Character-disordered patients generally do not possess the ego resources necessary to mobilize themselves for behavior change, especially
early in treatment. Their self-regulatory deficits are severe enough so
that symptom change should not be expected when they have little but
the symptom to rely on for tension reduction.

TREATMENT OF CHARACTER DISORDERS

Patients' ability to make use of directive interventions and the interpersonal therapeutic relationship are obviously going to be affected by
the nature and severity of their intrapsychic difficulties.

In general, the more disturbed the patient is, the greater the difficulty
she will have utilizing a symptom-focused approach. As we stressed earlier,
bulimics comprise a heterogeneous group, and many could be diagnosed
as having a borderline personality organization. These individuals are
often polysymptomatic, engaging in a variety of impulse-ridden behaviors,
including alcoholism, drug abuse, compulsive stealing, self-mutilation, and
suicide gestures/attempts. In a sense, in such patients bingeing and purging could represent one of their less dangerous mechanisms for tension
regulation.

In treating borderline patients with eating difficulties, therapists should
usually focus their energy on helping patients find ways to manage their
pervasive self-regulatory deficits. Efforts to engage these patients in active
interventions aimed at changing their disturbed eating behavior are usually
unsuccessful or very slow. For most of these patients the bingeing and
purging behavior serves as a self-integrating compensatory function. The
loss of the behavior may expose them to profoundly terrifying annihilation
anxiety. (This is in contrast to the type of signal anxiety more neurotic
patients experience when they are prevented from bingeing and purging.)
The action sequence of binge/purge behavior essentially has become the
glue that binds their intrapsychic world. In the absence of a highly struc-

tured and trusted holding environment, such as a hospital or long-term psychotherapeutic relationship, if threatened with the loss of behavior, these patients will often immediately substitute other, perhaps more destructive compensatory behaviors, such as self-mutilation, substance abuse, and so forth. This is not to say the therapist should not attempt to work with these patients using directive interventions. On the contrary, if the therapist does not actively help with life management issues, these patients will usually escalate symptomatic behavior until the therapist is provoked into active involvement.

In order to work effectively with this group, therapists must recognize that the patients will be able to utilize the therapeutic tools only after they have consolidated the long-term therapeutic alliance with the therapist and treatment team. This treatment alliance often does not consolidate until therapists have demonstrated in various ways that they are prepared to work with patients as long as desired.

Since the work with these patients can be so long and emotionally demanding, we have found it useful to encourage patients to develop significant relationships with as many members of the treatment team as possible (nurses, nutritionist, family therapist, group therapist, and so on). This provides patients with a number of resources to draw from when the individual therapist goes on vacation or is unavailable for one reason or another. For the individual therapist, having a solid team to work with can minimize guilt about leaving patients for vacations. It also provides a forum where he or she can compare thoughts and feelings about treatment, which is very useful in managing countertransference. Since many borderline patients often attempt to communicate their internal experience through the use of projective identification, which may be very provocative, the treatment team can help the therapist to avoid acting out or becoming lost or overwhelmed in the interactions with patients. This team approach in the treatment of borderline patients increases the possibility of their using the defensive mechanism of splitting. Continuous communication within the treatment team is essential in order to minimize this defensive adaptation.

Sometimes hospitalization of these patients is not only unavoidable but can be quite helpful. There are times, usually highly stressful situations for the patient, when the treatment team cannot provide adequate structure for her to feel safe. At these times the continuous structure of the inpatient setting can be very relieving to both therapist and patient. Depending on the severity of the patient's ego deficits, repeated brief hospitalizations can be an effective strategy. Medical monitoring with laboratory tests should also be conducted regularly with those patients who continue to engage in frequent purging behavior. If the patient's bulimic behavior is such that she is placing herself in significant medical danger, hospitalization is again indicated.

Suzanne. Thirty-two-year-old Suzanne had been in treatment for three years. In our first session she stated that I (M.C.) was her ninth "shrink" and that she wasn't even sure why she was attempting therapy again when it had never helped before. At that time she was bingeing and purging up to ten times per day, often stayed in bed all day because of severe depression, and felt that her life was constantly in a state of crisis.

Suzanne's developmental history made it quite clear how she came to be so disturbed; indeed, she had to have considerable strength to be functioning outside of a hospital at all. She was the middle child of three girls. Shortly after the birth of Suzanne's younger sister her parents divorced, and the girls lived with their mother, having no contact with their father. When Suzanne was two years old her mother believed herself and her daughters to be so evil that she thought she should kill them all and then herself. Fortunately, she never acted upon this belief, but told her daughters about it. There was a history of psychiatric disturbance and alcoholism on the maternal side of the family. Suzanne's maternal grandmother was probably schizophrenic; she was institutionalized and given a lobotomy, and never left the institution. Suzanne's own mother was alcoholic, as are the mother's two brothers. The mother seems to have organized her fragile character by compulsive cleaning rituals and incessant criticism of her children, especially Suzanne. She shouted at Suzanne that "You used me to get into the world!" and "You're the cross I bear in life."

Shortly after the divorce the mother remarried, to an alcoholic lawyer. He began abusing the girls physically soon after the marriage, and he and Suzanne's mother would go on alcoholic benders together. During one of these, they put the three girls and the family dog in the car and drove to a bar to continue drinking. The girls were told that they must not leave the car or they would be beaten. It was an extremely hot day and the children sweated in the car for hours while their parents drank. The dog began having convulsions due to the heat, but the girls were so terrified of leaving the car that they tearfully watched the dog die. When the parents came out at last, the stepfather was so drunk that he was not upset by the girls' condition or the dog's death; he drove to a nearby river and threw the dog's body in, proclaiming it a "burial at sea."

This stepfather was particularly sadistic to Suzanne and abused her in minor and major ways. When she would beg him to turn the radio down at night so that she could sleep, he would turn it up. He also devised a variety of physical punishments for her, including having her stand in a dark closet with several heavy encyclopedias in her arms until he allowed her to come out. When she was six, he began sexually abusing her as well. When they were alone in the house he would force her to come into his bed and fondle him. This went on until Suzanne was fourteen, at which time she arranged never to be home alone with her stepfather. She became involved with a boyfriend who was a gang member. At age sixteen she became pregnant by him, and her parents expelled her from the house. She lived on the streets for a while and finally moved in with her boyfriend's family. She had the baby and reported being very happy about the child. However, her boyfriend was physically abusive to her. He also committed violent and sadistic acts, such as shooting Suzanne's kitten in front of her. Several months after the baby's birth, the boyfriend was killed in a gang fight. Suzanne left the baby with his family and spent the next several years living with various men on the streets, and for several years was alcoholic and a cocaine abuser.

Suzanne finally became frightened by the extent of her addictions and went to Alcoholics Anonymous. After a year of sporadic drinking she was finally able to quit using alcohol and cocaine. She also entered college at this time and began seeing a therapist. However, without the cocaine to suppress her appetite, she began to gain weight and became panicky, since her slim figure had been a source of great pride to her. She learned about vomiting from a girl friend, and her eating quickly escalated out of control. She saw several more therapists as she spent the next few years dropping into and out of various local colleges. She revealed her eating problem to only one of these therapists, who laughed and said that she was so slim she couldn't have a weight problem. Suzanne terminated therapy and became increasingly depressed. She made a suicidal gesture (swallowing ten aspirin) and was referred to me by her college's counseling center.

Upon entering therapy Suzanne said that she wanted to be able to function better at school, be less depressed, and stop bingeing and purging. Several antidepressants were tried, but with each she would either complain of the side effects or state that it was having no impact on her depression. In addition, I was cautious about the possibility of her having any quantity of medication around, because of her suicide potential. Thus the initial focus of therapy was simply helping her to get out of bed each day and function. Much of her depression was linked to anxiety and hopelessness about ever being able to accomplish anything, so that when exam time came she typically was paralyzed and dropped out of school. After several months of making gradual small changes in her habits, she began to have a bit more self-esteem. She became more able to tolerate the anxiety about exams and remained in school.

My relationship with Suzanne was very stormy. Initially she felt very positively about me because I was the first to understand her eating disorder and to help her function better in school. She commented that I was one of the greatest women in the United States. This idealization quickly turned to rage when she became dissatisfied with her progress and felt it must be due to my incompetence. She assumed a very untrusting stance toward me and stated that I wanted her to come for therapy twice a week so I could make more money. She also changed her focus in therapy, stating that she wanted to work exclusively on the eating disorder. Gradually she eliminated the purging, and slowly her bingeing also began to subside. However, without these methods of tension regulation, she became suicidally depressed. Substituting more positive activities for the bingeing and purging proved unsuccessful with this patient, who commented that she hated herself so much that only another self-destructive and addictive activity could satisfy her. She began to use cocaine again and made frequent suicidal crisis calls to me at all hours. She felt as though I had taken something away from her and had left her with nothing (despite the fact that the eating disorder was not my focus in therapy, because this patient needed to address so many other issues).

By this time Suzanne was so angry at me that she terminated treatment after I suggested that she be hospitalized. Despite her ambivalence, however, she still felt connected to me and returned to treatment a month later. We discussed the fact that perhaps she was not yet ready to give up all of the bingeing and purging and that for the time being it might be less self-destructive than her other addictions. She has remained firm in her commitment not to purge, but does turn to bingeing when she feels terribly depressed, rather than to cocaine or suicidal gestures. This patient has been subjected to so many developmental traumas that she will probably need the bingeing for some time to help her regulate her depressive and self-depreciating affects. The primary goal of treatment at this point is for her to be able to tolerate remaining in treatment with me long enough to internalize more positive and less self-punitive ways of coping.

False Self/Narcissistic Character Disorders

As reviewed earlier (see chapter 5), patients who present with false self organizations have attempted to compensate for intrapsychic difficulties by creating an image of themselves as responsible, adequate, mature, in control, without needs, invulnerable, and very independent. Beneath this veneer of competency, however, they often feel quite needy and out of control. Their interpersonal world is marked by avoidance of intimate contact, which might result in exposure, and they continuously engage in activities to give the illusion of adequate functioning. Intrapsychically they generally struggle with what we have termed a wish/fear dilemma. On the one hand, they wish that someone would recognize and respond to their infantile needs. On the other hand, they fear that recognition and response to these needs would undermine the fragile psychological balance they have established. These patients generally recognize the discrepancy between how they feel about themselves and how the world sees them. Unfortunately, the more successful they are with effecting the false self presentation, the more fraudulent, cynical, and hopeless they feel.

Very little has been written about the treatment of these patients. In essence, they are distinguished by what we do not know about them. In our experience, during the initial interview their life histories seem uneventful and their current life adjustment often appears quite adequate. While they will compliantly answer direct questions, they rarely volunteer information, and as the interview proceeds the therapist progressively feels that the questions are painful and threateningly intrusive. These patients generally are very reluctant to talk about food-related behavior because it is an obvious exposure of a less than adequate aspect of themselves. In contrast to most patients, who seem to grow more comfortable as the interview proceeds, these patients appear to grow increasingly uncomfortable as the therapist learns more about them. Therapists generally leave the initial interview feeling that while the patient answered questions, they do not have a sense of who the person is. The patient has reported the facts, but there is an elusive, distant, almost empty quality to the presentation. One notable characteristic that seems common among these patients is the absence of long-term, intimate, heterosexual relationships.

If these patients enter treatment (it has been our experience that there is a very high dropout rate among this group), they generally are compliant, nondemanding, and very careful about becoming too involved.

The nature of the relationship these patients develop with the therapist seems to reflect the overall nature of their interpersonal world. They superficially accommodate to whatever treatment demands exist without ever becoming involved in intimate disclosure. They continue in treatment without complaint, but the therapist feels that he or she is not quite connecting with the patient in any significant way. The patients' compliance and avoidance of controversial issues seems to be an effort to avoid actually relating to the therapist. The therapist usually feels that he or she has a fragile alliance with a patient who wants to be in treatment but is very frightened about the potential development of the therapeutic relationship. It has been our experience that this ambivalence represents the basic wish/fear dilemma mentioned earlier.

We recommend long-term, relationship-oriented, individual psychotherapy for these patients. We have found that a nondirective, nonintrusive approach is most helpful. Directive interventions aimed at the food-related behavior are usually met with resistance until a consistent and stable relationship has been developed with the therapist. These patients usually refuse group therapy because of their fear of exposure.

CASE: FALSE SELF/NARCISSISTIC DISORDER

Kim. A twenty-two-year-old single female, Kim was in her first year of law school. She had come to treatment at the request of her mother, who was concerned about her disturbed eating behavior. When Kim entered my office she chose to sit on a couch that was several feet farther away from me (C.J.) than a chair patients normally use. She sat quite straight; while she was not rigid, it was clear that she had no intention of loosening her position. She compliantly answered my questions but her responses were guarded and remarkably unelaborated. She looked at me when she spoke but somehow avoided eye contact. She smiled occasionally and one sensed she was capable of being quite articulate. There was, however, very little spontaneity in her actions.

I learned she had begun binge eating and vomiting on a daily basis during her first semester of college, following a period of starvation. According to her there was no clear precipitant. When I asked her these questions she gave the impression that she had not reflected on this event and that she was not keen on my doing so now. Responses to questions about developmental history and family relations were similarly guarded. I finished the initial interview with a fair amount of basic information but did not have a sense of who Kim was. At the time my caseload was full, so normally I would have referred her to one of the other therapists. I found myself intrigued and challenged by her obscureness, however, and initiated twice-a-week treatment that lasted for four years.

The early stages of treatment were characterized by compliant attendance and a painful struggle on Kim's part to find things to talk about. The struggle appeared to be to find issues that were not obviously superficial but also not very revealing. For the most part the first year and one-half of treatment was spent reviewing her week, attending to life management issues, and occasionally learning something about her and her family. For me the sessions were generally tedious and boring. Silences were unbearable for her so I often found myself asking a lot of questions and feeling responsible for making the session tolerable for both of us. I later learned that at these times Kim felt I was taking care of her and protecting her from having to assume responsibility for how we both felt. When silences would develop I would often ask how she was doing with food. Although she was reluctant to talk specifically about it, she gradually gave me more details, which allowed me to offer her some tools that might be helpful to her. She respectfully listened to these suggestions, but they seemed to have little meaning to her. Later I learned that she actually made use of these suggestions but was reluctant to acknowledge it because she did not want to admit to herself or me that I was having any effect on her. In fact, throughout most of the treatment she actually attempted to minimize any suggestion that she was emotionally involved in the treatment. She never made phone contact outside of appointment times, denied any feelings about separations due to vacations, and never inquired about my life outside the office. I often felt at the end of each session that it was the last time I would see her. I also had to repeatedly control an episodic urge to confront her about whether the treatment relationship meant anything to her and, if not, why she was coming. On occasion she would allude to her family, who lived in the same city. Gradually I learned Kim had a younger sister who had cerebral palsy and an alcoholic father whom she felt distant and angry toward. When she would speak of her sister she would angrily devalue herself for jeopardizing her healthy body with symptomatic behavior. She would also chastise herself for being in therapy, saying that she had few and trivial problems compared to her sister. When issues would arise regarding her father, she would coldly withdraw and with much cynicism proclaim that things would never change. Her mother was portrayed as an exhausted caretaker of an alcoholic husband and a debilitated daughter.

Several moments in Kim's treatment seemed crucial to her. The treatment had been progressing along uneventfully until at one point I made a specific inquiry. Although Kim rarely missed sessions, after a time she began to consistently arrive ten to fifteen minutes late. I had assumed that she needed to control the boundaries of the hour, and frankly I'd been apprehensive to inquire about the lateness for fear she would feel pressured, which would subsequently drive her from treatment before we had a chance to process the inquiry. My decision to ask about her lateness came when I realized that I had come to look forward to it because it gave me an unexpected break in the day. So finally I asked how she thought I felt about her being late. She matter-of-factly responded that she thought I was glad she was late and that I valued the additional time. I then asked if she had ever felt before that her not being around was a valued relief from hectic demands. She then began to elaborate her early history.

Her sister had been born eleven months after the patient and her father had apparently begun to drink near this time. Kim's early memories were of beginning to take care of herself and how pleased everyone was that she was so independent. In fact, I learned that she was so competently mature that she was allowed to play unattended in her yard when she was two and a half years old and was struck by an automobile on one such occasion. She continued to maintain this pseudomature adaptation throughout high school, developing symptoms only when she separated from home. The separation exposed her to feelings of loss, depression, and anxiety that she had always been able to ward off and suppress. The emergence of the feelings made her acutely aware of the discrepancy between how the world viewed her and how she actually felt. The awareness of this discrepancy threatened the self-esteem that she had developed around the pseudomature adaptation. Her initial effort to starve herself was an attempt to gain control over her internal state. Paradoxically, the attendant starvation signaled to others that something was wrong.

It became clear to Kim that treatment with me represented an enormous wish/fear dilemma. On the one hand, she wanted to preserve the false self organization because the world had responded favorably to it and it had resulted in the illusion of success. On the other hand, the adaptation was at the expense of being able to rely on another human being to help meet some of her needs. She felt if people learned of her true feelings they would be disappointed or become overwhelmed by the burden of her needs.

A fair amount of the remaining time I spent with Kim centered around her ambivalence regarding my knowledge of her neediness. Interestingly, however, her bulimia disappeared while we were working through the issues of intimacy and interdependency.

Another important issue for Kim to work through was in fact a side effect from her false self organization. Over the years men in her social circle had come to interpret Kim's guardedness and avoidance of intimate contact as enigmatic and coy. Eventually her unavailability and obscureness became a passionate preoccupation of several of these men and resulted in a sense of challenge among them to "penetrate her" and "get inside her head." Paradoxically Kim's efforts to obscure the reality of her world was provoking men into aggressive pursuit of her. While she was annoyed and frightened by the potential penetration, she was also quite gratified by the attention. It was also an interesting adaptation in that she was able to engage people and yet protect herself from intimacy. Unfortunately, however, she had come to believe that her attractiveness and power resided in her ability to continue to be obscure.

Throughout the treatment it was very important for me to manage my own inclination to be challenged by her remoteness and not to be frustrated by her unresponsiveness. I sensed that if I became confrontive with her about her obscureness she would have had to flee the treatment. Patience, therapeutic neutrality, and durability were what seemed to allow her to make use of the therapeutic relationship.

After she had been symptom-free for one year and had finished law school and begun work as a trial attorney, she decided she wanted to end treatment. During termination she retreated somewhat into her hyper-competent stance. When she left my office after her final appointment I had a different sense of her leaving. In contrast to my early feelings that at the end of each appointment I would never see her again, this time I felt strongly that she would stay in touch.

The Use of Transitional Objects

In chapter 5 we noted Mahler's observations that toddlers often rely on transitional objects to help them navigate the demands of the rapprochement phase of separation-individuation. To briefly review, the rapprochement phase is a time of high separation anxiety as toddlers become particularly aware of their separateness, and hence aloneness, from the primary caregiver. During this time children will often invest some object with the power to soothe and comfort them. The importance of the transitional object is that it becomes a concrete symbolic representation of the mother's soothing and comforting function. It is not the mother, but it has the symbolic power to function like her, and, most important, it is something children can take with them and have control over in the physical absence of the mother. Food or the action of eating can also serve as transitional objects or transitional phenomena.

Given this developmental conceptualization, we have been impressed with the power of giving some patients things that are concrete representations of the therapeutic holding environment. These items can range from simply the therapist's handwriting on a list of alternative behaviors for avoiding binges to stuffed animals. We do not mean to suggest that therapists whimsically give things to their patients. We do believe, however, that under certain circumstances the therapist's providing the patient with something concrete can be quite useful. The patient can then take this object with her, control it, and use it to soothe herself when feeling overwhelmed. Initiating such a move should be well conceptualized and timed, and the therapist needs to be extremely alert to the patient's reaction to the intervention.

We became particularly interested in the power of transitional objects when we were conducting our early beeper studies. In these studies we had both anorexics and bulimics carrying electronic pagers that would beep once, at random, during every four-hour time period over the course of a week. When beeped, the subjects were to fill out a self-report diary about their activities, thoughts, and feelings at that time. Interestingly, at the end of the week the restricting anorexics could not give the beepers back to us fast enough. They generally experienced them as quite intrusive. In contrast, the bulimics were reluctant to separate from the beepers. The beeping gave them a sense of connectedness to the hospital. Since that time we have explored different aspects of this technique. The most common items we have given patients are handwritten lists of suggested alternatives to bulimic episodes and various information sheets. On occasion we have tape-recorded comments or had the patient record therapy sessions to play while at home. Some patients have found it helpful to place the tape recorder next to the refrigerator and play the tape before they begin binge eating. Recently at the conclusion of one of our short-term groups, we gave the patients refrigerator magnets that reminded them of what they had learned and the good feelings associated with the group. The following is a case example of how offering a transitional object was helpful in treatment.

Pat. A twenty-four-year-old woman, Pat had a ten-year history of anorexia nervosa and bulimia. She had been in numerous treatments since
she was fourteen, with marginal success. Throughout the ten years she
had been chronically underweight, resulting in amenorrhea. She also had
a long history of bingeing and vomiting several times daily. Despite her
symptom history she had graduated from college and was able to work.
She lived alone and was episodically involved in relationships. After a
year of outpatient therapy, Pat's weight began to drop into a critical range,
and hospitalization was recommended.

During the hospitalization we prevented her from binge/vomiting
and began restoring her weight. Deprived of her self-regulatory tools,
Pat became very agitated and panicky. This was worst at night when she
would go to sleep and experience night terrors. Occasionally she would
awaken, experience depersonalization, and then begin to frantically claw
her face to reintegrate. While medication was helpful in decreasing the
intensity of her panic, she would still awaken terrified.

Throughout the treatment Pat often spoke of wanting to be a turtle
so that she could simply pull her parts inside and be protected by the
outer shell. At one point I (C.J.) mentioned to her that I had recently
seen a stuffed turtle puppet that reminded me of our conversations. I
asked if she would allow me to give her one. She was pleased to accept.
Pat began sleeping with her hand in the puppet and her night terrors
abated. In an interesting postscript several years later, while still seeing
her in therapy, my wife and I had a child. Pat was aware of the event and
brought a gift for the new baby. It was a puppet washcloth that was labeled
a "tub buddy." Once again she was pleased.

Other Patient Characteristics

DRIVE FOR THINNESS

As mentioned earlier, patients with a powerfully entrenched drive for
thinness can be extremely resistant to change. We have already discussed
the current cultural obsession with thinness. When other factors interact
with the internalization of this cultural standard, the resulting drive for
thinness can be so deeply engrained that it is nearly impossible to change.
For example, we treated a patient with an obese mother who did not diet
herself but constantly scrutinized her daughter's caloric intake and con-
veyed to her that being fat entailed a life of misery. This patient later

became a model, thus entering a profession that required extreme thinness. She also repeated her family pattern of never being thin enough to suit others by dating men who encouraged her to lose more weight even when she was very slim. Thus this patient's mother, employers, and boyfriends all insisted on her thinness. The end result was her alternation between amphetamine and cocaine abuse and bingeing for a period of ten years. When she entered treatment, antidepressant medication was recommended in addition to psychotherapy because of her severe depression. Following the evaluation for medication, the patient called us in a panic after being told that the medication sometimes resulted in weight gain. In therapy the patient was encouraged to stop relying on the diet pills and to begin to normalize her eating. Evidently this patient was so overwhelmed and terrified by the prospect of any weight gain that she terminated treatment after only three sessions, despite great unhappiness about her current bingeing/starving regimen. Had she remained in treatment, it is possible that her drive for thinness could have been modified enough to permit some normalization of eating. However, it would probably have been quite a lengthy process, given that we were the first to suggest to her that being thin is not the most important thing in life.

It is our experience that an extremely entrenched drive for thinness in a patient who appears relatively healthy can be indicative of deeper pathology, even if it is not readily apparent. We treated in short-term therapy a young woman who was a binge-restrictor. Her relationships, job performance, and seeming lack of difficulty in regulating her affective states all indicated that she probably fell in the more high-functioning neurotic or identity-conflicted group of bulimics. However, despite these strengths, her drive for thinness was so rigid that she had a great deal of trouble implementing therapeutic suggestions concerning normalizing her eating. When this was discussed, she would literally wail that she couldn't bear to be fat. Therapy had to be terminated after twenty sessions because that was all her health service provided. Although a reasonable amount had been accomplished, we were struck by the intransigence of the need to be thin in an apparently well-functioning personality.

The patient requested hospitalization the next year because she felt her eating was out of control and she was very depressed. When her diagnostician recommended intensive outpatient treatment instead, the patient became quite upset. The following day she was brought to the hospital emergency room because her roommate had found a suicide note the patient had written (and left in an obvious place) in which she threatened to hang herself. The patient thus achieved her goal of hospitalization, although it was on a general psychiatry floor for suicidal tendencies rather than in an eating disorders program. We were struck by the patient's disturbed and manipulative behavior, little of which had been apparent in the brief treatment. Over time we have come to regard an intractable desire for thinness as a poor prognostic indicator, even when it first appears to be relatively circumscribed in a high-functioning individual. It generally suggests deeper pathology than might be apparent, often hidden by a well-developed false self organization.

EGO-SYNTONICITY OF THE SYMPTOM

The ego-syntonicity of the symptom refers to the patient's attitude toward her symptomatic behavior. Many (if not most) bulimics feel ashamed and disgusted by their bingeing and purging, and are motivated to change a behavior that is so discrepant with their ideal self; thus the bulimia is ego-dystonic. On the other hand, some patients may give lip service to a wish for change but are relatively undisturbed by their behavior. These individuals may enter treatment, often at the urging or the insistence of someone else, but will rarely make any changes.

One indicator of the ego-syntonicity of the bulimia comes from discussing with the patient who, if anyone, she has told about her symptom prior to the therapeutic interview. Patients who have told no one or only a few intimates are more likely to experience their bulimia as ego-alien and truly wish to change. Yet other individuals, for whom the behavior is much more acceptable, reveal their problem indiscriminately. For example, occasionally at parties and other social gatherings complete strangers, upon learning our occupation, regale us with the details of their eating disorder. The absence of shame or guilt and the consolidation of an identity as a bulimic implied by such indiscriminate self-disclosure are poor prognostic indicators.

Patients whose behavior is ego-syntonic may attend therapy sessions but make no effort to control their behavior. Often attendance is sporadic and the dropout rate is very high. Frequently these individuals go "therapist shopping" and blame their lack of progress on their inadequate therapists. These patients tend to externalize their difficulties and often have some degree of sociopathy. In treatment it is important for the therapist to continually assess progress or lack thereof, and to discuss with the patient her willingness to change. Sometimes the most therapeutic response is to frankly state that progress will not be made until the patient truly wishes to change, and that this does not seem to be the case at present.

For example, a young woman was referred for treatment by her fiance, with whom she lived. The patient was bingeing and purging regularly and was stealing food as well. As she became more open with us concerning her behavior, it became apparent that she was stealing *all* of the food that she and her fiance were eating, and that she used the words "bought" and "stole" interchangeably. When her fiance confronted her about any aspect of her behavior, she would deflect his concerns by assuring him that she was working on it in therapy. However, this was not the case, and she freely admitted to us that she had absolutely no guilt about the stealing and was relatively unconcerned about her eating behavior. Rather than collude with the patient in pretending that therapeutic work was being done, we informed her that because she appeared to have no interest in changing these aspects of her behavior, and unless she had other treatment goals that she did want to accomplish, the therapy could be of no use to her at that time.

Many bulimics steal food, but generally they express great shame and guilt concerning stealing, just as they do about the bingeing and purging. The degree of sociopathy exhibited by this patient's total lack of guilt about her behavior made therapeutic progress on these issues unworkable, at least at that time. It is impossible to conduct symptom-focused work with a patient who is less invested in the project than the therapist. Clearly this patient's agenda was to placate her fiance by pretending to be in treatment while her behavior remained unchanged.

Countertransference

Countertransference refers to feelings and reactions evoked in the therapist by the therapeutic interaction with a patient. Not surprisingly, it has been our experience that particular countertransference issues may arise in treating eating-disordered patients. We first turn to countertransference difficulties that may affect both male and female therapists in their work with bulimics. Later issues specific to each sex are discussed.

GENERAL COUNTERTRANSFERENCE ISSUES

Sharing Society's Obsession with Thinness. No one can be completely immune to the current cultural milieu that stigmatizes obesity and glorifies thinness. A therapist working with an obese patient may find that he or she is experiencing revulsion for the patient's fat. This could lead to a variety of countertherapeutic interventions, such as supporting the patient's dissatisfaction with her body and applauding plans for severe dietary restriction. The therapist whose patient makes a healthy decision to abandon restrictive dieting and accept what may be a natural body weight may feel dismayed that the patient is "giving up" in her quest for thinness. While the therapist's motives may be benign in the sense of wishing the patient to have an easier time by fitting into societal criteria for maximal attractiveness, any ambivalence about a patient's acceptance of herself could be counterproductive.

Revulsion at the Binge/Purge Behavior. Many individuals in our culture feel disgust and revulsion when they hear about bingeing and purging behavior, and therapists are not exempt from these feelings. Bingeing can connote all sorts of pejoratives to the therapist, including that the patient is out of control, greedy, and self-indulgent. Therapists with strong concerns for the state of the world might find themselves feeling moralistic at what they see as self-indulgence in the face of world hunger, particularly for wealthy patients. It is also not uncommon for therapists to feel a sense of superiority at their own "self-control" and lack of a need to indulge in binge eating.

Vomiting also has extremely negative connotations in our society. Unlike in ancient Rome, where vomitoriums provided a socially acceptable way to gorge oneself continuously, vomiting is now usually associated with being miserably ill or drunk. While young drinkers may boast about their drinking exploits and elaborate upon the quantity of beer they are able to consume, it would be very unusual indeed to expound upon the quantity vomited following consumption. Generally vomiting is regarded as revolting, and this is particularly true for self-induced vomiting.

The therapist must get past these attitudes so that vomiting behavior may be discussed matter-of-factly rather than in a judgmental fashion. An empathic stance concerning how the patient arrived at such a desperate adaptation must be maintained. This may involve a refusal to collude with the patient who uses euphemisms such as "I got sick" following a binge, and pointing out her active choice using the real words, like "you made yourself throw up then."

Impatience with Refusal to Change. The therapist who works with bulimic patients must be prepared to deal with their tremendous ambivalence about changing their behavior. It is easy to grow impatient with a bulimic whose intractable drive for thinness foils all therapeutic attempts to get her to normalize her eating. Again, empathy with this stance must be maintained. As Stern (1986) points out, the therapist must resist *needing* the patient to act in any particular way.

SPECIAL ISSUES FOR FEMALE THERAPISTS

Envy of the Patient. As we have discussed, women in our society are encouraged to work very hard at being attractive in certain culturally sanctioned ways. Lest we forget, a constant barrage of messages from television, magazines, and advertisements remind us of the cultural ideal toward which we should strive. It is likely that no woman in our society, including therapists, can escape having a certain measure of body dissatisfaction, which may or may not be related to weight. A number of our patients are stunningly beautiful women who may also have glamorous professions such as modeling, acting, and dancing. Thus the female therapist may have to deal with her feelings of envy around a patient's beauty and her impatience that the patient denigrates her body and does not realize her beauty. It is important to recognize that this envy can be present. The female therapist must come to terms with her own appearance, just as our patients must.

The Therapist with Eating and/or Weight Problems. Along these same lines of cultural attractiveness, many female therapists may struggle or have struggled with their own weight. Some female therapists are drawn to the eating disorders field because of personal experience with anorexia nervosa, bulimia, and/or obesity. On the other hand, female therapists who previously had not felt weight was an issue for them may come to find, as they begin to work with patients, that indeed it is. In these instances, it is important for the therapist to be very conscious of any weight-related issues of her own and to deal with them through her own therapy, supervision, and so forth.

Female therapists who are significantly overweight must be prepared for this to be an issue in treatment. Unlike recovered anorexics or bulimics, it is obvious that they do not fit society's ideal of thinness. It can be a wonderful modeling experience for the patient to see that an overweight woman can be successful and accomplished. However, because the fat is evident, it must be discussed explicitly. A number of patients we have seen have left treatment after one session with an obese therapist because they feared offending the therapist by talking about their feelings about her weight. When therapists are nondefensive about their weight and ask the patient how she might feel to have a fat therapist, the explicit permission they give opens the way for the necessary discussion of feelings.

Slender female therapists also have to deal with a variety of issues, often including the patient's envy and hostility that the therapist has something that the patient desperately wants. Patients might state that "It's easy for you to say I have to stop dieting before I can get control of my eating, but you don't know what it feels like to be this fat." Therapists must explore that patient's feelings about various body sizes and the patient's sense that therapists cannot understand her unless they are both the same size. Patients also tend to make the erroneous assumption that therapists keep their weight down through mighty willpower. When patients comment that "you're so slim—I bet you don't eat very much," therapists must provide reality testing by emphasizing that it is possible to eat normally and maintain weight when one is at a natural body weight.

These examples make it clear that at times female therapists working with bulimics must be prepared to face intense scrutiny regarding their weight and to discuss personal weight-related issues nondefensively when necessary. Often patients will ask how the therapist became interested in eating disorders, or will be more explicit and inquire if the therapist herself has ever had an eating disorder. If this is the case, we believe it can be helpful to tell the truth in brief, with an emphasis on the recovery period.

The revelation should be dictated by the patient's needs rather than by the therapist's wish to tell her story.

For therapists who have never had an eating disorder and are questioned about it, we recommend that they say something about having experienced societal pressures regarding attractiveness rather than a flat "no." It is important for therapists to ask if their lack of personal experience makes the patient feel that she cannot possibly be understood. This concern can generally be relieved by therapists consistently demonstrating that they have specific knowledge of the area.

COUNTERTRANSFERENCE ISSUES FOR THE MALE THERAPIST

The Empathic Connection. It may be difficult for the male therapist to appreciate the intensity of a bulimic woman's concerns about her weight. Dissatisfaction with one's weight is not normative for men as it is for women. Because he has never experienced cultural expectations mandating thinness as a prerequisite for success, the male therapist may feel baffled and perhaps impatient with the bulimic's weight preoccupation. Male therapists who have received little training in the treatment of bulimia may attempt to give "commonsense" advice, such as going on a diet to lose weight, which is completely countertherapeutic. The male therapist needs to do two things in order to avoid minimizing patients' concern about weight; first, he must allow the patient to describe her inner world to him in depth; and second, he should attempt to draw on some of his own experiences to find some basis for empathy with the patient.

A related difficulty for a male therapist is dealing with a patient's belief that, because he is a man, he will be unable to understand her fully. It would be easy for the therapist to feel angry and misunderstood that he is not even being given a chance. If from the start a patient is unable to regard a male therapist as a potential ally who could help her, however, she would probably feel best working with a female therapist. In treating bulimic women who are willing to see a male therapist, the therapist needs to be open to working with the patient's expectations of how well he will be able to understand her experiences. Presenting oneself as someone who has special knowledge about treating bulimia combined with a readiness to discuss the patient's feelings about the therapy often are sufficient to defuse the issue of males' supposed inability to understand females.

Concerns about Intrusiveness. Working with bulimic women involves discussing issues such as the patient's body weight, her feelings about various parts of her body, her menstrual cycle, and other body-related issues. Such inquiry and discussion may cause male therapists to feel uncomfortable about being intrusive and/or eroticizing their relationship with the patient. This may be particularly true since therapy with most other patients does not require such body-related discussions. Male therapists must recognize the necessity of gathering this information and knowing the feelings patients have concerning these issues, and be ready to discuss them in a matter-of-fact manner. If therapists can recognize that such inquiries are essential to the therapy, any feelings of intrusiveness or concerns that the topics are inappropriate can be mitigated.

12

Review of Treatment Studies: Methodology and Efficacy

The number of studies investigating various treatments for bulimia has increased geometrically over the last several years. In this chapter we offer a comprehensive review of the major published studies to date. The treatment methods have consisted primarily of behavioral, cognitive-behavioral, and psychopharmacological interventions. Although there is significant variability in methodology and reporting of findings, the response rates to the various interventions appear to be relatively comparable. The chapter concludes with methodological recommendations for future studies. These suggestions are offered in hopes of improving our ability to evaluate the relative effectiveness of the different treatment strategies.

Psychological Interventions

COGNITIVE-BEHAVIORAL AND BEHAVIORAL TREATMENT PACKAGES

Most psychological treatment studies have relied on cognitive-behavioral and behavioral interventions, and most have been "treatment packages" that incorporate a variety of different interventions, such as self-monitoring, goal setting, the provision of educational materials, group support, experimental exercises, suggestions for normalizing eating, assertiveness training, progressive relaxation, and cognitive restructuring. These interventions have been implemented in group settings as well as in individual psychotherapy, and the lengths of treatment have varied. Measures used and outcome criteria have also differed from study to study, making comparisons difficult. Nonetheless, it is useful to review these studies and reach some tentative conclusions concerning the efficacy of these interventions.

Boskind-Lodahl was the first to report on the effectiveness of a specific treatment program for bulimia (1978). The treatment involved gestalt-type experiential work coupled with techniques such as self-monitoring and goal setting within a feminist perspective. Her design included a pilot group of eleven, an experimental group of eleven, and an experimental group of thirteen who served as a waiting list control for three months while the first experimental group was conducted. The treatment program consisted of between eleven and eighteen weekly two-hour sessions plus one six-hour marathon session. Unfortunately, Boskind-Lodahl did not report in detail results regarding change in the binge/purge behavior. There was some reduction for most subjects by the end of the treatment, and at a three- to four-month follow-up the reduction had persisted for most. She reported that 11 percent had not changed or had become worse. In terms of psychological functioning, there were significant improvements for the experimental group on the Body Cathexis Test (Secord and Jourard, 1953) and on some subscales of the Sixteen Personality Factor Questionnaire (Cattell, 1972), such as emotional stability and assertiveness.

White and Boskind-White (1981) continued to use this treatment concept in a group format. In an uncontrolled study involving fourteen bulimics, they ran group meetings five hours a day for five days. Postgroup frequency of binge/purge episodes was not reported, but at six-month follow-up the authors reported three out of fourteen subjects (21 percent) were totally remitted, seven (50 percent) reported significant reduction, and four (28 percent) had little or no improvement. There was also significant psychological improvement on eight of sixteen subscales on the California Psychological Inventory (Gough, 1957) and on the Body Cathexis Test.

Fairburn (1981) conducted the first uncontrolled study involving cognitive-behavioral and behavioral techniques with binge-vomiters, utilizing individual therapy that included self-monitoring, goal setting, problem solving, and cognitive restructuring. Behavioral strategies such as the introduction of previously forbidden foods into the patients' diets were also included in the treatment. Length of treatment averaged seven months, with more frequent sessions at first then tapering to once a month. At the end of treatment nine of eleven subjects (82 percent) had reduced their binge/purge episodes to fewer than one per month. Data on six patients were available one year posttreatment. One (17 percent) was totally remitted, four (67 percent) had episodes every two to three months, and one (17 percent) did not change. No data were reported concerning psychological functioning.

Lacey (1983) achieved striking results in a large-scale controlled study involving the use of behavioral and cognitive techniques. His subjects were thirty females who met DSM-III criteria for bulimia. It is important to note that patients had to agree in advance to the demands of the program and had contracted to attend all sessions, maintain their current weight, and eat a prescribed diet (three meals a day at set times). They received weekly sessions involving one-half hour of individual therapy and one and one-half hours of group therapy over ten weeks, while an assessment-only control group was wait-listed. Twenty-four out of thirty subjects (80 percent) were totally remitted at the end of treatment, while an additional four remitted within four weeks, so that 93 percent of subjects were totally binge/purge-free. No changes were seen in the assessment-only control group, who were then offered treatment. Twenty-eight patients were monitored for up to two years posttreatment. Twenty out of twenty-eight (71 percent) remained totally binge-free, while eight (29 percent) reported occasional bingeing (on an average of three times a year). Psychological functioning was not reported in detail, although Lacey stated that while patients were depressed and angry before treatment, they seemed less angry and more depressed at the end of therapy, as though a masked depression had been uncovered.

In the same year Johnson, Connors, and Stuckey (1983) and Connors, Johnson, and Stuckey (1984) began reporting the results from a brief psychoeducational group treatment program. Subjects were twenty females meeting DSM-III criteria for bulimia. The study used a multiple baseline design with two groups receiving identical treatment but beginning three weeks apart. Subjects received twelve two-hour sessions over nine weeks, with sessions twice a week for the first three weeks and then tapering to once a week. The psychoeducational materials consisted of didactic information concerning bulimia, the effects of dieting, how to normalize eating, and other food- and weight-related issues. Additional techniques included self-monitoring, goal setting, relaxation, and assertion training. Results indicated that group treatment rather than assessment only and self-monitoring produced significant results. Two out of twenty subjects (10 percent) were totally remitted by the end of the group, nine (45 percent) had reduced their episodes by at least 50 percent, and nine (45 percent) showed little or no improvement. In terms of psychological functioning, there were significant positive changes on the Tennessee Self-Concept Scale (Fitts, 1964–65) and on several scales of the Multiscore Depression Inventory (Berndt, Petzel, and Berndt, 1980). Significant positive changes were also seen on the drive for thinness, bulimia, and ineffectiveness subscales of the EDI (Garner, Olmsted, and Polivy, 1983) and on the Assertion Inventory (Gambrill and Richey, 1975). While there was some improvement on the Body Cathexis Test, it was not significant. Follow-up of the symptomatic behavior one to two years after the group revealed that out of the seventeen patients located, eight (47 percent) were binge/purge-free, five (29 percent) maintained a 50 percent reduction from pretreatment, and four (24 percent) reported little change.

Another 1983 report (Abraham, Mira, and Llewellyn-Jones) described the results of uncontrolled trials of individual therapy with forty-three DSM-III–diagnosed bulimic females. Supportive and educational psychotherapy, supplemented in some cases by medication and/or marital therapy, was administered for between fourteen and seventy-two months. At the end of treatment fourteen (33 percent) of the subjects were considered "cured" (bingeing less than once a month and not purging at all); fourteen (32 percent) were binge/purging less than once a week; and fifteen (35 percent) were still having episodes more than once a week.

A plethora of reports emerged in 1984, primarily utilizing cognitive and behavioral interventions in group formats. Pyle, Mitchell, Eckert, Hatsukami, and Goff (1984) reported on an uncontrolled intensive group program with 104 bulimics. This eight-week program involved five nights of three-hour meetings the first week, four nights the second week, and finally tapered to twice a week for the remainder of the treatment. Cognitive-behavioral techniques as well as concepts from substance abuse treatment programs were utilized; thus patients were expected to be abstinent from bingeing and purging from the time they entered the program. Sessions included lectures, discussions, group meals, and group therapy. The results indicated that forty-nine (47 percent) of the patients were abstinent from the first night of the program, twenty-six (25 percent) had between one and three episodes, eleven (11 percent) had four or more, eleven (11 percent) failed to complete the program, and six (6 percent) were asked to leave for noncompliance. Psychological functioning was not reported in detail, although the authors suggested that self-esteem improved and depression decreased over the course of the program. Follow-up data were not presented.

Several reports of group therapy with small samples of bulimics were conducted in 1984 and 1985 (Bauer, 1984; Merrill, 1984; Roy-Byrne, Lee-Benner, and Yager, 1984; Schneider and Agras, 1985; Stevens and Salisbury, 1984). As these were all uncontrolled studies, they will not be reviewed in detail. They primarily utilized cognitive and behavioral interventions and reported varying degrees of positive results.

Yates and Sambrailo (1984) conducted a controlled study involving a comparison of two group treatments. Subjects were twenty-four females meeting DSM-III criteria for bulimia nervosa (Russell, 1979), sixteen of whom completed treatment. One group utilized cognitive-behavioral therapy and specific behavioral instructions, the other cognitive-behavioral therapy only. The cognitive-behavioral therapy included cognitive restructuring, assertion training, and relaxation training. The specific behavioral instructions focused on identification of antecedents and consequences of binge/purge behavior, with suggestions for stimulus control, response delay, and response prevention.

After a three- or six-week baseline period, subjects had six weeks of ninety-minute sessions and a six-week follow-up. The results indicated that there were no differences between the two groups. By follow-up two of sixteen subjects (12 percent) had remitted, seven (44 percent) had reduced by more than half, and seven (44 percent) had changed little. Posttreatment subjects were significantly better on the Carroll Rating Scale for Depression (Carroll et al., 1981). There were no significant changes on the Eysenck Personal Inventory Rating (Eysenck and Eysenck, 1975) or the IPAT Anxiety Scale (Krug, Schreier, and Cattell, 1976). On the Coopersmith Self Esteem Inventory (Self Esteem Institute, 1975) subjects were significantly below norms at pretest but were within the normal range at the end of follow-up.

Kirkley, Schneider, Agras, and Bachman (1985) compared the relative effectiveness of two group treatments of bulimia. Subjects were twenty-eight females meeting DSM-III criteria for bulimia. Both groups met weekly for sixteen weeks, and both utilized extensive self-monitoring and weekly charting of vomiting. However, the cognitive-behavioral group received specific instructions concerning normalizing eating, delaying vomiting, and other techniques that have generally been found useful in altering bulimic behavior. The nondirective group discussed food-related issues but received no instructions; the group's emphasis was on self-disclosure and self-discovery. Results showed significant differences between groups in terms of reduced bingeing and vomiting, with the cognitive-behavioral group reducing significantly more. While both treatments resulted in decreased binge/purge episodes from pre- to posttreatment, the within-group changes were significant only in the cognitive-behavioral condition. There were also fewer dropouts in that group. After treatment, both groups reported significantly lower levels of depression on the BDI (Beck, 1967), less anxiety on the Spielberger State Trait Personality Inventory (Spielberger, 1979), and improvements on the EAT and the EDI. At three-month follow-up, there were significant differences between groups regarding bingeing and purging. Five of thirteen (38 percent) in the cognitive-behavioral group were abstinent, while only one in nine (11 percent) in the nondirective group was abstinent. Overall, both treatments resulted in reduction of bingeing and purging at follow-up, with over three-quarters of the members of both groups decreasing their vomiting rate by more than 60 percent.

Ordman and Kirschenbaum (1985) conducted a controlled study of twenty bulimic females comparing full intervention individual therapy to a brief intervention wait list. The brief intervention consisted of three assessment sessions plus some recommendations, such as exposure plus response prevention. The full intervention was individual therapy over an average of fifteen sessions, ranging from four to twenty-two. Interventions included cognitive-behavioral therapy, process-oriented therapy with some behavioral techniques, and exposure plus response prevention. Results indicated that the full intervention was significantly more effective than the brief treatment. Of the full intervention group, two of ten patients (20 percent) remitted, five (50 percent) reduced by more than half, and three (30 percent) had changed little. On a pre-post behavior test where subjects were asked to eat snack foods without purging and rate their feelings of discomfort and urge to vomit, the full intervention group ate significantly more food after treatment than the brief group. They also had significantly less discomfort with food and a significantly shorter duration of the urge to vomit. Significant changes occurred on the EAT, Body Cathexis, BDI, and SCL-90 (Derogatis et al., 1974) for the full intervention group compared to the brief group, although neither group fell within a normal range on the SCL-90 or the BDI after intervention.

Of the fifteen studies we reviewed involving cognitive-behavioral and behavioral therapy that consisted of more than one case, only five had some sort of control (multiple baseline, two-group comparison, or wait-list control). There are problems with most of these studies: many are uncontrolled pilot programs with small samples, lack follow-ups, omit measures of psychological functioning as well as binge/purge behavior, and do not specify their results clearly. Nonetheless, as a group these studies suggest that cognitive-behavioral and behavioral interventions are relatively effective in their impact on binge/purge behavior and psychological functioning. The five controlled studies utilizing assessment-only controls or multiple baselines seem to indicate that the intervention programs themselves are producing the results.

These fifteen studies indicate that at the end of a treatment program, approximately 40 percent of patients will be binge/purge-free, around 30 percent will have reduced their binge/purge episodes by half, and about 30 percent will show little change. It is important to note, however, that these are very rough estimates, and there is a great deal of variability between studies.

At this point, it is difficult to say which specific interventions or combinations are most effective. The treatment programs reviewed were almost exclusively treatment packages. As yet we do not know which elements of these programs were active in producing changes. Component analyses are needed to control for nonspecific effects and to tease out truly effective interventions. Fortunately, several studies have investigated the effects of more specific components.

EXPOSURE WITH RESPONSE PREVENTION

As mentioned, Rosen and Leitenberg (1982) have hypothesized that the primary reinforcer in bulimia may be vomiting rather than binge eating. They suggested that vomiting may serve an anxiety-reducing function similar to that of compulsions, such as hand washing, in obsessive-compulsive disorders. Once the bulimic learns that vomiting reduces the anxiety concerning weight gain, the vomiting response is reinforced, and subsequently there are fewer inhibitions to overeating (Johnson and Larson, 1982). Thus their response-prevention method focused on the vomiting component of bulimia rather than the uncontrolled eating. In their 1982 single-case study Rosen and Leitenberg employed a multiple baseline design involving exposure to preferred binge foods and prevention of the vomiting response. The treatment resulted in complete cessation of both bingeing and vomiting.

These promising results led to several other studies investigating the efficacy of exposure plus response prevention (ERP). Leitenberg, Gross, Peterson, and Rosen (1984) treated five subjects who met DSM-III criteria for bulimia. After a three-week baseline period, subjects received between twelve and eighteen individual sessions. Sessions were divided into two-week phases in which subjects were exposed to various foods according to their self-rated degree of difficulty with them. Subjects were instructed to eat until they felt a strong urge to vomit, and then would confront anxiety-provoking cognitions with the therapist. Generally the subjects ate more and reported less anxiety over time. At the end of treatment two of the five subjects (40 percent) had ceased vomiting entirely, two (40 percent) had reduced by more than half, and one (20 percent) had not changed. At a three- to six-month follow-up these results were maintained. Regarding psychological functioning, positive changes were reported on the BDI, the EAT, the Rosenberg Self-Esteem Scale (Rosenberg, 1979) and the Lawson Self-Esteem Scale (Lawson, Marshall, and McGrath, 1979), although no statistics were reported.

Johnson, Schlundt, Kelly, and Ruggiero (1984) designed a study in which ERP and energy balance interventions were compared. Energy balance was defined as the self-regulation of eating and exercise in order to maintain an acceptable weight and included scheduling balanced meals and cognitive restructuring. Subjects were six bulimics, five of whom completed treatment, who were randomly assigned to the treatment they would receive first in a multiple baseline design. Length of treatment was variable, with weekly individual sessions up to twelve weeks. While ERP was intended to target vomiting and energy balance to address the bingeing, the patients reduced both bingeing and vomiting during both interventions. Neither technique proved superior to the other in this pilot data. At the end of treatment one of five completers was in remission (20 percent), three (60 percent) were "considerably improved," and for one (20 percent) there was no change. No follow-up data or information on psychological functioning were reported.

Hoage and Gray (1984) conducted ERP treatment in a group setting. Their subjects were eight bulimic females who received group treatment and were compared to five wait-list controls. The group treatment program consisted of twelve two-hour sessions over six weeks and included such techniques as self-monitoring, cognitive restructuring, and eating habit stabilization as well as ERP. At the beginning of each session subjects ate amounts of food that were moderately anxiety provoking, then spent the rest of the session using the techniques just mentioned. Posttreatment there were "significant reductions" in the binge/purge behavior for seven of eight subjects (88 percent). At a six-month follow-up, 75 percent had reduced their vomiting to one time per week or less, one had relapsed (12 percent), and one (12 percent) was unchanged. There were no changes in the wait-list control group during this time. For the experimental group statistically significant improvements were reported on the BDI and Binge Eating Scale (Hawkins and Clement, 1980).

Kelly (1984) also reported on a group treatment involving ERP as well as refutation of irrational beliefs. Subjects were five female bulimics who received twenty-three weekly sessions after a three-week baseline period. Subjects ate various foods, and then their anxiety-provoking irrational cognitions were challenged. Two of five subjects (40 percent) had "virtually eliminated" binge/purge behavior by the end of treatment, and one (20 percent) had ceased for four weeks with a slight increase in the last session. Two subjects (40 percent) who reported little behavior change were erratic in attendance and admitted to lack of motivation. No follow-up data were reported.

Because exposure plus response prevention is a relatively new form of treatment for bulimia, these are the only data-based reports available. Among them there is the usual difficulty of comparing results, but generally they seem to suggest that between 60 to 80 percent of subjects will remit or markedly reduce their vomiting by the end of treatment and that these results will be maintained at a brief (three to six month) follow-up. Thus ERP seems a promising form of treatment.

It must be remembered, however, that these studies are based on very small samples of patients. Fewer than twenty-five subjects were assessed in the five studies combined. Further studies employing larger samples with longer follow-up periods are necessary. In addition, it also must be remembered that like many of the behavioral and cognitive-behavioral treatment packages reviewed, ERP is hardly a "pure" treatment involving a single component. It involves other cognitive-behavioral techniques, such as self-monitoring and cognitive restructuring in the postconsumption period. Some studies employing ERP have also utilized still other techniques, such as psychoeducational materials, group support, problem solving, and eating habit stabilization.

SELF-HELP

While vast numbers of self-help groups and associations have emerged in the last several years to aid bulimics and their families, by their very nature such groups tend to exclude mental health professionals and their research questions. Thus little is known concerning the efficacy of these various organizations (although Enright, Butterfield, and Berkowitz [1984] present a detailed analysis of their structures and functions). Recently, however, Huon (1984) has detailed the success of a self-help program by mail in Australia. Subjects were ninety females who met DSM-III criteria for bulimia who responded to an invitation in a magazine to participate in a study. Subjects were divided into three groups: group 1 was sent the mail component and offered mail or phone contact with a "cured" bulimic; group 2 also received the mail component but was offered contact with an "improved" bulimic; group 3 received only the mail component. An additional thirty subjects were used as wait-list controls. The mail self-help component consisted of task-oriented suggestions for eating behavior changes sent to each individual monthly over seven months. Most participants in all three experimental groups improved, with no comparable improvements in the wait-list groups. Seventeen out of ninety (19 percent) were symptom-free at the end of seven months, while sixty-one (68 percent) improved to the point that they were binge/purging less than once per week. At a six-month follow-up twenty-nine (32 percent) were symptom-free and forty (45 percent) reported "significant improvement." At the end of the program there was little difference between the three experimental groups, but at follow-up there were more symptom-free subjects in the two conditions where there was contact with another bulimic. Psychological functioning also improved, with significant differences before and after intervention on the Body Cathexis Test. Huon noted that those willing to self-monitor tended to remain in the program, while those unwilling to comply with this request dropped out. This study speaks to the efficacy of providing bulimics with psychoeducational materials and the ability of some to make use of them, even in the absence of therapeutic contact.

FAMILY THERAPY

While there have been a number of reports of the use of family therapy with anorexia nervosa patients (for example, see Minuchin, Rosman, and Baker, 1978), very few data-based reports have appeared concerning its use for bulimia. In 1982 Schwartz published a single case study involving a seventeen-year-old bulimic and her family in which positive results were obtained. Schwartz, Barrett, and Saba (1984) reported on a larger-scale study of family therapy. The patients were thirty bulimics and their families who were seen for an average of thirty-three sessions over nine months, with a range of from two to ninety sessions. The primary interventions were structural family therapy and symptom-focused directives. Before treatment, authors considered all thirty bulimics to be "level 4"; that is, they were binge/purging more than five times per week and feeling out of control. At the close of treatment twenty (66 percent) were considered to be at "level 1," having less than one binge/purge episode per month and feeling nearly always in control. Three (10 percent) were at "level 2," having two episodes per month to once per week but feeling usually in control; three (10 percent) were at "level 3," having between two and four episodes weekly; and four (14 percent) remained at "level 4." The mean follow-up was sixteen months. All the cases that had reached level 1 remained there through the follow-up period. Two out of the three patients at level 2 had relapsed to level 3, and those at levels 3 and 4 had maintained. The authors noted that cases with the worse outcomes tended to be those bulimics who had begun and ended treatment still living at home and those who dropped out prematurely.

This one study points to the efficacy of family therapy with bulimia. While the outcome figures are positive, this treatment modality must be investigated further. There are many unanswered questions concerning selection criteria for family treatment.

Psychopharmacological Interventions

Over the last several years more pharmacologically oriented clinicians have suggested that bulimia may simply be a symptomatic expression of a biologically mediated affective disorder. This speculation arises from reports that many bulimics present with symptoms that are characteristic of unipolar and bipolar illness (Hudson, Laffer, and Pope, 1982; Johnson and Larson, 1982; Pyle, Mitchell, and Eckert, 1981; Russell, 1979; Walsh, Roose, and Glassman, 1983); that there is a high incidence of major affective disorder among first- and second-degree relatives of bulimics (Hudson, Laffer, and Pope, 1982; Hudson, Pope, Jonas, and Yurgelun-Todd, 1983; Strober, 1981; Strober, Salkin, Burroughs, and Morrell, 1982); and, finally, that laboratory findings from the dexamethasone suppression test and sleep architecture studies indicate that bulimics present with abnormal DST and sleep profiles that are similar to those of patients with histories of affective disorder (Gwirtsman, Roy-Byrne, Yager, and Gerner, 1983; Hudson, Laffer, and Pope, 1982; Katz et al., 1984). These findings have prompted several investigations into the effectiveness of pharmacological treatment of bulimia. Most investigations have focused on the use of antidepressant medication (tricyclics and MAOIs).

TRICYCLIC ANTIDEPRESSANTS AND MAOIs

The effectiveness of tricyclic medication was initially investigated through open trial administration. Pope and Hudson (1982) administered imipramine (150 mg) to eight patients who met DSM-III criteria for bulimia. The medication was administered over a four-week period, and serum levels were obtained after the patients had reached a maximum daily dose for at least seven days. Results indicated that at follow-up (ranging from two to sixteen months), three of eight (38 percent) patients reduced their frequency of binge eating by greater than 90 percent; three (38 percent) had reductions greater than 50 percent; and two (25 percent) reported no response. The study did not include any measures of change in eating attitudes.

Another open trial study that reported on the effectiveness of MAOIs appeared at the same time. Walsh and associates (1982) administered phenelzine (60–90 mg) and tranylcypromine (45 mg) to six patients who also met DSM-III criteria for bulimia. Although the follow-up period was not reported, the results indicated that four (67 percent) of the patients were completely symptom-free and two (33 percent) had reduced their binge frequency by greater than 90 percent. Walsh and his colleagues also demonstrated that the patients' disturbed eating attitudes, as measured by the EAT, significantly decreased following the medication trial.

Not all of the preliminary open trial reports found antidepressant medication effective in the treatment of bulimia. Brotman, Herzog, and Woods (1984) retrospectively reported on twenty-two patients who met DSM-III criteria for bulimia and who were treated with at least one trial of antidepressant medication. These investigators selectively administered the medication to bulimic patients who had major depression or dysthymic disorder or who were treatment failures with psychotherapy. The therapeutic trial consisted of drug treatment for a minimum of four weeks with either a tricyclic (125 mg), trazedone (150 mg), or phenelzine (45 mg). Serum levels were not monitored, and it should be noted that the dosages of the medications were in the average to low-average range. The results of this retrospective, open trial report are seriously compromised by questions regarding the medication dosage levels used.

Results indicated that at two- to twelve-month follow-ups, five of the twenty-two (23 percent) patients were in remission and four (18 percent) decreased their binge eating by greater than 50 percent. Thirteen (59 percent) showed no improvement. Brotman and his colleagues concluded that while pharmacotherapy should play a role in the treatment of bulimia, the disorder is multidetermined. To stress this they pointed out that sixteen of twenty-two patients in their study also had a DSM-III Axis II diagnosis, indicating that they had significant personality disturbance. The authors felt that the level of personality disturbance was a major factor in the chronicity of the symptomatic eating behavior.

These preliminary uncontrolled reports stimulated considerable interest in further understanding the effectiveness of antidepressant pharmacotherapy in treating bulimia. Over the last several years a number of controlled investigations of these medications have appeared.

Pope, Hudson, Jonas, and Yurgelun-Todd (1983) were the first to conduct a well-controlled medication trial. Using a double-blind, placebo-controlled design, they administered imipramine (200 mg) to eleven bulimic patients and a nonactive placebo to a control group of ten bulimic patients over a six-week period. At two- to eight-month follow-up, results indicated that within the active drug group, two patients had withdrawn from the study after developing side effects (photosensitivity and maculopapular rash); three of the nine who completed the trial (33 percent) were in remission, four (44 percent) had reduced their binge frequency by greater than 75 percent, and two (22 percent) had improved by greater than 50 percent. Additional results indicated a significant difference between the active drug and placebo group on measures of self-control, food preoccupation, intensity of binge eating, depression, and global improvement.

Among the ten placebo subjects, one (10 percent) reported a decrease in binge frequency by greater than 50 percent, eight (80 percent) were unchanged, and one (10 percent) worsened. At the end of the six-week trial period, the placebo patients were offered imipramine or another antidepressant medication. After receiving the active medication, three of nine (33 percent) subjects in the placebo group stopped binge eating entirely, two (22 percent) decreased by greater than 50 percent, and two (22 percent) showed no improvement. When the active drug and placebo group were combined, the results showed that six of eighteen (33 percent) were in complete remission; six (33 percent) decreased binge frequency by greater than 75 percent; four (22 percent) decreased 50 percent; and two (11 percent) showed no improvement. It is also important to note that six of the eighteen patients had to be given several different antidepressant medications before an adequate response was achieved.

Similarly impressive results were reported by Hughes, Wells, Cunningham, and Ilstrip (1986). Using a double-blind, placebo-controlled design once again, desipramine (200 mg) was administered to ten patients meeting DSM-III criteria for bulimia. A control group of twelve patients meeting the same criteria received a nonactive placebo. Although adequate posttrial follow-up data were not reported, results indicated that at completion of the six-week trial, nine of ten (90 percent) patients receiving the active drug had reduced their binge frequency by 80 percent, compared to zero of twelve in the placebo group. When the placebo group was offered active drug treatment, ten of twelve (83 percent) reduced their binge eating by greater than 80 percent. At the end of the ten weeks, when both groups were receiving active medication, fifteen of twenty-two (68 percent) patients were in total remission. Significant improvement was also reported regarding depression and global improvement.

In addition to the overall findings regarding symptomatic behavior, several dimensions of this study warrant mentioning. The authors provided a detailed report of the relationship between serum levels of the medication and change in symptomatic behavior. Serum-to-desipramine levels were drawn at week 5 of the study after the patients had attained a target dose of 200 mg. Laboratory results indicated that only six of twenty patients had levels within the reported therapeutic range for depression, 125 to 275 nanograms per milliliter (Nelson, Jatlow, Quinlan, and Bowers, 1982). Ten patients were subtherapeutic, with a range of 44 to 116 nanograms per milliliter. Four of these had attained complete remission, and consequently dosage was not changed. Of the six who were still partially symptomatic, dosage was increased until the therapeutic serum level was reached. Four of the six subsequently achieved complete remission and the other two improved markedly. These findings support speculation that poor response may often be the result of inadequate serum levels of the different medications.

Another notable dimension of the Hughes, Wells, Cunningham, and Ilstrip study was that their selection criteria involved excluding patients who also met *Research Design Criteria* for major depression. Consequently their study essentially demonstrated the effectiveness of desipramine in reducing binge frequency in a group of bulimic patients who did not manifest major depression. The authors' explanation for this effectiveness was that the nature of the affective disorder is more similar to anxiety-based disorders, such as panic attack, in which imipramine, desipramine, and MAO medications have been very effective. In fact, Hughes and his colleagues offer preliminary hints about what might predict medication responders: many of their patients described their binges as being spontaneous, unrelated to identifiable stressors, or "out of the blue." The authors point out that panic attack patients offer strikingly similar descriptions of symptom onset. Although a fair number of bulimic patients do not report spontaneous unplanned binges, it is possible that those who report this particular type of phenomenological experience prior to binge eating may be particularly responsive to these medications.

Walsh, Stewart, Roose, Gladis, and Glassman (1984) also argued for an anxiety-based disorder and felt that the use of MAOIs would be particularly useful in the treatment of bulimia because of the drugs' effectiveness in the treatment of anxiety and agitated depressions. Following up on their original open trial report, they conducted a double-blind, placebo-controlled trial with phenelzine. Nine randomly assigned patients received phenelzine (60 mg per day) and eleven received an inert placebo. Results indicated that at the end of eight weeks, five of the nine (56 percent) patients in the active drug group were in remission and the other four (44 percent) had reduced their binge eating by 50 percent. Interestingly, eating attitudes as measured by the EAT scale also significantly decreased.

Among the placebo group, no patients had stopped bingeing and only two of eleven (18 percent) reduced their frequency by 50 percent. Seven patients in the group subsequently were tried on a regimen of phenelzine. Three reportedly experienced marked improvement, one had a transient response, and three showed no benefit. Three- to fifteen-month follow-up data on eight of the nine patients in the active drug group were reported. Five patients who had responded well later discontinued phenelzine; three of these suffered clear relapses after stopping medication, while two continued to do well. Of the three who remained on the medication, two continued in full remission, and one had partially relapsed.

Other controlled trials of antidepressant medication have not yielded comparably effective results. Sabine and associates (1983) conducted a placebo-controlled, double-blind trial using mianserin (60 mg). Fifty patients, who met the criteria for bulimia nervosa (Russell, 1979) plus a frequency criteria of weekly or greater binge eating, were randomly assigned to either drug ($N = 20$) or nonactive placebo ($N = 30$). Of the twenty subjects in the active drug group, six dropped out as did eight in the placebo group. All patients monitored food behavior on a daily basis and met regularly (frequency unspecified) with a psychiatrist over the trial period. At the end of eight weeks results indicated both groups showed improvement, but the improvement did not differ between active drug and placebo treatment (serum levels were not reported). Neither group improved significantly regarding binge/purge frequency, but both groups showed significant improvement in depression, anxiety, and disturbed eating attitudes.

It is difficult to compare the results of the Sabine and coworkers' study to those of the other studies for several reasons. Foremost, their data were poorly presented. Pre-post data related to frequency of binge/purge episodes were not presented, nor was the frequency of contact with the psychiatrist. Second, the group did not use DSM-III criteria, which makes it unclear how comparable their population was to those in the other studies.

Mitchell and Groat (1984) reported similarly equivocal results comparing active drug treatment to nonactive placebo. Once again using a placebo-controlled, double-blind design, they administered amitriptyline (150 mg) to sixteen patients who met DSM-III criteria for bulimia (eight of whom met criteria for depression using the Hamilton Rating Scale [Hamilton, 1967] and eight of whom were not depressed) and placebo to sixteen patients (eight of whom met the same criteria for depression as the active drug group and eight of whom were not depressed). A two-by-two analysis of variance was performed on four cells. All patients also received a minimal behavioral treatment program that focused on self-monitoring and instructions concerning normal eating.

Results indicated that although depressive symptoms decreased significantly more among the active drug groups, change in symptomatic eating behavior was not significantly different between the two groups. It is important to note that both groups reported substantial improvement in bulimic behavior, and while differences between the two groups were not statistically significant, the drug group did report substantially more improvement (79 percent reduction of vomiting) compared to the placebo group (53 percent reduction).

Comparisons between depressed versus nondepressed patients on symptom improvement yielded particularly interesting results. The depressed groups, whether on active drug or placebo, improved considerably less than the nondepressed group. Actual results of the number of binge/purge episodes per week by group were not available. These findings led Mitchell and his colleagues to conclude that while the differential improvement between active drug and placebo did not reach statistical significance in terms of eating behavior, all differences favored active drug. The authors also suggest, however, that the presence of depression among bulimic patients may indicate a poor prognosis.

Assessment of the effectiveness of the medication in this study was complicated by the absence of information regarding serum levels. Serum levels were not tested until the end of the study, and then on only a few patients. Consequently medication ineffectiveness may have been a result of inadequate dosage.

LITHIUM CARBONATE

One noncontrolled, open trial investigation of the use of lithium with bulimic patients has been reported. In response to findings that lithium is helpful to character-disordered patients who experience emotional lability (Gram and Rafaelson, 1972; Rifkin et al., 1972), Hsu (1984) administered lithium carbonate (450 mg per day to 1,350 mg per day; lithium level maintained between 0.6 and 1.2 mg per liter) to fourteen patients who met DSM-III criteria for bulimia. Eight patients received lithium carbonate in combination with behavioral therapy, and six patients were treated with the drug either after their response to behavioral therapy was unsatisfactory or after they had relapsed from initial improvement with behavioral therapy. Results indicated that at follow-up (six to sixteen months), among the eight who received both treatments concurrently, six (75 percent) were in complete remission and two (25 percent) had reduced their binge frequency by 50 percent. Among the six who had not responded to behavior therapy, at six- to fourteen-month follow-up, three (50 percent) were in remission, one (17 percent) had improved moderately, and two (33 percent) showed no response. Eating attitudes improved, as did depression. It is also important to note that Hsu reported that all of the patients indicated feeling calmer with the lithium treatment.

PHENYTOIN

There has been considerable speculation in recent years that anorexia nervosa and bulimia may be related to certain neurophysiological abnormalities. One reason for this hypothesis has been the demonstrated association between abnormal eating behaviors and certain neurological conditions, such as partial complex seizures (Remick, Jones, and Compos, 1980) and certain central nervous system tumors (Kirschbaum, 1951). Another line of evidence suggesting this hypothesis has been the presence of electroencephalogram (EEG) abnormalities in patients with eating disorders. Crisp, Fenton, and Strotton (1968) found an increased incidence of EEG abnormalities in patients with active anorexia nervosa compared to controls.

Much of the recent research in this area has been reported by Rau and Green (1974, 1975, 1977, 1978, and 1979). A total of forty-seven patients were reported to have had adequate trials of phenytoin, an anticonvulsant often used in the treatment of epilepsy. Operational criteria based on patients' reports of their progress were included. Analysis revealed a higher percentage of abnormal EEGs among compulsive eaters when compared to normal controls. The authors concluded that patients with abnormal EEGs were more likely to respond to drug treatment. With the exception of four patients described in 1977 and two patients described in 1979, all subjects reported by Rau and Green were treated in open and nonblind protocols. Blood levels of anticonvulsants were not reported.

The work of Wermuth, Davis, Hollister, and Stunkard (1977) addressed some of the methodological problems in the Rau and Green studies. This group originally reported EEG abnormalities in four or five patients with bulimia. A subsequent trial compared phenytoin to placebo and double-blind design among nineteen bulimic women, one of whom had anorexia nervosa. The study involved a cross-over design with random assignment to treatment groups. The treatment phase lasted six weeks. Three subjects had definitely abnormal EEGs and four had questionably abnormal EEGs. There was no significant relationship between drug response and EEG abnormality. Phenytoin was found to be associated with fewer eating binges overall. Eight of nineteen (42 percent) patients showed "marked" to "moderate" improvement, while eleven (58 percent) showed "slight" to "no" improvement. Interestingly, the authors reported that patients with anorexic histories were among the least improved. In the phenytoin-to-placebo sequence, the number of binge-eating episodes decreased during drug treatment; however, this improvement continued when the subjects were placed on placebo. This finding complicates the result interpretation. Five additional cases of phenytoin treatment of bulimia have appeared, all unsuccessful (Greenway, Dahms, and Brag, 1977; Weiss and Levitz, 1976).

The available studies indicate that phenytoin may be helpful in treating some patients with eating disorders. However, the research to date has not been particularly helpful in identifying specific patient characteristics that might distinguish those patients who will be more responsive to the drug. It must also be noted that the types of EEG abnormalities that Rau and Green described in patients with bulimia are considered by some electroencephalographers to be normal variants and not indicative of neurophysiological dysfunction (Wermuth, Davis, Hollister, and Stunkard, 1977).

In reviewing the medication literature, it appears that pharmacological interventions are promising. It seems reasonable to conclude that many bulimic patients have affect regulation difficulties and that for some a biological vulnerability plays a predominant role in the etiology of the disorder (Johnson and Maddi, 1986). What is unclear at this point is who is responsive to the medications and what the medication is treating. Interestingly, some preliminary indications suggest that patients with significant character pathology (Axis II diagnosis) or, paradoxically, significant depressive symptoms are the poorest responders. Those patients who perhaps have more predominant anxiety-based disorders seem to respond most favorably.

It is important to urge caution in interpreting these early medication studies. Their significance is compromised by the small sample sizes, inadequate long-term follow-up data, and failure to monitor serum levels. Effective monitoring of serum levels may prove to be one of the most critical factors in future evaluation of the effectiveness of the different medications. The Hughes, Wells, Cunningham, and Ilstrip (1986) study and the Mitchell and Groat (1984) study suggest that it is necessary to achieve a certain serum level for the medication to be effective. While it is currently unclear what that range is for bulimia, preliminary information from the former study indicates that the therapeutic range may be similar to that of depression.

Greater attention to the use of placebo groups will also become increasingly more important, since two of the five controlled studies found comparable benefit from the placebo treatment. More detailed reporting of the frequency of contact and effects of the intervention (self-monitoring of food intake, binge/purge frequency, feeling state) in the placebo groups will be necessary to assess the comparability of the treatments. There have been no comparisons of active versus nonactive medication placebos. This may prove to be an important avenue of research, since some bulimics appear to have cognitive styles that render them vulnerable to suggestion. This impressionable style could result in the interpretation of any shift in their biological milieu as positive and curative.

DRUG VERSUS PSYCHOLOGICAL INTERVENTIONS

In an effort to compare the effectiveness of drug versus psychological interventions, we pooled subjects across studies and calculated improvement in binge/purge behavior at the conclusion of the treatment intervention. Obviously such a comparison is complicated by numerous methodological problems, but we felt that the comparison allowed for a "flash report" on the relative treatment effectiveness.

Controlled studies of both psychological and pharmacological intervention are presented in tables 12.1 and 12.2. Among the psychological treatment studies, five reported their results in a way that allowed for cross-sample comparison. Pooling patients resulted in a sample of eighty-one individuals. Results indicated that thirty-one (38 percent) were in remission, twenty-four (30 percent) had decreased their binge frequency by more than 50 percent, and twenty-six (32 percent) had reduced their binge frequency by less than 50 percent. Three medication studies could be compared. Pooling patients resulted in a combined sample of forty-nine. Results indicated that twenty-six (53 percent) were in complete remission, fourteen (28 percent) had reduced their binge frequency by more than 50 percent, and nine (19 percent) showed little response.

This preliminary and crude comparison suggests that pharmacological and psychological interventions yield roughly comparable results. Yet this raises the very interesting question of why two very different interventions have similar outcomes. Clearly, the next stage of research on treatment of bulimia requires a controlled comparison of drug versus psychological treatment within a single design.

Conclusions

While data-based treatment studies of bulimia have proliferated over the last several years, the data thus far permit us to draw very limited conclusions. Most studies and treatment interventions reviewed have been methodologically deficient. Overall these studies have been pilot projects involving small numbers of subjects, no control or comparison groups, unclear methods of reporting outcome, and brief or no follow-up. While the methodologies have improved significantly over the last few years, it is clear that this research remains in its beginning stages.

The three methods of intervention that have been investigated the most—behavioral and cognitive-behavioral treatment packages, psychopharmacological treatment, and exposure with response prevention—seem to lead to significant reductions in the binge/purge behavior of

TABLE 12.1

Controlled Studies of Psychological Treatment of Bulimia

Author	N	Treatment	Duration	Post-treatment Findings		
				Remitted (%)	Greater than 50% Reduction (%)	Less than 50% Reduction (%)
Lacey, 1983[a]	30	Individual and group therapy	10 weeks	24/30 (80)		6/30 (20)
Connors, Johnson, and Stuckey, 1984[a]	20	Psychoeducational group therapy	9 weeks	2/20 (10)	9/20 (45)	9/20 (45)
Hoage and Gray, 1984	13	Group exposure plus response prevention	6 weeks		"Significant reductions for 7/8 (88)"	
Huon, 1984	120	Mailed self-help materials	7 months	17/90 (19)		
Johnson, Schlundt, Kelly, and Ruggiero, 1984[a]	5	Individual exposure plus response prevention	Up to 12 weeks	1/5 (20)	3/5 (60)	1/5 (20)
Yates and Sambrailo, 1984[a]	16	Two group comparison	6 weeks	2/16 (12)	7/16 (44)	7/17 (44)
Ordman and Kirschenbaum, 1985[a]	20	Individual therapy	Average of 15.3 sessions	2/10 (20) (full intervention only)	5/10 (50)	3/10 (30)

[a] These studies were selected for comparison.

TABLE 12.2

Controlled Studies of Psychopharmacological Treatment of Bulimia

Author	N	Treatment	Duration	Post-treatment Findings			
				Remitted (%)	Greater than 50% Reduction (%)	Less than 50% Reduction (%)	
Wermuth, Davis, Hollister, and Stunkard, 1977	19	Phenytoin	6 weeks		8/19 (42) (marked to moderate improvement)	11/19 (58) "slight to no improvement."	
Pope, Hudson, Jonas, and Yurgelun-Todd, 1983[a]	18	Imipramine (200 mg)	6 weeks	6/18 (33)	10/18 (55)	2/18 (11)	
Sabine et al., 1983	50	Mianserin (60 mg)	8 weeks	Neither group significantly reduced binge/purge behavior.			
Mitchell and Groat, 1984	32	Amitriptyline (50 mg)	10 weeks	Drug group reduced vomiting by 79%, placebo group by 53%. Depressed group improved less than nondepressed.			
Walsh et al., 1984[a]	9	Phenelzine (60 mg)	8 weeks	5/9 (56)	4 (44)	0	
Hughes, Wells, Cunningham, and Ilstrip, 1986[a]	22	Desipramine (200 mg)	6 weeks	15/22 (68)		7/22 (32)	

[a] These studies were selected for comparison.

most subjects. In nearly every study there were a minority of subjects who changed very little, showed no response, or became worse after treatment. While follow-up data are sketchy, treatment gains seem for the most part to be maintained, and in some cases further improvements are made.

Outcome differs greatly when all of the studies using that particular form of intervention are compared. At this point it is not possible to say that one of the three main treatments investigated is clearly superior to the others. More well-controlled studies comparing these forms of treatment to one another coupled with long-term follow-up will be necessary before any such conclusion can be drawn. Also, additional research needs to be done in areas like family therapy where the small amount of data that exists is promising.

The complex issue of which treatment might be suitable for what type of patient has hardly begun to be addressed. It may well be that a subgroup of patients with a true biological vulnerability will respond only to medication, while another group will respond to a larger variety of interventions. The fact that such variability in outcome results was obtained even using similar intervention methods raises the question of patient variables. Several different patient variables have been found to be associated with poorer treatment outcome. These include anorexic tendencies (Stevens and Salisbury, 1984); higher EAT and EDI scores (Leitenberg, Gross, Peterson, and Rosen, 1984); level of personality disorder (Brotman, Herzog, and Woods, 1984); borderline personality organization (Johnson, 1984); major depression (Hughes, Wells, Cunningham, and Ilstrip, 1986; Mitchell and Groat, 1984); and continuing to live at home throughout treatment (Schwartz, Barrett, and Saba, 1984). Most investigators seem to agree that, predictably, the general level of psychopathology influences outcome.

An additional but related issue is the degree to which patients comply with the demands of a particular treatment group and self-select in or out of various treatments. In the psychoeducational group (Johnson, Connors, and Stuckey, 1983; Connors, Johnson, and Stuckey, 1984), the best predictor of improvement was compliance with the different aspects of the treatment program; however, patients could and did remain in the group while being noncompliant. This is in contrast to Lacey's treatment format (1983), where patients agreed in advance to comply with all program demands, including such anxiety-provoking requirements as eating three meals a day. Patients who are capable of entering a program where this level of change is contracted for, or who select an intensive program such as that of Pyle and associates (1984) where abstinence is demanded from the first night of the program, are likely to be a healthier group with higher motivation and less ambivalence about relinquishing their disturbed behavior. This issue of patient character structure and the resulting ability and/or motivation to comply with the anxiety-provoking demands of a particular treatment program is probably a very important variable, and one that remains relatively unexplored.

In addition, the issues of general level of psychopathology, compliance, and motivation certainly influence patient dropout rates. This represents another relatively unexplored area, as few investigators have followed up their treatment dropouts. In a number of studies reviewed the dropout rates have been relatively high. Other studies fail to provide this information, making comparisons difficult.

Methodological Recommendations

After reviewing the treatment literature, there are several suggestions concerning the collecting and the reporting of data that we believe would contribute to more meaningful interpretation of results.

SAMPLE DESCRIPTION

Detailed reporting of methods by which patients were recruited, selected, and included in or excluded from the study are essential to allow for cross-sample comparisons. All patients should meet the latest DSM-III criteria for bulimia, and any other applicable DSM-III diagnosis should be reported as well. Details of program requirements must be specified, including level of compliance required, any contractual agreements entered into, exclusion criteria for noncompliance after the commencement of the treatment program, and the degree of behavior change required compared to the patient's initial condition. Since certain clinical features (such as age of onset, duration of illness, weight history, previous history of anorexia nervosa, and previous treatment) probably have prognostic significance, they should routinely be reported in detail.

CONTROLLED TRIALS

Adequately controlled designs with random assignment are essential. Dropout rates and level of compliance should be reported, and treatment dropouts should be followed up whenever possible. In drug studies serum levels should be routinely monitored, and the use of active versus nonactive placebos should be explored.

SYMPTOMATIC BEHAVIOR

Objective indices of symptom change should be reported in detail pre- and posttreatment and at follow-up. Symptom change can be divided into eating and non–eating-related variables. Eating-related variables include frequency of binge-eating episodes and type and frequency of purging behavior. We urge that studies continue to compute this on a weekly basis. We also recommend reporting the number of binge-free days during the week or number of meals eaten without subsequent purging.

The actual number of episodes should be reported rather than percentage reductions, which can be misleading since the percentage is influenced by the original baseline frequency. For example, it is our experience that a patient's reduction of binge episodes from seven times per week to once per week is much more clinically significant than a patient who reduces her binge eating from forty-two to six times per week. Both of these figures reflect an 86 percent reduction, which is statistically but may not be clinically comparable.

This example also hints at a central problem in bulimia research: the definition of a binge episode. There have been various attempts to provide definitional criteria for binge eating; these include amount consumed, duration of episode, speed of eating, affective state during and after eating, and whether the individual purges following the food consumption. We have concluded that the patient's subjective report of distress appears to be the best variable distinguishing between normal eating and binge eating. Further, in a large sample of women reporting difficulties with binge eating, Johnson and Love (1985) have found that the patient's self-report of feeling out of control during binge eating was the best single predictor of impairment in life adjustment. Consequently a scale measuring the patient's experience of control during food consumption should be included in the assessment.

Pre- and posttreatment and follow-up changes in attitudes about food and weight preoccupation, drive for thinness, and body dissatisfaction should also be reported. Specialty scales such as the EDI (Garner, Garfinkel, and O'Shaughnessy, 1983) and the Diagnostic Survey for Eating Disorders-Revised (Johnson, 1984, Love and Johnson, 1984) allow for measurement of psychological change in these areas. Non–eating-related symptom change should also be reported. This would include objective indices of depression, anxiety, self-esteem, and overall work and social adjustment.

FOLLOW-UP DATA

Most treatment studies reviewed lacked follow-up data of any duration. Sophisticated follow-up data are crucial to our understanding of the long-term relative effectiveness of different treatment strategies. They also enlighten us about various patterns of outcome among bulimic patients. Follow-up data should be collected on both food-related and life adjustment variables.

In reporting follow-up results, terminology must be clearly defined. For example, some workers currently use the term remission to indicate a total absence of binge/purge episodes, while others allow for some relapse. Remission has generally been defined as less-than-monthly episodes of binge eating and purging. Given the episodic nature of bulimia, it is also crucial that the follow-up period be specified. When assessing binge/purge frequency, we suggest that the patient be asked to report the number of episodes per week over the last month. We recommend that patients be assessed pre- and posttreatment, six months after treatment, then at yearly intervals.

Concluding Comments

This is an exciting time in the area of research on the treatment of bulimia. Now that the small-sample pilot work has been conducted, larger-scale controlled studies with long-term follow-up are needed. More rigorous methodological studies can provide us with the best information on the most efficacious treatment, how to match patients and treatments optimally—and perhaps how to help those patients who have not responded to treatment at all.

REFERENCES

ABRAHAM, S., BENDIT, N., MASON, C., MITCHELL, H., O'CONNOR, N., WARD, J., YOUNG, S., and LLEWELLYN-JONES, D. (1985). The psychosexual histories of young women with bulimia. *Australian and New Zealand Journal of Psychiatry, 19,* 72–76.

ABRAHAM, S., and BEUMONT, P.J.V. (1982a). Varieties of psychosexual experience in patients with anorexia nervosa. *International Journal of Eating Disorders, 1,* 10–19.

ABRAHAM, S., and BEUMONT, P.J.V. (1982b). How patients describe bulimia or binge eating. *Psychological Medicine, 12,* 625–635.

ABRAHAM, S. F., MIRA, M. E., and LLEWELLYN-JONES, D. (1983). Bulimia: A study of outcome. *International Journal of Eating Disorders, 2,* 175–180.

ABRAMSON, L. Y., SELIGMAN, M.E.P., and TEASDALE, J. D. (1978). Learned helplessness in humans: Critique and reformulation. *Journal of Abnormal Psychology, 87,* 49–74.

ADLER, A. G., WALINSKY, P., KRALL, R. A., and CHO, S. Y. (1980). *Journal of the American Medical Association, 243,* 1927–1928.

AHOLA, S. (1982). Unexplained parotid enlargement. A clue to occult bulimia. *Connecticut Medicine, 46,* 156–185.

ALBERTI, R. E., and EMMONS, M. L. (1978). *Your perfect right* (3rd ed.). San Luis Obispo, CA: Impact Publishing.

ALLON, N. (1975). Latent social services in group dieting. *Social Problems, 32,* 59–69.

AMERICAN PSYCHIATRIC ASSOCIATION. (1980). *Diagnostic and Statistical Manual of Mental Disorders* (3rd ed.). Washington, DC: Author.

BANDURA, A. (1977). Self-efficacy: Toward a unifying theory of behavior change. *Psychological Review, 84,* 191–215.

BARDWICK, J. (1971). *Psychology of women: A study of bio-cultural conflicts.* New York: Harper & Row.

BAUER, B. G. (1984, May). Bulimia: A review of a group treatment program. *Journal of College Student Personnel,* 221–227.

BECK, A. T. (1967). *Cognitive therapy and the emotional disorders.* New York: International Universities Press.

BECK, A. T., RUSH, J., SHAW, B., and EMERY, G. (1979). *Cognitive therapy of depression.* New York: Guilford Press.

BECK, A. T., WARD, C. H., MENDELSON, M., MOCK, J., and ERBAUGH, J. (1961). An inventory for measuring depression. *Archives of General Psychiatry, 5,* 561–571.

References   307

BEM, S. L. (1974). The measurement of psychological androgyny. *Journal of Consulting and Clinical Psychology, 42,* 155–162.

BENEDEK, T. (1936). Dominant ideas and their relation to morbid cravings. *International Journal of Psycho-Analysis, 17,* 40–56.

BENJAMIN, L. S. (1974). Structural analysis of social behavior. *Psychological Review, 81,* 393–425.

BENJAMIN, L. S. (1983). *INTREX questionnaires.* Madison, WI: INTREX Interpersonal Institute.

BENNETT, W., and GURIN, J. (1982). *The dieter's dilemma.* New York: Basic Books.

BERNDT, D. J., PETZEL, T. P., and BERNDT, S. M. (1980). Development and initial evaluation of a multiscore depression inventory. *Journal of Personality Assessment, 44,* 396–403.

BEUMONT, P.J.V., GEORGE, G.C.W., and SMART, D. E. (1976). "Dieters" and "vomiters and purgers" in anorexia nervosa. *Psychological Medicine, 6,* 617–622.

BIGMAN (1985). Personal communication.

BINSWANGER, L. (1958). The case of Ellen West. In R. May, E. Angel, and H. Ellenberger (Eds.), *Existence* (pp. 237–364). New York: Basic Books. (Original work published 1944)

BLATT, S. (1974). Levels of object representation in anaclitic and introjective depression. *Psychoanalytic Study of the Child, 29,* 40–56.

BLITZER, J. R., ROLLINS, N., and BLACKWELL, A. (1961). Children who starve themselves: Anorexia nervosa. *Psychosomatic Medicine, 23,* 369–383.

BLOCK, J. H., and VAN DER LIPPE, A. (1973). Sex role and socialization patterns: Some personality concomitants and environmental antecedents. *Journal of Consulting and Clinical Psychology, 41,* 321–341.

BLOS, P. (1967). The second individuation process of adolescence. *Psychoanalytic Study of the Child, 22,* 162–186.

BO-LINN, G. W., SANTA ANA, C. A., MOROWSKI, S. G., and FORDTRAN, J. S. (1983). Purging and calorie absorption in bulimic patients and normal women. *Annals of Internal Medicine, 99,* 14–17.

BOND, D. D. (1949). Anorexia nervosa. *Rocky Mountain Medical Journal, 46,* 1012–1019.

BOSKIND-LODAHL, M. (1976). Cinderella's stepsisters: A feminist perspective on anorexia nervosa and bulimia. *Signs: Journal of Women in Culture and Society, 2,* 342–356.

BOSKIND-LODAHL, M. (1978). The definition and treatment of bulimarexia: The gorging/purging syndrome of young women (Doctoral dissertation, Cornell University, 1977). *Dissertation Abstracts International, 38,* 717A.

BOSKIND-WHITE, M., and WHITE, W. (1983). *Bulimarexia: The binge/purge cycle.* New York: W. W. Norton.

BOWLBY, J. (1969). *Attachment and loss.* New York: Basic Books.

BOYD, J. H., and WEISSMAN, M. M. (1982). Epidemiology. In E. S. Paykel (Ed.), *Handbook of affective disorders* (pp. 109–125). New York: Guilford Press.

BRADY, W. F. (1980). The anorexia nervosa syndrome. *Oral Surgery, 50,* 509–516.

BROTMAN, A. W., HERZOG, D. B., and WOODS, S. W. (1984). Antidepressant treatment of bulimia: The relationship between bingeing and depressive symptomatology. *Journal of Clinical Psychiatry, 45,* 7–9.

BROTMAN, M. C., FORBATH, W., GARFINKEL, P. E., and HUMPHREY, H. J. (1981).

Ipecac syrup poisoning in anorexia nervosa. *Canadian Medical Association Journal, 125*, 453–454.

BROWNMILLER, S. (1984). *Femininity.* New York: Linden Press.

BRUCH, H. (1961). Conceptual confusion in eating disorders. *Journal of Nervous and Mental Disease, 133*, 46–54.

BRUCH, H. (1962). Perceptual and conceptual disturbances in anorexia nervosa. *Psychosomatic Medicine, 24*, 187–194.

BRUCH, H. (1970). Family background in eating disorders. In E. J. Anthony and C. Koupernik (Eds.), *The child in his family* (pp. 66–97). New York: Wiley.

BRUCH, H. (1973). *Eating disorders: Obesity, anorexia nervosa, and the person within.* New York: Basic Books.

BRUCH, H. (1977). Antecedents of anorexia nervosa. In R. A. Vigersky (Ed.), *Anorexia nervosa* (pp. 1–10). New York: Raven Press.

BRUCH, H. (1978). *The golden cage: The enigma of anorexia nervosa.* Cambridge, MA: Harvard University Press.

BUTLER, P. (1981). *Talking to yourself.* New York: Harper & Row.

BUTLER, P. (1981). *Self-assertion for women.* New York: Harper & Row.

BUTTON, E. J., and WHITEHOUSE, A. (1981). Subclinical anorexia nervosa. *Psychosomatic Medicine, 11*, 509–516.

CANNING, H., and MAYER, J. (1966). Obesity: Its possible effect on college acceptance. *New England Journal of Medicine, 275*, 1172–1174.

CARROLL, B. J., FEINBERG, M., SMOUSE, P. E., RAWSON, S. G., and GREDEN, J. F. (1981). The Carroll Rating Scale for Depression, I. Development, reliability and validity. *British Journal of Psychiatry, 138*, 194–200.

CARROLL, K., and LEON, G. (1981). *The bulimic-vomiting disorder within a generalized substance abuse pattern.* Paper presented at the annual meeting of the Association for the Advancement of Behavior Therapy, Toronto, Canada.

CASPER, R. C. (1983). On the emergence of bulimia nervosa as a syndrome: A historical view. *International Journal of Eating Disorders, 2*, 3–16.

CASPER, R. C., ECKERT, E. D., HALMI, K. A., GOLDBERG, S. C., and DAVIS, J. M. (1980). Bulimia: Its incidence and significance in patients with anorexia nervosa. *Archives of General Psychiatry, 37*, 1030–1035.

CATTELL, R. (1972). *The 16 personality factor questionnaire.* Champaign, IL: Institute for Personality and Ability Testing.

CAUWELS, J. (1983). *Bulimia: The binge purge compulsion.* New York: Doubleday.

CHARONE, J. K. (1982). Eating disorders: Their genesis in the mother-infant relationship. *International Journal of Eating Disorders, 1*, 15–42.

CHERNIN, K. (1981). *The obsession.* New York: Harper & Row.

CHERNYK, B. (1981). *Sex differences in binge eating and related habit patterns in a college student population.* Paper presented at the meeting of the Association for the Advancement of Behavior Therapy, Toronto.

CODDINGTON, R. D., and BRUCH, H. (1970). Gastric perceptivity in normal, obese, and schizophrenic subjects. *Psychosomatics, 11*, 571–579.

COLLINS, M., KREISBERG, J., PERTSCHUK, M., and FAGER, S. (1982). Bulimia in college women: Prevalence and psychopathology. *Journal of Adolescent Health Care, 3*, 144.

CONNORS, M. E. (1983). *Structured group treatment of normal weight bulimic women.* Unpublished doctoral dissertation, DePaul University, Chicago, IL.

CONNORS, M. E., JOHNSON, C. L., and STUCKEY, M. K. (1984). Treatment of bulimia with brief psychoeducational group therapy. *American Journal of Psychiatry, 141,* 1512–1516.

CONTE, H. R., PLUTCHIK, R., KARASU, T., and JERRETT, I. (1980). A self-report borderline scale: Discriminative validity and preliminary norms. *Journal of Nervous and Mental Disease, 168,* 428–435.

COOPER, P. J., and FAIRBURN, C. G. (1983). Binge eating and self-induced vomiting in the community: A preliminary study. *British Journal of Psychiatry, 142,* 139–144.

CRAWLEY, J. N., and BEINFELD, M. C. (1983). Rapid development of tolerance to the behavioral effects of cholecystokinin. *Nature, 302,* 703–706.

CRISP, A. H. (1980). *Anorexia nervosa: Let me be.* London: Academic Press.

CRISP, A. H. (1981). Anorexia nervosa at a normal weight!: The abnormal-normal weight control syndrome. *International Journal of Psychiatry in Medicine, 11,* 203–233.

CRISP, A. H., FENTON, G. W., and STROTTON, L. (1968). A controlled study of the EEG in anorexia nervosa. *British Journal of Psychiatry, 114,* 1149–1169.

CRISP, A. H., HARDING, B., and McGUINNESS, B. (1974). Anorexia nervosa. Psychoneurotic characteristics of parents: Relationship to prognosis. *Journal of Psychosomatic Research, 18,* 167–173.

CROWN, S., and CRISP, A. H. (1966). A short clinical diagnostic self-rating scale for psychoneurotic patients. *British Journal of Psychiatry, 112,* 917.

CROWTHER, J. H., POST, G., and ZAYNOR, L. (1985). The prevalence of bulimia and binge eating in adolescent girls. *International Journal of Eating Disorders, 4,* 29–42.

CURRY, C. E. (1982). Laxative products. In American Pharmaceutical Association, *Handbook of non-prescription drugs* (pp. 69–92). Washington, DC: American Pharmaceutical Association.

DALLY, P. J., and GOMEZ, J. (1979). *Anorexia Nervosa.* London: Heinemann.

DAVIS, K. L., QUALLS, B., HOLLISTER, L., and STUNKARD, A. J. (1974). EEG's of "binge eaters." *American Journal of Psychiatry, 131,* 1409.

DAVIS, R., FREEMAN, R., and SOLYOM, L. (1985). Mood and food: An analysis of bulimic episode. *Journal of Psychiatric Research, 19,* 331–335.

DEISHER, R. W., and MILLS, C. A. (1963). The adolescent looks at his health and medical care. *American Journal of Public Health, 53,* 1928–1936.

DEROGATIS, L. R., and CLEARY, P. (1977). Confirmation of the dimensional structure of the SCL-90: A study in construct validation. *Journal of Clinical Psychology, 33,* 981–989.

DEROGATIS, L. R., LIPMAN, R. S., RICKELS, K., UHLENHUTH, E. H., and COVI, L. (1974). The Hopkins Symptom Checklist (HSCL): A measure of primary symptom dimensions. In P. Pichot (Ed.), *Psychological measurements in psychopharmacology: Modern problems in pharmacopsychiatry* (pp. 79–110). Basel, Switzerland.

DRUSS, R. G., and SILVERMAN, J. A. (1979). Body image and perfectionism of ballerinas: Comparison and contrast with anorexia nervosa. *General Hospital Psychiatry, 2,* 115–121.

DUBOIS, A., GROSS, H. A., EBERT, M. H., and CASTELL, D. O. (1979). Altered gastric emptying and secretion in primary anorexia nervosa. *Gastroenterology, 77,* 319–323.

DUNN, P. K., and ONDERCIN, P. (1981). Personality variables related to compulsive eating in college women. *Journal of Clinical Psychology, 37,* 43–49.

DWYER, J. T., FELDMAN, J. J., SELTZER, C. C., and MAYER, J. C. (1969). Body image in adolescents: Attitudes toward weight and perception of appearance. *American Journal of Clinical Nutrition, 20,* 1045–1056.

ENRIGHT, E. F., BUTTERFIELD, P., and BERKOWITZ, B. (1984). Self-help and support groups in the management of eating disorders. In D. M. Garner and P. E. Garfinkel (Eds.), *Handbook of psychotherapy for anorexia nervosa and bulimia* (pp. 491–512). New York: Guilford Press.

EPSTEIN, L., and WING, R. (1980). Aerobic exercise and weight. *Addictive Behaviors, 5,* 371–388.

EYSENCK, H. J., and EYSENCK, S.B.G. (1975). *Manual of the Eysenck Personality Inventory.* Kent, UK: Hodder & Stroughton.

FAIRBURN, C. G. (1981). A cognitive behavioral approach to the treatment of bulimia. *Psychological Medicine, 11,* 707–711.

FAIRBURN, C. G. (1982). *Binge-eating and bulimia nervosa.* London: Smith, Kline, & French.

FAIRBURN, C. G., and COOPER, P. J. (1982). Self-induced vomiting and bulimia nervosa: An undetected problem. *British Medical Journal, 284,* 1153–1155.

FAIRBURN, C. G., and COOPER, P. J. (1984a). Binge-eating, self-induced vomiting and laxative abuse: A community study. *Psychological Medicine, 14,* 401–410.

FAIRBURN, C. G., and COOPER, P. J. (1984b). The clinical features of bulimia nervosa. *British Journal of Psychiatry, 144,* 238–246.

FALLON, A. E., and ROZIN, P. (1985). *Sex differences in perceptions of body shape*: Manuscript submitted for publication.

FICHTER, M. M., and PIRKE, K. M. (1984). Hypothalmic pituitary function in starving healthy subjects. In K. M. Pirke and D. J. Ploog (Eds.) *The psychobiology of anorexia nervosa* (pp. 124–135). Berlin: Springer.

FITTS, W., 1964–65. *Manual: The Tennessee Self-Concept Scale.* Nashville, TN: Counselor Recordings and Tests.

FLETCHER, C. M., and OLDHAM, P. D. (1959). Diagnosis in group research. In L. J. Witts (Ed.), *Medical surveys and clinical trials* (pp. 25–49). London: Oxford University Press.

FREEMAN, R. J., BEACH, B., DAVIS, R., and SOLYOM, L. (1985). The prediction of relapse in bulimia nervosa. *Journal of Psychiatric Research, 19,* 349–353.

FRISCH, R. E. (1983). Fatness and reproduction: Delayed menarche and amenorrhea of ballet dancers and college athletes. In P. L. Darby, P. E. Garfinkel, D. M. Garner, and D. V. Coscina (Eds.), *Anorexia nervosa: Recent developments.* (pp. 343–363). New York: Alan R. Liss.

GALLO, L., and RANDEL, A. (1981, Sept.-Oct.). Chronic vomiting and the effect on the primary dentition: Report of case. *Journal of Dentistry for Children,* 382–384.

GAMBRILL, E. D., and RICHEY, C. A. (1975). An assertive inventory for use in assessment and research. *Behavior Therapy, 6,* 550–561.

GARFINKEL, P. E., and GARNER, D. M. (1982). *Anorexia nervosa: A multidimensional perspective.* New York: Brunner/Mazel.

GARFINKEL, P. E., and GARNER, D. M. (1984). Bulimia in anorexia nervosa. In R. C. Hawkins, W. J. Fremouw, and P. F. Clement (Eds.), *The binge-purge syndrome* (pp. 27–46). New York: Springer.

GARFINKEL, P., GARNER, D., ROSE, J., DARBY, P., BRANDES, J. S., O'HANLON, J., and WALSH, N. (1983). A comparison of characteristics in the families of patients with anorexia nervosa and normal controls. *Psychological Medicine, 13,* 821–828.

GARFINKEL, P. E., MOLDOFSKY, H., and GARNER, D. M. (1979). The stability of perceptual disturbances in anorexia nervosa. *Psychological Medicine, 9,* 703–708.

GARFINKEL, P. E., MOLDOFSKY, H., and GARNER, D. M. (1980). The heterogeneity of anorexia nervosa. *Archives of General Psychiatry, 37,* 1036–1040.

GARFINKEL, P. E., MOLDOFSKY, H., GARNER, D. M., STANCER, H. C., and COSCINA, D. V. (1978). Body awareness in anorexia nervosa: Disturbances in body image and satiety. *Psychosomatic Medicine, 40,* 487–498.

GARNER, D. M. (1985). Iatrogenesis in anorexia nervosa and bulimia nervosa. *International Journal of Eating Disorders, 4,* 701–726.

GARNER, D. M., and BEMIS, K. M. (1982). A cognitive-behavioral approach to anorexia nervosa. *Cognitive Therapy and Research, 6,* 123–150.

GARNER, D. M., and BEMIS, K. M. (1984). Cognitive therapy for anorexia nervosa. In D. M. Garner and P. E. Garfinkel (Eds.), *Handbook of psychotherapy for anorexia nervosa and bulimia* (pp. 107–146). New York: Guilford Press.

GARNER, D. J., and GARFINKEL, P. E. (1979). The Eating Attitudes Test: An index of the syndrome of anorexia nervosa. *Psychological Medicine, 9,* 273–279.

GARNER, D. M., and GARFINKEL, P. E. (1980). Socio-cultural factors in the development of anorexia nervosa. *Psychological Medicine, 10,* 647–656.

GARNER, D. M., GARFINKEL, P. E., and BEMIS, K. M. (1982). A multidimensional psychotherapy for anorexia nervosa. *International Journal of Eating Disorders, 1,* 3–46.

GARNER, D. M., GARFINKEL, P. E., and OLMSTED, M. (1983). An overview of sociocultural factors in the development of anorexia nervosa. In P. L. Darby, P. E. Garfinkel, D. M. Garner, and D. V. Coscina (Eds.), *Anorexia nervosa: Recent developments in research* (pp. 65–82). New York: Alan R. Liss.

GARNER, D. M., GARFINKEL, P. E., and O'SHAUGHNESSY. (1983). Clinical and psychometric comparison between bulimia in anorexia nervosa and bulimia in normal-weight women. *Report of the Fourth Ross Conference on Medical Research* (pp. 6–13). Columbus, OH: Ross Laboratories.

GARNER, D. M., GARFINKEL, P. & O'SHAUGHNESSY, M. (1985). The validity of the distinction between bulimics with and without anorexia nervosa. (1985). *American Journal of Psychiatry, 142,* 581–587.

GARNER, D. M., GARFINKEL, P. E., SCHWARTZ, D., and THOMPSON, M. (1980). Cultural expectations of thinness in women. *Psychological Reports, 47,* 483–491.

GARNER, D. M., OLMSTED, M. P., and POLIVY, J. (1983). Development and validation of a multidimensional eating disorder inventory for anorexia nervosa and bulimia. *International Journal of Eating Disorders, 2,* 15–34.

GARNER, D. M., OLMSTED, M. P., POLIVY, J., and GARFINKEL, P. E. (1984). Comparison between weight-preoccupied women and anorexia nervosa. *Psychosomatic Medicine, 46,* 255–256.

GARNER, D. M., ROCKERT, W., OLMSTED, M. P., JOHNSON, C., and COSCINA, D. V. (1985). Psychoeducational principles in the treatment of bulimia and anorexia nervosa. In D. M. Garner and P. E. Garfinkel (Eds.), *A handbook of psychotherapy for anorexia and bulimia* (pp. 513–572.) New York: Guilford Press.

GARROW, J. S. (1974). *Energy balance and obesity in man.* New York: Elsevier.

GERSHON, E., HAMOVIT, J. R., SCHREIBER, J. L., DIBBLE, E., KAYE, W., NURN-BERGER, J., ANDERSON, A., and EBERT, M. (1983). Anorexia nervosa and major affective disorders associated in families: A preliminary report. In S. Guze, F. Earls, and J. Barrett (Eds.), *Childhood psychopathology and development* (pp. 279–286). New York: Raven Press.

GLUCKSMAN, M. L., and HIRSCH, J. (1969). The response of obese patients to weight reduction. *Psychosomatic Medicine, 31,* 1–7.

GOLDBLATT, P. B., MOORE, M. E., and STUNKARD, A. J. (1965). Social factors in obesity. *Journal of the American Medical Association, 192,* 1039–1044.

GOLDSTEIN, H. J. (1981). Family factors associated with schizophrenia and anorexia nervosa. *Journal of Youth and Adolescence, 10,* 385–405.

GOODE, E. T. (1985). Medical aspects of the bulimic syndrome and bulimarexia. *Transactional Analysis Journal, 15,* 4–11.

GOODSITT, A. (1984). Self psychology and the treatment of anorexia nervosa. In D. M. Garner and P. E. Garfinkel (Eds.), *Handbook of psychotherapy for anorexia nervosa and bulimia,* pp. 55–82. New York: Guilford Press.

GORMALLY, J., BLACK, S., DASTON, S., and RARDIN, D. (1982). The assessment of binge eating severity among obese persons. *Addictive Behaviors, 7,* 47–55.

GOUGH, H. G. (1957). *Manual for the California Psychological Inventory,* Palo Alto, CA: Consulting Psychologist Press.

GRAM, L. F., and RAFAELSON, O. J. (1972). Lithium treatment of psychotic children and adolescents. *Acta Psychiatrica Scandinavica, 48,* 253–260.

GRAY, J. J., and FORD, K. (1985). The incidence of bulimia in a college sample. *International Journal of Eating Disorders, 4,* 201–210.

GRAY, S. H. (1977). Social aspects of body image: Perception of normalcy of weight and affect of college undergraduates. *Perceptual and Motor Skills, 45,* 1035–1040.

GREEN, R. S., and RAU, J. H. (1974). Treatment of compulsive eating disturbances with anticonvulsant medication. *American Journal of Psychiatry, 131,* 428–432.

GREEN, R. S., and RAU, J. H. (1977). The use of diphenylhydantoin in compulsive eating disorder: Further studies. In R. A. Vigersky (Ed.), *Anorexia Nervosa* (pp. 377–382). New York: Raven Press.

GREENWAY, F. L., DAHMS, W. T., and BRAG, D. A. (1977). Phenytoin as a treatment of obesity associated with compulsive eating. *Current Therapeutic Research, 21,* 338–342.

GRINKER, R. R., WERBLE, B., and DRYE, R. (1968). *The borderline syndrome: A behavioral study of ego functions.* New York: Basic Books.

GUIORA, A. (1967). Dysorexia: A psychopathological study of anorexia nervosa and bulimia. *American Journal of Psychiatry, 124,* 391–393.

GULL, W. W. (1874). Apepsia hysteria: Anorexic nervosa. *Transactions of the Clinical Society, 7,* 22–28.

GUNDERSON, J. G., and SINGER, M. T. (1975). Defining borderline patients: An overview. *American Journal of Psychiatry, 132,* 1–10.

GWINUP, G. (1975). Effect of exercise alone on the weight of obese women. *Archives of Internal Medicine, 135,* 676–680.

GWIRTSMAN, H. E., ROY-BYRNE, P., YAGER, J., and GERNER, R. H. (1983). Neuroendocrine abnormalities in bulimia. *American Journal of Psychiatry, 140,* 559–563.

HALEY, J. (1963). *Strategies of psychotherapy.* New York: Grune & Stratton.

HALMI, K. A., FALK, J. R., and SCHWARTZ, E. (1981). Binge-eating and vomiting: A survey of a college population. *Journal of Psychological Medicine, 11,* 697–706.

HAMBURGER, W. W. (1951). Emotional aspects of obesity. *Medical Clinics of North America, 35*, 483–499.

HAMILTON, M. (1967). Development of a rating scale for primary depressive illness. *British Journal of Social and Clinical Psychology, 6*, 278–296.

HARRIS, R. T. (1983). Bulimarexia and related serious eating disorders with medical complications. *Annals of Internal Medicine, 99*, 800–807.

HARTMANN, H. (1958): *Ego psychology and the problem of adaptation.* New York: International Universities Press.

HASLER, J. (1982). Parotid enlargement: A presenting sign in anorexia nervosa. *Oral Surgery, Oral Medicine, Oral Pathology, 53*, 567–573.

HATSUKAMI, D., OWEN, P., PYLE, R., and MITCHELL, J. (1982). Similarities and differences on the MMPI between women with bulimia and women with alcohol and drug abuse problems. *Addictive Behaviors, 7*, 435–439.

HAWKINS, R. C. II, and CLEMENT, P. F. (1980). Development and construct validation of a self-report measure of binge eating tendencies. *Addictive Behaviors, 5*, 219–226.

HAZARD, C. (1985). *Feminine self-concept in bulimic women.* Unpublished manuscript, Texas A & M University.

HEALY, K., CONROY, R., and WALSH, N. (1985). The prevalence of binge eating and bulimia in 1063 college students. *Journal of Psychiatric Research, 19*, 161–166.

HERMAN, C. P., and MACK, D. (1975). Restrained and unrestrained eating. *Journal of Personality, 43*, 647–660.

HERMAN, C. P., and POLIVY, J. (1980). Restrained eating. In A. J. Stunkard (Ed.), *Obesity* (pp. 208–225). Philadelphia: W. B. Saunders.

HERZOG, D. (1982). Bulimia: The secretive syndrome. *Psychosomatics, 23*, 481–487.

HOAGE, C. M., and GRAY, J. J. (1984). *Bulimia: Group behavior therapy with exposure and response prevention.* Paper presented at the annual convention for the Advancement of Behavior Therapy, Philadelphia.

HOLLINGSHEAD, A. B. (1957). *Two factor index of social position.* (Available from author, 1965 Yale Station, New Haven, CT)

HSU, L.K.G. (1984). Treatment of bulimia with lithium. *American Journal of Psychiatry, 141*, 1260–1262.

HSU, L.K.G., CRISP, A. H., and HARDING, B. (1979). Outcome of anorexia nervosa. *Lancet, 1*, 61–65.

HUDSON, J. I., LAFFER, P. S., and POPE, H. G. (1982). Bulimia related to affective disorder by family history and response to the dexamethasone suppression test. *American Journal of Psychiatry, 137*, 695–698.

HUDSON, J. I., POPE, H. G., JR., JONAS, J. M., and YURGELUN-TODD, D. (1983). Family history study of anorexia nervosa and bulimia. *British Journal of Psychiatry, 142*, 133–138.

HUDSON, J. I., POPE, H. G., JR., and JONAS, J. M. (1983). Phenomenologic relationship of eating disorders to major affective disorder. *Psychiatry Research, 9*, 345–354.

HUENEMANN, R. L., SHAPIRO, L. R., HAMPTON, M. C., and MITCHELL, B. W. (1966). A longitudinal study of gross body composition and body conformation and their association with food and activity in a teen-age population. *American Journal of Clinical Nutrition, 18*, 325–338.

HUGHES, P. L., WELLS, L. A., CUNNINGMAN, C. J., and ILSTRIP, D. M. (1986). Treating bulimia with desipramine: A double-blind placebo-controlled study. *Archives of General Psychiatry, 43,* 182–186.

HUMPHREY, L. L. (1987). Family-wide distress in bulimia. In D. Cannon and T. Baker (Eds.), *Addictive disorders: Psychological assessment and treatment.* New York: Praeger.

HUON, G. F. (1984). *Validation of a self-help treatment program for bulimia.* Paper presented at the International Conference on Eating Disorders, Swansea, Wales.

JOHNSON, C. (1984). The initial consultation for patients with bulimia and anorexia nervosa. In D. M. Garner and P. E. Garfinkel (Eds.), *Handbook of psychotherapy for anorexia nervosa and bulimia* (pp. 19–51). New York: Guilford Press.

JOHNSON, C. L, and BERNDT, D. M. (1983). Preliminary investigation of bulimia and life adjustment. *American Journal of Psychiatry, 140,* 774–777.

JOHNSON, C., CONNORS, M., and STUCKEY, M. (1983). Short-term group treatment of bulimia. *International Journal of Eating Disorders, 2,* 199–208.

JOHNSON, C., and FLACH, A. (1985). Family characteristics of 105 patients with bulimia. *American Journal of Psychiatry, 142,* 1321–1324.

JOHNSON, C. L., and IRVIN, F. S. (1983). Depressive potentials: Interface between adolescence and mid-life transition. In H. L. Morrison (Ed.), *Children of depressed parents: Risk, identification, and intervention* (pp. 115–137). New York: Grune & Stratton.

JOHNSON, C. L., and LARSON, R. (1982). Bulimia: An analysis of moods and behavior. *Psychosomatic Medicine, 44,* 333–345.

JOHNSON, C., LEWIS, C., LOVE, S., LEWIS, L., and STUCKEY, M. (1983). A descriptive survey of dieting and bulimic behavior in a female high school population. *Report of the Fourth Ross Conference on Medical Research* (pp. 14–18). Columbus, OH: Ross Laboratories.

JOHNSON, C., LEWIS, C., LOVE, S., LEWIS, L., and STUCKEY, M. (1984). Incidence and correlates of bulimic behavior in a female high school population. *Journal of Youth and Adolescence, 13,* 15–26.

JOHNSON, C. L., and LOVE, S. Q. (1985). Bulimia: Multivariate predictors of life impairment. *Journal of Psychiatric Research, 19,* 343–347.

JOHNSON, C. L., and MADDI, K. L. (1986). The etiology of bulimia: A bio-psychosocial perspective. *Annals of Adolescent Psychiatry, 13,* 253–273.

JOHNSON, C., STUCKEY, M., LEWIS, L., and SCHWARTZ, D. (1982). Bulimia: A descriptive survey of 316 cases. *International Journal of Eating Disorders, 11,* 1–16.

JOHNSON, C., STUCKEY, M., LEWIS, L. D., and SCHWARTZ, D. (1983). Bulimia: A descriptive survey of 509 cases. In P. L. Darby, P. E. Garfinkel, D. M. Garner, and D. V. Coscina (Eds.), *Anorexia nervosa: Recent developments* (pp. 159–172). New York: Alan R. Liss.

JOHNSON, W. G., SCHLUNDT, D. G., KELLY, M. L., and RUGGIERO, L. (1984). Exposure with response prevention and energy regulation in the treatment of bulimia. *International Journal of Eating Disorders, 3,* 37–46.

KAGAN, D., and SQUIRES, R. (1983). Dieting, compulsive eating, and feelings of failure among adolescents. *International Journal of Eating Disorders, 3,* 15–26.

KALUCY, R. S., CRISP, A. H., and HARDING, B. (1977). A study of 56 families with anorexia nervosa. *British Journal of Medical Psychology, 50,* 381–395.

KATZ, J. L., KUPERBERG, A., POLLACK, C. P., WALSH, B. T., ZUMOFF, B., and

WEINER, H. (1984). Is there a relationship between eating disorder and affective disorder? New evidence from sleep recordings. *American Journal of Psychiatry, 141,* 753–759.

KATZMAN, M., and WOLCHIK, S. (1984). Bulimia and binge eating in college women: A comparison of personality and behavioral characteristics. *Journal of Consulting and Clinical Psychology, 52,* 423–428.

KAUFER, J., and KATZ, J. (1983). Rorschach responses in anorectic and non-anorectic women. *International Journal of Eating Disorders, 3,* 65–74.

KEESEY, R. E. (1980). A set point analysis of the regulation of body weight. In A. J. Stunkard (Ed.), *Obesity* (pp. 144–165). Philadelphia: W. B. Saunders.

KEESEY, R. E. (1983). A hypothalamic syndrome of body weight regulation at reduced levels. In *Report of the Fourth Ross Conference on Medical Research* (pp. 60–66). Columbus, OH: Ross Laboratories.

KELLY, S. C. (1984). A group treatment of bulimia: *Exposure and response prevention with refutation of irrational beliefs.* Paper presented at the annual meeting of the American Psychological Association, Toronto, Canada.

KERNBERG, O. (1975). *Borderline conditions and pathological narcissism.* New York: Jason Aronson.

KERNBERG, O. (1976). *Object relations theory and clinical psychoanalysis.* New York: Jason Aronson.

KEYS, A., BROZEK, J., HENSCHEL, A., MICKELSON, O., and TAYLOR, H. L. (1950). *The Biology of Human Starvation: Vol. 1.* Minneapolis, MN: University of Minnesota Press.

KIRKLEY, B. G., SCHNEIDER, J. A., AGRAS, W. S., and BACHMAN, J. A. (1985). Comparison of two group treatments for bulimia. *Journal of Consulting and Clinical Psychology, 53,* 43–48.

KIRSCHBAUM, W. R. (1951). Excessive hunger as a symptom of cerebral origin. *Journal of Nervous and Mental Disease, 113,* 95–114.

KLEIN, M. (1946). Notes on some schizoid mechanisms. *International Journal of Psycho-Analysis, 33,* 433–438.

KLESGES, R. C., BARTSCH, D., NORWOOD, J. D., KAUTZMAN, D., and HAUGRUD, S. (1984). The effect of selected social and environmental variables on the eating behavior of adults in the natural environment. *International Journal of Eating Disorders, 3,* 35–41.

KOG, E., and VANDEREYCKEN, W. (1985). Family characteristics of anorexia nervosa and bulimia: A review of the research literature. *Clinical Psychology Review, 5,* 159–180.

KOG, E., VERTOMMEN, H., and DE GROOTE, T. (in press). Family interaction research in anorexia nervosa: The use and misuse of a self-report questionnaire. *International Journal of Family Psychiatry.*

KOHUT, H. (1971). *The analysis of the self.* New York: International Universities Press.

KORNHABER, A. (1970). The stuffing syndrome. *Psychosomatics, 11,* 580–584.

KRUG, S. E., SCHREIER, I. H., and CATTELL, R. B. (1976). *Handbook for the IPAT Anxiety Scale.* Champaign, IL: Institute for Personality and Ability Testing.

LACEY, J. H. (1982). The bulimic syndrome at normal body weight: Reflections on pathogenesis and clinical features. *International Journal of Eating Disorders, 2,* 59–66.

LACEY, J. H. (1983). Bulimia nervosa, binge eating, and psychogenic vomiting: A controlled treatment study and long-term outcome. *British Medical Journal, 286,* 1609–1613.

LACEY, J. H., and GIBSON, E. (1985). Does laxative abuse control body weight? A comparative study of purging and vomiting bulimics. *Human Nutrition: Applied Nutrition, 39,* 36–42.

LARKIN, J. E., and PINES, H. A. (1979). No fat persons need apply. *Sociology of Work Occupations, 6,* 312–327.

LARSON, R., and JOHNSON, C. L. (1985). Bulimic: Disturbed patterns of solitude. *Addictive Behaviors, 10,* 281–290.

LAWSON, J. S., MARSHALL, W. L., and McGRATH, P. (1979). The social self-esteem inventory. *Educational and Psychological Measurement, 39,* 803–811.

LEON, G. R., PHELAN, P. W., KELLY, J. T., and PATTEN, S. E. (1984). *Binge eating relationships with the menstrual cycle and cyclothymia.* Paper presented at the 15th European Conference on Psychosomatic Research, London, England.

LEITENBERG, H., GROSS, J., PETERSON, J., and ROSEN, J. C. (1984). Analysis of an anxiety model and the process of change during exposure plus response prevention treatment of bulimia nervosa. *Behavior Therapy, 15,* 3–20.

LERNER, H. D. (1983). Contemporary psychoanalytic perspectives on gorge-vomiting: A case illustration. *International Journal of Eating Disorders, 3,* 47–63.

LEVIN, P. A., FALKS, J. M., and DIXON, K. (1980). Benign parotid enlargement in bulimia. *Annals of Internal Medicine, 93,* 827–829.

LEWIS, L., and JOHNSON, C. (1985). A comparison of sex role orientation between women with bulimia and normal controls. *International Journal of Eating Disorders, 4,* 247–257.

LICHTENSTEIN, H. (1964). The role of narcissism in the emergence and maintenance of a primary identity. *International Journal of Psycho-Analysis 45,* 49–56.

LIDZ, T. (1976). *The person: His or her development throughout the life cycle.* New York: Basic Books.

LIEBOWITZ, M. R., and KLEIN, D. F. (1979). Hysteroid dysphoria. *Psychiatric Clinics of North America, 2,* 555–575.

LIZDAS, P., and ABRAMSON, E. (1984, April). *Prevalence of bulimia in a California state university.* Paper presented at the annual meeting of the Western Psychological Association, Los Angeles.

LORO, A. D., JR., and ORLEANS, C. S. (1981). Binge eating in obesity. Preliminary findings and guidelines for behavioral analysis and treatment. *Addictive Behaviors, 6,* 155–166.

LOVE, S. Q., & JOHNSON, C. L. (1984). A preliminary investigation on the reliability and validity of the Diagnostic Survey of Eating Disorders. Manuscript submitted for publication.

LOVE, S. Q., OLLENDICK, T., JOHNSON, C. L., and SCHLESINGER, S. (1985). A preliminary report of the prediction of bulimic behaviors: A social learning analysis. *Bulletin of the Society of Psychologists in Addictive Behaviors, 4,* 93–101.

LUYCKX, A., and DE AGUILAR, M. (1972–73). Anorexis mentale (Anorexia nervosa). *Psychotherapy and Psychosomatics, 21,* 278–281.

MAHLER, M. (1968). *On human symbiosis and the vicissitudes of individuation. Vol. 1: Infantile Psychosis.* New York: International Universities Press.

MAHLER, M. (1971). A study of the separation-individuation process and its possible application to borderline phenomena in the psychoanalytic situation. *Psychoanalytic Study of the Child, 26,* 403–424.

References   317

MAHLER, M., PINE, F., and BERGMAN, A. (1975). *The psychological birth of the human infant.* New York: Basic Books.

MALMQUIST, J., ERICSSON, B., HULTEN-NOSSLIN, M. B., JEPPSSON, J. O., and LJUNGBERG, O. (1980). Finger clubbing and aspartylglucosamine excretion in a laxative abusing patient. *Post Graduate Medicine, 56,* 862–864.

MARLATT, G. A. (1979). Alcohol use and problem drinking: A cognitive behavioral analysis. In P. C. Kendall and S. P. Hollon (Eds.), *Cognitive behavioral interventions: Theory, research, and procedures* (pp. 319–355). New York: Academic Press.

MARLATT, G. A., and GORDON, J. R. (1978). Determinants of relapse: Implications for the maintenance of behavior change. In P. Davidson (Ed.), *Behavioral medicine: Changing health lifestyles* (pp. 410–452). New York: Brunner/Mazel.

MASSERMAN, J. (1941). Psychodynamics in anorexia nervosa and neurotic vomiting. *Psychoanalytic Quarterly, 10,* 211–242.

MASTERSON, J. F. (1976). *Psychotherapy of the borderline adult.* New York: Brunner/Mazel.

MASTERSON, J. (1977). Primary anorexia in the borderline adolescent: An object relations view. In P. Hartocollis (Ed.), *Borderline personality disorders.* (pp. 475–494). New York: International Universities Press.

MATIKAINEN, M. (1979). Spontaneous rupture of the stomach. *American Journal of Surgery, 138,* 451–452.

MERRILL, C. A. (1984). *Cognitive techniques in the group treatment of bulimia.* Paper presented at the annual meeting of the American Psychological Association, Toronto.

Metropolitan Life Insurance Company (1959). How you can control your weight. (Available from Metropolitan Life, One Madison Avenue, New York)

MILLMAN, M. (1980). *Such a pretty face.* New York: Berkley Books.

MINUCHIN, S., ROSMAN, B. L., and BAKER, L. (1978). *Psychosomatic families: Anorexia nervosa in context.* Cambridge, MA: Harvard University Press.

MITCHELL, J. E., and BANTLE, J. (1983). Metabolic and endocrine investigation in women of normal weight with the bulimia syndrome. *Biological Psychiatry, 18,* 355–365.

MITCHELL, J. E., DAVIS, L., and GOFF, G. (1985). The process of relapse in patients with bulimia. *International Journal of Eating Disorders, 4,* 457–463.

MITCHELL, J. E., and GOFF, G. (1984). A series of twelve adult male patients with bulimia. *Psychosomatics, 25,* 909–913.

MITCHELL, J. E., and GROAT, R. (1984). A placebo-controlled, double-blind trial of amitriptyline in bulimia. *Journal of Clinical Psychopharmacology, 4,* 186–193.

MITCHELL, J. E., HATSUKAMI, D., ECKERT, E., and PYLE, R. L. (1985). Characteristics of 275 patients with bulimia. *American Journal of Psychiatry, 142,* 482–485.

MITCHELL, J. E., PYLE, R. L., and ECKERT, E. D. (1981). Frequency and duration of binge-eating episodes in patients with bulimia. *American Journal of Psychiatry, 138,* 835–836.

MITCHELL, J. E., PYLE, R. L., ECKERT, E. D., HATSUKAMI, D., and LENTZ, R. (1983). Electrolyte and other physiological abnormalities in patients with bulimia. *Psychological Medicine, 13,* 273–278.

MITCHELL, J. E., PYLE, R. L., and MINER, R. A. (1982). Gastric dilatation as a complication of bulimia. *Psychosomatics, 23,* 96–99.

Moos, R. (1974). *Family Environment Scale Manual*. Palo Alto, CA: Consulting Psychologists Press.

Morgan, H. G., and Russell, G.F.M. (1975). Value of family background and clinical features as prediction of long-term outcome in anorexia nervosa: Four-year follow-up study of 41 patients. *Psychological Medicine, 5*, 355–372.

Morley, J. E. (1980). The neuroendocrine control of appetite: The role of endogenous opiates, cholecystokinin, TRH, gamma-amniobutyric-acid and the diazepam receptor. *Life Science, 27*, 355–368.

Moron, P., and Bruno, Y. 91972–73). Tests et troubles psychosomatiques chez l'enfant. [Tests and psychosomatic troubles in children]. *Psychotherapy and Psychosomatics, 21*, 321–324.

Moulton, R. (1942). A psychosomatic study of anorexia nervosa including the use of vaginal smears. *Psychosomatic Medicine, 4*, 62–74.

Mrosovsky, N., and Powley, T. L. (1977). Set points of body weight and fat. *Behavioral Biology, 20*, 205–223.

Nagelberg, D., Hale, S., and Ware, S. (1984). The assessment of bulimic symptoms and personality correlates in female students. *Journal of Clinical Psychology, 40*, 440–445.

Nelson, J. C., Jatlow, P., Quinlan, D. M., and Bowers, M. B., Jr. (1982). Desipramine plasma concentration and antidepressant response. *Archives of General Psychiatry, 39*, 1419–1422.

Nemiah, J. C. (1950). Anorexia nervosa: A clinical psychiatric study. *Medicine, 29*, 225–268.

Neuman, R. O. (1902). Experimentelle Beitragezurhehre von dem Taglichen Nahrungsbedarfdes Menschen unter besonderer Berucksichtigung der notwendigen Eiweissmenge. *Archives fur Hygiene, 45*, 1–87.

Nevo, S. (1985). Bulimic symptoms: Prevalence and ethnic differences among college women. *International Journal of Eating Disorders, 4*, 151–168.

Nicolle, G. (1939). Prepsychotic anorexia. *Proceedings of the Royal Society of Medicine, 32*, 153–162.

Nisbett, R. E. (1972). Eating behavior and obesity in men and animals. *Advances in Psychosomatic Medicine, 7*, 173–193.

Norman, D. K., and Herzog, D. B. (1983). Bulimia, anorexia nervosa, and anorexia nervosa with bulimia: A comparative analysis of MMPI Profiles. *International Journal of Eating Disorders, 2*, 43–52.

Norman, D. K., and Herzog, D. B. (1984). Persistent social maladjustment in bulimia: A 1-year follow-up. *American Journal of Psychiatry, 141*, 444–446.

Nylander, I. (1971). The feeling of being fat and dieting in a school population: Epidemiologic interview investigation. *Acta Sociomedica Scandinavica, 3*, 17–26.

Ogden, T. G. (1979). On projective identification. *International Journal of Psycho-Analysis, 60*, 357–373.

Olson, D. H., Bell, R., and Portner, J. (1978). *Family Adaptability and Cohesion Evaluation Scale*. St. Paul: University of Minnesota, Family Social Science.

Ondercin, P. A. (1979, March). Compulsive eating in college women. *Journal of College Student Personnel*, pp. 153–157.

Orbach, S. (1978). *Fat is a feminist issue*. New York: Berkley Books.

Orbach, S. (1982). *Fat is a feminist issue II*. New York: Berkley Books.

Ordman, A. M., and Kirschenbaum, D. S. (1985). Cognitive-behavior therapy for bulimia: An initial outcome study. *Journal of Consulting and Clinical Psychology,* *53,* 305–313.

OSLER, W. (1892). *Principles and practice of medicine.* New York: D. Appleton and Co.

PALAZZOLI, M. (1971). Anorexia nervosa. In S. Arieti (Ed.), *The world biennial of psychiatry and psychotherapy: Vol. 1* (pp. 197–218). New York: Basic Books.

PALAZZOLI, M. S. (1974). *Self-starvation.* London: Chaucer.

PALAZZOLI, M. (1978). *Self-Starvation: From individual to family therapy in the treatment of anorexia nervosa.* New York: Jason Aronson.

PALMER, J., MENSCH, I., and MATARAZZO, J. (1952). Anorexia nervosa: Case history and psychological examination data with implications for test validity. *Journal of Clinical Psychology, 8,* 168–173.

PALMER, R. L. (1979). The dietary chaos syndrome: A useful new term? *British Journal of Medical Psychology, 52,* 187–190.

PATTON, S. G. (1982). *Stop dieting, start living.* New York: Dodd, Mead, & Co.

PIAGET, J. (1954). *The construction of reality in the child.* New York: Basic Books.

POLIVY, J., and HERMAN, P. (1983). *Breaking the diet habit.* New York: Basic Books.

POPE, H. G., JR., and HUDSON, J. I. (1982). Treatment of bulimia with antide-pressants. *Psychopharmacology, 78,* 176–179.

POPE, H. G., and HUDSON, J. I. (1984). *New hope for binge eaters.* New York: Harper & Row.

POPE, H. G., JR., HUDSON, J. I., JONAS, J. M., and YURGELUN-TODD, D. (1983). Bulimia treated with imipramine: A placebo-controlled, double-blind study. *American Journal of Psychiatry, 140,* 554–558.

POPE, H. G., HUDSON, J. I., and YURGELUN-TODD, D. (1984). Anorexia nervosa and bulimia among 300 suburban women shoppers. *American Journal of Psychiatry, 141,* 187–190.

POPE, H. G., HUDSON, J. I., YURGELUN-TODD, D., and HUDSON, M. S. (1984). Prevalence of anorexia nervosa and bulimia in three student populations. *International Journal of Eating Disorders, 3,* 45–51.

PYLE, R. L., MITCHELL, J. E., ECKERT, E. D. (1981). Bulimia: A report of 34 cases. *Journal of Clinical Psychiatry, 42,* 60–64.

PYLE, R. L., MITCHELL, J. E., ECKERT, E. D., and HALVORSON, P. A. (1983). The incidence of bulimia in freshman college students. *International Journal of Eating Disorders, 2,* 75–85.

PYLE, R. L., MITCHELL, J. E., ECKERT, E. D., HATSUKAMI, D. K., and GOFF, G. M. (1984). The interruption of bulimic behaviors: A review of three treatment programs. *Psychiatric Clinics of North America, 7,* 275–286.

RAHMAN, L., RICHARDSON, H. B., and RIPLEY, H. S. (1939). Anorexia nervosa with psychiatric observations. *Psychosomatic Medicine, 1,* 335–365.

RAPAPORT, D. (1967). *The collected papers of David Rapaport* (M. Gill, Ed.). New York: International Universities Press.

RAU, J. H., and GREEN, R. S. (1975). Compulsive eating: A neuropsychologic approach to certain eating disorders. *Comprehensive Psychiatry, 16,* 223–231.

RAU, J. H., and GREEN, R. S. (1978). Soft neurologic correlates of compulsive eating. *Journal of Nervous and Mental Disorders, 166,* 435–437.

RAU, J. H., STRUVE, F. A., and GREEN, R. S. (1979). Electroencephalographic correlates of compulsive eating. *Clinical Electroencephalography, 10,* 180–188.

REMICK, R. A., JONES, M. W., and COMPOS, P. E. (1980). Postictal bulimia [letter to the editor]. *Journal of Clinical Psychiatry, 41,* 26.

RIFKIN, A., QUITKIN, F., CARRILLO, C., BLUMBERG, A. G., and KLEIN, D. F. (1972). Lithium carbonate in emotionally unstable character disorder. *Archives of General Psychiatry, 27,* 519–523.

RODIN, J., SILBERSTEIN, L., and STRIEGEL-MOORE, R. (1984). Women and weight: A normative discontent. *Nebraska Symposium on Motivation,* 267–307.

ROE, D. A., and EICKWORT, K. R. (1976). Relationships between obesity and associated health factors with unemployment among low income women. *Journal of the American Medical Women's Association, 31,* 193–204.

ROSEN, J., and LEITENBERG, H. (1982). Bulimia nervosa: Treatment with exposure and response prevention. *Behavior Therapy, 13,* 117–124.

ROSEN, J., and LEITENBERG, H. (1984). Exposure plus response prevention treatment of bulimia. In D. M. Garner and P. E. Garfinkel (Eds.), *A handbook of psychotherapy for anorexia and bulimia* (pp. 193–209). New York: Guilford Press.

ROSENBERG, M. (1979). *Conceiving the self.* New York: Basic Books.

ROTH, G. (1982). *Feeding the hungry heart.* New York: Signet.

ROTH, G. (1984). *Breaking free from compulsive eating.* Indianapolis: Bobbs-Merrill.

ROWLAND, C. V. (1970). Anorexia nervosa: A survey of the literature and review of 30 cases. *International Psychiatric Clinics, 7,* 37–137.

ROY-BYRNE, P., LEE-BENNER, K., and YAGER, J. (1984). Group therapy for bulimia: A year's experience. *International Journal of Eating Disorders, 3,* 97–116.

RUDERMAN, A. (1985). Restraint, obesity, and bulimia. *Behavior Research and Therapy, 23,* 151–156.

RUSSELL, G.F.M. (1979). Bulimia nervosa: An ominous variant of anorexia nervosa. *Psychological Medicine, 9,* 429–448.

RYBICKI, D. J., LEPKOWSKY, C. M., and ARNDT, S. (In press). An empirical assessment of bulimic patients using multiple measures. *International Journal of Eating Disorders.*

SABINE, E. J., YONACE, A., FARRINGTON, A. J., BARRATT, K. H., and WAKELING, A. (1983). Bulimia nervosa: A placebo controlled double-blind therapeutic trial of mianserin. *British Journal of Clinical Pharmacology, 15,* 195S–202S.

SAUL, S. H., DEKKER, A., and WATSON, C. G. (1981). Acute gastric dilatation with infarction and perforation: Report of a fatal outcome in a patient with anorexia nervosa. *Gut, 22,* 978.

SCHACHTER, S. (1971). *Emotions, obesity, and crime.* New York: Academic Press.

SCHACHTER, S., and RODIN, I. (1974). *Obese humans and rats.* Hillsdale, N.J.: Lawrence Erlbaum.

SCHNEIDER, J. A., and AGRAS, W. S. (1985, January). A cognitive-behavioral group treatment of bulimia. *British Journal of Psychiatry,* 66–69.

SCHWARTZ, D. M., THOMPSON, M. G., and JOHNSON, C. (1982). Anorexia nervosa and bulimia: The sociocultural context. *International Journal of Eating Disorders, 1,* 23–25.

SCHWARTZ, R. (1982). Bulimia and family therapy: A case study. *International Journal of Eating Disorders, 2,* 75–82.

SCHWARTZ, R. C., BARRETT, M. J., and SABA, G. (1984). Family therapy for bulimia. In D. M. Garner and P. E. Garfinkel (Eds.), *Handbook of psychotherapy for anorexia nervosa and bulimia,* (pp. 280–307). New York: Guilford Press.

SECORD, P., and JOURARD, S. (1953). The appraisal of body-cathexis; body cathexis and the self. *Journal of Consulting Psychology, 17,* 343–347.

Self-Esteem Institute. (1975). *Coopersmith Self-Esteem Inventory.* Toronto, Canada: Self-Esteem Institute.

SELIGMAN, M.E.P. (1975). *Helplessness.* San Francisco: W. H. Freeman.

SELLING, L. S., and FERRARO, M. A. (1945). *The psychology of diet and nutrition.* New York: W. W. Norton.

SHAINESS, N. (1984). *Sweet suffering: Woman as victim.* Indianapolis: Bobbs-Merrill.

SIFNEOS, P. E. (1973). The prevalence of "alexithymic" characteristics in psychosomatic patients. In J. Reusch, A. Schmale, and T. Sperri (Eds.), *Psychotherapy in Psychosomatics* (pp. 255–262). White Plains, NY: Karger.

SIMS, E.A.H., GOLDMAN, R., GLUCK, C., HORTON, E. S., KELLEHER, P., and ROWE, D. (1968). Experimental obesity in man. *Transactions of the Association of American Physicians, 81,* 153–170.

SKINNER, H. A., SANTA-BARBARA, J., and STEINHAUER, P. D. (1983). The family assessment measure. *Canadian Journal of Community Mental Health, 2,* 91–105.

SKYNNER, A. C. (1981). An open-system, group-analytic approach to family therapy. In A. S. Gurman and D. P. Kniskern (Eds.), *Handbook of family therapy* (pp. 39–80). New York: Brunner/Mazel.

SMALL, A. (1984). The contribution of psychodiagnostic test results toward understanding anorexia nervosa. *International Journal of Eating Disorders, 3,* 47–59.

SMALL, A., MADERO, J., GROSS, H., TEAGRO, L., LEIB, J., and EBERT, M. (1980). A comparative analysis of primary anorexics and schizophrenics on the MMPI. *Journal of Clinical Psychology, 37,* 733–736.

SMALL, A., TEAGNO, L., MADERO, J., GROSS, H., and EBERT, M. (1982). A comparison of anorexics and schizophrenics on psychodiagnostic measures. *International Journal of Eating Disorders, 1,* 49–56.

SMITH, G. P. (1980). Satiety effect of gastrointestinal hormones. In R. F. Beers and E. G. Bassett (Eds.), *Polypeptide hormones* (pp. 413–420). New York: Raven Press.

SOLTMAN, O. (1894). Anorexia cerebralis and centrale nutritions neurose. *Jahrbuch der Kinderheilklinik, 38,* 1–13.

SOURS, J. A. (1980). *Starving to death in a sea of objects.* New York: Jason Aronson.

SPENCE, J., HELMREICH, R., and STAPP, J. (1975). Ratings of self and peers on sex role attributes and their relation to self-esteem and conceptions of masculinity and femininity. *Journal of Personality and Social Psychology, 32,* 29–39.

SPENCER, J. A., and FREMOUW, W. J. (1979). Binge eating as a function of restraint and weight classification. *Journal of Abnormal Psychology, 38,* 262–267.

SPERLING, E., and MASSING, A. (1970). Der familiar Hintergrund der Anorexia Nervosa und die sich daraus ergebenden therapeutischen schwierigkieten. *Zeitschrift fur Psychosomaticsche Medizin, 16,* 130–141.

SPIELBERGER, C. D. (1979). *Preliminary manual for the State-Trait Personality Inventory.* Unpublished manuscript.

SQUIRE, S. (1983). *The slender balance: Causes for bulimia, anorexia and the weight-loss, weight-gain seesaw.* New York: Putnam.

STAFFIERI, J. R. (1967). A study of social stereotype of body image in children. *Journal of Personality and Social Psychology, 7,* 101–104.

STAFFIERI, J. R. (1972). Body build and behavior expectancies in young females. *Developmental Psychology, 6,* 125–127.

STANGLER, R. S., and PRINTZ, A. M. (1980). DSM III: Psychiatric diagnosis in a university population. *American Journal of Psychiatry, 137,* 937–940.

STERN, S. (1986). The dynamics of clinical management in the treatment of anorexia nervosa and bulimia: An organizing theory. *International Journal of Eating Disorders, 5,* 233–254.

STERN, S., WHITAKER, C. A., HAGEMANN, N. J., ANDERSON, R. B., and BARGMAN, G. J. (1981). Anorexia nervosa: The hospital's role in family treatment. *Family Process, 20,* 395–408.

STEVENS, E. V., and SALISBURY, J. D. (1984). Group therapy for bulimic adults. *American Journal of Orthopsychiatry, 54,* 156–161.

STORY, I. (1976). Caricature and impersonating the other: Observations from the psychotherapy of anorexia nervosa. *Psychiatry, 39,* 176–188.

STROBER, M. (1981). The significance of bulimia in juvenile anorexia nervosa: An exploration of possible etiological factors. *International Journal of Eating Disorders, 1,* 28–43.

STROBER, M., and GOLDENBERG, I. (1981). Ego boundary disturbance in juvenile anorexia nervosa. *Journal of Clinical Psychology, 37,* 433–438.

STROBER, M., SALKIN, B., BURROUGHS, J., and MORRELL, W. (1982). Validity of the bulimia-restrictor distinction in anorexia nervosa. *Journal of Nervous and Mental Disease, 170,* 345–351.

STUNKARD, A. J. (1959). Eating patterns and obesity. *Psychiatric Quarterly, 33,* 284–292.

STUNKARD, A. J. (1978). Behavioral treatment of obesity: The current status. *International Journal of Obesity, 2,* 237–248.

SUGARMAN, A., and KURASH, C. (1982). The body as a transitional object in bulimia. *International Journal of Eating Disorders, 1,* 57–67.

SUGARMAN, A., QUINLAN, D., and DEVENIS, L. (1982). Ego boundary disturbance in anorexia: Preliminary findings. *Journal of Personality Assessment, 46,* 455–461.

SWIFT, W. J., and STERN, S. (1982). The psychodynamic diversity of anorexia nervosa. *International Journal of Eating Disorders, 2,* 17–35.

SWIFT, W., and LETVEN, R. (1984). Bulimia and the basic fault. *Journal of the American Academy of Child Psychiatry, 23,* 489–497.

TANSEY, M. H., and BURKE, W. F. (1985). Projective identification and the empathic process. *Contemporary Psychoanalysis, 21,* 42–69.

THIELGAARD, A. (1965). Psychological testing of patients with anorexia nervosa. In J. Meyer and H. Feldmann (Eds.), *Anorexia nervosa* (pp. 122–129). Stuttgart: G. Thieme.

THOMAS, A., and CHESS, S. (1977). *Temperament and development.* New York: Brunner/Mazel.

THOMAS, S., and CORDEN, M. (1970). Tables of composition of Australian foods. Canberra: Australian Government Publishing Service.

THOMPSON, M. G., and SCHWARTZ, D. M. (1982). Life adjustment of women with anorexia nervosa and anorexic-like behavior. *International Journal of Eating Disorders, 1,* 47–60.

WAGNER, E., and WAGNER, C. (1978). Similar Rorschach patterning in three cases of anorexia nervosa. *Journal of Personality Assessment, 42,* 426–432.

WALSH, B. T., ROOSE, S. P., and GLASSMAN, A. H. (1983). *Depression and eating disorders.* Paper presented at the annual meeting of the American Psychiatric Association, Los Angeles.

WALSH, B. T., STEWART, J. W., ROOSE, S. P., GLADIS, M., and GLASSMAN, A. H. (1984). Treatment of bulimia with phenelzine. *Archives of General Psychiatry, 41,* 1105–1109.

WALSH, B. T., STEWART, J. W., WRIGHT, L., HARRISON, W., ROOSE, S. P., and GLASSMAN, A. H. (1982). Treatment of bulimia with monoamine oxidase inhibitors. *American Journal of Psychiatry, 139,* 1629–1630.

WEBB, W. L., and GEHI, M. (1981). Electrolyte & fluid balance: Neuropsychiatric manifestations. *Psychosomatics, 22,* 199–202.

WEINER, H. (1983). The hypothalamic-pituitary-ovarian axis in anorexia and bulimia nervosa. *International Journal of Eating Disorders, 2,* 109–116.

WEISS, S., and EBERT, M. (1983). Psychological and behavioral characteristics of normal-weight bulimics and normal-weight controls. *Psychosomatic Medicine, 45,* 293–303.

WEISS, T., and LEVITZ, L. (1976). Diphenylhydantoin treatment of bulimia [Letter to the editor]. *American Journal of Psychiatry, 133,* 1093.

WEISSMAN, M. M. (1975). The assessment of social adjustment. *Archives of General Psychiatry, 32,* 357–364.

WEISSMAN, M. M., PRUSOFF, B. A., THOMPSON, W. D., HARDING, P. S., and MYERS, J. K. (1978). Social adjustment by self report in a community sample and in psychiatric outpatients. *Journal of Nervous and Mental Disease, 166,* 317–326.

WERMUTH, B. M., DAVIS, K. L., HOLLISTER, L. E., and STUNKARD, A. J. (1977). Phenytoin treatment of the binge-eating syndrome. *American Journal of Psychiatry, 134,* 1249–1253.

WHITE, W. C., and BOSKIND-WHITE, M. (1981). An experiential-behavioral approach to the treatment of bulimarexia. *Psychotherapy: Theory, Research, and Practice, 18,* 501–507.

WILSON, C. P. (1983). *Fear of Being Fat.* New York: Jason Aronson.

WINNICOTT, D. W. (1965). *The maturational process and the facilitating environment: Studies in the theory of emotional development.* New York: International Universities Press.

WINSTEAD, M. (1984). *Cognitive behavioral factors of relapse among bulimics.* Paper presented at the annual meeting of the American Psychological Association, Toronto, Canada.

WOOLEY, S., and WOOLEY, O. (1979). Obesity and women—I: A closer look at the facts. *Women's Studies International Quarterly, 2,* 69–79.

YATES, A. J., and SAMBRAILO, F. (1984). Bulimia nervosa: A descriptive and therapeutic study. *Behavior Research and Therapy, 22,* 503–517.

ZINCAND, H., CADORET, R. J., and WIDMAN, R. B. (1984). Incidence and detection of bulimia in a family practice population. *Journal of Family Practice, 18,* 555–560.

NAME INDEX

Kelly, J. T., 56
Kelly, M. L., 288, 300
Kelly, S. C., 289
Kernberg, O., 80, 89
Keys, A., 143*n*, 228
Kirkley, B. G., 286
Kirschbaum, W. R., 297
Kirschenbaum, D. S., 131, 286, 300
Klein, D. F., 296
Klein, M., 168
Klesges, R. C., 24
Kog, E., 126, 132
Kohut, H., 89, 113, 141
Kornhaber, A., 5
Krall, R. A., 54
Kreisberg, J., 17
Krug, S. E., 286
Kuperberg, A., 55, 60, 291
Kurash, C., 104*n*

Lacey, J. H., 33, 53, 284, 302
Laffer, P. S., 59–60, 291
Larkin, J. E., 140
Larson, R., 24, 45, 47, 50, 59, 149, 245, 291
Lawson, J. S., 288
Lee-Benner, K., 285
Leitenberg, H., 149, 206, 287–88, 302
Lentz, R., 53, 164
Leon, G. R., 42*n*, 43–44, 48, 56–59, 161, 163
Lepkowsky, C. M., 73–74
Lerner, H. D., 104*n*
Letven, R., 104*n*
Levin, P. A., 54
Levitz, L., 297
Lewis, C., 17, 20–25, 27
Lewis, L. D., 7, 11, 21–25, 27, 32–38, 40–42, 42*n*, 43, 49, 56, 58, 77–78, 138, 141*n*, 143, 159, 163–64, 210*n*
Lichtenstein, H., 91
Lidz, T., 105, 166
Lipman, R. S., 287
Lizdas, P., 15, 18, 21
Ljungberg, O., 54
Llewellyn-Jones, D., 285
Loro, A. D., 5
Love, S. Q., 12, 17, 20–25, 27, 67, 155, 254, 304
Luyckx, A., 79

Mack, D., 143*n*, 230
Maddi, K. L., 226, 298
Madero, J., 79

Mahler, M., 89, 89*n*, 90–94, 100, 272
Malmquist, J., 54
Marlatt, G. A., 250–52
Marshall, L., 210*n*
Marshall, W. L., 288
Masserman, J., 88
Massing, A., 127
Masterson, J. F., 80, 89
Matarazzo, J., 79
Matikainen, M., 53
Mayer, J. C., 64, 140
McCulough, P., 218*n*
McGrath, P., 288
McGuiness, B., 126, 129
Mendelson, M., 155
Mensch, I., 79
Merrill, C. A., 285
Mickelson, O., 143*n*, 228
Millman, M., 200, 223, 225*n*, 240
Mills, C. A., 25
Miner, R. A., 53
Minuchin, S., 128–30, 290
Mira, M. E., 285
Mitchell, B. W., 26, 64
Mitchell, J. E., 7, 11, 17, 20–26, 32–36, 38–42, 42*n*, 43–45, 47, 48, 50, 53, 55–59, 74–75, 141*n*, 143, 163–64, 251, 285, 291, 295–96, 298, 301–2
Mock, J., 155
Moldofsky, H., 9–10, 51, 57, 62, 75, 127, 158
Moore, M. E., 140
Moos, R., 130, 155
Morgan, H. G., 129
Morley, J. E., 136–37
Moron, P., 79
Morowski, S. G., 54, 165
Morrell, W., 10, 59, 75, 126, 291
Moulton, R., 88
Mrosovsky, N., 144, 237
Myers, J. K., 28, 48–49

Nagelberg, D., 18, 20, 67
Nelson, J. C., 294
Nemiah, J. C., 5
Neuman, R. O., 237
Nevo, S., 19, 21, 23–24
Nicolle, G., 5
Nisbett, R. E., 62, 144, 237
Norman, D. K., 10, 49, 74–75, 141*n*
Norwood, J. D., 24
Nurnberger, J., 127
Nylander, I., 26

Ogden, T. G., 168
O'Hanlon, J., 126–27
Oldham, P. D., 14–15
Ollendick, T., 67, 254
Olmsted, M. P., 27–28, 61–62, 138, 143*n*, 144, 155, 239, 284
Olson, D. H., 131
Ondercin, P. A., 16, 77
Orbach, S., 260
Ordman, A. M., 131, 286, 300
Orleans, C. S., 5
O'Shaughnessy, M., 10, 64, 132, 304
Osler, W., 3
Owen, P., 75

Palazzoli, M. S., 79–80, 99, 128, 138
Palmer, J., 79
Palmer, R. L., 7
Patten, S. E., 56
Patton, S. G., 260
Pertschuk, M., 17
Peterson, J., 206, 288, 302
Petzel, T. P., 200, 284
Phelan, P. W., 56
Piaget, J., 89, 94
Pine, F., 89, 92, 94
Pines, H. A., 140
Pirke, K. M., 55, 230
Plutchik, R., 156
Polivy, J., 27–28, 61–62, 143*n*, 144, 155, 237–39, 259, 284
Pollack, C. P., 55, 60, 291
Pope, H. G., 10, 15, 18, 21–22, 24–25, 59–60, 81, 219, 260, 291–93, 301
Portner, J., 131
Post, G., 19, 21, 25, 27
Powley, T. L., 144, 237
Printz, A. M., 15–16, 22, 25
Prusoff, B. A., 28, 48–49
Pyle, R. L., 7, 11, 17, 20–26, 32–36, 38, 40–42, 42*n*, 43–45, 47–48, 50, 53, 56–59, 74–75, 141*n*, 143, 163–64, 285, 291, 302

Quinlan, D. M., 79, 294
Quitkin, F., 296

Rafaelson, O. J., 296
Rahman, L., 5
Rapaport, D., 88–89

SUBJECT INDEX

Abdominal distension, 53
Abnormal normal weight control syndrome, 7
Abstinence violation effect (AVE), 251, 253
Achievement expectations, 142
Acting, 278
Adolescence: binge eating and purging behaviors in, 5, 11, 14, 21, 39, 136; concern about weight during, 25–27; onset of dieting and, 29; separation-individuation and, 99
Adversarial relationship with body, 4
Affect, awareness and regulation of, 101, 165
Affective disorders, 59–60; anorexia nervosa as, 9–10; biogenetic predisposition to, 166; bulimia nervosa as, 9–10, 44–48, 50, 59, 137, 141, 149–50; in first- and second-degree relatives of bulimics, 127, 138
Agitation, 75
Alcoholics Anonymous, 267
Alcoholism, 5, 44, 49, 57–58, 60, 127, 250, 264, 266–67
Alexithymia, 62
Alienation, 75
All-or-none thinking, *see* Dichotomous thinking
Alprazolam, 221
Amenorrhea, 108; in anorexia nervosa, 56; associated with low body weight, 38; in bulimia nervosa, 13, 55–56, 158, 274
Amphetamines: abuse of, 6, 57–58, 112, 275; side effects of, 55
Anger, 43, 46–47, 75, 245
Anorexia nervosa: body-image disturbance and, 63–64; boundary disturbance and, 79; bulimic features in, 4; chronicity of, 10; control as issue in, 68, 116–17; demographic characteristics of, 126–27; developmental considerations in, 88–101, 103–6, 108–10, 113–18, 122, 125; disturbed satiety clues and, 62; drive for thinness and, 70; DSM-III criteria for, 38; duration of, 10; family systems perspective for, 128–30; family therapy for, 290; group therapy for, 208–10;

impulsive behavior in, 10; interoceptive awareness and, 61; interpersonal distrust and, 68; maternal overinvolvement and, 99; maturity fears and, 71; menstrual cycle in, 100; neurological complications in, 55–56; neurotic conflicts and, 122–23; onset of, 10, 114; overdiagnosis of, 195–96; overspecificity and, 79; perfectionism and, 72; relationship to bulimia nervosa, 5, 7, 10, 51; relationship to developmental deficits, 95–101; relationship to restricting anorexic borderline personality, 108; resistance to therapy by anorexic patients, 68; restricting false self patients and, 116; restricting neurotic patients and, 123–24; self-esteem and, 67; self-mutilation and, 10; sexual acting out and, 10; shoplifting and, 10; socioeconomic status and occurrence of, 34, 126; subclinical variant of, 29
Anxiety, 44, 55, 59, 64, 75, 143, 166, 267
Appetite control, lack of in bulimia nervosa, 44
Assertion Inventory, 200, 284
Assertiveness training, 200–205, 283–85
Assessment of bulimia nervosa, 263–64, 284; data base development for, 154; developmental considerations, 88; DSED-R, 174–94; ego-syntonicity of symptom and, 276; initial consultation for, 153
Attachment theory, 89
Auditory disturbances, 143
Autonomy, 107

Barbiturates, 58
Beck Depression Inventory (BDI), 155, 286–89
Behavior therapy, 49, 282–87
Bem Sex Role Inventory (BSRI): androgeny subscale, 77; femininity subscale, 77; masculinity subscale, 77; undifferentiated subscale, 77
Benzodrazepines, 221; *see also specific drugs*